VOCATIONALISM AND SOCIAL CATHOLICISM IN TWENTIETH-CENTURY IRELAND

Vocationalism and Social Catholicism in Twentieth-Century Ireland

The Search for a Christian Social Order

DON O'LEARY

IRISH ACADEMIC PRESS
DUBLIN • PORTLAND, OR

First published in 2000 by
IRISH ACADEMIC PRESS
44, Northumberland Road, Dublin 4, Ireland

and in the United States of America by
IRISH ACADEMIC PRESS
c/o ISBS, 5804 NE Hassalo Street,
Portland, OR 97213–3644

Website: www.iap.ie

British Library Cataloguing in Publication Data
O' Leary, D. J. (Donal J.)
Vocationalism and social catholicism in twentieth-century Ireland
1. Catholic Church 2. Vocation – Christianity 3. Ireland – Social conditions – 20th century
I. Title
282.4'17
ISBN 0–71652–667–0

Library of Congress Cataloging-in-Publication Data
O'Leary, Don, 1955–
Vocationalism and social catholicism in twentieth-century Ireland: the search for a Christian social order / Don O'Leary.
p. cm.
Includes bibliographical references and index.
ISBN 0–7165–2667–0 (hardback)
1. Ireland—Politics and government—1922–1949. 2. Corporate state—Ireland—History—20th century. 3. Sociology, Christian (Catholic)—Ireland—History—20th century. I. Title.

JN 1415.044 2000
320.9417'09'04—dc21 99–059621

Typeset in 10.5 pt on 12.5 pt Palatino
by Carrigboy Typesetting Services, County Cork
Printed by Creative Print and Design (Wales), Ebbw Vale

Contents

List of Illustrations

Illustrations appear between pp. 146 and 147

Acknowledgements

The writing of this book depended considerably on the goodwill and assistance of many individuals and organisations. My first debt of gratitude is to Professor Dermot Keogh (Department of History, University College Cork). He supervised the doctoral thesis on which the book is based. His guidance and constructive criticism proved to be of crucial importance.

Obtaining the primary source documentation was a difficult but rewarding process. In regard to the examination of archival collections I wish to express my appreciation of the assistance which I received from the staffs of various institutions and organisations. In particular I wish to thank: Brian Donnelly, Ken Hannigan, Gregory O'Connor and Tom Quinlan, National Archives, Dublin; Rev Noel Mullin and Thomas M. May, Galway (RC) Diocesan Archives; Fr Stephen Redmond SJ, Jesuit Archives, Dublin; David C. Sheehy, Dublin (RC) Diocesan Archives; the Council of Trustees and the staff of the National Library of Ireland; Tom FitzGerald, Muintir na Tíre; Peadar Cranitch, The Boole Library, University College Cork; Fr Leo Layden CSSp, Archives of the Holy Ghost Congregation (Irish Province), Dublin; Fr Seán Farragher and Caroline Mullan, Blackrock College, Dublin; Séamus Helferty, Archives Department, University College Dublin; Dr Breandán Mac Giolla Choille, Fr Ignatius Finnerty OFM, and Mark Farrell, Franciscan Archives, Killiney, Co. Dublin. Items from the Éamon de Valera papers at the Franciscan Library, Killiney, are quoted with the kind permission of the trustees. I am indebted to the late Dr Thomas Morris (then retired Archbishop of Cashel) for allowing me to examine his papers in the Muintir na Tíre Archives (Tipperary).

A section of the Bishop Michael Browne papers, concerned with the Commission on Vocational Organisation, proved to be a rich archival source. I wish to thank the former Bishop of Galway, Dr Eamonn Casey, for giving me access to these documents. I am grateful to the present Bishop of Galway, Dr James McLoughlin, for granting me permission to use the information in this publication.

The staff of the Boole Library of University College Cork assisted me in my search for official documentation and facilitated my acquisition of secondary source material. I am grateful to them for their friendly and efficient service. I also wish to thank Tim Cadogan of Cork County Library. He assisted me in gaining access to a number of obscure but useful publications.

Unpublished documents and publications, collectively, do not yield a full account of any historical topic. Motivations, ideas, conversations, and events are not always put on record – hence the importance of interviewing, where possible, those who were contemporary observers, or had a role to play, in the historical process being studied. I am grateful to Dr Maurice Moynihan, Tom Barrington and Tom FitzGerald for granting me interviews. They provided me with valuable insights and information which I would otherwise have missed.

The study of history is usually, if not always, best served by an interdisciplinary approach to the subject matter under discussion. A number of my co-workers in University College Cork provided me with information and advice which enabled me to broaden the scope of my analysis of vocationalism in Ireland. I am grateful to Fr Pádraig Corkery (RC Chaplaincy), Joseph Ruane (Department of Sociology), and Raymond O'Connor (Department of Geography) for their interest and for their help. I also benefited considerably from discussions I had with Finín O'Driscoll who was at the time a postgraduate student in the Department of History.

In the course of my research it was necessary for me to become competent in the use of computers. Donal Kingston (the Computer Centre) and Deirdre McGlynn (Department of Anatomy) helped me to solve some of my technical problems. I am indebted to other members of staff in the Department of Anatomy who were very supportive throughout my period of study. Miriam Bogan typed most of the script and Angela Marsh assisted with proofreading.

My wife Kate bore the burden of my neglect of domestic duties while this book was being written. I am indebted to her for her support, and to my children, Karen, Kevin, Sarah, and Claire, for creating an oasis of tranquillity at home which proved conducive to scholarly work.

DON O'LEARY
University College Cork
March 1999

Terms and Abbreviations

The terms 'church', 'Catholic Church', and 'Roman Catholic Church' all refer to The Holy Catholic Apostolic and Roman Church. Members of this Church are referred to as 'Catholics' and 'Roman Catholics'.

The terms 'Catholic social movement' and 'social Catholicism' are generally regarded as synonymous. Social Catholicism refers to those socially conscious Roman Catholics who responded to the repercussions of the Industrial Revolution and expanding capitalism in Europe during the nineteenth and twentieth centuries. However, it does not apply to those Roman Catholics who engaged only in traditional charitable activities in order to alleviate the poverty created by industrial capitalism. Rather it pertains to organised Roman Catholics who advocated, and worked for, social and economic reforms to treat the causes rather than the effects of injustice.[1] The impact of social Catholicism was not limited to the socio-economic sphere of community life; it also had profound political implications which become evident in this study. Political Catholicism has been defined, by Alfred Diamant, as the attempts by Roman Catholics to solve the political problems arising from the neutral republican state created by the French Revolution.[2]

The concept of vocational organisation (i.e. vocationalism), notwithstanding its political ramifications, is considered to lie mainly within the realm of social Catholicism. There is no standard definition of 'vocational organisation' or of 'functional organisation'. The Commission on Vocational Organisation (1939–1944) regarded both terms as synonymous but it gave priority of usage to 'vocational organisation'.[3] The commission regarded vocational organisation as

> a form of organisation of human beings based on their occupation or vocation and designed to enable them to fulfil some activity concerned with the occupation . . . when members of a vocation associate for some purpose concerned with their vocation and form an organic body with power to speak and act for the vocation we have a vocational organisation. It may be limited in area by including only those practising the vocation in a single town; it may be limited in scope by concerning

> itself with only some of the interests of the vocation: but with all its limitations it is a vocational organisation.[4]

Vocationalism, sometimes referred to as papal corporatism, prescribed the organisation of society on a vocational basis. It envisaged that the various occupational groups would regulate their own affairs in accordance with the principle of subsidiarity. State intervention in the socio-economic aspects of national life was to be minimal.

AN EXPLANATION OF CORPORATISM

Corporatism (sometimes called corporativism), like the concept of vocationalism, has persistently resisted precise definition. Consequently, a plethora of definitions have been put forward by various writers. Philippe C. Schmitter has defined corporatism as

> a system of interest representation in which the constituent units are organised into a limited number of singular, compulsory, non-competitive, hierarchically-ordered and functionally differentiated categories, recognised or licensed (if not created) by the state and granted a deliberate representational monopoly within their respective categories in exchange for observing certain controls on their selection of leaders and articulation of demands and supports.[5]

Corporatism may also be regarded as 'a system of self-regulation by autonomous groups, on the model of the medieval corporations of producers or the franchised mercantilist corporations'.[6] L.P. Carpenter proposes a fluid definition where

> corporatism is the unification of self-governing industries by a national committee representing them and other interests, including the state. Within this broad description, individual models vary considerably by making the unification tight or loose, and by making the state, the coordinating machinery, or industries dominant.[7]

Corporatism, apparently, requires the state to be sufficiently strong to maintain its autonomy from interest groups. Yet, if the state is so strong that interest groups are not able to participate in decision making, then there is little room for genuine corporatist arrangements. Two types of corporatism may be identified. When corporatist organisations develop naturally within society this is known as societal corporatism. State corporatism occurs where the state imposes corporatist structures and may be described as

> a system of political representation in which geographical parliamentary constituencies are replaced by industrial/occupational/functional

> groups organised in national syndicates. It is the formalisation of economic interest groups into a political institution.[8]

Taken to its extreme it was envisaged that this could lead to the evolution of a pervasive bureaucracy where the state attempts to control everything. Exponents of Roman Catholic social teaching, stridently opposed to the growth of state power, vigorously opposed the idea of a corporatist state. They proposed instead a societal variant of corporatism which was not imposed but somehow developed voluntarily by a natural process.

The absence of a broadly accepted definition of corporatism creates a vagueness which is further compounded by the fact that an extraordinary variety of activists, ideologues and theorists have advocated corporatism for widely different reasons, motives and interests. These included Friedrich Schlegel, Adam von Müller, G.W. Friedrich Hegel, Wilhelm von Kettler, Karl von Vogelsang, the Marquis de la Tour de Pin, Albert de Mun, Popes Leo XIII and Pius XI, Oliveira Salazar, and G.D.H. Cole.[9] If consensus is ever achieved across the theoretical spectrum, a core descriptive definition may prove to be of little advantage. Such a formal definition would unduly restrict, and may confuse rather than clarify the various strands of corporatist thought.[10] Therefore, when attempting to present an analytical description of corporatist ideology, it may be helpful to emphasise the characteristics of corporatism rather than becoming preoccupied with definitions.

Corporatism represents an effort to deal with the reality of interest groups in society and a prime objective is for power to be shared between them rather than letting it be monopolised by one group. Society is seen as a number of constituent parts unified into one body or corpus, hence the word corporatism. Corporatism represents an economic system where the state directs and controls business which is mainly privately owned. Of central importance is the idea that economic goals can be best achieved by co-operation rather than in the free market where competition is the driving force. Corporatism sees little merit in the price mechanism and views market economies as inherently anarchic. Co-operation is seen as a duty where workers and employers are obliged to collaborate. Strikes and lockouts are anathema to the corporatist ideal, which recommends the compulsory arbitration of disputes: the emphasis is on discipline not on liberty.

Corporatism is not an individualistic system. The general welfare of the national community has moral primacy over the rights of social class, ethnic group, family and individual rights. Corporatism, in accepting the inevitability of sectional interests, also accepts that different functions may be differentially rewarded and because of this it tends to be anti-egalitarian by nature.[11] Therefore, corporatism, by advocating inequality and illiberal ideas, rejected the central tenets of the French Revolution.

Corporatism, as an economic system of private ownership and state control, has important theoretical links with capitalism and socialism. In the case of capitalism both ideologies involve the ownership of private property but the ownership of private property is significantly altered by corporatist controls designed to protect the common good. In the corporatist system the state may limit the rights of private owners to use or direct the use of their property. Corporatism is opposed to free market economics and this represents a fundamental difference with capitalism.

Socialism and corporatism share common ground in that both oppose the fluctuations, wastes and excesses of capitalism. The two systems envisage a state-regulated economy. However, corporatism embraces none of the three most common defining characteristics of socialism, neither public ownership, nor egalitarianism – or workers' control. Thus, it may be regarded as a hybrid of capitalism and socialism or as a distinct economic system.[12] Alternatively, corporatism may be regarded as

> a variant of co-ordinated capitalism in which interest organisations, especially those representing the interests of labour, play important roles in the organisation of economic activities and, consequently, in the economic performance of a nation.[13]

Proponents of corporatism criticised the ideals of socialism and liberalism. They envisaged that a new corporate order – based on functional rather than on class or individual forms of representation – would guarantee order, stability, and national self-reliance.

Abbreviations

A.S.T.I.	Association of Secondary Teachers in Ireland.
C.H.A.	Catholic Headmasters' Association.
C.I.O.	Committee on Industrial Organisation.
C.S.V.O.C.	Catholic Societies' Vocational Organisation Conference.
C.Y.M.S.	Catholic Young Men's Society.
F.U.E.	Federated Union of Employers.
I.B.S.C.	Irish Banks Standing Committee.
I.C.T.U.	Irish Congress of Trade Unions.
I.N.T.O.	Irish National Teachers' Organisation.
I.R.A.	Irish Republican Army.
N.E.S.C.	National Economic and Social Council.
N.H.I.S.	National Health Insurance Society.
N.I.E.C.	National Industrial and Economic Council.
R.C.	Roman Catholic.
T.C.D.	Trinity College, Dublin.

Introduction

The vocationalist ideas expressed in Pope Pius XI's *Quadragesimo Anno* (1931) appealed strongly to those in the Irish Free State who felt that Roman Catholicism should play a more central role in the country's future development. In the 1930s there was an upsurge of interest in studying Catholic social teaching and the Irish Catholic social movement entered a phase of vigorous growth. An influential sector of this movement pressed for the application of vocationalist principles. Those who advocated vocationalism condemned communism and socialism and were also critical of *laissez-faire* capitalism and liberal democracy. Their opinions were expounded at length in Catholic periodicals and considerably influenced public opinion. This book evaluates the impact of their ideas on Irish society and it presents a comprehensive explanation of the origins, development and decline of vocationalism in twentieth-century Ireland.

Basil Chubb's 'Vocational Representation and the Irish Senate', published in 1954, is the first substantial academic work on the history of vocationalism. In his article Chubb explains how, and why, the vocationalist concept was abandoned because of party political interests.[1] Since then vocationalism has been discussed in several publications. These include, most notably, John H. Whyte's *Church and State in Modern Ireland 1923–1970*[2] and Joseph Lee's 'Aspects of Corporatist Thought in Ireland: The Commission on Vocational Organisation, 1939–43.'[3] In his cogent analysis Lee advised that further research should be undertaken to ascertain, more thoroughly, the implications of the reaction to the *Commission on Vocational Organisation Report*. Furthermore, he stated: 'This paper does not pretend to exhaust the research potential either of corporatist thinking in Ireland or of the Commission on Vocational Organisation. There are other patterns to be discerned, and innumerable loose threads to be tied.'[4] There is still much to be learned about vocationalism – notwithstanding the considerable volume of research which has taken place since Lee's words were published. Fortunately, the increased availability of primary source material has created the opportunity for undertaking a reappraisal of the vocationalist movement.[5]

This book begins with an examination of the origins and development of vocationalist ideology. Vocationalism originated from Catholic social teaching, drawing inspiration in particular from Pope Leo XIII's *Rerum Novarum* (1891) and *Quadragesimo Anno*. These encyclicals were written as a response to the social, economic and political problems which profoundly affected the wellbeing of the Roman Catholic Church at the time. Considerable attention, therefore, is focused on western Europe, mainly from the late nineteenth century to 1931.

The impact of the papal encyclicals extended far beyond mainland Europe and stimulated the development of social Catholicism in Ireland. However, before 1931 the Irish Catholic social movement was conspicuously underdeveloped in comparison to its counterparts in western Europe. Social Catholicism made no significant impact on Irish society and there was no organisation to press for the implementation of vocationalist ideas. Furthermore, political upheaval and armed conflict from 1919 to 1923 did not seem conducive to the promotion of reforms based on papal social teaching. Despite these unfavourable conditions the vocationalist concept was expressed in the *Constitution of the Irish Free State* (1922). After the foundation of the southern Irish state the people of the twenty-six counties enjoyed considerable control over their own affairs. The population was about 90% Roman Catholic and expectations of radical reforms, inspired by papal social teaching, seemed reasonable. But the anticipated social reconstruction did not occur and vocationalism remained dormant and obscure between 1923 and 1931. The reasons for this require explanation.

After the publication of *Quadragesimo Anno* in 1931 there was a strong and sustained public interest in Catholic social teaching for several years. In this context vocationalism emerged as a theme of major importance. In this book a number of factors, which militated for and against the popular acceptance of vocationalism, are identified. The effects of vocationalist demands on party politics, and on constitutional change, are examined. That vocationalism impacted strongly on political thinking in 1930s Ireland is probably most clearly indicated by its expression in the *Constitution of Ireland* (1937) which made provision for the establishment of the Senate on a vocational basis. The taoiseach (prime minister), Éamon de Valera, felt the need to acknowledge the importance of the vocationalist concept and in 1938 he decided to establish the Commission on Vocational Organisation. Its terms of reference included an obligation to investigate, and report on, the best means of promoting the development of vocational organisation. The commission, he stated, was the most important one since the foundation of the state.

De Valera was the unchallenged leader of Fianna Fáil – the largest political party in the state, and he served as taoiseach continuously from March 1932 to February 1948. He was the most formidable Irish politician when the vocationalist lobby was sufficiently influential to warrant a very cautious response. No radical reforms, such as those envisaged by the vocationalists, could take place without his consent. Therefore his attitude towards vocationalism receives particular attention in this study. Although it becomes clear that de Valera's political interests would not have been well served by the emergence of a new vocationalist order this observation does not lead to a complete explanation of his motives. He was an astute politician but he was also a devout Roman Catholic – mindful of Catholic social principles. His Catholic conscience had to be satisfied.

The commission, despite the problems it had to contend with, managed to complete its voluminous *Commission on Vocational Organisation Report* and presented it to the taoiseach in August 1944. Civil servants in the state departments were instructed to evaluate the report and to submit their observations to the Department of the Taoiseach. From their submissions it becomes increasingly evident why the recommendations of the commission were so untenable in a liberal parliamentary democracy. Public statements by prominent Fianna Fáil politicians, from October 1944 to April 1945, strongly indicated the government's disapproval of the commission's findings.

The government's rejection of vocationalist proposals did not escape public attention and it received national press coverage, especially in March 1945. At the height of the controversy the main opposition party, Fine Gael, attempted to use the commission's report for its own political advantage. This tested de Valera's political skills – although not to the extreme. Care had to be taken to avoid creating the impression that the government was repudiating an important principle of Catholic social teaching.

The vocationalists did not abandon their aspirations when they failed to win government support for their ambitious scheme of radical reforms. In May 1945 they formed the Catholic Societies' Vocational Organisation Conference to press for the implementation of the commission's proposals. But they were unable to win any significant degree of support for their demands, either from the political parties or from the general public. Sweeping changes in post-war Europe militated against their aspirations for a new Christian social order. However, it is important to emphasise that the slow decline of the vocationalist movement in the 1940s and 1950s does not bring the discussion of vocationalism to an end. It has been claimed that vocationalist aspirations were realised – although in a way that was very different from the scheme put forward by the Commission on Vocational Organisation. Such a claim needs to be critically evaluated if the history of vocationalism is to be comprehensively dealt with. In this context a number of issues are studied, including the revival of corporatism or neo-corporatism, the overcentralisation of political power, the growth of bureaucracy, and changes in social Catholicism.

In summary, this work, based on a wide range of primary source material from state and ecclesiastical archives, provides a systematic analysis of the vocationalist movement. This has entailed the examination of a number of cognate topics, extending from social Catholicism in nineteenth-century Europe to neo-corporatism in late twentieth-century Ireland. The study is set in a broad European context, taking cognisance of changes on the continent which stimulated the emergence and influenced the development of vocationalism in the new Irish state.

DON O'LEARY
Mallow, Co. Cork,
January 2000

CHAPTER ONE

Social Catholicism, the Papacy and the Continental Origins of Vocationalism

THE EMERGENCE OF SOCIAL CATHOLICISM AND ITS EARLY DEVELOPMENT

The development of Catholic social thought was not dictated by purely theological considerations, rather it was a response by the Roman Catholic Church to the external forces of social, economic and political change throughout western Europe. These transformations profoundly influenced the formation of Catholic social teaching, inducing a fear of state power, and a condemnation of bureaucracy, unbridled *laissez-faire*, liberalism, socialism and communism. The historical background to the formation of modern Catholic social teaching extends back to medieval times. Those who were to the forefront of social Catholicism tended to praise the distant past. They harked back to the guilds of the Middle Ages, to an era when the church enjoyed considerable power in the early corporative state or *Ständesstaat* which had replaced the medieval feudal state. In the *Ständesstaat* the power of the monarch was curtailed by the legislative and judicial rights of semi-independent provinces, municipalities, *Estates* (or Diets, Parliaments, Cortes etc.), universities, guilds and the church.[1]

During the seventeenth and eighteenth centuries the *Ständesstaat* was in turn superseded by 'absolutist' states.[2] The growing centralisation of power was accompanied by the growth of bureaucracy which enabled the state to function without the detailed personal intervention of the ruler. As powerful monarchs gained more control in the second half of the eighteenth century the Roman Catholic Church suffered a considerable loss of power and privilege.[3]

The increasing power of the centralised state was paralleled by the emergence of the Enlightenment (the 'Age of Reason'). A major trait of the Enlightenment was its malevolent anti-Catholicism. The published works of Baron Charles-Louis de Montesquieu, Voltaire (pen name of François Marie Arouet), Denis Diderot and other *philosophes* (i.e. 'enlightened' writers) denounced the Roman Catholic Church. Its teachings, organisation and privileges were stigmatized and ridiculed and the church itself was proclaimed to be the greatest hindrance to the dissemination of progressive ideas.[4] The *philosophes* appealed to rationality rather than to religious belief and their ideas, which spread far beyond the borders of France, were popularised by the press, public libraries, salons, coffee houses, reading societies and by the academies.[5] Enlightenment principles featured prominently in the political rhetoric of the French Revolution which in turn traumatised the Roman Catholic Church, especially in France.

Eighteenth-century Europe experienced rapid and revolutionary changes which prepared the way for political centralisation and economic modernisation throughout the continent. The guilds or corporations which had existed throughout Europe since the Middle Ages were virtually obliterated by the onslaught of industrial capitalism and the repercussions of the French Revolution. Each trade had its own guild and these organisations regulated prices, conditions of work, standards of materials and workmanship. With the ascent of mercantile capitalism and the rise of the factory system, the wealthier master craftsmen sought release from the restrictions of the guilds. The French Revolution coincided with an era in which the guilds were declining in both influence and number. It reinforced this trend when, in 1791, the *loi Chapelier* abolished the guilds in order to promote the ideal of individual liberty. Freedom, it was believed, would be enhanced by the absence of any intermediate organisation between the individual citizen and the state. In Britain and Ireland the legal powers of the guilds were abolished by the Corporation Acts of 1835 and 1840.[6] In other European countries, especially in Germany, the guilds declined at a slower rate due to the later onset of economic liberalism.

Another major development in Europe was the Industrial Revolution. In the late eighteenth century the factory system expanded rapidly and productive output increased to levels previously undreamed of. Unfortunately, the lower income sector of society did not benefit proportionally. Men, women and children worked long hours for low wages. As the traditional way of life broke down they migrated in large numbers to the industrialised cities where they lived in abject poverty. Under liberal capitalism the factory system all but enslaved some of the working classes. *Laissez-faire* was not kind to the Roman Catholic Church either. With its power already diminished from above by the emergence of stronger central government it was now to find its authority further eroded from below as the working classes left the church in large numbers.[7] The church was, to a large extent, the author of its own misfortune when it failed to respond constructively to the social changes induced by industrialisation and urbanisation.[8] In the cities it did little to ease the plight of the new urban poor. Excessive time spent on the factory floor left little time for religion. Many workers turned to the trade unions to improve their conditions of work. The ideologies of socialism and communism often exerted a strong appeal where workers felt ruthlessly exploited by the capitalist system.

The Roman Catholic hierarchy did not look favourably upon the new Europe. Concerned Catholics, who were conscious of the intricate relationship between their religion and the other aspects of their lives, attempted to confront the problems created by modern developments. In western mainland Europe a number of influential Catholic intellectuals and social activists attempted to create a new philosophy and a new social order to counteract ideologies and developments which were perceived to be incompatible with the teachings of the Roman Catholic Church. Social Catholicism was a response to the consecutive waves of modernisation that ruptured and eventually swept away the traditional patterns of economic and social life.[9]

The origins of social Catholicism can be traced back to the romanticism of the early nineteenth century.[10] The romantic school of thought was extremely diverse[11] and that part of it which was sympathetic to Catholicism was relatively small. Notwithstanding this, these romanticists helped to shape the foundations of modern Catholic social teaching. Romanticists shunned the mechanisation of the Industrial Revolution. They used the organic rather than the mechanical metaphor when they described society.[12] Emphasis was placed on medieval institutions *(Estates or Stände)* rather than on individuals when discussing the organisational structure of the state. Romanticists supported monarchical rule and defended the notion of hierarchy. They opposed absolutism, the rationalism and ideas of the Enlightenment, *laissez-faire* capitalism and modern liberalism.[13] Romanticism impressed many Catholics with its idealised portrayal of the Christian Middle Ages.[14] The ideology was inspired by the nostalgic yearning for a return to a patriarchal and corporative past instead of a realistic adaptation to the new conditions created by the Industrial Revolution. The political romanticism exemplified by Adam Müller and Bishop von Kettler of Mainz[15] reflected the failure of Catholicism to come to terms with the host of revolutionary changes that were taking place in the various facets of west European life in the early nineteenth century.

Up to 1870 social Catholicism failed to attract any significant degree of public support in western Europe. The vast majority of Catholics were utterly heedless. Those who were active in promoting Catholic social values met with little success.

> Unfortunately Catholic opinion had remained indifferent to their efforts. Nobler souls clung to standard forms of charity; the rest, as Albert de Mun observed, were 'a little worse that worthless' in the field of social endeavour. About 1870 there were scarcely a dozen socially minded bishops.[16]

After the Franco-Prussian War (1870–1871) the Catholic social movement began to gain momentum.[17] Gaspar Mermillod, the bishop of Fribourg-Lausanne-Geneva, played an important role by establishing lines of communication between Catholic social activists in Austria, France and Rome.[18] In the following decade corporatist ideology came to prominence in social Catholicism. The corporatist idea, which had been expressed by the romanticists, was developed further by a small number of individuals, especially by Karl von Vogelsang in Germany and by Count Albert de Mun and the Marquis René de la Tour de Pin in France.[19] But the writings of these and other individuals active in social Catholicism had little effect on mainstream philosophical thought or on public opinion.

As social Catholicism continued its crusade on behalf of the church the papacy maintained a reactionary stance. Throughout most of the nineteenth century the papacy had steadfastly refused to reconcile itself with the new Europe. Pope Gregory XVI (1831–1846) even banned railways in the Papal States. In 1864 Pope Pius IX (1846–1878) issued the *Syllabus of Errors*, condemning the popular ideas and trends which had gained momentum throughout nineteenth century Europe. In particular the document repudiated the principles of liberty and equality which were so central to the ideology of the French Revolution.[20] From the time of the Jacobin Terror, liberalism had become associated with anticlericalism and the papacy reacted by supporting the *anciens régimes*. This created another barrier between it and the ordinary people who were growing less tolerant of archaic political systems.[21]

In the late nineteenth century the Roman Catholic Church found itself very much on the defensive. The Papal States were lost to a united Italy. In Germany the power of Protestant Prussia dominated the southern Catholic states and there was friction between church and state in Germany throughout the 1870s. In Catholic France the anti-clericalism of the republican parties also created trouble for the Roman Catholic Church there. The development of a more secular society, scientific progress, materialism, the growth of state power, liberal capitalism, anticlerical radicalism, and atheistic revolutionary communism all seemed to threaten the faith and power of the Roman Catholic Church.[22]

POPE LEO XIII'S CONTRIBUTION TO THE GROWTH AND DEVELOPMENT OF SOCIAL CATHOLICISM

In 1878 Gioacchino Pecci was elected pope and took the name Leo XIII. His pontificate (1878–1903) was to be of major importance for the development and orientation of social Catholicism. Like the exponents of romanticism Leo looked back to an idealised past, to an age which pre-dated the Reformation, the Scientific Revolution and the Industrial Revolution. His social outlook was not influenced by the Enlightenment; rather it was based on the Bible and on the written works of the medieval theologian, St Thomas Aquinas. Leo had issued the encyclical *Aeterni Patris* on 4 August 1879. It laid the foundation of the programme that he intended to pursue during his pontificate and it was intended to promote the Aristotelian-Scholastic philosophy as expounded by St Thomas.[23] Thomism was an enduring phenomenon within the intellectual life of the church and although Leo did not initiate its revival he did give it a powerful stimulus.[24]

Thomism harmonised Aristotelian philosophy with Christian theology.[25] Leo's endeavours to promote Thomistic philosophy received considerable assistance from two powerful religious orders, the Jesuits and the Dominicans.[26] His objective was to use a revived blend of ancient and medieval philosophy for the purpose of presenting a universal solution to the diversity of problems afflicting the modern world.[27] He attempted to find a way whereby the church could reach a *modus vivendi* with a world that had become radically secularised. Thomism enabled him to reach back in time in order to link the modern church with its historical heritage. Leo's intention was to provide a sound base for Catholic theology and to protect the church against the rationalism of the Enlightenment. However, his heavy reliance on Thomistic theology was not an adequate response to the problems of the nineteenth century.[28] But despite this shortcoming Leo XIII was more progressive in his thinking than previous popes. He was more sympathetic and sensitive to the trends of the modern world than his predecessors.[29]

As the 1880s drew to a close Leo came under increasing pressure to provide guidance on a number of pressing social issues. He was motivated to commit the church to the creation of a more just society because many workers had left the church[30] and he felt compelled to devise an ideological framework to guide the activities of influential Catholic intellectuals who were active in promoting social reform. In England, Cardinal Henry Manning had found it necessary to intervene in the London Dock Strike of 1889 and had encouraged Catholic involvement in the labour movement. In America, Cardinal James Gibbons and Archbishop John Ireland had supported the newly emerged trade union movement and persuaded the Vatican not to condemn the Knights of Labour. Even Leo himself, when Bishop of Perugia, had felt compelled to speak out against the ruthless exploitation of women and children in the factories and mines.[31] As the plight of workers deteriorated several governments in Europe, throughout the 1880s, took the initiative to address the broad issue of social justice against the background of growing demands for social reform.[32] Leo came under mounting pressure to speak out against the evils of liberal-capitalism but the ideological divisions in the Catholic social movement presented serious problems for him, and of course for the church. Socially conscious Catholics wished to find a middle way between two repugnant extremes – *laissez-faire* and socialism, between Adam Smith and Karl Marx. However they differed over the nature of the *via media*.[33] Contradictory concepts within Catholicism became more intense at the international congresses of Liège in 1886, 1887 and 1890.[34]

Other influences also impinged on Leo's thinking as he searched for a universal remedy. The French industrialist, Leon Harmel, owned a spinning factory at Val-de-Bois and shared authority and responsibility with his workers. By transcending divisions between left and right, between liberal and conservative, he made an important contribution to the development of Christian Democracy. His pioneering work may have influenced Leo considerably.[35] The discussions of the Fribourg Union were probably of greater significance. This organisation was composed of a number of Catholic social leaders who met annually to debate the formation of a Christian social order. Cardinal Gaspar Mermillod played a leading role in the proceedings. The Union prepared a charter for industry and in 1888 Leo discussed their recommendations with some of the members. Subsequently, at his request, they submitted a memorandum to him and this document profoundly influenced the writing of *Rerum Novarum*.[36]

Since the time of Pius IX the encyclical had become the preferred method for bringing important papal statements to public notice. Throughout his pontificate Leo had issued a series of these documents. When he decided to produce an encyclical his method was to entrust the writing of it to a reliable author in papal Rome. Oral instructions were given and he would have it revised until it was in accordance with his objectives. Matteo Liberatore, a Jesuit writer, who was prominent in the neo-Thomist movement, was given the task of writing the first draft of *Rerum Novarum*.[37] When the encyclical was published in 1891 it laid the foundation for the modern social teaching of the Roman Catholic Church. It was a response to the growth of trade unionism and socialism amongst the working classes. Its publication was an important part of Pope Leo's plan to stimulate the growth of Catholic Action, which in turn was intended to restore, indirectly, church power and influence, much of which had been lost with the Papal States.[38] *Rerum Novarum* also served another important function. Catholic social activists had been deeply divided by two main schools of thought – *Rerum Novarum* settled the dispute in favour of the more liberal of the two.[39]

Leo was intensely aware of the urgency of finding a solution to the misery and suffering endured by the majority of the working classes. He attributed five causes to this grave injustice:

- The abolition of the guilds;
- The abandonment of the 'ancient' religion;
- The excesses of free competition;
- Rapacious usury;
- The concentration of economic power and wealth in the hands of a relatively small number of very rich men.[40]

Leo repudiated the socialist solution of transferring property from private individuals to the community. Private property was defended as a natural right and the faithful were admonished not to covet what belonged to their neighbour.[41] The wealthy classes were urged not to reduce workers' wages and Leo advocated a wider distribution of wealth.[42] Although the right to possess private property was sacrosanct the state had the right to control its use if this was necessary to protect the common good.[43]

The concept of private ownership and public control is an important feature of corporatist ideology. Leo also articulated other corporatist concepts. Inequality and harmony between classes and occupational groups were accepted as beneficial to the community.[44] Conflict between classes was condemned as a great mistake and Leo hoped that, because capital and labour were interdependent, co-operation would prevail. But he did not endorse a radical programme of corporatist reforms. Instead he advocated changes within the existing capitalist system. This may have been deliberate. Few people were familiar with the concept of corporatism. Where corporatist organisations did exist they were associated with monopolistic practices rather than serving the common good. Furthermore, workers lacked organisational discipline and employers were not anxious to reform the capitalist system which was serving them so well.[45]

The pope reiterated Vogelsang's teaching on the rights of association and he expressed support for both employers' and workers' unions. He envisaged the organisation of individuals in associations or 'lesser societies'. The merits of association were upheld with reference to scripture (Ecclesiastes IV, 9–10; and Proverbs XVIII, 19) and the writings of St Thomas Aquinas.[46] The right of associations to exist, free of excessive state interference, was vigorously defended. These associations would act as a mechanism to secure co-operation between employers and workers. Precise organisational structures, procedures and rules were not specified in detail. Instead, Leo acknowledged that the numerous organisations would vary due to the circumstances of time and place.[47]

The principle of subsidiarity was articulated rather obliquely when Leo emphasised the need for the state to adopt an overall co-ordinating role in society. The state was not to interfere in the internal affairs of the associations or it would destroy the social harmony which they promoted. Finally, Leo asserted that no progress could be achieved if the supernatural authority of the church was ignored because the success of the new order could only take place if the teachings of the Gospel were observed – and the church was the supreme authority on Gospel truth.[48]

In 1891 the foundation of modern Catholic social teaching was completed. Negative concepts were expressed – egalitarianism, liberalism, socialism and communism were all condemned; and excessive state intervention in the social and economic aspects of community life was declared anathema. Positive proposals were also put forward. These included the notion of a just wage, respect for private property, subsidiarity, social harmony based on Christian morality (as defined by the papacy), co-operation between the various occupational groups in society, and a state mindful of its duties and limitations. These ideological traits were embraced by a church seeking to reconcile itself with a world that had been utterly transformed by revolution. The church's response, however, was inadequate. *Rerum Novarum* was a cautious document and it left many social and economic issues open to question.[49]

> Although this basic orientation was clear enough, Leo XIII's other attitudes often were not. His views on the right ordering of society were not so systematically presented as were his opinions on other social questions and were often distressingly vague.[50]

Although Leo proclaimed his desire that the poor should rise above poverty he still expected them to accept their wretched conditions. Suffering was glorified and scripture was quoted to assure those who were poor and heavily burdened that they were closer to God.[51] *Rerum Novarum* insisted that the state had a duty to protect those who were poor. In practice the state was not a vigilant promoter of social justice. Those who held political power held economic power also. Therefore the state was not neutral in addressing the labour problem and displayed a distinct bias against the poor. Economic action alone was not enough to bring about constructive reform. Political or quasi-political action was also necessary but Leo failed to give guidelines for this. He had an overriding concern for public order and this severely reduced the effectiveness of *Rerum Novarum*.[52]

However, Leo's encyclical, despite its defects, did address some of the important issues. Its teachings, despite the many questions it left unanswered, were developed enough to provide sufficient guidance for the next generation of Catholics who were anxious to apply Christian social principles to their particular circumstances. Catholics in western Europe developed a network of organisations which were motivated, in part, by a desire for constructive social change. Another objective was to prevent Catholic workers and farmers from succumbing to the appeal of socialism. These organisations included co-operatives, friendly societies, farmers' organisations, trade unions, adult education schemes and youth movements. The intellectual aspect of the movement, which had a reinforcing effect, was manifested by a growing number of study circles, specialist periodicals and meetings such as the *semaines sociales*, which started in France in 1904 and were imitated in other countries shortly afterwards. The extent and success of the movement varied throughout Europe. It was weak in much of southern and eastern Europe but in France, in parts of Italy, and in the Catholic regions of Germany, Austria and Switzerland, it was strong. The movement was probably at its most advanced stage of development in Belgium and Holland.[53] Ireland, in contrast to the rest of western Europe, had a remarkably weak Catholic social movement up to the early 1930s.

In mainland Europe the appeal of Catholic social thought was that it combined a reactionary nostalgia for the demise of the medieval guilds with a forward looking aim of seeking socio-economic harmony within the framework of a modern industrial society.[54] Catholic social activists began campaigns to establish the modern analogues of the extinct guilds and corporations. In 1891, when Pope Leo XIII published *Rerum Novarum*, their efforts benefited from a much needed stimulus but the corporatist idea did not gain widespread acceptance until after World War I.[55] This was due in no small measure to the suppressive actions of Leo XIII's successor, Pius X (reigned 1903–1914).

Leo had encouraged scholars to become more venturesome in their studies. His liberal gestures 'opened a window to the world which permitted a whiff of secularity to drift through a church that, for centuries, reeked of incense'.[56] For the first time since the Enlightenment, Catholic intellectuals felt not only free but also compelled to reconcile church teaching with modern science. Leo's pronouncements gave great encouragement to the modernists but he was unable to make provision for institutional support without seriously endangering the structure of the church.[57]

The modernists wished to revise some traditions of the church because of the new insights emanating from the scientific and historical discoveries of the previous century. Pius X, afraid of where this might lead, set himself the task of exterminating social as well as doctrinal modernism. He was determined to secure hierarchical and clerical control over all Catholic organisations concerned with social reform.[58] He suppressed much of the enthusiasm which had been generated by *Rerum Novarum*. The social question was not high on his list of priorities. Demands for socio-economic reforms were 'supported in word but stifled in deed'.[59] Pius X's successor, Benedict XV (reigned 1914–1922), was less regressive in his thinking. Shortly after his election he set about subduing the anti-modernist crusade although for political reasons he reiterated the condemnation of modernism. However, despite the fact that he was not as conservative as his predecessor, he failed to encourage the practical application of principles enunciated by Leo.[60]

In 1922 Achille Ratti was elected pope and took the name of Pius XI (reigned 1922–1939). His espousal of the Leonine social programme stimulated the popularisation of interest in corporatism in western Europe and this was to have a profound effect on the Catholic social movement in Ireland.

THE STIMULATING EFFECT OF *QUADRAGESIMO ANNO* ON SOCIAL CATHOLICISM

As the fortieth anniversary of *Rerum Novarum* drew near Europe was in turmoil. The Great Depression created severe poverty and social strife. Prices and wages were falling rapidly and international trade was drying up. Thousands of employers faced bankruptcy and unemployment was rampant. Farmers were destroying produce which they could not sell and there was a loss of confidence in capitalism.[61] Economic instability led to political instability. Critics of the existing order became more vociferous and militant. Democracies fell prey to dictatorships and by the end of 1938 only 12 of the 28 states in Europe remained democratic.[62] Communism and fascism won many supporters in the 1930s and each promised successful alternatives to the capitalist system. Communists continued to be enemies of the church because they taught the need for incessant class warfare and the complete abolition of private property. Totalitarian movements, whether right or left of the political spectrum, frightened many people who had lost faith in capitalism. Caught between the brutality and loss of liberty, inherent in dictatorial systems, and the anarchy of the capitalist system, many Catholics turned to the church for guidance. The papacy, claiming to have answers to social and economic problems, had to speak out – but Pius was in need of inspiration. This was reflected by the fact that, since the publication of *Rerum Novarum* forty years earlier, Catholic social thinkers had become divided into two main groups – *Sozialpolitik* and *Sozialreform*. *Sozialpolitik* accepted the basic structure of the capitalist system and wished to reform it in the interests of social justice. *Sozialreform* advocated radical change on a corporatist basis and, due to the crisis in capitalism at the beginning of the 1930s, this school of thought gained considerable support.

In this time of crisis Pius turned to the Jesuits for assistance.[63] The pope bypassed all Vatican offices and through Fr Wlodimir Ledochowski, the Superior General of the Society of Jesus, Fr Oswald von Nell-Breuning was commissioned to write the main part of the document. It was hoped that this document would not only be a fitting tribute to *Rerum Novarum* but would also address the many changes which had taken place since 1891. Von Nell-Breuning was a well known Jesuit economist and a student of law. He was obliged to work under strict conditions of secrecy. This placed him at a severe disadvantage because he had to seek advice and information from those who did not know his purpose. Von Nell-Breuning benefited from his participation in the discussions of the Konigswinter Group *(Koenigswinterer Kreis)*. This group of Catholic intellectuals were particularly interested in issues pertaining to political economy and it had a profound influence on him.[64] So also had Gustav Gundlach, a Jesuit colleague of von Nell-Breuning's, who unwittingly contributed much to the sociological and philosophical aspects of *Quadragesimo Anno*. Gundlach's social and philosophical outlook was 'soaked up like a dried out sponge' and the encyclical was 'well saturated' with his ideas.[65]

Although von Nell-Breuning was aware that the encyclical was not covered by the decree of infallibility he did not seriously contemplate the possibility that any error of his would find its way into the final draft – 'the presence of the Holy Spirit would protect the Pope.'[66] A greater influence on the pope, it seems, was a desire not to antagonise Mussolini.[67] While under the direct obedience of the pope and the superior general of his order there was little room for doubt. This failure to exercise his critical faculties had unfortunate consequences. Pius carried out some of the editorial work and, apart from the note on fascism, only a few statements in the encyclical are attributable to him. When Pius XI submitted his note on fascism for insertion into the encyclical the Jesuit priest failed to adequately scrutinize it – despite the order of Fr Ledochowski to express any doubts which might arise.[68] With the benefit of hindsight Von Nell-Breuning was forced to the conclusion that Pius did not understand the social and political aspects of fascism. Furthermore, he came to believe that the insertion of the pope's note on fascism was mainly responsible for the widespread misunderstanding of the encyclical after it was published.[69]

Quadragesimo Anno was published when Europe was in turmoil. It is understandable that in such circumstances Pius XI felt compelled to prescribe specific socio-economic remedies for universal application. The proposals for reform, promulgated in his name, were more radical than those of any of his predecessors. That he was ill-advised is now not seriously in doubt. The misinterpretation of *Quadragesimo Anno* was a cause of much anguish to von Nell-Breuning and he gradually came to realize that he had been called upon to complete a task far beyond his ability.[70] It was this encyclical which was to feature so prominently in vocationalist ideology.

The encyclical did not win the approval of many academic and political experts.[71] Instead it was misused by dictators such as Salazar and Dollfuss to justify their economic and social policies.[72] In the 1930s, therefore, two radically different types of corporatism can be identified, one being animated by political leaders, the other by papal social teaching. The more secular and statist brand of corporatism found its most public expression in the *corporazioni* of fascist Italy, followed by imitations in Portugal and Austria. In the corporatist state, corporations were merely instruments of power for the state and responded to its will. The corporations did not enjoy self-government whereas the corporations proposed by Pius XI were to be autonomous and not subject to any political interference. More often than not this fundamental distinction was not understood and the papal plan was confused with its statist counterpart.[73] This in turn counteracted the broad acceptance of societal corporatism.

A substantial amount of the blame for the widespread misunderstanding which linked fascism and societal corporatism may be attributable to Pius XI, notwithstanding his severe criticisms of dictatorial regimes.[74] Pius was not averse to dealing with dictators when he felt it was to the advantage of the church.[75] The Lateran Treaty (1929) restored the Vatican City to papal sovereignty and helped Mussolini's fascist government win greater support from the Catholics of Italy.[76] In Germany, Hitler's consolidation of power was enhanced considerably when the Vatican and the German hierarchy readily sacrificed organised political Catholicism in order to safeguard the church's influence in that state.[77] The Vatican under Pius XI preferred authoritarian regimes to the liberal democracies – the latter he was inclined to criticise excessively.[78] His dealings with dictators probably militated against a broader acceptance of his social teaching in democratic countries.[79] Indeed those who believed that the Vatican supported fascist regimes were not without some degree of justification. Pius XI publicly supported Mussolini's involvement in the Spanish conflict on the basis that the dictator was helping to defend Christianity.[80] Nazi Germany, Fascist Italy and the Vatican all supported the Spanish Fascists led by General Franco.[81] In Ireland the Catholic bishops also sympathised with the Nationalist side and attempted unsuccessfully to persuade Éamon de Valera's government to support Franco's cause. This may have caused some confusion amongst the general public, creating the idea in some quarters that the papal message of social reform was in some way supportive of fascism.[82]

Despite the widespread misunderstandings about papal corporatism, *Quadragesimo Anno* gave great encouragement to many Catholics, in different countries, to promote the development of vocational organisations. It served the important function of restoring unity to social Catholicism when it distinctly favoured the *Sozialreform* school of thought.[83] This in turn instilled within the Catholic social movement throughout the world a new self-confidence and induced a new precision in the formulation of objectives. *Quadragesimo Anno*, published exactly forty years after *Rerum Novarum*, represented a modern version of the older encyclical and corrected it on some minor points.[84] Both encyclicals were fundamentally the same.[85] The emphasis was on harmony between different social groups – the Christian in contrast to the political philosophy of class war. However, *Quadragesimo Anno* was more precise about how this aim might be achieved and was more explicit in its advocacy of vocational organisation. The encyclical proposed that the members of each industry or profession should be organised in vocational groups or corporations so that employers and workers would co-operate to further their common interests.

Vocationalists, inspired by *Quadragesimo Anno*, frequently invoked the organic metaphor in their writings where the nation was likened to a higher organism like the human body – something which was alive, active and growing. Tissues, organs and systems in the human body, although quite distinctive in their characteristics, all functioned in co-operation to ensure good health. Similarly, different levels of organisation existed in the modern nation-state. The state was perceived as a corporate organisation of individuals, families, occupational groups, trade unions, employers associations, and various other groups. The reformed 'social body' was to form 'the mystical body of Christ' with Christ as the 'head.'[86] Like the human body the state could only retain or attain good health if its component parts functioned co-operatively for the common good. According to the organic concept of society, the duty of the state was not to direct the functions of its components but merely to ensure that they worked in harmony with each other.

The purpose of the state was not to try to do everything itself. Pius declared that the principle of subsidiary function was of crucial importance: 'it is an injustice, a grave evil and a disturbance of right order for a larger and higher organisation to arrogate to itself functions which can be performed efficiently by smaller and lower bodies'.[87] State power would have to be curbed but, ironically, Pius relied heavily on state intervention to bring about the changes he had in mind. His encyclical declared

> Now this is the primary duty of the State and of all good citizens, to abolish conflict between classes with divergent interests, and thus foster and promote harmony between the various ranks of society. The aim of social legislation must therefore be the re-establishment of vocational groups.[88]

The state had the primary responsibility of restoring the intermediate associations which were once more to unite society. The development of vocational organisation was to lead to the formation of occupational groups analogous to the medieval guilds. This was presented as a demand for social justice and would not only provide an alternative to class conflict – it was also to restore the state to its rightful place by relieving it of an excessive number of duties. Heavy government control, which might be necessary for the foundation of a harmonious society, was to be only temporary. *Quadragesimo Anno's* corporate reconstruction of society required state guidance because of the magnitude of the reform but the increased state economic control was more likely to be long-term than temporary. Subsequent events in countries such as Austria, Italy and Portugal tend to confirm this where the state dominated the corporations. This was ironical because the purpose of constructing a corporatist society was to relieve the state of burdens threatening to crush it.

Pius, like Leo XIII, insisted that economic life should be inspired by Christian principles. Charity, justice, love of neighbour and love of God were to be the predominant motives.[89] He implied that the structure of society was so much in conflict with Christian principles that fundamental changes were necessary. He compared the labour market of the capitalist system to a battlefield which was 'leading society to ruin'. Nothing less than a restructuring of society on a corporatist or a vocationalist basis could effect a 'perfect cure'.[90] Liberalism, socialism, communism, and the free competition of the capitalist system all stood condemned.[91] Free competition had to be limited by public authority for the common good. The state had no right to abolish private property but it had the right to control its use in order to protect the welfare of society.[92]

Quadragesimo Anno and corporatism had much in common. Both wanted to restructure society according to professional or economic activity. Collaboration between management and labour was stressed but there were also some sharp differences between the encyclical and the corporatists. According to *Quadragesimo Anno* existing trade unions and employer associations were still beneficial but they needed to be more fully developed. Corporatists thought that social construction would render these organisations obsolete. Most corporatists believed that the new organisations should be compulsory, both in membership and in the enforcement of policies. This seems to be contrary to Pius XI's teaching but there is a vague passage in *Quadragesimo Anno* indicating that these new organisations should be accorded the status of semi-public authorities with the power to limit free competition and control the economy in other ways.[93] If the new associations were to be given semi-public regulatory powers there would have to be some element of compulsion involved. Even if membership of these associations was not compulsory, their regulations would have to be complied with.

A major weakness of the encyclical was the assumption that vocational organisations could be trusted to subordinate their own interests to the common good. Furthermore, it was assumed, rather naively, that class conflict could be lessened or even eliminated by the simple expedient of bringing employers and employees together in the same organisations. The issue of power was not addressed and it was not clear whether or not management would share power equally with labour. *Quadragesimo Anno* did not indicate how these new associations were to be integrated with existing trade unions and employer associations which were based on very different policies.

Rerum Novarum and *Quadragesimo Anno*, notwithstanding their deficiencies, were favourably received in Ireland. In the following chapters it will become clear how the encyclicals influenced the formation of Irish social Catholicism and stimulated the development of the vocationalist movement.

CHAPTER TWO

Social Catholicism and the Vocationalist Ideal

SOCIAL CATHOLICISM IN IRELAND BEFORE THE WAR OF INDEPENDENCE

At the close of the nineteenth century *Rerum Novarum* was less relevant to Ireland than to the rest of western Europe because the associated processes of industrialisation and urbanisation were not at an advanced stage.[1] The church pursued its mission in a socio-economic environment which did not threaten its position and the encyclical had no significant impact on the country. There were also a number of other reasons why Ireland remained almost impervious to the social message of Leo XIII. There were important differences between Ireland and other European countries where the Catholic social movement was strong. Germany, France, Belgium and Holland, unlike Ireland, were not preoccupied with a struggle for national independence at the end of the nineteenth century. Neither were these countries burdened with a social problem comparable with the Irish land question up to the Wyndham Act of 1903. Furthermore, the Irish Catholic Church, unlike its European counterparts, had suffered extreme suppression under the Penal Laws. Consequently, the Catholic Church in Ireland, throughout the nineteenth century and the first quarter of the twentieth century, had to put enormous effort into reconstructing the basic institutions – churches, schools and charitable organisations.

When comparing social Catholicism in Ireland to Catholic social movements in continental Europe, cognisance has to be taken of the different traditions in Catholicism. In western mainland Europe, many trade unions were formed by socialists who were highly critical of the churches. The hostility of the socialists had the effect of impelling the more religiously inclined workers to form Catholic organisations as a bulwark against socialism. They tended to organise themselves on a confessional basis and were under strong clerical guidance. They also formed Catholic political parties that received support only from the Catholic sector of the population. In the Anglo-American world, of which Ireland was a part, Catholics, in general, did not form professedly Catholic organisations, probably because they did not feel so threatened by secular ideologies such as socialism.[2] The Catholic trade union movement was strong in mainland Europe and was weak to the point of insignificance in the Anglo-American world. Developments in Ireland reflected the distinctiveness of Anglo-American social Catholicism. For example, the Irish Agricultural Organisation Society, which was an important rural association in Ireland in the early years of the twentieth century, was non-confessional. The Irish parliamentary party, although it sometimes acted in the best interests of Catholics, was concerned to emphasise that it was a nationalist and not a Catholic party.[3]

The Irish Catholic social movement lacked organisational and numerical strength. Furthermore, it was weak on the intellectual front because of the general intellectual weakness of Irish Catholicism. This, to a large extent, can be attributed to the fact that seminarians in Ireland received a poor standard of education in the late nineteenth and early twentieth centuries. Severe discipline, rote-learning, and an anti-intellectual bias militated against the emergence of indigenous social theory. The emphasis was on strenuous pastoral work rather than on the innovative application of Christian principles.[4] Consequently, priests were ill-equipped to adopt leadership roles in social Catholicism.

The education of the Catholic clergy and laity left much to be desired. The French writer, Louis Paul-Dubois observed in 1907 that

> . . . secondary education is so inadequate . . . and higher education still so cruelly defective, that among the Catholics of Ireland, even among the liberal classes, there are but few to be found who possess any real culture. We find, on the contrary, a certain form of intellectual apathy very widespread, a distaste for mental effort, a certain absence of the critical sense. . . .[5]

Paul-Dubois deplored the fact that Irish Catholicism was 'unhealthy and abnormal' because it lacked an educated laity.[6] He believed that this problem was an evil consequence of the Penal Laws. This oppressive legislation, in his opinion

> deprived Ireland of her directing classes, and thereby assured the supremacy of the clergy. It reduced the people as inevitably to ignorance as to poverty; and there followed necessarily the results that are seen today, inertia, lethargy of opinion, lack of liberty of mind, of energy, and of power of moral resistance.[7]

The lack of progressive social thought, so characteristic of Irish Catholicism, was also a trait of the Irish Protestant mentality. The Irish Protestant churches were much slower than their associated institutions in Britain in applying new concepts to alleviate social problems.[8]

A major obstacle to the emergence of a dynamic Catholic social movement was the scarcity of educated Catholics. In the early years of the twentieth century, the educated class in Ireland was disproportionately made up of Protestants and its relatively few Catholic members were more concerned with imitating their Protestant counterparts than attempting to establish a new Catholic culture. The Catholic Church in Ireland did not improve matters when it persistently disapproved of the existing Irish universities and discouraged the entrance of its members. Consequently, before the Irish Universities Act of 1908, conditions militated against the emergence of a Catholic university-educated elite in Ireland.[9]

Some priests were acutely aware of the intellectual deficit in Irish Catholicism. In 1895–96 a small group of influential clerics in Maynooth had organised an association of graduates for the purpose of rectifying this problem. Prominent among the newly formed Maynooth Union were Dr Walter McDonald, Dr William Moran and Fr Michael Hickey.[10] These men, and other like-minded clerics, attempted to induce a social consciousness amongst their colleagues as a first step in creating a Catholic social movement in Ireland. Their efforts did not meet with resounding success. The bishops were extremely cautious about priests involving themselves in social issues and the majority of the clergy did not respond positively to appeals that they should adopt a more active social role. The educational training of priests did not enable them to cope with the social and economic changes around them. By 1910 Irish Catholicism was still confined to the moral sphere – despite the growing interest of priests in social problems.[11] However, it was becoming increasingly difficult for the church in Ireland to neglect the social and economic aspects of community life. Since the turn of the century Belfast, Dublin and Cork had grown in size. Urban expansion brought with it poor housing, inadequate sanitation and unjust conditions of employment. In response to their plight, workers organised themselves into trade unions and the Irish labour movement grew in strength. With trade unionism came socialism – an ideology that, according to the papacy, was irreconcilable with Christianity.

Pope Leo's sweeping condemnation of socialism did not contribute to the development of a Catholic social movement in Ireland. The word 'socialism' covered a diversity of beliefs and of people working towards social and economic reform. This broad condemnation caused confusion among middle class and working class Catholics, particularly in the English-speaking world.[12] In Ireland it tended to counteract the formation of associations that Leo had advocated. The anti-socialist concepts expressed in *Rerum Novarum* served to increase rather than alleviate conflict between the social classes in the country.[13] This, in combination with the weakness of the Catholic social movement, militated against the development of vocational organisation in Ireland in the early twentieth century.

Rerum Novarum vindicated the rights of workers but many felt it left them dependent on the benevolence of employers, which was not forthcoming. Furthermore, the encyclical was used to condemn their leaders who were demanding fair wages and improved working conditions. The encyclical intensified the fear of socialism amongst the clergy and middle class Catholics. Contrasting attitudes were sharply evident during the great Dublin Lock-Out in August 1913–January 1914.[14] *Rerum Novarum* elicited mixed feelings in trade union circles. It was held in high esteem by many Dublin trade unionists[15] but it did not escape scathing criticism during the labour troubles.[16] The church's hostility towards socialism, and its tendency to condemn trade union leaders, created problems for the few priests who worked for social justice and who shared with Pope Leo XIII the sense of urgency in alleviating the poverty of the workers.[17]

When the workers were defeated and returned to work in January 1914 many Catholics felt that the church's stance left much to be desired.[18] There was a growing realisation amongst some of the clergy that a programme of Catholic social action was necessary. The publication, in 1914, of Charles Plater's work *The Priest and Social Action* heightened the social consciousness of Catholic clergy in the English-speaking world and it was instructive on some of the practical aspects of social Catholicism. The fundamental difference between charity and social action was emphasised by the young Jesuit. The publication of Plater's book in the wake of the bitter labour dispute in Dublin reinforced the conviction, held by the more progressive-minded clergy in Ireland, that there was a pressing need for a new approach to social action. The Jesuits were quick to rise to the challenge of devising a Catholic social programme. From 1913 to 1918 their Irish Messenger Office published a series of 28 pamphlets covering different aspects of Catholic social teaching. The order's most influential writer on social issues was Lambert McKenna.[19] Other individuals who embraced the cause of social Catholicism included Alfred O'Rahilly and the Waterford priest, Rev John Kelleher.

O'Rahilly was to play a key role in the vocationalist movement. He had entered St Mary's College (Stonyhurst, England) in 1908, intending to become a Jesuit priest but came to realise that the restrictions of the order were not compatible with his temperamental independence of character.[20] On 10 May 1914 O'Rahilly left the order after a troubled period of study at Milltown Park, Dublin. His years with the Society of Jesus, especially at Stonyhurst, had a profound and enduring effect on his intellectual formation. It was there that Charles Plater influenced him.[21] As a Jesuit scholastic he came to believe that the social teaching of the church, as expounded in *Rerum Novarum*, was of central importance in providing an alternative to the ideologies of fascism, capitalism and communism.[22] From his study of the Schoolmen[23] and the medieval guilds came a strong belief in functional democracy (more commonly known as vocationalism after 1931).[24]

In October 1914 O'Rahilly joined the academic staff of University College Cork as a lecturer of mathematics and mathematical physics. Shortly afterwards he began working towards the implementation of Catholic social teaching in Cork city. However, his endeavours met with a dismal response.[25] He was an active member of the Society of St Vincent de Paul until late 1917 and he tried to convince his colleagues that the alleviation of poverty demanded more than a charitable response. To this end he invoked the writings of the organisation's founder, Frederick Ozanam, but his appeals were futile. The dominant middle class attitude was that the type of social activism advocated by O'Rahilly would bring the Society of St Vincent de Paul into conflict with the authorities and this in turn, it was feared, would detract considerably from its primary objective of giving charitable assistance to the poor.[26] O'Rahilly's exceptional intellectual abilities, his broadness of vision, and his dedication to social justice distinguished him from his co-religionists, and also serves to indicate the weakness of social Catholicism at the time.

In addition to the inhibitory factors within Irish Catholicism, the external factors of war and political upheaval were to stifle the growth of social Catholicism for several years to come. The effects of the First World War and the 1916 Rising in Dublin distracted public attention and frustrated the efforts of O'Rahilly and others who wished for the formation of a new social order based on Catholic principles. Where public opinion was concerned priority was given to addressing the national question and the social question was pushed to the background. The momentous political developments between 1918–1923 were to create a similar effect but it was in these barren years for social Catholicism that vocationalism came to feature in Irish constitutional change.

THE CONSTITUTIONAL ENSHRINEMENT OF THE VOCATIONALIST IDEAL

In the general election of December 1918 Sinn Féin[27] won 73 of the 105 Irish parliamentary seats but the party's parliamentarians refused to take their seats at Westminster. Instead they assembled in Dublin to form the Constituent Assembly of Ireland (Dáil Éireann) – in January 1919. Ireland then slipped gradually into a state of war with Britain. It was, of course, most inopportune in the midst of war to press for social reforms. Some clerical commentators contemplated what developments might take place after the war. Rev Myles V. Ronan was aware of the potency of propaganda in politics and he expressed the opinion that Catholic Action could benefit greatly from an organised dissemination of information. He noted that the Irish Catholic Truth Society, the Messenger Office, and the English Catholic Truth Society all produced 'excellent' publications on social problems but these did not 'sufficiently penetrate the popular masses.'[28] What was required, he asserted, was a Catholic Social Union of Ireland, composed of priests and well educated laymen, who would produce pamphlets concerned with social problems in the country. Ronan believed that 'a great Catholic social propaganda' could emanate from a concerted campaign involving 'pulpit, press, platform, and pamphlet.' He went on to predict 'social issues will soon dominate the situation; and, it must be remembered, that religion is not confined to church. Irish Catholics must necessarily apply Catholic principles to the labour programme.'[29]

Appeals for social reform were not made only on the basis of Catholic values. During the War of Independence some socially conscious Catholics were anxious to ensure that Catholic social teaching was seen to be in harmony with Irish nationalism. Rev Patrick Boylan, in a pamphlet entitled *Catholicism and Citizenship in Self-Governed Ireland*, argued that charity and justice, which were the most familiar themes of Catholic teaching, were essential to the practise of the highest civic virtues. He believed that only Catholic teaching provided the correct foundation for the politics of social reform.[30] A glimmer of corporatist thought was evident when he emphasised the Christian concept of community life. Citizenship implied 'public and corporate, in contrast with merely individual and private, action.'[31]

A small number of Catholic social activists continued to strive for the implementation of the principles enunciated in *Rerum Novarum*. Alfred O'Rahilly did not abandon his pursuit of social justice despite the failure of his earlier initiatives. When he became involved in Irish politics he continued to advocate the principles espoused in Pope Leo XIII's encyclical – even when the country was faced with great political uncertainty. He had joined Sinn Féin in 1916 and was imprisoned on Spike Island from January to June 1921 by the British. The War of Independence ended on 11 July 1921 and, after protracted negotiations, the Anglo-Irish Treaty was signed on 6 December of that year.

After the signing of the treaty the Provisional Government, under the leadership of General Michael Collins, set about the task of drafting a constitution. Collins selected nine men to serve on the drafting committee. Its members included: Darrell Figgis, James Douglas, James MacNeill, C.J. France, Kevin O'Shiel, Hugh Kennedy, John O'Byrne, James Murnaghan, and Alfred O'Rahilly.[32] Collins held the position of chairman but he did not have time to participate in the drafting process. Figgis acted as deputy chairman and secretary of the committee. At the draft committee's first meeting on 25 January 1922 Collins outlined the general parameters and objectives. The constitution was to be democratic, practicable, short, simple, and easy to revise.[33]

From an early stage in the committee's proceedings there was much disagreement among the members, and the difficulties experienced may have been aggravated by outside interference. When the acting chairman, Darrell Figgis, submitted a draft constitution to the committee for consideration O'Rahilly's caustic comment was that it was merely an English translation of the Weimar constitution. O'Rahilly was dissatisfied with the committee's resistance to innovative proposals. When he learned that the committee had met without him, and had agreed not to include any religious provisions in the final draft, he left it for a time to write his own document.[34] However, he was not content with just producing his own alternative draft. Feeling ignored by his colleagues, he suggested to Archbishop Edward Byrne of Dublin that the Catholic hierarchy should set up an episcopal committee for 'consultation, suggestion and criticism' of the draft constitution.[35] On 12 February the archbishop wrote to O'Rahilly, politely declining the invitation to become involved.

The divided committee proceeded with its task but failed to reach agreement on a wide range of issues and split into three factions. The 'conservative' group was composed of Figgis, MacNeill and O'Byrne and produced 'Draft A'. The 'liberal' wing, made up of Douglas, Kennedy and France, produced 'Draft B'. The 'radicals', O'Rahilly and Murnaghan (both university professors) signed 'Draft C' which was written by O'Rahilly.[36] O'Rahilly saw much merit in functional democracy as an adjunct to geographical democracy. Article 37 of his draft constitution read as follows

> In addition to territorial autonomy, legislation shall institute a measure of functional autonomy for the different branches of social service and economic life. In particular a Council of Education, a Council of Agriculture, a Council of Transport and a Council of Industry, shall be established; and in each of these Councils the relevant occupational groups shall be represented according to their social and economic importance. Legislation shall determine the advisory, supervisory and administrative capacity of such Councils.
>
> Drafts of important laws, involving social and economic policy, shall be submitted by the Executive Council to the Council to which they appertain, for consideration and criticism, before they are introduced into the House of Representatives. Bills may also be referred by the House of Representatives to a Council. The Councils have the right of proposing such Bills themselves. Should the Executive Council disapprove of them, it must nevertheless introduce them into the House of Representatives, with a statement of its own views.[37]

His advocacy of vocational councils was inspired by the principle of subsidiarity put forward by Pope Leo XIII in *Rerum Novarum*.[38] In a document entitled 'Footnotes to the Draft Constitution of 1922' he added

> These functional councils, with power to criticise and originate Bills, are the natural successors of the English Boards in this country and will be a powerful agent in preventing political incompetence and bureaucracy.[39]

Article 67 of O'Rahilly's draft constitution gave further expression to Catholic social teaching when it stated

> It shall be the aim of social legislation to promote the association of employees with employers in the management and control of industry, and to encourage co-operative ownership and organisation.[40]

O'Rahilly's strong Catholic beliefs and his innovative political ideas profoundly influenced the writing of Draft C and, with the exception of Murnaghan, set him apart from his colleagues on the drafting committee. He was of the opinion that the constitution should take cognisance of Roman Catholic values in a country that was predominantly Roman Catholic. Unlike the other two drafts some articles in his document were explicitly Roman Catholic.[41] He endeavoured to persuade his colleagues to give serious consideration to the parliamentary structures of Switzerland and Denmark. This initiative was based on the belief that a small country like Ireland would have more in common with these countries than with the much wealthier states such as Britain or the United States of America.

O'Rahilly urged the limitation of the powers of central government and a reduction of bureaucratic controls. He wished to grant the people more power than any political party was willing to concede.[42] Antidotes to the overcentralisation of power were, in his opinion, a federal state, the senate as the guardian of the people's interests, vocational councils with statutory powers, external government ministers, the right of the people to initiate legislation, and a system which would enable the people's wishes to be complied with through referenda.[43] His disregard for the British parliamentary system contrasted with his admiration for the federal constitution of Switzerland.

O'Rahilly's views received little attention and he was regarded as an 'eccentric academic'.[44] However, he may have influenced his colleagues to make constitutional provision for the establishment of vocational councils.[45] Other members of the drafting committee advocated the constitutional enshrinement of the vocationalist concept. Hugh Kennedy was in favour of vocational councils with statutory powers. He also gave consideration to the creation of vocational councils with the power to nominate government ministers.[46] James Douglas was in agreement with Kennedy and declared

> I am strongly in favour of the creation of vocational councils, and believe that Ministers should be members of such councils, and be nominated with their approval. Some such system will do more to curb an autocratic executive than any I can conceive of and I contend that it will only be really workable if Ministers acting in conjunction with such councils are chosen without regard to Party and have no Party in the House dependent on their votes.[47]

Douglas envisaged a political system whereby some government ministers would not be members of the Oireachtas (parliament). The advantage of these ministers would be their political neutrality with regard to the Anglo-Irish Treaty. Article 53 of Draft B, signed by Kennedy, Douglas and France, specified that only the President, Vice-President, the Minister of Finance, and the Minister of External Affairs, had to be members of Dáil Éireann (the lower house of parliament).[48] As many as eight external ministers could be appointed for responsibility on a range of internal matters.[49] This system, Douglas argued, would be free of party politics. He believed that the integration of vocational councils with the parliamentary system would facilitate the proposal of alternative policies by Éamon de Valera and others across the political divide, without reference to the Anglo-Irish Treaty.[50]

In drawing up a constitution for the Irish Free State (Saorstát Eireann) the three factions of the drafting committee studied a number of foreign constitutions including those of Germany, Poland, the United States of America, Denmark and Switzerland. Some of these constitutions contained articles which allowed for the establishment of vocational councils and, furthermore, allowed for the possibility of such councils with an influence over the passing of legislation. Notable examples were Article 68 of the *Constitution of the Polish Republic* (1921) and Article 165 of the *Constitution of the German Realm* (1919).[51] Evidently, the vocational concept was widely favoured in the much divided committee because the three drafts which were produced made provision for the establishment of functional/vocational councils.[52]

Some of the main features of vocationalist ideology, had been articulated i.e. the principle of subsidiarity, the notion of self-governing occupational groups in society, a contempt for civil servants and a disdain for politicians. On 8 March 1922, Michael Collins received the three drafts but O'Rahilly's document did not receive serious consideration; it was used only as an aid to the amendment of Draft B. When O'Rahilly discovered that the Provisional Government was giving priority to Draft B he tried again to involve the Catholic bishops. He wrote to Archbishop John M. Harty of Cashel, urging that a committee, formed by the hierarchy, should examine the drafts then before the government. He also sought assistance from the Catholic Truth Society of Ireland but all his lobbying was in vain.[53] The church authorities were extremely reluctant to become involved in such a sensitive political issue, notwithstanding the fact that O'Rahilly was endeavouring to have put in place a Catholic constitution.

Collins undertook the preparation of a draft constitution mainly from Drafts A and B. His draft was an amended conflation of the two but with a preference for Draft B.[54] British approval of the final draft was required before submission to the Irish electorate. On 27 May 1922 Collins delivered the draft proposal to the British government; two days later it was rejected. Acrimonious negotiations ensued and the British demanded and 'forced a complete and radical revision of the Irish draft' in accordance with the terms of the treaty.[55] The revised draft of the constitution was finally accepted on 15 June and published the following day – the same day as the general election which was to decide whether or not the Irish people rejected the treaty. The election results favoured acceptance of the treaty.

O'Rahilly did not approve of the draft constitution which was to be submitted to the Provisional Parliament. He believed that it was not in accordance with the ethos of the Catholic majority. There was no mention of God and the document, in his opinion, did not reflect Catholic principles, either moral or social.[56] He decided to publicise his own views on what a constitution should contain and informed Darrell Figgis of his intentions. Figgis advised O'Rahilly that he was bound to secrecy in regard to the proceedings and documentation of the draft committee.[57] O'Rahilly did not feel constrained by what he believed to be an unjust restriction. After leaving the Jesuits he had remained in contact with the order and had written a number of articles for *Studies*. He now intended to have his draft C of the constitution published and submitted a copy of it to Fr Patrick J. Connolly, editor of the Jesuit magazine. Connolly was pleased with O'Rahilly's submission and the document was scheduled for publication in the September 1922 issue. However, he decided to seek official permission to publish what might prove to be a very controversial document.[58] The government withheld permission.[59] O'Rahilly was outraged and disputed the government's right to censor him and he demanded the right to put his views before members of the Provisional Parliament. If a positive response was not forthcoming he would publish his own draft constitution.[60] However, he did not succeed in having his document published.

The vocationalist idea had survived the extensive changes imposed by the British government and its succinct expression went virtually unaltered.[61] The draft which had been agreed by the British and Irish governments in June was submitted to Dáil Éireann on 22 September and underwent further amendment before approval by the Dáil on 25 October. This draft was favourably received by the British Parliament on 4 December. Article 45 of the *Constitution of the Irish Free State* (1922) stated

> The Oireachtas may provide for the establishment of Functional or Vocational Councils representing branches of the social and economic life of the Nation. A law establishing any such Council shall determine its powers, rights and duties, and its relation to the government of the Irish Free State (Saorstát Éireann).

Furthermore, Article 56 of the constitution (corresponding to Article 55 of Draft B) allowed for the possibility that these vocational/functional councils would be authorised to nominate external ministers.

Article 45 did not arise from the fervent espousal of Catholic social principles, rather it seems to have been inspired by Article 165 of the German Constitution (1919), or by Article 68 of the Polish Constitution (1921), or by both.[62] It catered for an unusual convergence of interests between Southern Unionism and social Catholicism – the limitation of the powers of central government was of fundamental importance to both. Furthermore, it was in accordance with the popular concern to curtail the authority of central government.[63] The enactment of the constitution arose from one of the provisions of the Anglo-Irish Treaty and was designed to give reassurance to Southern Unionists who felt vulnerable in a predominantly Catholic state.[64] It granted protection to social, political and religious minorities. Personal rights were expressly guaranteed. Religious freedom, freedom of expression and freedom of association were also safeguarded.

On 5 December 1922 the Irish Free State Constitution Act received the royal assent. The following day, exactly one year after the signing of the Anglo-Irish Treaty, the Irish Free State formally came into existence. At its inception the state had to endure civil war because there was strong opposition to the treaty. Peace was restored in May 1923. The prospects for vocationalist developments now appeared full of promise.

SOCIAL CATHOLICISM IN THE IRISH FREE STATE 1923–1931

In 1923 those who hoped for extensive social reforms, on the basis of Catholic social principles, found themselves in a political environment which differed radically from that of the previous decade. The Irish Free State had much more independence than what had been envisaged in the third Home Rule Bill but it fell far short of the aspirations for a 32 county republic. Over 90% of its population was Roman Catholic and, despite the religious neutrality of its constitution, its future was destined to be profoundly influenced by a Catholic ethos. Roman Catholicism exerted a powerful unifying influence within Irish society. It embraced all social classes and spanned the political divide in post civil war Ireland.

All members of the new government were Roman Catholic, except the Minister for Finance, Ernest Blythe. Irish Catholics, when under British rule, had little scope for developing a distinct socio-economic system in harmony with church social teaching. Now that the foreign flag had, to a large extent, been cast off the majority of the Irish people were free to shape their own future. Some Catholic commentators believed that self-government allowed for the possibility of social and economic experimentation on the basis of Catholic social teaching. Their aspirations were unduly optimistic.

There was a lack of consensus among those who hoped for a new social order. Furthermore, neither church nor state, for different reasons, were prepared to facilitate their wishes. The main aim of the government was to maintain law and order and the question of social reforms did not feature prominently on their agenda. The Irish bishops, who had supported the government during the Civil War, enjoyed an influential and privileged position in the new state. Their sense of loyalty to Cosgrave, and their overriding concern for the preservation of moral standards amongst the Catholic majority, influenced them to discourage the few clergymen who were inclined to involve themselves in social initiatives. What they wished for was moral renewal – not social reform.[65] Their negative attitude towards social Catholicism was probably also conditioned by the fear of an investigation from the Vatican if they were seen to support demands for an alternative economic system.[66] The anti-modernist crusade of Pope Pius X was still fresh in the memories of many Catholics.

Proponents of social Catholicism pressed ahead with their demands, unaware of the consensus that existed between church and state. In 1923 Alfred O'Rahilly addressed the congress of the Irish National Teachers' Organisation (I.N.T.O.). He stressed the need for functional democracy and stated that the most urgent and important educational reform was the creation of a council of education.[67] The idea of a council of education was not new, it had been advocated before the foundation of the Irish Free State.[68] O'Rahilly observed that there were already precedents for the establishment of functional councils endowed with statutory powers. The Incorporated Law Society and the General Medical Council exercised a large measure of control over their respective professions with very beneficial results. Evidently he was dissatisfied with the new Irish state when he expressed the opinion

> after the French Revolution the pseudo-democratic dictators sought to abolish all corporate life and combination, so, in a small way, after our little revolution there is a distinct tendency to abolish all councils and boards and consultative bodies in education, agriculture and other departments. One of the first fruits of liberty is apparently to be ministerial bureaucracy. It is not altogether without significance that the proposal to establish such functional councils, which I made in my draft of the Constitution, was suppressed and rejected.[69]

O'Rahilly urged the I.N.T.O. to give priority to the establishment of a council of education when formulating its new educational policy.[70] This body was to be broadly representative of all those engaged in education and was to have advisory and administrative powers. Furthermore, it was to have initiatory and critical functions concerning the passing of legislation. Such a council, he believed, was essential as a mechanism for making badly needed improvements in the educational system. O'Rahilly's advocacy of a council of education met with general approval from the I.N.T.O.[71] but the time had not yet come for any significant degree of public interest in vocational proposals.

By 1924 the bishops' pastoral letter of February 1914, which had emphasised the importance of *Rerum Novarum*, was long forgotten by the general public. One observer of social matters, Pádraig Ua Murcada, noted with regret in *The Catholic Bulletin* that the First World War, the War of Independence, and the Civil War had all distracted public interest from the social teaching of the church.[72]

Throughout the 1920s social Catholicism lacked cohesion and a sense of direction. The November 1923 editorial of *The Catholic Bulletin* reflected this when it declared:

> The fact is that there can be no one policy, whether as regards business transactions, or labour organisation, or public life, that can be definitely stamped as 'the Catholic policy' . . . For there are many Catholic solutions, and the Church never commits herself to the imposition of any one solution as exclusively and specially Catholic. Within the broad and essential limits fixed for Catholic social action by Popes Leo XIII and Pius X, individual Catholics and groups of Catholics are quite free to act and to plan.[73]

Those who did make precise proposals for socio-economic reforms, in accordance with the precepts outlined in *Rerum Novarum*, failed to achieve consensus. A clear example of this can be found in the comments on Henry Somerville's 'An Alternative to Capitalism'. Somerville's article, published in the December 1925 issue of *Studies*, argued that exponents of Catholic social teaching were obliged to condemn both capitalism and socialism. The positive consequence of this was the requirement to put forward an alternative system. His preferred scheme was a guild system, based on private ownership, which had been favoured by Pope Leo XIII in *Rerum Novarum*.[74] For the purpose of substantiating his proposal he described, at length, the formation, composition and functioning of a railway guild. Somerville's article elicited different responses, indicative of the divergent strands of Catholic social thought.

Rev John A. Ryan was of the opinion that Somerville's scheme was well constructed in regard to both ethics and economics but he was not convinced about the practicability of extending the plan to cover a broad range of industrial activities.[75] Hilaire Belloc believed that the guild system was important but he argued that the main mechanism for constructive reform was a redistribution of property.[76] Rev John Kelleher, adopting a more flexible approach, disagreed with Somerville on the basis that neither the natural law nor supernatural revelation specified a particular type of organisation. His contention was that organisations should be formed in accordance with principles of justice and charity, regardless of what type they were.[77] George O'Brien argued strongly that the guild system, as proposed by Somerville, was unlikely to succeed, did not take due cognisance of human nature, would require an excessive amount of state intervention, and would work against the interests of owners. He vigorously defended the capitalist system which Somerville had denounced; it needed to be reformed, not abolished. Despite the fact that the capitalist 'may be an inhuman oppressor and an unchristian brute' his redeeming quality was that he did at least 'provide the filthy lucre without which even the most idealistically controlled business cannot be undertaken.'[78]

Catholic social thought in Ireland was rich in principles but was poor in specifics. This was due to the fact that *Rerum Novarum* did not prescribe a new social order in exact detail; rather it had only given attention to basic principles of Christian social behaviour. Broad consensus was achieved in the acceptance of some of the fundamental concepts of papal social teaching, such as the notion of a just wage, the freedom of workers and employers to form associations, and the right to own private property. Precise proposals, such as the formation of a guild system, did not command much support in the 1920s.

The Catholic hierarchy was too preoccupied with moral renewal to give constructive guidance and support to social Catholicism. Despite the power and influence of the church in Irish society the Catholic bishops and priests were deeply apprehensive about preserving the faith. Their concern focused mainly on issues relating to sexual morality. Books and newspapers, mainly from England, were seen as a major corrupting influence on the youth of the country. Motion pictures and radio programmes were held in similar contempt.[79]

Some social commentators, however, perceived that moral renewal and social reform were related concerns. Rev John Kelleher believed that the drift towards anti-Christian attitudes and practices was largely attributable to the withdrawal of the clergy from the secular life of the people after the War of Independence.[80] The great antidote to neo-pagan immorality was energetic clerical participation in a wide range of social and economic activities. It was anticipated that this strategy would bring the priests and the people closer together, thus consolidating the faith.[81] Yet no consensus was reached on a well-defined scheme for Catholic social reform. Even if widespread agreement had been secured there was no strong Catholic social movement to bring it into effect. Furthermore, the Catholic bishops, as stated earlier, did not wish to reform a system that served them so well. Their cautious attitude towards social Catholicism was evident in the proceedings of the Synod of Maynooth (August 1927) when they declared that

> All should bear constantly in mind the often repeated warning of Pius XI that Catholic Action is concerned with the pastoral ministry and the Christian rule of life, that it is not a political but a religious activity, and, therefore, that it should be amenable to ecclesiastical authority.[82]

The restrictions imposed by this decree were not conducive to the development of social Catholicism in Ireland. Throughout the remainder of the decade the movement remained conspicuously underdeveloped relative to its counterparts in western Europe. Some contemporary observers were acutely of this. Fr Edward Cahill put forward a partial explanation when he wrote

> In Ireland a Catholic social movement in the ordinary sense was practically impossible up to very recent times. The land struggle, the fight for educational freedom, the national contest, the work of church building and religious organisation, engaged the energies of the priests and people during the nineteenth and the first quarter of the twentieth centuries.[83]

In 1930, Cahill saw evidence of a nascent social Catholicism. Some professional organisations, such as the Irish Guild of Catholic Nurses (formed in 1922), were set up on the basis of a Catholic ethos. The periodical, *Studies*, which began publication in 1912, contained articles on social topics in its early issues. The foundation of the Central Catholic Library in Dublin in 1922 and the expanding activities of the Irish Catholic Truth Society were also regarded by Cahill as important developments in the formation of an Irish Catholic social movement. In 1930, attempts were being made to co-ordinate the activities of the Catholic Young Men's Societies so that the new organisation, like *An Ríoghacht*, would be able to work more efficiently towards the implementation of Catholic social teaching.[84]

Despite the efforts of individual priests and laymen the social record of Irish Catholicism remained, if not insignificant, unremarkable. There were no periodicals specialising in social issues. Neither was there study weeks, and there was no equivalent in Ireland of the Catholic Social Guild which English Catholics had founded in 1909. Article 45 of the Free State Constitution (1922), which made provision for the establishment of vocational councils, had not been activated. No influential sector of Irish society clamoured for its implementation and the Cumann na nGaedheal government did nothing to activate it. The lack of interest amongst politicians provoked sharp criticism from John Busteed, professor of economics at University College, Cork. He stated that 'for all our wagging of Papal flags, we insist on discussing our economic problems on a purely agnostic platform'. In his opinion the vast majority of legislators in Dáil Éireann were not familiar with the contents of *Rerum Novarum*. Busteed believed that any politician who publicly advocated the implementation of policies, based on the encyclical, would be undermined by all Irish political parties. This would be done by covert action – not openly. Otherwise there was the fear that the offended politician might 'wag a big woolly-minded unrealistic Papal stick' at his detractors.[85]

The vocationalist ideology, which Alfred O'Rahilly had articulated from 1922 onwards, was still only an aspiration. There was no organisation, commanding widespread support, attempting to put it into effect. However, changes were afoot which were to dredge vocationalism from the depths of obscurity – vocationalism was destined for the arena of public debate. By the late 1920s some inhibiting factors, which had previously restrained the development of the Catholic social movement in Ireland, were no longer present or were not quite so formidable.[86] Ireland was by then a self-governing country, and although the Civil War had left a legacy of deep divisiveness, this was outweighed by the end of the bloodshed and disruption that accompanied the struggle for political independence. The Catholic Church had a network of churches, schools, and other buildings now in place and the construction of its infrastructure was virtually completed. The National University of Ireland had been in operation since 1908 and a university educated Catholic elite was emerging. Thus, by 1930, there was evidence of an embryonic Catholic social movement which was primed for rapid growth.

The growth of social Catholicism was a prerequisite for the popularisation and implementation of vocationalist ideas. A new development in Catholic social teaching was also required to provide an ideological stimulus, and to enable Catholic social activists to reach substantial agreement on social objectives. Such a development occurred on 15 May 1931 when *Quadragesimo Anno* was published.

CHAPTER THREE

Vocationalism, Party Politics and Constitutional Change: 1931–1938

In the general election of 16 February 1932, Cumann na nGaedheal, the political party which which had governed the Irish Free State since its foundation, was defeated by Fianna Fáil. Under the leadership of Éamon de Valera, Fianna Fáil went on to win the next five general elections, retaining power until 1948. Vocationalism did not feature as an important election issue but nevertheless it could not be easily ignored. The publication of *Quadragesimo Anno* in May 1931 had given a new impetus to social Catholicism in western Europe, especially in Ireland. It was mainly responsible for the popularisation of the term 'vocational organisation' in the new state.[1] In Irish parlance papal corporatism came to be known as vocationalism. Many Catholics, who were conscious of the urgent need for constructive reforms, believed that papal corporatism was the great elixir for the pressing social, political and economic problems of their time. The newly issued encyclical bestowed a sharper ideological focus on Catholic social teaching. Never before had the papacy been so precise in advocating a particular economic system. *Quadragesimo Anno* provided social Catholicism with a document of vital importance that was to serve as the ideological basis for a programme of socio-economic reconstruction. Due to the previous weakness of the Catholic social movement in Ireland, its progress after 1931 was even more evident than in other countries.

Vocationalism, it seemed, was destined to have a strong impact on the Irish Free State – a state with an overwhelming Roman Catholic majority anxious to shape its own future independent of Britain. An ideology which appealed simultaneously to nationalism, and to a sense of Catholic loyalty, required a considered response. The 31st Eucharistic Congress, held in Dublin in June 1932, indicated the major importance of Catholicism in the celebration of national identity. On that occasion de Valera, President of the Executive Council, was eager to publicise internationally 'the nation's loyalty to Catholicism and to Rome'.[2] De Valera was the most formidable southern Irish politician of his time and his support was crucial for the success of any vocationalist initiatives which might be undertaken. His attitude towards vocationalism was less than straightforward – this will become evident as the discussion progresses. Party political considerations, his programme of constitutional reform, his commitment to parliamentary democracy, and his sense of Catholicism, were all to play a role in influencing how he dealt with the newly emergent vocationalist lobby.

THE POPULARISATION OF VOCATIONALISM AND ITS IDEOLOGICAL TRAITS

The publication of *Quadragesimo Anno* gave Irish Catholicism a rejuvenated version of *Rerum Novarum* and it served as a great source of inspiration to those who hoped to induce fundamental changes in society. Catholic social teaching in general received more media attention.[3] A number of organisations, societies and periodicals appeared that advocated the adoption of corporatist or vocationalist ideals. It was hoped that the establishment of a new vocational order would end the conflict between social classes, reduce the power of the state, and usher in an era of co-operation and social harmony. Writers, in periodicals such as *Studies, United Ireland, Hibernia* and *The Irish Monthly* praised the concept. A popular weekly newspaper, *The Standard*, frequently advocated the vocationalist ideal.[4]

Vocationalists, inspired by the social encyclicals of Popes Leo XIII and Pius XI, endeavoured to induce radical changes in society on the basis of Christian moral renewal. Dr Cornelius Lucey, who had been Professor of Ethics at Maynooth since 1929, reiterated papal teaching when he stated

> Without vocational organisation we cannot hope to have a healthy social order. Such is the teaching of the encyclical *Quadragesimo Anno*. But we must not think that all will become right once we establish the organisation. Something more is required. We must have good conscientious men to represent us on these vocational councils . . . the reform of morals and manners in our trade union leaders and business men is as indispensable as the reform of the machinery of our social organisation.[5]

When emphasising the urgent need for social reform vocationalists frequently praised the medieval guilds and regretted the passing of a system which supposedly had secured peace, stability, and justice. The Middle Ages were looked upon as an era where moral principles took priority over economic motives. Vocationalists were not of course trying to recreate a medieval society. Lucey emphasised that

> a return to medieval theory does not imply a return to medieval conditions. We do not want to stay or put back the hands of the clock of civilisation and progress. What we want is to dynamise and regulate them with the saner outlook of pre-Reformation days.[6]

Vocational organisations were to be the modern analogues of the extinct guilds and were seen as a mechanism to establish social justice and economic efficiency. There was, however, a distinct tendency amongst vocationalists to express reactionary views which were highly critical of modern ideas and developments. The expressed opinions of a Jesuit priest, Fr Edward J. Coyne, provides a clear example of this. He was a well known exponent of Catholic social teaching and he traced the origins of vocationalism to the romantic movement which had emerged in western Europe in the early nineteenth century.[7] He wrote extensively on social issues and had very strong views on the crisis facing the church in the nineteenth and twentieth centuries. His conservative and anachronistic beliefs were conditioned by a loyal adherence to the tenets of Catholic social teaching as enunciated in the papal encyclicals, and were probably reinforced by an awareness that the Sociey of Jesus had suffered much persecution due to the twin forces of Enlightenment philosophy and absolutist rulership.[8] His social outlook is highly significant because, in later years, he played a central role in the work of the Commission on Vocational Organisation (1939–1944).

Coyne perceived the European society of his time as the end product of European thought which had evolved after the Reformation. According to Coyne, European thought was dominated by a 'whole brood of errors hatched out in the corruption of sane philosophical thought'. From a conservative Catholic point of view error was everywhere. In this context Coyne stated the church's position

> She has always refused to admit that it makes no difference what a man thinks, that there should be complete licence or liberty of thought, that She must be indifferent to or tolerant of all views. Error is an unnatural thing, something which is an intellectual disease or wound in man, and if allowed to exist or spread must produce effects which like itself will be unnatural and evil.[9]

Error had no rights. Thus, according to Coyne; 'it is one of the best known characteristics of the Church that She has always dreaded error, hated it and persecuted it'.[10] The works of René Descartes, Benedictus de Spinoza, Immanuel Kant, Georg Hegel and other intellectuals were not merely of academic interest. With the spread of printing and the increased literacy amongst the masses, error had taken on the qualities of a plague. All this had induced the secularisation of society, a 'half-doubting belief in materialistic evolution', and a sceptical attitude towards religion.[11]

According to Coyne, philosophical errors had inflicted havoc on European society. Jean Jacques Rousseau, Thomas Hobbes, Auguste Comte, Herbert Spencer and Emile Durkheim were identified as the major contributors to the diverse conglomeration of social philosophies which were contrary to Catholic teaching. Maximilien Robespierre was named as the main author of the political philosophy which had a dominating influence over Europe from the time of the French Revolution. This 'very insidious type of philosophy' had been consolidated in the nineteenth century and it had 'seriously infected' many Catholics. Coyne believed that the majority of the population had been led astray and it was on this basis that he questioned the merit of rule by majority and the supremacy of parliament.[12] On the economic front all was not well either. Marxism, like the theory of evolution articulated by Charles Darwin, exerted an 'enormous, if unconscious, influence on the average man'.[13] Thus, by the end of the nineteenth century the philosophical errors of centuries had been disseminated from the study and lecture halls to the masses. Human thought and attitude in turn shaped and transformed society, either by passive tolerance or by militant action.[14]

Coyne believed that Ireland was in dire need of change because Irish society owed 'little or nothing to distinctively Irish thought and not very much to distinctively Catholic thought'.[15] He expressed the view that the economic and political aspects of Irish national life were not just a legacy of English rule but had developed also under the influence of 'the false principles of European philosophy'. In his opinion the Irish political and economic mentality was 'saturated with ideas and principles completely foreign to Catholic philosophy'.[16] Most Irish Catholics were unaware of their erroneous ways. According to Coyne this unintentional divergence from Catholic doctrine was due to the fact that the Catholic majority in Ireland did not have a university of their own for centuries.

Coyne's condemnation of secular philosophies, and his tendency to excessively criticise the institutions of western parliamentary democracies, was typical of those who advocated vocationalism. Another important feature of vocationalism was its affinity for rural fundamentalism. As well as being mainly Roman Catholic, Irish society was predominantly agrarian. In the late nineteenth century the struggle for political independence had become intertwined with the campaign for land reform. This induced the formation of a very potent strain of rural fundamentalism that was to endure into the early years after the Second World War.[17] Rural fundamentalism embraced a set of values that elevated farming and rural life to a high ideological plateau. Agriculture was perceived as essential to national prosperity. Family owned farms were advocated as the basic units of agricultural production. In accordance with distributist principles, which underpinned so much of Catholic social thought, a numerically strong class of landowners was favoured. Rural or small-town life was seen as idyllic.

A strong bond developed between the Roman Catholic Church and the rural community in Ireland. The majority of priests were recruited from the countryside. The church was wary of rapid industrialisation because it invariably led to greater urbanisation and the church's influence tended to be much weaker in urban areas.[18] Consequently, some Irish Catholic intellectuals and social activists indulged in deprecating the twin phenomena of industrialisation and urbanisation that so strongly characterised the socio-economic landscape of Protestant England.

A number of organisations supported the vocationalist movement, most notably Muintir na Tíre (People of the Land). It was founded in 1931 by Fr John Hayes, then a curate in Castleiny, County Tipperary. Although Hayes founded his organisation one week before the publication of *Quadragesimo Anno* he adopted the principles enunciated in the encyclical as the as the basis of its activities. A stated aim of Muintir na Tíre was to promote vocational organisation amongst the rural population. Hayes was a member of the Knights of St Columbanus.[19] This conservative Catholic lay organisation was dedicated to the extension of practical Christianity in all aspects of life. The Knights had, apparently, a profound influence in the shaping of Muintir na Tíre because it was from discussions at Primary Council meetings that the programme of Muintir na Tíre was drafted.[20]

Muintir na Tíre started as an economic organisation, a producers' co-operative movement, modelled on the *Boerenbond Belge* which represented the dominant form of agricultural organisation in the Flemish districts of Belgium. However, the emphasis soon shifted. In the years 1933–1937 Muintir na Tíre transformed itself from a marketing organisation to a movement dedicated to the socio-economic uplift of Irish rural life. Hayes sought advice in setting up the new organisation. Fr E.J. Coyne submitted recommendations concerning the reformation of Muintir na Tíre and outlined a plan for its expansion.[21] The unit of organisation was the parish and parish guilds were left free to choose whatever projects they regarded as most appropriate to their particular circumstances. The organisation gave added impetus to the Catholic social movement and Hayes' own speeches frequently referred to the teaching of *Quadragesimo Anno*.[22]

The espousal of *Quadragesimo Anno* in Ireland was sometimes accompanied by an antagonistic attitude towards Protestantism. Rev M.J. Browne, who was later to serve as chairman of the Commission on Vocational Organisation, asserted that there was nothing basically wrong with industrial capitalism. Nevertheless, he condemned the prevailing capitalist system because he believed it had developed on the basis of a Protestant ethos that had its origins in Reformation principles.[23] However, he did not call for the abolition of capitalism. Instead he stressed the need for reform. In repudiating the evils of a system dominated by Protestantism he invoked the tenets of Catholic social teaching which were to be found in *Quadragesimo Anno*. Browne rejected the Protestant notion that religion was a matter for the individual conscience only and claimed that the serious social and economic problems that were so prevalent at the time were within the realm of morals and therefore the guidance of the Catholic Church was essential.[24] In view of the historical conflict, hostility and suspicion between Catholicism and Protestantism in Ireland, Browne's opinion was more than a voice in the wilderness.

Vocationalists, basing their ideology on the papal encyclicals, were harshly critical of the British system of parliamentary democracy. They expressed an extreme distrust of the state. It was perceived as a dangerous force and it was thought that any attempt to strengthen it could lead to totalitarianism. This was an understandable fear at a time when most of Europe had succumbed to dictatorships. But it was taken so far that even the social welfare system of a liberal democracy such as Ireland, based on the British model, was looked upon with suspicion.[25] The vocationalists' extreme fear of excessive state intervention coincided with a deep and widespread suspicion of officialdom which had inadvertently been implanted during the long years of British rule.[26] Careful provision had been made in the *Constitution of the Irish Free State* (1922) for legislation by referendum as well as by parliament. The constitution, based on an earlier and more individualist way of thinking, provided, not so much for a representation of the people's will, but rather to protect the rights of the individual.[27] The nationalist tradition, political inexperience, Catholic social philosophy and economic exigencies all indicated a state whose role would be less interventionist than in most European nations.[28]

Vocationalists came from different backgrounds, including university lecturers, journalists, trade unionists, businessmen, political activists and priests. They varied widely in their political loyalties. For example, professors Michael Tierney and James Hogan were actively supportive of Fine Gael. Dr Michael Browne was known to be sympathetic towards Fianna Fáil. Vocationalists also varied widely in their understanding of Catholic social teaching. The Blueshirt leader, General Eoin O'Duffy, did not appreciate the distinction between the corporatism of Mussolini and the corporatism of Pope Pius XI. This would have distinguished him from those who were more discerning (such as E.J. Coyne and Michael Browne) and who believed in societal, as distinct from state, corporatism. Fr John Hayes, in contrast to Fr Coyne, was not a theoretician – his social outlook was 'instinctive rather than academic'.[29] Nevertheless, Hayes did more than any other vocationalist in Ireland to give practical effect to *Quadragesimo Anno*.

Vocationalist ideology lacked clarity and 'the precise manner in which a vocational system might function, and its implications for the general governance of Irish society, remained shrouded in a haze of generalities.'[30] The vocationalist movement, therefore, was not monolithic; it developed extremes of left and right. The right wing included the Blueshirts who were inclined to attach greater importance to the state than to smaller organisational units. In contrast those who constituted the left wing tended to anticipate the practices of modern social democracy. They were far more liberal than their right wing counterparts in that they stressed the importance of organisations lower than the state. A notable example is Fr Hayes of Muintir na Tíre, despite the fact that he was an admirer of Mussolini.[31] This wing also included theoreticians such as Fr Edward Coyne and Dr John Dignan, Bishop of Clonfert. Coyne stressed the importance of free vocationalism, growing from within society rather than being imposed by the state.

In the 1930s it seemed that the Catholic social movement in Ireland was assured of success – there seemed to be no major obstacles to the implementation of Catholic teaching. Throughout the decade unchristian ideologies did not pose a threat to social Catholicism in the new state. The Labour Party's brief flirtation with the idea of a 'Workers' Republic' clearly demonstrates this. At its annual conference of 1936 the Labour Party adopted a new party constitution declaring its determination to bring about the establishment of a 'Workers' Republic'. However there was far from unanimous support for Labour's swing to the left within the party. Furthermore, there was much unease about how the new party constitution related to Catholic social teaching.[32] Arising from this the party leadership, in early 1937, decided to seek advice on the matter. A letter was sent to the Catholic hierarchy who in turn referred the matter to a Committee of Experts. The committee of four included two outspoken vocationalists, Dr Michael Browne (then Bishop-Elect of Galway) and Dr Cornelius Lucey.[33] The aspiration for a 'Workers' Republic' was found to be opposed to Catholic principles and was eventually abandoned.[34] There was no strong secular ideology to challenge social Catholicism. Communists were rare in Ireland and even social democrats and liberals were scarce. The vast majority of Irish men and women were practising Catholics. Therefore, it was understandable that many individuals anticipated that a movement based on Catholic social philosophy would gain wholehearted and widespread support.

THE POLITICISATION OF VOCATIONALISM

In the volatile and bipolar political world of Treatyites and anti-Treatyites, Catholicism played a major role in the new state and became the dominant feature of Irish nationalism. There was a tendency, not least in political circles, to declare respect and support for the social teaching of the church. In 1933, the Minister for Local Government and Public Health, Seán T. O'Kelly, publicly stated, in reference to *Quadragesimo Anno*, that 'in no country was this inspiring pronouncement read and studied with greater eagerness and interest than in Ireland'.[35] On the same occasion he announced that the Irish government's programme of economic and political reform was based on Catholic principles. O'Kelly's statement epitomised the influence of Catholicism over Irish society and the Irish political system. It would then have seemed reasonable to expect that Fianna Fáil, when it came to power in March 1932, would embark on a programme of socio-economic reform in accordance with the principles proclaimed in *Quadragesimo Anno*. Such an expectation, however, would not have taken due consideration of the complexities of Irish politics in the early 1930s. In this context the brief ascendancy of the Blueshirts in Fine Gael is of major significance.

Fine Gael was formed in September 1933 when the largest opposition party, Cumann na nGaedheal, joined the National Centre Party and the Blueshirts (National Guard) to form the United Ireland Party, later to be known as Fine Gael. The new party held its first Ard-Fheis on 10 February 1934 under the presidency of the leader of the Blueshirts, General Eoin O'Duffy. The policy of Fine Gael supported demands for a united Ireland within the British Commonwealth. Other party objectives were the ending of the economic war with Britain and the abolition of the existing system of proportional representation. In conformity with the vogue of corporatism, the party advocated the establishment of industrial and agricultural corporations with statutory powers. Despite their minority status the corporatists in Fine Gael enjoyed an influence disproportionate to their numbers during the leadership of Eoin O'Duffy.

The social and political policies of the Blueshirts were developed by Michael Tierney and James Hogan and formed the basis of O'Duffy's corporatist rhetoric during 1933 and 1934. Hogan and Tierney hoped to use the Blueshirts as a means to promote the social and political reconstruction of the Irish state. Their ideas were based mainly on the principles expressed in *Quadragesimo Anno* but they were also influenced by developments in the Catholic fascist states of Europe.[36] General O'Duffy was a keen admirer of the Italian corporate state and was quick to quote *Quadragesimo Anno* as a prop for his political ideology. His failure to distinguish between the fascism of the corporate state in Italy and the societal corporatism preached by the Roman Catholic Church could only have contributed substantially to public apathy towards vocationalism.[37] The connection between fascism and corporatism was widely perceived. That this was so is evident from the persistent tendency of vocationalists to emphasise the difference between the state corporatism of Mussolini and the societal corporatism advocated by the papacy.[38] The political opponents of the Blueshirts regarded the organisation as the Irish counterpart of fascism and a grave threat to democracy. However, the Blueshirts were not fascists despite the outward signs.[39]

Notwithstanding their leader's zeal for corporatism the majority of Fine Gael parliamentary representatives remained unconvinced of its merits and this reflected the overall lack of support within the party. Fine Gael Dáil deputies and Senators did not make reference to corporatism in the course of parliamentary debates. Neither did corporatism influence the formation of party policy in such areas as agriculture or local government.[40] Ironically, the Blueshirts, who were most closely identified with corporatism, knew little about it. Their fascist strutting and paraphernalia caused much public disquiet and their contempt for parliamentary democracy aroused widespread opposition – not just amongst the general public but also within Fine Gael itself. Accusations of fascism put O'Duffy and his supporters on the defensive and considerably weakened the corporatist cause.[41] The main problem with O'Duffy was not his potential to become a dictator. His weakness lay in his political ineptitude and following one blunder after another a deeply embarrassed Fine Gael Party forced him to resign the leadership. O'Duffy, after his departure from Fine Gael, was bitter about the party's lack of genuine commitment to corporatism. After the split corporatist proposals disappeared promptly from Fine Gael policy – this suggests that the commitment of the party had never been strong.

The replacement of democratic governments by dictatorial regimes in mainland Europe caused much apprehension in Irish trade union circles. The militant posturing of the Blueshirts had alarmed those in Labour – the threat to their freedom and even to their very existence was a source of serious concern.[42] Blueshirt advocacy of corporatism tended to reinforce Labour ambivalence towards the ideology. Trade union leaders and Labour party politicians generally refrained from condemning vocationalism outright. The primary reason was that vocationalism was a central feature of Catholic social teaching. Secondly, syndicalist and socialist ideologies also embraced corporatist ideas. The former leader of the Labour Party, Thomas Johnson, was aware that corporatism had been supported by a wide variety of groups such as French and Italian syndicalists, the industrial unionists and the Socialist Labour party of America, and the Guild Socialists of England. Even the social democracy of James Connolly had included corporatist ideas.[43] Johnson equated the corporatism of O'Duffy with the corporatism of Mussolini and of Hitler. These corporatist bodies, real or proposed, were all unacceptable because they were 'ruled from above'.[44] In this regard they differed radically from the ideas put forward by the Guild Socialists and by the syndicalists. While Johnson felt that the corporate idea had much to commend it, the stumbling block was in finding the means to 'apply a democratic conception' so that it could be 'fitted into the wider scheme of civic representation'.[45] Johnson's views highlighted the main problem for those in Labour who were prepared to consider the pursuance of corporatist developments as potentially beneficial.

As Fine Gael and the Blueshirt movement espoused, with varying degrees of emphasis, the merits of vocationalism, Fianna Fáil remained unenthusiastic. Its wariness of radical proposals throughout the 1930s (and early 1940s) was probably due to the widespread political instability in Europe. Furthermore, the bitter legacy of the Civil War did not encourage the party to respond positively to vocationalist demands. Suspicion and distrust characterised the relationship between Fianna Fáil and Fine Gael. Anything so radical as the vocationalisation of Irish society was extremely unlikely to elicit co-operation between the two main political parties. A successful outcome to such a risky undertaking was most improbable in the absence of a broad consensus. The advocacy of corporatism by Fine Gael, especially by the Blueshirts, was seen by Fianna Fáil as an ideological weapon to be used against them and was resisted as such.[46] Fianna Fáil politicians did not frequently discuss corporatist ideology. When they did give their opinions it was in reference to the actions of its advocates at home and abroad. Patrick J. Ruttledge, Minister for Justice, had misgivings about the corporative system and spoke of it in the context of Blueshirt militancy and continental fascism.[47] The Minister for Finance, Seán MacEntee felt that the idea of a corporate state was a euphemism for fascism and resented the verbal onslaught on parliamentary democracy which had been carried out by O'Duffy and his colleagues.[48]

After General O'Duffy resigned as leader of Fine Gael the corporatists were marginalised in the party. Thus, the fate of corporatism came to depend on Fianna Fáil but de Valera did not see fit to 'engage in any radical experimentation or social engineering'.[49] The corporatists had demanded the establishment of a national vocational council which would advise or even supersede parliament. From de Valera's viewpoint this had to be avoided because a national vocational council would restrict the power of political parties. Fianna Fáil, as the largest party, had the most to lose.[50]

De Valera's attitude towards vocationalism was not dictated entirely by political self-interest. He was committed to the democratic process and reports from Irish diplomats serving abroad probably discouraged him from embarking on a programme which had become confused with corporatist experiments in Italy and Portugal. Yet, he could not publicly criticise an ideology based on the papal encyclicals. He was unable to completely reject corporatist ideology but his concept of corporatism was fundamentally different from that of the Blueshirts. It was based on voluntary action rather than on state intervention. De Valera clearly stated his understanding of the vocationalist concept at the Fianna Fáil Ard Fheis on 3 November 1936. He declared

> I would like personally to see such an organisation developed, but I would like to see it developed voluntarily – I don't believe in State-imposed organisations of that kind. I believe they only last for a while. The regime may support them with its power, but once the regime breaks they break. There is nothing permanent about them, and they are not natural. I hope, therefore, to see developed gradually here a functional organisation of our society by voluntary action . . .[51]

De Valera approved of vocationalism in principle but he, and his ministers, were to reject demands to grant statutory powers to vocational organisations. A cautious strategy, reinforced, if not induced by

Blueshirt rhetoric, was adopted. De Valera was prepared to make symbolic gestures of approval but no concrete action would be taken to assist the vocationalisation of Irish society. His outlook was shared by the Irish Catholic bishops. Their antipathy towards vocationalism become evident as early as 1933–1934 when they opposed the proposal to form a vocational council of education.

THE BISHOPS AND THE VOCATIONALIST IDEAL

Alfred O'Rahilly had advocated, at the 1923 Congress of the Irish National Teachers' Organisation (I.N.T.O.), the formation of a vocational council of education. He continued to do so[52] and the I.N.T.O. adopted it as an important policy objective. On 3 October 1933 the executive of the I.N.T.O. issued invitations to several educational associations, training colleges and universities to send representatives to a meeting for the purpose of discussing the formation of a council or federation.[53] This council was to serve the Minister for Education in an advisory or consultative capacity. Without such a council it was feared that the Department of Education would 'tend to become bureaucratic and more or less divorced from public opinion.'[54] This proposal did not seem to pose any fundamental problems because, it was claimed, advisory councils were already giving assistance to the Departments of Local Government, Agriculture, Industry and Commerce, Posts and Telegraphs, and Fisheries.

On 9 November 1933 the Catholic Headmasters' Association (C.H.A.) selected its chairman, Dr John Charles McQuaid and its secretary, Canon James Staunton, as its representatives to attend the convention organised by the I.N.T.O. On 11 November approximately 40 delegates assembled for discussions in response to the I.N.T.O. initiative.[55] McQuaid, appeared determined to prevent the the I.N.T.O. from achieving its objective. He did not contribute constructively to the proceedings and he forcefully articulated his objections. He felt that an advisory council, composed of representatives from over a dozen educational bodies, would be unwieldy. The priorities of the constituent organisations would tend to cause conflict rather than consensus and McQuaid expressed his concern that the C.H.A. would be drawn into a succession of controversies.[56]

McQuaid and the C.H.A. were of the opinion that, since 1922, successive ministers of education had improved the secondary sector of the educational system. Furthermore, the problems of secondary education could be more equitably dealt with by the department than by the majority vote of an advisory council. Thus, the C.H.A. would oppose the formation of a council if it did not receive the approval of the Minister for Education.[57] That such approval would be obtained was most unlikely. The C.H.A., according to McQuaid, had 'clear evidence' that two successive ministers of education had refused to establish an advisory council.[58] The C.H.A. adopted a negative stance and was supported by representatives of both the Christian Brothers and the De La Salle Training College. The attitude of the C.H.A. delegates aroused 'much dissatisfaction' and, due to the continuous opposition of McQuaid and Staunton, the meeting was adjourned.[59] However it was agreed that a second convention would be held. After the meeting McQuaid spoke to the Minister for Education. Thomas Derrig approved of the stance of the C.H.A. and, according to McQuaid, expressed dissatisfaction with the 'big stick' behaviour of the I.N.T.O.[60] Understandably, the Minister for Education would not welcome the erosion of his authority which was likely to occur if the I.N.T.O. was successful in forming an advisory council. The Executive of the I.N.T.O. had anticipated that if a council was formed it would be able to exert a strong influence on departmental policies, even if the council was not officially appointed.[61] The proposed council would also diminish the authority of the Irish Catholic hierarchy over the educational system. McQuaid was to observe that

> It does not appear, either from official correspondence or from private conversations or from the convention proceedings that either the I.N.T.O. or the A.S.T.I. consider it in any way opposed to Catholic principles to constitute a Federation of any and every religious body.[62]

McQuaid was not surprised at the attitudes of the I.N.T.O. and the A.S.T.I. (Association of Secondary Teachers of Ireland) because, as he observed, both organisations were constituted on a non-denominational basis. He perceived that the two teaching associations were 'strongly organised'. In contrast, the professedly Catholic organisations had no joint organisation and McQuaid feared that the lay organisations would dominate the council. Despite his strong opposition to the I.N.T.O. proposal he thought it prudent to treat the invitation with 'sympathetic courtesy, lest offence be given to teaching organisations of lay persons, who are mainly Catholic.'[63]

The second meeting was convened on 24 March 1934. The I.N.T.O. now proposed the formation of a 'loose Federation' of educational bodies because of the strong opposition to the formation of an advisory council. McQuaid's opposition was facilitated by the fact that fewer delegates attended. Furthermore, since November he had obtained the support of delegates representing the Christian Brothers and the De La Salle Brothers. Arising from a motion put forward by McQuaid, and seconded by a representative of De La Salle College (Waterford), the burden of responsibility was placed on the I.N.T.O. to draw up a memorandum for the next meeting which would explain to delegates the objectives, functioning and constitution of the proposed federation. The I.N.T.O. document was then to serve as the basis for further discussions.[64] McQuaid was careful to act with the approval of Archbishop Edward Byrne. Shortly before the third meeting he conveyed to the archbishop his intention to attend the meeting, 'watch carefully, but make no proposals whatever other than that of referring the memorandum to our Association'.[65]

A third meeting was held on 26 May 1934 with only 16 delegates in attendance. The memorandum issued by the I.N.T.O. was confidential and any amendments decided on were to be included in a final memorandum which would be issued later 'entirely on the responsibility of the I.N.T.O.'[66] The system of representation on 'The Federation of Irish Educational Associations' was questioned, first by McQuaid, then by Canon James Staunton. Difficulties arose over attempts to define the term 'association' relating to representation. It was agreed that each Training College would have one member in the federation. Each university college and Trinity College were to have two members each. The I.N.T.O., with 12,000 members, did not press for representation proportional to their numerical strength and agreed to limit their representation on the federation to six.

The C.H.A. delegates did not put forward any constructive proposals. Neither did Brother Ryan of the Christian Brothers.[67] However, despite their negative stance the final draft of a proposal for a federation of educational associations was issued on 15 June. At this point the formation of a federation, composed of the I.N.T.O., A.S.T.I. and the Protestant associations seemed certain. The next convention was scheduled for November.[68] On 26 September McQuaid met Archbishop Byrne and secretly sought permission to conduct 'private and personal negotiations' with the A.S.T.I. and the I.N.T.O.[69] The previous day McQuaid had interviewed T.J. Burke, Secretary of the A.S.T.I. He recorded

> As Mr Burke has been for years a member of our teaching Staff, I have had an opportunity of observing him closely and of proving that he is a very worthy Catholic. When the situation was explained he agreed at once to secede from the proposed Federation. He anticipates little difficulty in persuading his Executive. I believe he will fully succeed, for I know that his opinion is greatly valued by his Association, and this year, all the members of his Executive happen to be Catholics.[70]

Six days later McQuaid met T.J. O'Connell, Secretary of the I.N.T.O., and persuaded him to abandon the scheme. However, O'Connell anticipated opposition from some members of the organisation. Nevertheless he was confident that 'by deft arrangement and without giving all the reasons' he would at least persuade 'the reasonable element' of the I.N.T.O. He was of the opinion that the other associations would not have either the motivation or the ability to form a federation.[71] O'Connell's confidence and optimism were well founded. On 5 October McQuaid wrote to senior members of the hierarchy informing them that the scheme had been abandoned.[72]

The C.H.A. had been in a strong position to make or break the attempt to form a council of education. The Chairman of the I.N.T.O., Cormac Breathnach, had acknowledged this.[73] McQuaid and his colleagues in the C.H.A. not only had the support of the Minister for Education – their obstructionist strategy was also approved of by the Catholic hierarchy.[74] The perceived danger of a non-denominational federation had been averted. McQuaid had been careful to avoid antagonising or offending Catholic lay teachers. Both Burke and O'Connell had informed him that there was considerable dissatisfaction amongst the membership of their respective organisations concerning the 'aloofness of the clerical element' in the educational system. McQuaid emphasised that the opposition to setting up a federation of educational associations was not a refusal to co-operate with the lay organisations. He anticipated that the I.N.T.O. and the A.S.T.I. would press for more active collaboration from the clerical associations and he felt that this should be forthcoming if 'the Catholic position' was to be consolidated.[75]

McQuaid had dutifully carried out the wishes of the hierarchy in undermining the initiatives of the I.N.T.O. The I.N.T.O. scheme was regarded as a threat to clerical control. It would lead to a greater secularisation of the educational system and for this reason it had to be strenuously opposed. The Roman Catholic bishops were determined to place Catholic education 'under the closer guardianship' of the hierarchy.[76]

The rejection of a vocational council of education indicated an opposition to vocationalism in general. It would be untenable for the bishops to advocate vocationalism in other social and economic aspects of community life while opposing it in the educational system. Yet the bishops, like the politicians, could not criticise an ideology promulgated by the papacy. In public they eulogised *Quadragesimo Anno* without reservation. In practise they either opposed or failed to support vocationalist schemes. The hazardous contradiction between public statements and private practice required shrewd diplomacy. A veil of secrecy had been drawn over the convention proceedings from the onset of negotiations between the educational associations. McQuaid had been anxious to 'prevent useless or hurtful discussions' in the newspapers when, at the third meeting, he formally proposed that secrecy be maintained. Prior to this himself and Staunton had succeeded in keeping the proceedings 'as private as possible'.[77] Failure to secure confidentiality would probably have caused a sharp deterioration in relations between Catholic lay teachers and the clergy. Furthermore there was the risk that public opinion would look unfavourably on the heavy-handed methods of McQuaid and his superiors. However, a disadvantage of the secretive approach was that some loyal Catholics (most notably Alfred O'Rahilly), who espoused vocationalist principles, continued to advocate the establishment of a council of education – unaware that the hierarchy was hostile to such a proposal.[78]

Only a small minority of the clergy genuinely supported the attempts of lay Catholics to bring about changes on the basis of the social principles expressed in the encyclicals.[79] The Catholic social movement was further disadvantaged because it was fragmented into different groups.[80] There was a broad spectrum of opinion in regard to the interpretation and application of the papal encyclicals. By 1937–38 the endeavours of socially conscious Catholics to achieve their objectives had proven to be a dismal failure.[81] Furthermore, with the notable exception of Muintir na Tíre, there were no encouraging signs for future development.

The Irish Catholic bishops continued to oppose the radical aspirations of social Catholicism and this was indicated by the role of Bishop William MacNeely of Raphoe in the proceedings of the Commission of Inquiry into Banking, Currency and Credit (1934–38). When B. Berthon Waters and Cox Gordon, both members of *An Ríoghacht* (a Catholic Action organisation), submitted evidence to the commission MacNeely took issue with them. Waters and Cox Gordon had based their submissions on the papal encyclicals but MacNeely asserted that these papal documents were not applicable to the specific points of detail which had been put forward for consideration.[82] Two other members of *An Ríoghacht*, Brian J. McCaffrey and James O'Rourke, also gave written and oral evidence to the commission. They received a frosty response from MacNeely. The bishop was quick to state that their views did not represent those of the church. Moreover, he added that they were not competent to interpret Catholic social teaching.[83]

Evidently, MacNeely did not welcome the introduction of the social encyclicals into the discussions of the commission. He disagreed with a minority of his colleagues on the commission who believed that the principles outlined in the social encyclicals should form the basis of their findings. In Appendix No.15 of the majority report, jointly signed with George O'Brien, he made his views clear. With the *Constitution of Ireland* (1937) in place MacNeely and O'Brien were confident that 'institutions that offend against social justice will not be tolerated . . .'[84] They maintained that '. . . it is easy to show that the aims of the encyclicals are being achieved – slowly and imperfectly, no doubt – by existing leglislation.'[85] They claimed that Portugal was the only country in Europe to seriously attempt to give legislative effect to the teachings of the papal encyclicals. This had not involved 'attempts at monetary or financial experimentation.' On the contrary, Salazar's government had been 'very conservative.'[86] The authors of Appendix No.15 were clearly against any radical proposals and were favourably disposed towards the maintainence of the *status quo*. Furthermore, they asserted that only those with advanced training in theology and cognate subjects were competent to interpret the social encyclicals.[87]

Alfred O'Rahilly repudiated the majority report and wrote what became Minority Report no. I. He persuaded two of his colleagues, Seán Campbell and William O'Brien, to sign it.[88] In appendix B of the minority report O'Rahilly maintained that the majority of his colleagues had not taken due cognisance of the papal encyclicals. He derived no comfort from the 1937 constitution because he was of the opinion that 'the road to social chaos is paved with high-sounding Constitutions . . . the abstract acceptance of the social Encyclicals does not lead us anywhere.'[89] He believed that there was a 'considerable' amount of social injustice in Ireland which was not being adequately addressed.[90] The time had come to implement the ideals of both the constitution and the papal encyclicals. In a robust refutation of Appendix No.15 he disputed the claim that the encyclicals were so complicated and obscure that the laity were incapable of understanding the contents of the documents. He pointed out that *Quadragesimo Anno* was addressed, not only to the bishops, but also to 'all the faithful of the Catholic world.'[91]

Another member of the commission, Peadar J. O'Loghlen, submitted Minority Report Number III. This document had been prepared by Fr Edward Cahill, SJ, B. Berthon Waters and Bulmer Hobson.[92] These individuals were associated with two Catholic Action organisations; *An Ríoghacht* and the League for Social Justice.[93] O'Loghlen declined to sign the Majority Report because he was of the opinion that the principles expressed in papal social teaching had been 'mentioned only to be dismissed as not having any special bearing on conditions in Ireland'.[94] The proposals put forward in his name were designed to assist the application of the encyclicals in Ireland.

O'Loghlen, O'Rahilly, O'Brien and Campbell formed only a small minority in a commission of 21 members. They received no support from Bishop William MacNeely in invoking the social encyclicals. MacNeely, like the majority of his colleagues, was content to endorse the prevailing fiscal theory and practice of the Department of Finance.[95] The two minority reports were not well received by the department.[96]

The Catholic bishops remained steadfast in their conservative outlook. Matters of personal morality remained their dominant concern. They made no serious attempt to stimulate an interest in the social encyclicals and they were opposed to any radical changes that might disturb the harmonious relationship between church and state. Nevertheless, some prominent Catholic intellectuals, motivated by a desire to reform society on the basis of Catholic social principles, greeted *Rerum Novarum* and *Quadragesimo Anno* with zeal. The reform of the monetary system was an important aspect of Catholic teaching. Vocationalist ideology also featured prominently in social Catholicism. Because its underlying principles emanated from the Vatican loyal Catholics who stridently advocated its acceptance and implementation did not subject it to rigorous critical analysis. Vocationalism was sufficiently plausible and had a certain appeal that evoked a popular response in some Catholic circles. Consequently, the popularisation of the vocationalist concept impacted strongly on Irish politics.

VOCATIONALISM AND CONSTITUTIONAL REFORM

De Valera and Fianna Fáil regarded the 1922 constitution as a document imposed by the British that had legitimised the most repugnant provisions of the Anglo-Irish Treaty. This view persisted despite the fact that Cumann na nGaedheal had successfully endeavoured to bring about a number of constitutional reforms which had resulted in a greater degree of independence for the Irish Free State. De Valera wished to give to the Irish people a constitution that they could call their own, free of imperial symbols and accretions.[97] His accession to office in 1932 gave him the opportunity to rewrite the Anglo-Irish Treaty of 1921. Simultaneously, this involved the destruction of the Irish Free State and a fundamental change in the law of the state to accommodate his view of Anglo-Irish relations. The 1922 constitution had to go. It was time to begin to replace the old with the new but first the Senate (Seanad Éireann, the upper house of parliament) had to be abolished because the process of constitutional change would be much easier under a unicameral parliamentary system.

When the first Fianna Fáil government took office in March 1932 it promptly put through the Dáil a Bill for the removal of the Oath of Allegiance. This Bill was blocked by the Senate. De Valera anticipated that the Senate would obstruct constitutional change and he decided to remedy this problem.[98] Therefore in March 1934 he introduced a Bill for its abolition and on 29 May 1936 the Senate of the Irish Free State ceased to exist. Under a unicameral parliamentary system, Éamon de Valera carried through legislation which defined the external association of the Irish Free State with the British Commonwealth. However, there was considerable support for the establishment of a bicameral parliament. Fine Gael, sections of the Catholic Church, commercial interests and ex-Unionists all favoured the idea.[99] De Valera took cognizance of their demands and this is why on 9 June 1936 the Second House of the Oireachtas Commission was appointed to examine the possibilities of forming a new Senate as part of the new constitution. It reported on 1 October of the same year.

The commission was unable to come to an agreed conclusion and produced three minority reports as well as several reservations to the majority report. It was one of the minority reports which most appealed to de Valera and which he made the basis of his own proposals. D.A. Binchy, Sir John Keane, E. Lynch, F. MacDermot, J. Moynihan, A. O'Rahilly, M. Tierney and R. Wilson signed this minority report.[100] The minority report advocated that the Second Chamber should be established on a functional basis.[101] It was envisaged that a vocational Senate would serve as an adjunct to geographical democracy. A new method of selection, based on the principle of organised functional democracy, was intended to soften the conflict between political parties. It was designed to induce highly qualified individuals to become active in public life who would normally not do so despite their outstanding abilities to constructively criticise and improve particular legislative proposals. The report emphasised the importance of not challenging the primacy of the Dáil – this obviously appealed to de Valera; otherwise there would be an inevitable conflict between the two Houses of Parliament. The signatories of the report therefore rejected any popular electoral procedure that would merely duplicate the composition of the Dáil.

The report acknowledged that vocational organisation was still insufficiently developed to facilitate representation entirely on the basis of existing vocational organisations.[102] Consequently, the commissioners felt compelled to recommend that the forty elected members of the Second Chamber should be elected by Dáil Éireann. The members were to be elected from panels formed before each general election and would be drawn mostly from vocational organisations of 'a substantially representative character'.[103] It was hoped that, eventually, vocational organisations would proliferate and develop to such an extent that the constitution would make provision for direct election to the Second Chamber by functional councils.[104] But first the new constitution had to be drafted and put before the people.

The task of making constitutional provision for the establishment of a vocational Senate was of minor importance in comparison to the overall scheme of drafting a new constitution. Despite this, the number of individuals involved in the drafting process was relatively small. De Valera excluded many of his cabinet ministers from the project. Furthermore, in a political environment where the bitter legacy of the Civil War was still conspicuously evident, he felt unable to make use of a wide range of legal expertise that would otherwise have been available to him. Some eminent lawyers, for example Daniel Binchy and Patrick McGilligan, were associated with the opposition.[105] Many of de Valera's academic friends were clergymen and, in view of the scarcity of expert advice open to him, he availed of their counsel.

The drafting of the constitution was a risky undertaking and de Valera was careful to keep himself informed about issues pertaining to Catholic moral and social teaching. When the constitution was being drafted he carefully studied the published and private views of Dr Cornelius Lucey and Dr Michael Browne[106] – both were outspoken advocates of vocationalism. He also sought and obtained advice from other Catholic clergymen. Fr Edward Cahill and his Jesuit colleagues were 'quietly influential' in the drafting of the document.[107] The Holy Ghost priest, John Charles McQuaid (then president of Blackrock College, became Archbishop of Dublin in 1940), was much more influential in the drafting process than the Jesuits. He was a close advisor to de Valera and he spent a considerable amount of time 'rummaging in the heads of the last few Popes' in this capacity.[108] Although de Valera sought guidance from a carefully selected number of clergymen it was he who made the final decisions about what was included in the final draft of the constitution.

Fr Cahill advised de Valera that the new constitution 'should mark a definite break with the Liberal and non-Christian type of State' and '. . . should be, if not confessedly Catholic . . . at least definitely and confessedly Christian'.[109] De Valera found Cahill's submission 'very useful as indicating the principles which should inspire all governmental activity so as to make it conform with Catholic teaching'. However, a major problem for de Valera was deciding to what extent Catholic teaching could be, or should be, given legal expression in the new constitution.[110]

Cahill informed de Valera that it was possible to have a Christian constitution under any one of several political systems. Cornelius Lucey, although acknowledging that democracy had much to commend it, was extremely generous in allowing for possibilities when he stated

> it is ethically certain that no citizen has a natural right that he be consulted through his vote as to who shall be his ruler. The only natural right he has in this respect is that his ruler, however selected, shall rule for the common good . . . Just as there is no Divine Right of Kings, there is no Divine Right of Democracy. The principles of Political Autonomy, Majority Rule, The Will of the People, The Supremacy of the People and the rest are principles of order, not fundamental moral principles.[111]

De Valera was hardly impressed by the wide range of political options which this assertion seemed to offer. He realized that Catholic social teaching demanded a more complex approach to the formation of political structures than Lucey's exposition indicated. The exponents of Catholic teaching who advised de Valera did not always agree with each other.[112] While this tested his intellectual capability it did not present him with any insurmountable problems.

On 1 July 1937 the constitution was submitted to the electorate. The result of the referendum favoured acceptance by 685,105 votes to 526,945.[113] De Valera had won popular acceptance for his constitution. The contents of the *Constitution of Ireland (Bunreacht na hÉireann)* reflected the fact that he had been deeply influenced by Catholic teaching. Its preamble, its provision for vocational councils, its articles on religion, the family, personal rights and education – all reflected both the moral and social teaching of the Catholic Church.

The constitution, which became effective on 29 December 1937, had popular legitimacy by virtue of the referendum and it elicited a favourable response from the international community. It was influenced by two very different concepts – the liberal and secular tradition of parliamentary democracy and the notion of a state based upon Catholic principles. The document gave expression to the contemporary ideas of Catholic sociologists with particular reference to vocational organisation. However, the relationship between democracy and vocationalism was debatable. De Valera's attitude towards vocationalism, therefore, was one of extreme caution. Consequently, the vocationalists gained only a symbolic gesture, a constitution with a vocationalist veneer, not a firm commitment from the government to assist in the creation of a new vocationalist order.

A VOCATIONAL SENATE?

De Valera did not really have the option of excluding the vocationalist ideal from the new constitution. Although Article 45 of the 1922 constitution was never activated it did at least genuflect to vocationalism. When so much from the 1922 constitution had been retained it would have been unwise to exclude vocational organisation. Fianna Fáil was politically vulnerable and it would have been imprudent to risk difficulties with the Catholic hierarchy. Article 15.3 of the 1937 constitution, repeating almost verbatim article 45 of the 1922 constitution, declared

> The Oireachtas may provide for the establishment or recognition of functional or vocational councils representing branches of the social and economic life of the people. A law establishing or recognising any such council shall determine its rights, powers and duties, and its relation to the Oireachtas and to the Government.

Further to this Articles 18 and 19 appeared to envisage the new Senate as a vocational chamber. Article 19 stated

> Provision may be made by law for the direct election by any functional or vocational group or association or council of so many members of Seanad Éireann as may be fixed by such law in substitution for an equal number of the members to be elected from the corresponding panels of candidates constituted under Article 18 of this Constitution.

Alfred O'Rahilly was not impressed by de Valera's apparent commitment to the vocationalist concept and denounced Article 15.3 as 'pious claptrap.'[114] He believed that Fianna Fáil did not take *Quadragesimo Anno* seriously and drew attention to the fact that the government had refused to set up a council of education despite repeated demands by the I.N.T.O. and other educationalists to do so. He was of the opinion that de Valera was not serious about Article 19. If he was then, O'Rahilly urged,

> let him make a few Councils mandatory in the Constitution – say, councils of Education, Agriculture and Industry – and give them certain powers. I proposed this fifteen years ago, as he is perfectly aware. But he still takes refuge in the platitudes with which my dissident colleagues of 1922 politely turned me down.[115]

O'Rahilly regarded the Senate as 'a very bad one' and not in accordance with the minority report (of the Second House of the Oireachtas Commission) which he had signed, notwithstanding de Valera's claim to the contrary. It was unlikely to be reformed by any serious attempts to implement Article 19. He posed the rhetorical question: 'are the Government and Party likely to abandon the power of election and patronage which the delightfully elastic method of Senate-election puts into their hands?' He did not think so because 'there is altogether too much may-be, or endeavouring to direct policy towards, about parts of this Constitution. A further dose of shall-be would be most welcome to some of us.'[116] O'Rahilly's scathing criticisms were to prove remarkably perceptive.

In retrospect it is clear that de Valera was not enamoured with vocationalism. It was not that he was unsympathetic to papal teachings in general, or to *Quadragesimo Anno* in particular. On the contrary, there was much in the encyclical that appealed to him. The *Constitution of Ireland* (1937) bears testimony to this; the document was, to a large extent, a reflection of his personal philosophy.[117] Article 45, which is dedicated to 'Directive Principles of Social Policy' echoes some of the teaching from *Quadragesimo Anno*. Herein, for example, can be found a commitment to regulate free competition (45, 2.3) and control financial credit (45, 2.4) in order to safeguard the common good. Yet, despite his declared affinity for Catholic social teaching, de Valera was reluctant to put in place a constitutional imperative for its implementation.

A common criticism of Article 45 was that it had no legal effect.[118] It is likely that De Valera repudiated this criticism on the basis that

> A Constitution purports to lay down the directive lines along which the Nation shall strive, in unity of mind and will, to attain the common good. A constitution is not a thesis of philosophy and theology. It is an enactment guided and delimited by the teachings of Catholic philosophy and theology. It enshrines and sets forth the aim of what ought to be our Christian endeavour in social policy.
>
> The intention of this Draft Constitution – to one who carefully studies it – is clearly set forth: it means seriously to endeavour to create those circumstances of temporal life which shall realize the Christian ideal of Society. We desire – within the vast freedom of the Social Encyclicals – to achieve the common good of this Nation on Christian lines and by Christian methods.[119]

Yet it was difficult to dismiss the assertion that the article was no more than a collection of 'pious aspirations, devoid of effective force'.[120] Articles 15, 18 and 19, which made provision for the formation of vocational councils and the establishment of a vocational senate, were to prove equally ineffective because supporting legislation was not forthcoming.

The decision to restore the bicameral system was a controversial feature of the 1937 constitution. The vast majority of members of both Fianna Fáil and the Labour Party, and probably most of the electorate, were at least apathetic if not hostile to the idea of a Second Chamber.[121] When cognizance is taken of de Valera's attitude towards the bicameral system in general, and towards the old Senate in particular, it seems strange that constitutional provisions were made for the establishment of a new Senate. When discussing the Seanad Electoral (Panel Members) Bill of 1937 he exclaimed 'it would pass the wit of man to devise a really satisfactory Second Chamber'.[122] This conviction was based on the Abbé Sieyès' dilemma which meant that if two chambers are in agreement then one does not serve a useful purpose. If they disagree then one of them is 'mischievous'.[123]

Despite all his objections to a Second Chamber he felt unable to reject the creation of a new Senate on the basis of abstract logic alone. He had a 'certain sort of hankering' for a Senate which he could not explain.[124] As if to justify this rather vague thinking on the issue he stated that most other nations had established a Second Chamber. He felt that there might be some benefit in having a Second Chamber but, because he could not devise a satisfactory method for constituting a new Senate, he omitted from the constitution specific guidelines that would determine electoral procedure. The ambiguity that arose from this failure created problems for the legislature later on.

The signatories of the minority report of the Second House of the Oireachtas Commission, which de Valera apparently favoured as a basis for establishing a vocational Senate, were not government supporters. The Fianna Fáil leader declared that he was not interested in implementing the ideas of a particular political party.[125] He reiterated some of the views expressed in the minority report. The advantage of a Senate formed on a vocational basis meant that the Senate would not be an imitation of the Dáil.[126] It was to be complementary rather than antagonistic towards geographical democracy. He declared that any system now proposed could be amended later because the constitution was flexible enough to allow functional organisations, when formed, to elect their members directly to the Senate. In the meantime, another method had to be found and the best that could be hoped for was a transitional Senate.[127]

De Valera felt that a Second Chamber could be justified by its function of checking, redrafting and amending legislation.[128] What he hoped for was the independent criticism of Bills. He considered that the vocational method would give to the Oireachtas valuable expertise and specialist information. Yet, he was not so naive to expect that it was possible to devise a Senate which would be non-political.[129] He was determined that the Senate would be subordinate to the Dáil and would be incapable of obstructing government policy, especially in foreign affairs. He warned that the Senate would be 'taught a very good lesson' if it caused a general election without ample reason.[130] The Senate was created by an Act of Parliament and could be disposed of by repealing the legislation.

Under the terms of the constitution there were, and still is, three different types of Senator. Eleven are nominated by the taoiseach (prime minister). Six are elected by two Irish Universities – three from the National University of Ireland, and three from the University of Dublin. Article 18 provided that the remaining forty-three were to be elected on a vocational basis. This seemed to be a major move in the corporatist direction. The forty-three members were to be elected from five panels of candidates. The formation of these panels was to be determined by future legislation and they were to represent the following sectors:

- Education and Culture,
- Agriculture and Fisheries,
- Labour,
- Industry and Commerce,
- Public Administration and Services.

The Seanad Electoral (Panel Members) Act, 1937, provided for the nomination of candidates for the above panels by Dáil Deputies, and by vocational organisations within the category concerned. The Irish Agricultural Organisation Society, for example, could nominate for the Agricultural Panel and the Irish Trade Union Congress could nominate for the Labour Panel. The assignment of employers and trade unions to separate Senate panels represents an important difference between Irish vocationalism and continental corporatism. In Italy 'corporations' were associations that combined employers and trade unions from the same profession or trade.[131]

Although nominations came in part from some vocational bodies, the actual electorate for the forty-three panel members was entirely political – consisting of Dáil deputies and County Borough councillors.[132] Vocational organisations could nominate outstanding men from their ranks but they had nothing whatever to do with the final choice. Owing to the fact that the electoral process was almost entirely in the hands of politicians, the nominating bodies tended only to choose those who were most likely to be acceptable to the political parties, rather than those who were most accomplished in their professions. The vocational principle in the Senate elections was rendered inoperable. Those bodies who ignored the political parties were generally unsuccessful and under the 1937 Act, non-political nominees often failed to acquire even a single first preference vote.[133]

Article 18 of the constitution provided that eleven members of Seanad Éireann were to be nominated by the taoiseach. De Valera defended this for two reasons. Firstly, the taoiseach would be empowered to give representation to minorities or particular interests, if he believed they deserved representation. Secondly, these nominations would virtually guarantee a government majority and greatly reduce the probability of a Senate which would be hostile to the Dáil or to a Dáil majority.[134] The latter consideration took priority. De Valera consistently nominated a majority of loyal party members and the representation of minority groups or special interests received little attention.[135] He was assured of a docile Senate by being able to manipulate its composition. As if he had not been cautious enough in this regard, the 1937 constitution gave the Senate very little power – it was a mere shadow of its predecessor.[136]

Article 18.7.1 was not conducive to the creation of a satisfactory process of nomination and election, since no one could define in legal terminology what constituted 'knowledge and practical experience'. Consequently, many of those elected from the five panels described in Article 18.7 had only very tenuous connections with the interests they were supposed to represent. Nor could the term 'vocational' (used in Articles 15.3.1 and 19) be defined.[137] The situation, which arose from the vagueness of Articles 18 and 19, was exacerbated by the subsequent legislation. The Seanad Electoral (Panel Members) Act 1937, provided for a complicated system of nomination together with election by proportional representation. The Act was badly flawed. Consequently, the quota was so low, the electorate so easy to manipulate, and the voting arrangements so unsatisfactory, that not only were the political parties able to monopolise the electoral process but there was also opportunity for bribery and corruption. Allegations of bribery in the first elections were dismissed by de Valera in the Dáil.[138] He resisted pressure – even from within Fianna Fáil – to initiate urgent reforms.

The outcome of placing the electoral system in the hands of politicians was that the parties controlled the elections to the exclusion of almost all the genuine vocational groups. De Valera clearly sacrificed the small measure of vocational representation which, apparently, he had intended in favour of political expediency and the Senate became an inferior imitation of the Dáil. Indeed, as one historian stated, 'it would require a suspension of critical faculties to assume that Mr de Valera did not know what he was doing'.[139] De Valera did know, and it was plain to see, as his political opponents pointed out, that party political considerations would take precedence over vocational interests.[140]

Éamon de Valera did not pretend to advocate a scheme which provided for a comprehensive representation of vocational organisations but he indicated his intention of taking the first tentative steps towards the vocationalist ideal.[141] Apparently he regarded his proposals as a means of giving a limited amount of vocational representation by allowing for nominations by a substantial number of representative bodies. He was unable to provide a vocational basis of representation because vocational organisation in the state was insufficiently developed to allow for a Senate to be elected mainly by vocational bodies. But this does not constitute an adequate defence of his system of nomination and election because those organisations which were satisfactorily organised on a vocational basis were not given effective representation.[142]

The new Irish Senate, which convened for the first time on 27 April 1938, had become discredited shortly after its foundation. With the exception of the university seats, the political parties controlled the electoral process from the beginning. The dismal failure of vocational candidates was highlighted by the national press.[143] De Valera had used vocational ideas as an excuse to establish a new Senate because 'he was more motivated by the desire to institutionalise Fianna Fáil patronage than support the gospel of corporatism'.[144] The composition of the Senate therefore came to represent a large number of party candidates (defeated at the previous Dáil election), party members and prominent supporters. Naturally these members tended to speak and vote on party lines and they even sat in party groups.[145]

De Valera sacrificed the vocationalist ideal in the formation of the Senate but he did not do so lightly. The fact that the constitution provided for the formation of the Senate on a vocational basis shows how influential the idea of vocational organisation had become in the Ireland of 1937. De Valera could not ignore vocationalism nor could he completely reject it. His intellectual curiosity about the subject had not yet been satisfied. Furthermore, the practical aspects of vocationalism had still to be elucidated.

CHAPTER FOUR

De Valera's Appeasement of the Vocationalist Lobby

DE VALERA AND VOCATIONALISM

From an analysis of the formation and functioning of the Senate, established under the provisions of the 1937 constitution, it would be reasonable to assume that Éamon de Valera was disingenuous in his professed acceptance of the vocationalist concept. There was, and still is, a striking difference between the notion and the reality of a vocational Senate. Furthermore, it is difficult to refute the assertion that de Valera regarded vocationalism as an aggravation with the potential to become politically disruptive.[1] However, this assessment does not completely explain de Valera's attitude towards vocationalist demands. Different strands of his social, political and religious beliefs need to be considered in order to attempt a comprehensive account of his reasoning and actions.

De Valera hoped that the state would achieve economic self-sufficiency; a Gaelic autarky endowed with frugal comforts.[2] Vocationalism implied the attainment of social harmony that would assist in the achievement of self-sufficiency while at the same time giving expression to Catholic social teaching. Besides, self-sufficiency was fast becoming a necessity rather than a policy option because of the deterioration in international relations and the perceived inevitability of war in 1938. Therefore, de Valera's interest in vocationalism can be seen as deriving, not only from his commitment to Catholicism, but also from his desire for a self-sufficient Gaelic state; a desire accentuated by economic exigencies – both real and anticipated.

A fundamental requirement for any vocationalist scheme was that there had to be a reasonable prospect of economic benefit to the national community. The vocationalists, however, had not clearly demonstrated, by empirical research and objective analysis, how the vocationalisation of Irish society would benefit the country. De Valera was anxious to extract from them a scheme whereby abstract principles could be applied to the pressing socio-economic problems without yielding any measure of political power to a new order. In early 1938 he suggested that there should be a series of broadcasts on vocational organisation.[3] Alfred O'Rahilly too exercised his considerable influence in persuading the management of Radio Éireann to organise the series of lectures.[4]

An insight into de Valera's personal feelings concerning vocationalism can be ascertained from a letter written by Maurice Moynihan, dated 10 February 1938, and addressed to T.J. Kiernan. Moynihan told the director of broadcasting

> From what I know generally, however, of the Taoiseach's mind in the matter, I think that he would like to have lectures of a rather practical nature included in the proposed series. He is particularly interested in the actual working of Vocational Organisation where it has been tried. He has expressed interest from time to time in the Whitley system of Industrial Councils in Great Britain, feeling, as he does, that in some respects conditions in that country are more nearly akin to our own than conditions in Continental countries. I think, therefore, that he would like some attention to be given to the Whitley system, and to the question whether Whitley Councils form a useful basis for the development of Vocational Organisation.[5]

Where vocationalism was concerned the taoiseach wished to separate the socio-economic from the political. The corporatism of O'Duffy, Mussolini and Salazar could only have strengthened such a resolve. In contrast, the Whitley Councils of Britain functioned on a voluntary basis and were not endowed with statutory powers.[6] However, despite the widespread distribution of vocational organisations, no country was governed or functioned on the basis of societal corporatism. There were no clear examples to light the way. Ireland had more in common with Britain than any other country and, because of this, de Valera focused his attention on the Whitley Councils which formed a highly developed and extensive network of vocational organisations.

In mainland Europe obstacles to corporatist planning were overcome by the assertion of the coercive powers of the state and this usually involved the suppression of the working classes. The majority of vocationalists did not approve of the linkage between corporatism and dictatorship and were anxious to stress that vocationalism, so closely related to corporatism, was compatible with democracy.[7] De Valera's affinity for democracy precluded him from drawing any positive conclusions from such dictatorial systems of governance. His commitment to parliamentary democracy formed the basis of his political outlook. There were no clear examples from Europe or elsewhere to cause him to seriously contemplate the idea of promoting the development of vocational organisation in Ireland which involved the devolution of statutory powers. The system of Whitley Councils offered the only sign of encouragement from abroad.

Whitley councils had been formed on the basis of the recommendations of the Whitley Committee (which had been set up by the British government in 1916–1917). The committee's objective was to address the issue of industrial relations and it recommended a hierarchy of councils. The function of these councils was to bring management and workers together so as to facilitate the settlement of disputes in order to promote harmony and efficiency in production. Whitley Councils put the onus of responsibility on management and trade unions to make this system of voluntary conciliation work. Agreements reached by the councils were not registered by the state or by law. The policy of the state was not to interfere with the councils and it was hoped that the Whitley system would promote a greater commitment to self-government in industry. Whitley Councils grew in number and the system proliferated.[8] From de Valera's viewpoint they were worthy of serious enquiry.

Nine radio broadcasts on vocational organisation were transmitted between 20 March and 15 May 1938.[9] Those who spoke on different aspects of vocational organisation included Alfred O'Rahilly, Michael Tierney, and Fr John M. Hayes. Hayes expressed views which were sharply critical of industrial capitalism and he decried 'the tinselled achievements of industrialism' which had left widespread unemployment in its wake.[10] In contrast to the industrialised cities, which were so severely affected by the Great Depression of the early 1930s, rural life was invested with an almost utopian quality. His speculative venture into the future conjured up a vista where factories would lie in ruins while the 'broad acres will still be kissed by the sun, and bountiful nature will still be opening her treasures to the hands who seek them in the spirit of honest toil.'[11] This romantic view was sharply at variance with the hardships of rural life in Ireland during the 1930s. Hayes believed that 'in this country we cannot think of vocational organisation without giving our first thoughts to agriculture'. He stressed the importance of vocational organisation to the rural community when he stated 'the rural population need vocational organisation more than any others, because of their paramount importance'.[12]

De Valera shared some of the ideas expressed by Hayes – this is evident from Article 45.2(v.) of the *Constitution of Ireland* (1937) which states: 'That there may be established on the land in economic security as many families as in the circumstances shall be practicable'. Years later, in a flight of fantasy, de Valera spoke of a rustic utopia complete with 'athletic youths', 'comely maidens' and 'cosy homesteads'.[13] Despite his vision of rural bliss de Valera shared little common ground with the vocationalists. The Whitley Councils, which he had expressed such a strong interest in, were not discussed. This omission epitomised the tendency of the vocationalists to look to mainland Europe, rather than to Britain, for inspiration. The Irish vocationalists were not enamoured with Britain – it appealed to their nationalist feelings to denounce the failures of a capitalist system that had been founded mainly on a Protestant ethos. Yet de Valera, whose nationalist credentials were not in question, was not handicapped by an aversion to things British or Protestant.

Notwithstanding the vocationalist veneer of the new Senate, the structure and functioning of the Irish parliament was deeply influenced by British parliamentary democracy. Michael Tierney's lecture, entitled 'Vocationalism and Parliamentary Democracy: Are They Reconcilable?' denounced the British political system. When Britain was mentioned it served only to illustrate what was wrong with society where vocational organisation was absent or insufficiently developed.[14] Tierney went so far as to declare in the radio broadcast of 3 April 1938 that

> The whole conception of economic freedom, which by an amazing misplaced act of faith identified the public good with the satisfaction of private greed, is an English conception. Born of English Puritanism, it has conquered the whole world . . .[15]

Other vocationalists shared Tierney's contempt for Protestant Britain. Fr Hayes depicted a rather grim scenario in England when he declared that the collapse of uncontrolled industrialisation had led to unemployment and a flight from the land on a massive scale.[16] Ireland had not yet suffered the same fate.

Not only did the broadcasts ignore an aspect of vocationalism that was of particular interest to de Valera – views were also expressed which were sharply critical of, or at variance with, the policies of his government. Vocationalists frequently articulated contempt for the civil service, equating it with a pervasive and pernicious bureaucracy. By denouncing the civil service, based on the British model, the vocationalists may have hoped to appeal to Irish nationalist feelings. Michael Tierney was of the opinion that in a modern parliamentary democracy such as Ireland, 'the real authority is shared between the party, the ministers, and the bureaucracy, with the first having the smallest share and the third by far the greatest'.[17] De Valera was hardly impressed by this extreme view. Ironically, a few weeks after the Tierney lecture, the Fianna Fáil government was defeated in the Dáil on the issue of an Arbitration Board for the civil service. In the general election campaign which followed, de Valera defended his party's position by arguing that the government, as guardian of the public interest, had the duty and the right to retain effective control over the civil service.[18]

John J. Horgan's lecture entitled 'A Vocational Second Chamber', was broadcasted on 8 May 1938. Horgan noted that the professions, which were the best organised vocational bodies, gained less than any of the other organisations in the recent elections. Political rather than vocational considerations had taken priority.[19] Horgan believed that the Senate could not function on a vocational basis because, with the exception of the professions, vocational organisations were scarce in Ireland. He doubted that these organisations would develop naturally from the various vocations. Therefore, vocational organisations had to be legislated for and had to be fostered by the state if a vocational Senate was ever to be realised.[20] This view diverged widely from de Valera's version of vocationalism – which was based on voluntary commitment and spontaneous growth. But if de Valera was to retain a shred of credibility concerning his professed belief in the merits of the vocational ideal he had to grant another concession, real or apparent, to the vocationalist lobby. He had to be seen to have a positive approach. The discredited Senate, and one of his own nominees to it – Senator Frank MacDermot – provided him with the opportunity of dealing effectively with the vocationalists.

MacDermot had left Fine Gael in late 1935 and he served as an independent TD until 1937. In 1938 de Valera appointed him to the new Senate. MacDermot played a significant role in the formation of the Senate, having served as a member of the Second House of the Oireachtas Commission. He was one of eight signatories to one of the minority reports which de Valera professed to use as the basis of his own scheme. This minority report advocated the setting up of a Second Chamber on a functional or vocational basis. The Senate did not operate on a vocational basis and MacDermot was anxious to remedy this. On 13 July 1938 he proposed in the Senate: 'That in the opinion of the Seanad a small commission should be appointed by the Government to examine and report on the possibility of extending vocational organisation by legislative or administrative action.'[21] MacDermot's proposal was primarily motivated by his desire to create 'a firm foundation for a vocational Seanad'.[22] However, he stated that his motion had broader objectives than this but he dwelt only briefly on the much wider subject of vocationalism. He regretted that the papal encyclicals had been greeted with much uncritical acclaim in Ireland.

There was a marked tendency in some quarters to regard encyclicals as infallible documents.[23] In the August 1938 issue of *The Irish Ecclesiastical Record* Dr Cornelius Lucey conceded that 'Encyclicals are not usually made the vehicle for infallible pronouncements'. Lest this encourage a liberal attitude amongst the laity, he went on to say 'still their teaching has to be accepted as the official teaching of the Church. All Catholics, therefore, are bound to abide by it loyally'.[24] Not surprisingly, therefore, *Quadragesimo Anno* had served as a conduit for the uncritical acceptance of corporatist ideas – greatly facilitated by the triumphalism so characteristic of Irish Catholicism in the 1930s. Confident that they had all the answers many Catholics closed their minds to any idea or argument which challenged official church teaching.[25] Few were courageous enough, or perhaps foolish enough, to openly question what emanated from the Vatican. However, passive acceptance did not lead to the widespread implementation of the principles enunciated in the social encyclicals. This was reflected in Frank MacDermot's speech to the Senate on 13 July 1938 when he observed

> I would say that the Encyclical in question has been much more praised in this country than it has been read, more read than it has been understood, and more understood than it has been put into practice. There are some obvious questions that arise out of it that are not even being asked in this country.[26]

Notwithstanding the fact that vocationalism was an ideal praised by the papacy, few bishops or clergymen supported it. Therefore, few amongst the laity were well disposed towards giving practical effect to Catholic social teaching.[27]

MacDermot declared that the pope's demand for the abolishment of disputes between classes lay within the domain of morals. Yet he was careful to point out that the promotion of vocational organisation, which the papacy put forward as the solution to this pressing problem, was within the domain of politics and economics and there was no obligation upon Catholics to accept it as an infallible doctrine. He was critical of those supporters of Catholic social teaching who stridently condemned the democratic traditions of Britain and France while placing Ireland and other Catholic countries above reproach.[28] He did not claim to be an expert on the subject of vocationalism and had formed no firm opinions about its potential advantages nor was he convinced that the societies of western Europe could be radically reorganised on a vocationalist basis.[29] MacDermot did not approve of the type of corporatism which existed in Italy or Portugal. His objective was to strengthen parliamentary democracy – not to weaken it. To this end a reformed Senate would make available to the legislature expertise which could not be otherwise obtained.[30]

Senator Michael Tierney, who seconded MacDermot's motion, took a different approach to the issue of vocational organisation. He regarded the vocationalisation of the Senate as an issue of secondary importance. For him the vocationalisation of the whole of Irish society was by far a more important objective.[31] Tierney's outlook probably commanded more support that MacDermot's in vocationalist circles.

De Valera reacted cautiously to the Senate proposal put forward by MacDermot and Tierney. Vocationalism was based on Catholic social teaching and de Valera was not able to reject it outright. The dictates of his Catholic conscience (albeit a conscience modified by political perceptions) had to be satisfied. Vocationalist aspirations were not clearly compatible with the existing system of parliamentary democracy. Therefore, he was confronted with a serious dilemma. There is evidence to suggest that he contacted Fr John Charles McQuaid for advice on this issue. When the commission was established, or was about to be established, McQuaid expressed the view that

> . . . no functional organisation can truly be imposed from above by the State. Rather it must grow upwards after it has taken deep root in the true understanding of the common good as the end of social organized life . . . In this Christian State . . . when a Constitution was evolved for the citizens, no structure of vocational groups was imposed but room was left for the slow uprise of what it was hoped our Christian conscience would certainly evolve: a framework within which each person and group could effectively work towards achievement of a social order truly conformable with the laws of nature and Christian teaching. Such is the hope that this Commission, I am sure, will attempt to realize.[32]

McQuaid's concept of vocational organisation posed no problems for Fianna Fáil because it did not call for radical reforms in the political system. McQuaid was of the opinion that 'vocational structure is not, as I understand it, in itself concerned with any particular political or economic form of State'.[33] This type of vocational organisation, motivated by Christian commitment rather than by state intervention, was clearly compatible with parliamentary democracy and did not represent any threats to the primacy of Fianna Fáil in the political arena of Irish national life. If fundamental changes were to occur then the motivating force would be voluntary action. This highly improbable development did not present de Valera with a dilemma. He had nothing to fear from vocational organisations which arose from Christian efforts to promote the common good. He could confidently reject, in the light of Catholic social teaching, any proposals for the artificial creation of powerful vocational organisations, such as a national vocational assembly, which would tend to undermine the supremacy of parliament.

His attitude to the establishment of a commission on vocational organisation was passive and tactical rather than enthusiastic. He acceded to the Senate motion of MacDermot and Tierney because he could not see any harm in setting up a commission to investigate the feasibility of extending vocational organisation by legislative or administrative action.[34] It would have been difficult for him to refuse the request because the Senate was theoretically based on the vocationalist concept. His opposition would have risked the provocation of harsh criticism from the vocationalists and was likely to place him in a predicament with the clergy. The decision to establish such a commission would not commit him, or anyone else, to any particular policy because no one knew what the commission's findings would be.[35] Accordingly, the motion to set up the Commission on Vocational Organisation was passed by Seanad Éireann on 21 July 1938 and de Valera promised to implement it.[36]

De Valera, like Tierney, favoured broad terms of reference.[37] The taoiseach's motivation, however, was more complex than Tierney's and was typical of the machinations of his labyrinthine intellect – anxious to reconcile divergent objectives. An extensive enquiry would satisfy his intellectual curiosity about vocationalism while simultaneously determining whether or not it had any practical value. It would satisfy his Catholic conscience that he was doing everything reasonably possible to promote the practical application of Catholic social teaching. Furthermore, a broad agenda would preoccupy the vocationalists during a critical time in the nation's history and leave the Fianna Fáil government free to attend to the exigencies of a great European war which was drawing closer.

The vocationalist lobby had stubbornly persisted in its strident demands for radical reforms and, despite its diminished popularity, it still required a prudent response. With the threat of war on the horizon the disruptive potential of the vocationalists was enhanced and it may have been thought necessary to divert the main thrust of the movement along a route calculated to diminish the probability of conflict with the government. It is most likely that this was one of de Valera's motivations when he decided to set up the Commission on Vocational

Organisation.[38] He was short of political options when it came to the appeasement of the vocationalist lobby.[39] One senior Fianna Fáil politician, Seán MacEntee, felt that a committee of self-declared experts would be useful in deflecting vocationalist zeal in a direction which would not cause problems for the Fianna Fáil government.[40] John Swift's polemical article on vocationalism supports MacEntee's observation. Swift noted that when a government is troubled by the strident demands of an influential and persistent lobby a favoured tactic is to appoint a commission to research and report. This strategy can be particularly effective if the task assigned to the commission is complicated and broad in its terms of reference. In these circumstances the government is likely to calculate that the commission's enquiry will take years and, by the time the report is submitted, events will have either discredited its recommendations or the process of change will have made the report irrelevant. This in turn will enable the government to quite effectively and confidently resist proposals pressed on it by influential interest groups.[41] Therefore, commissions can serve as a means of deflecting the activities of a lobby away from the danger of causing problems for government.

De Valera's attitude towards the formation of the new Senate indicates his line of logic in regard to the setting up of the commission. He believed that it was the duty of those who clamoured for a second chamber to show how it might be constituted and to explain what powers should be given to it. Simply pointing to two chambered parliaments abroad was not good enough.[42] Setting up a commission on vocational organisation was consistent with this type of reasoning. Those who advocated vocationalist initiatives were obligated to show how such schemes could be practicable, economically beneficial, and compatible with a liberal parliamentary democracy.

Maurice Moynihan, who served as Secretary to the Government between 1937 and 1960, worked closely with de Valera for most of this period. In conversation with the author he made a number of perceptive statements concerning de Valera's attitude towards vocationalism. In making constitutional provision for a vocational Senate de Valera was simply allowing for possibilities. He was never 'welded' to the idea of vocational organisation. However, he did harbour an intellectual curiosity about the subject. He had a sound understanding of Catholic social teaching and he understood the fundamental difference between the societal corporatism (i.e. vocationalism) advocated by the papacy and the state corporatism of fascist regimes.[43] Some people in Ireland, and throughout Europe also, became confused about the distinction between the two ideologies. Consequently, the popular appeal of vocationalism, which had reached its zenith in the early 1930s, declined considerably near the end of the decade. Why then did de Valera wait until 1938 to set about establishing the Commission on Vocational Organisation? Why not 1933 or 1934? Moynihan's answer is surprisingly straightforward. There were far more pressing matters to be attended to – such as the deterioration of Anglo-Irish relations, widespread unemployment, and the subversive activities of the I.R.A.[44]

THE ESTABLISHMENT OF THE COMMISSION ON VOCATIONAL ORGANISATION

On 21 July 1938 de Valera announced in the Senate that his government was prepared to acquiesce to the motion of MacDermot and Tierney. His department took responsibility for setting up the Commission on Vocational Organisation. The necessary procedures were initiated without delay and by 26 July the draft terms of reference, which were virtually identical in wording to the final terms of reference, had been formulated.[45] Tierney, although suggesting a slight change in the wording, regarded the draft terms of reference as 'excellent'.[46] Little did he appreciate the implications. A serious disadvantage with wide terms of reference was that a broadly based enquiry was called for. This would place an extremely heavy burden on the commission. The study would take years to complete and might even end in confusion. The commission's terms of reference were

> to examine and report on:
> - the practicability of developing functional or vocational organisation in the circumstances of this country;
> - the means best calculated to promote such development;
> - the rights and powers which should be conferred and the duties which should be imposed on functional or vocational bodies and, generally, the relations of such bodies to the Oireachtas and to the Government, and
> - the legislative and administrative measures that would be required.[47]

De Valera insisted that the commission should be a large one. He justified this on the basis that it was

> desired to have on the Commission, in addition to persons who have studied the theory of Vocational Organisation, representatives of various classes of the community who have personal experience of the problems

> which confront those whom they represent and who are, therefore, in a position to examine these problems from the practical as distinct from the purely theoretical point of view.[48]

A communication from the Taoiseach's Office, addressed to the private secretary of each minister (except External Affairs), conveys a hint of embarrassment when it was admitted that the proposed list of personnel for the commission was 'rather extensive'.[49] The reason, allegedly, was that it was 'impossible to reduce the membership if representation is to be accorded to the various individuals and interests who have a claim to consideration'. This difficulty could have been avoided if de Valera had not devised very broad terms of reference.

De Valera sought advice in setting up the commission. On 26 July 1938 Maurice Moynihan, on his instructions, wrote to Senators Tierney and MacDermot requesting names of persons who, in their opinion, would be suitable to act as members of the proposed commission. The Right Rev W.J. Curry of the Presbyterian Church in Ireland and the Most Rev J.A.F. Gregg (Church of Ireland, Lord Archbishop of Dublin) were contacted in pursuance of the intention to have clergymen of the main Christian denominations included in the membership of the commission.[50] Government ministers were also asked for their views on the list of proposed personnel. Seán Lemass's lack of interest is noteworthy. An insight into his vision of the future can be obtained from a speech which he gave to the Drapers' Chamber of Trade on 21 April 1938. He expressed the view that the complexity of modern life and the increasing intervention of the state in the economy would make the creation of voluntary associations for sectional interests a vital necessity. Lemass believed that

> it was inevitable that future years would see the transfer, in whole or in part, of legislative functions, in matters affecting the conduct of industrial and mercantile activities, from the national parliament to special bodies comprised of persons with special intimate knowledge of particular branches of trade and representative of all interests affected.[51]

Apparently, he supported the notion of subsidiary function so espoused by the vocationalists. He stated that until the above legislative changes had taken place, government departments would pursue a policy of maintaining close relations with voluntary trade associations for the purpose of helping legislators to make informed decisions. Yet, despite his expressed neo-vocationalist opinions, he had no views to put forward about who should be invited to join the commission.

The only opinion offered by the Minister for Posts and Telegraphs, P.J. Little, was that the chairman of the commission should be a layman. The Minister for Finance, Seán MacEntee, proposed that Professor Daniel Binchy be chosen in preference to Professor O'Rahilly as a member of the churches and universities group of the commission. MacEntee drew attention to paragraph 623 of *The Majority Report of the Commission of Inquiry into Banking, Currency and Credit*. Apparently, O'Rahilly had withheld his minority report until the last meeting of the commission and even then refused to allow discussion on it.[52] Furthermore, McEntee noted that the professor had attended only about one-quarter of the meetings of the commission.[53] As if all this was not enough to indicate O'Rahilly's unsuitability to serve on a government commission MacEntee stated that since the Commission of Inquiry into Banking, Currency and Credit had finished its work O'Rahilly had criticised, at length, his former colleagues. Allegedly, O'Rahilly proceeded to express his views in great detail in journals and other publications. Previously, it was claimed, he had declined to give his opinions during the three and a half years in which the commission was carrying out its work.[54] MacEntee's account, although substantially true, was not unbiased.[55] O'Rahilly's deviation from economic orthodoxy had incensed the civil servants in the Department of Finance. As far as MacEntee and his officials were concerned O'Rahilly was now *persona non grata*. However, despite MacEntee's opposition, O'Rahilly was invited to serve on the commission.

The Minister for Education, Thomas Derrig, was anxious to forestall renewed demands for a vocational council of education when he offered his views on the list of proposed personnel. He was strongly opposed to the setting up such a council and feared that the majority of the proposed personnel in the churches and universities group were biased in favour of establishing it. Fr Edward J. Coyne, SJ, was singled out as a possible exception.[56] Derrig then proposed that the Professor of Education of Maynooth College and some representatives of the Catholic Headmasters' Association, such as their chairman (Fr John Charles McQuaid), should be added to the list. McQuaid had already opposed the establishment of such a council. However, Derrig's advice had little or no effect.

The only member of the cabinet who seemed to have any influence on the selection of personnel was the Minister for Agriculture, James Ryan. Four members of the commission, Lucy Franks, Patrick Gallagher, John Hayes, and Henry Kennedy were recommended by the minister.[57] Senators Tierney and MacDermot were apparently more influential – no less than eight members of the commission were appointed, although not exclusively, on the strength of their recommendations.[58] Perhaps this was in keeping with the strategy of letting the self-appointed experts get on with the job of seeking solutions to the country's pressing socio-economic problems – beginning with finding suitable members for the commission. Of course de Valera, as taoiseach, had the predominant input into determining the final composition of the commission.

On 29 August 1938 de Valera had visited Dr Browne in Galway, requesting him to accept the post of chairman of the commission. The Bishop of Galway was well known for his Fianna Fáil sympathies although it should be noted that the two opposition Senators, Tierney and MacDermot, recommended his appointment to the commission. Browne did not give the taoiseach a decision on that occasion but he intimated that his answer would be forthcoming within a few days. On 6 September a telegram was received from Browne stating that his acceptance was 'most probable'.[59] The bishop had been extremely cautious about accepting the invitation. Before doing so he contacted the papal nuncio, Mgr Paschal Robinson, who advised him to accept the chairmanship.[60] Browne had also contacted Cardinal Joseph MacRory and Archbishop Thomas Gilmartin of Tuam and it seems that they also advised him to accept.[61] Refusing to be rushed he delayed in making his reply. De Valera found it necessary to write again on 14 October, inquiring whether he was now in a position to give his decision. Browne finally agreed to serve on the commission after receiving an assurance from de Valera that its establishment was not merely a tactic to shelve the issue of vocational organisation.[62] He confirmed his acceptance to the taoiseach on 17 October.

As de Valera proceeded with setting up the commission there was much unease in Labour circles. This was due to the fact that corporatism was closely associated with fascism in the public mind, especially amongst those in Labour. Many supporters of the trade unions were deeply suspicious and hostile towards any concept that had appeared to elicit Blueshirt or fascist approval. The Blueshirts had expressed support for both fascism and corporatism. By late 1938 the Blueshirts had long ceased to trouble Irish domestic politics but memories of Eoin O'Duffy's garbled rhetoric probably helped to sustain Labour's misgivings about vocationalism, which had become confused with state corporatism. The representatives of Labour were, therefore, less than enthusiastic about the setting up of the commission. On 2 December, Browne wrote to de Valera stating 'It is common gossip in Dublin that a certain number of people have been nominated on a Commission on Vocational Organisation who misunderstand and detest it as a species of dictatorship'.[63] It is most likely that this gossip emanated from Labour circles. On 7 December the taoiseach met

Browne to discuss the matter. On the same day Browne had discussions with O'Rahilly and Coyne. No information was obtained about these conversations but it is likely that greater cognisance was taken of Labour's sensitivities.

James Larkin was suspicious that the commission might advocate a type of corporatism similar to that of Italy or Portugal. He urged his trade union colleagues to be vigilant when the commission issued its recommendations because he feared that the corporatist proposals would not be compatible with democracy.[64] Louie Bennett was more moderate in her views but she was still wary of corporatism. She could see no reason for completely rejecting the concept of corporative organisation which she equated with vocationalism. The merit of corporatism, as she saw it, was that it had the potential to induce a greater democratization of the political system. However, she was not confident that the commission would advocate the right type of corporatism. Therefore, her role, and that of her trade union colleagues, was to ensure that a scheme was devised in conformity with the aspirations of the trade union movement.[65]

Doubts about the merits of setting up the commission extended beyond the ranks of Labour. Browne had 'effectively nominated' Coyne, O'Rahilly and Tierney to serve with him. Coyne and Tierney readily agreed but O'Rahilly was cautious about accepting the invitation which de Valera had issued on 30 November 1938.[66] He was 'wary and sceptical' due to his 'recent experience'.[67] This was, presumably, due to his former membership of the banking commission which had presented its report to the government in the spring of 1938.

O'Rahilly feared that the commission would be composed of members who did not share a common set of principles. Consensus, therefore, would be difficult to achieve. He envisaged the production of a majority report and a number of minority reports. With its unwieldy composition there was always the danger that the commission might degenerate into a mere forum for debate at the public expense. Furthermore, he had serious doubts about the intentions of the Fianna Fáil government. He suspected that the commission might be a poisoned chalice – 'set up to stultify itself, to break up into irreconcilable factions, and to lead to a triumphant justification of the *status quo*'.[68] Because of his doubts and suspicions O'Rahilly was anxious to obtain assurances regarding personnel and principles. He wanted to be assured that those appointed to the commission would be committed to the implementation of a workable scheme in accordance with the papal encyclicals. It pleased O'Rahilly that Browne had been chosen as chairman. He had also heard the rumour that one or two Catholic sociologists were included.

However, he perceived that there was 'another category of men, rare and difficult to find, namely men who not only accept fully the principle of functional organisation but have a detailed practicable knowledge of business' which was lacking in himself and in his clerical colleagues. Not one for modest self-evaluation, O'Rahilly believed that he was more competent than de Valera to indicate who these men were.[69]

O'Rahilly's suspicions and lack of information about the composition and objectives of the commission prompted him to decline acceptance of de Valera's offer of membership until more information was supplied – especially regarding personnel. He was anxious to co-operate only with those who embraced Catholic social teaching. With this purpose in mind he pressed for the inclusion of two Cork colleagues whom he valued for their business experience. On 1 December he hurriedly wrote to Browne advocating the appointment of T. O'Mahony (Secretary and Director of Dowdall O'Mahony and Company) and C.P. McCarthy who was an auditor.[70] Both O'Rahilly and Browne wrote to de Valera (on 8 December and 10 December respectively) urging the addition of O'Mahony and McCarthy to the commission.[71] Browne also advised the Taoiseach to include James Larkin and Senator Thomas Foran.

De Valera did not reply promptly to the recommendations of O'Rahilly and Browne. O'Rahilly again communicated his proposal to de Valera. He had not yet agreed to serve on the commission and did not intend to change his stance until invitations were extended to O'Mahony and McCarthy.[72] O'Rahilly's demands were eventually met and, by 3 January, O'Mahony and McCarthy had been included in the list of personnel. So too was O'Rahilly who had been eventually persuaded by Browne to participate.[73] O'Rahilly's reason for serving on the commission was to help the chairman when requested to do so. This included giving advice and assistance to Browne so that he could 'meet opposition from certain schools of thought.'[74]

On 10 January 1939, the government approved of the terms of reference and the personnel of the commission. (See Appendix 1 for a list and classification of personnel).

The employers' group, by far the largest, was more than twice the labour representation. The reason for this was that de Valera thought it necessary to 'get people with a sufficiently varied knowledge of industry in its various branches'.[75] In contrast to the employers' group the agricultural group seems to have been grossly under-represented in view of the central importance of agriculture in the Irish economy. De Valera's excuse for the relatively low representation given to agriculture was that 'agricultural conditions in all parts of the country were very much the same, and one representative would have as much knowledge – talking generally – as another.'[76] He then went on to say: 'In regard to agriculture, however, the commission would fail if it was not able to deal with rural organisation.' The prospect of a successful outcome was poor; it was even less promising when cognisance was taken of the size of the commission – 25 members in all. Furthermore, the commission was composed of individuals who were not noted for their flexibility and readiness to change their minds.[77]

On 10 January the government had decided that the appointment of a vice-chairman to the commission should be considered and determined by the taoiseach.[78] De Valera intended to ask the Church of Ireland bishop, Dr Thomas A. Harvey, to serve in that capacity. However, he prudently decided to consult Browne before communicating his decision to Harvey.[79] Browne was not satisfied with the way the taoiseach had set up the commission and he did not feel inhibited from bluntly stating his views. In his reply of 20 January he stated that he did not object to the proposal to appoint a vice-chairman but he did convey his lack of enthusiasm by drawing attention to the fact that such an appointment had not been made when the Dublin Housing Commission was set up. Moreover, it was not possible for him to give his opinion as to who would be most suitable because he had not been informed about the final composition of the commission. The most recent information on personnel that he had received was from the meeting with de Valera on 7 December. On that occasion he had been surprised to learn that the membership of the commission had been almost completed.[80] A few days later he wrote to de Valera on the subject of commission members. Presumably, this was the letter of 10 December when Browne had advocated the inclusion of Thomas Foran, Timothy O'Mahony, C.P. McCarthy, and James Larkin.

The bishop bitterly complained that 'though six weeks have elapsed I have received neither reply nor acknowledgement.' Browne concluded his letter with biting sarcasm, declaring: 'If, when the Commission is established it will be ignored in a similar fashion by Government Departments, I suggest that the most suitable person for your purpose would be a representative of the Christian Scientists.'[81] Obviously Browne was angered by the lack of consultation but his indignation was probably also aroused by an expectation of having a greater say in the selection of the commissioners. It was indeed strange that Browne had not been informed of the final composition of the commission by 20 January when its membership had been completed on or before 3 January (although not formally approved by the government until 10 January).[82]

De Valera replied to Browne's complaint, expressing regret that the letter of 10 December was not duly acknowledged. Browne was informed that the secretary to the government had been instructed to send him a list of individuals who had agreed to serve on the commission.[83] De Valera also noted that Browne did not oppose the proposal to appoint a vice-chairman – despite the latter's obvious lack of enthusiasm for the idea. On 23 January a list of members of the commission was forwarded to Browne. The bishop was also informed that the issue of the vice-chairmanship was to be discussed by the government the following day.[84]

De Valera seems to have been anxious to placate Browne. The government acknowledged, rather condescendingly, that the chairman might not be absent from any meeting of the commission as had occurred in the case of the Commission of Inquiry into Banking, Currency and Credit. Therefore, it would be unnecessary to deputise for the chairman. If the need did arise then the commission had the option of appointing one of its members to act in that capacity.[85] In the aftermath of the bishop's verbal salvo de Valera seems to have adopted a very cautious approach and the issue of the vice-chairmanship did not represent an important compromise on his part.

The setting up of the commission did not elicit unanimous support from the vocationalist lobby. The editor of *The Standard*, Peadar O'Curry, looked upon its composition with extreme disfavour. The weekly newspaper had not highlighted the establishment of the commission. O'Curry disapproved of a commission which he perceived as being nearly 60% non-Catholic in personnel in a state which was 93% Catholic. Furthermore, he alleged that some of the commissioners were anti-Catholic and even hostile to the Irish nation. Browne's position was not one to be envied, placed as he was in the company of 'a Protestant Bishop, a Prince Mason (Mr Lowe), a non-Catholic spinster Feminist (in the worst sense – Ms. Louie Bennett) and an academic bigot of the calibre of Professor Duncan of Trinity College'. O'Curry believed that the commission was destined to waste the time of busy men because its terms of reference did not explicitly specify the study of vocationalism in conformity with Catholic social teaching. However, he refrained from expressing his views in *The Standard* because he did not want to create difficulties for Browne and a 'few' other Catholics who were actively supportive of the vocationalist cause and who might achieve some degree of success.[86]

O'Curry's suspicions that the commission might be a waste of effort were not without foundation – although not for the reasons he expressed. The size of the commission was diametrically opposed to the motion put forward by MacDermot and Tierney in the Senate. Senator MacDermot had advised against the establishment of a large commission. He recommended a commission of approximately ten members. He believed that a small commission would be an efficient one. If it was much larger than ten members then it would tend to become a mere forum for debate. The senator warned that large commissions encouraged members to become careless in their attendance because they felt that there were so many others who could substitute for them. He feared that proceedings would become unnecessarily prolonged and that there would be a tendency for procrastination and confusion.[87] It is difficult to escape the conclusion that this was exactly what de Valera wanted. In common with the bishops he publicly approved of vocational organisation in principle but he was not to support it in practice.

De Valera may have been informed by John Charles McQuaid that there was no genuine support amongst the bishops for vocationalist schemes. It is most unlikely that Bishop Michael Browne, new to episcopal office, was aware of this crucial fact when he accepted the chairmanship of the commission. The opposition of the government and the Catholic hierarchy to vocationalism was indicated by the failure of the I.N.T.O. to form a vocational council of education in 1933–34. It seems the hierarchy's devoted servant, McQuaid, had kept de Valera informed about what was happening at private meetings.[88] The hierarchy of course could not openly criticise those loyal Catholics who espoused an ideology based on the social encyclicals but, nevertheless, their opposition was formidable. It is likely that Éamon de Valera was fully aware of the bishops' difficult position and accordingly resorted to deceitful methods in the interests of both church and state. Even as he was recruiting personnel for the commission his Minister for Education, Thomas Derrig, was co-operating with John Charles McQuaid to obstruct another attempt to form a vocational council of education.

In April 1938 the Association of Secondary Teachers (Ireland) had decided to press for the formation of such a council. Its general secretary, Florence Quirke, wrote to McQuaid requesting his assistance.[89] McQuaid's reply did not reveal his hostility to the proposal of the A.S.T.I. As before he enquired about the purpose, constitution and practical functioning of the proposed council.[90] When the Catholic Headmasters' Association held its half-yearly meeting on 13 October 1938 the council of education was on the agenda. McQuaid, who presided as chairman, told the members that the council would give those involved in educational work a greater influence over educational policy while at the same time diminishing the dominant position of civil servants who were sometimes out of touch with working conditions. Nevertheless, he asserted that these advantages would not compensate for, nor outweigh, the disadvantages of the council.

A number of points were made at the meeting. Education was regarded as a 'delicate and exceptional activity' that 'should not be selected for experiment'. Before a council of education could be considered it was deemed necessary to explain how it was to be integrated into a fully developed system of vocational organisation. The existing system of administration was held to be 'very near to the perfect Catholic system' and it was feared that the proposed council would work against it. The hierarchy was opposed to the formation of a non-denominational council which would have so much power that it could 'determine absolutely' the courses and textbooks to be studied. McQuaid and his colleagues felt that the A.S.T.I., and those who supported its proposal, failed to distinguish the difference between a vocational organisation of teachers (which would be concerned with salaries, working conditions, qualifications, etc.) and a council of education which would influence the minister on broader issues of educational policy. They were of the opinion that the existing educational associations could still advise the Department of Education – 'without the disadvantage of nondenominational control'.[91] The A.S.T.I. proposal suffered the same fate as the I.N.T.O. initiative. Once again McQuaid found a staunch ally in the Department of Education.[92]

The department had a number of reasons for objecting to the establishment of a council of education. The prevailing opinion was that a vocational council was not likely to act responsibly if it was to be merely an advisory body. Like a parliamentary opposition too small to ever become a government it would tend to carelessly propose schemes in the knowledge that it would not have the responsibility for implementing policy. If the council did have authority then it would undermine the minister's position, thus violating the sovereignty of parliament. This rigid outlook was, in effect, an insuperable objection to a long-standing vocationalist aspiration.

The department's opposition to the establishment of a council of education was also due to ideological motives that emanated from Fianna Fáil's brand of republicanism. During the 1930's Fianna Fáil placed a high priority on the restoration of the Irish language and culture. From 1934 a pass in Irish (Gaelic) became essential for the school leaving examinations. Article 8.1 of the new constitution designated Irish as the first official language despite the fact that the vast majority of the population spoke English. The teaching profession became more and more uneasy about compulsory teaching through Irish – especially to children whose home language was English. Despite this concern Fianna Fáil pressed ahead with the compulsory Gaelicisation policy and resisted any attempts to critically evaluate its impact.[93]

The attitude of the Department of Education was that a council of education would be likely to oppose the Irish policy in the schools. According to Thomas Derrig the leaders of the Church of Ireland and the Presbyterian Church had strongly supported the formation of a council of education on general principles and also because they hoped that it might be used to slow the advancement of Irish in the school system.[94] He thought that their representatives on the council, in combination with other representatives who held similar opinions, might constitute a majority opposed to the amount of compulsion deemed necessary for the survival of the language.

With the power of church and state allied against it the commission was doomed to failure from its inception and its establishment put the vocationalists at a severe disadvantage. The onus of responsibility was now put on the self-declared experts to devise an effective scheme whereby society and the economy could be reformed in accordance with the principles enunciated in the papal encyclicals without conflicting with the democratic process and the common good. A very large commission with extremely broad terms of reference was unlikely to achieve consensus and produce a single report. Even if it did succeed the government was only obliged to consider its findings – not necessarily to implement them. Given such a broad agenda the commission, which was now the flagship of the vocationalist cause, would find itself open to criticism on many fronts as it presented detailed proposals on various aspects of Irish socio-economic life. Even if the findings of the commission were substantially sound the report was likely to be rendered obsolete in a volatile Europe, threatened by war, and destined for transformation – unprecedented in its rapidity and magnitude. All the advantages were with the government as the commission set about its onerous task.

CHAPTER FIVE

The Commission on Vocational Organisation, 1939–1944

PROBLEMS ENCOUNTERED BY THE COMMISSION, 1939–1941

The Commission on Vocational Organisation held its inaugural meeting on 2 March 1939. The taoiseach, Éamon de Valera attended to address those present and he expressed the opinion that the commission was the most important one since the foundation of the state.[1] The commission was unique in that it took the whole spectrum of Irish economic and social life as its field of enquiry, and attempted to construct a new system of regulation and governance. However, it was ill-equipped to pursue such an enquiry. A thorough knowledge and understanding of the economic history of modern Ireland was essential for success but there was no published work available which came even close to satisfying the need. Neither was there any advanced Irish school of social studies.[2]

The commission began its investigations by studying memoranda on the theory and history of vocational organisation prepared by members and by the secretary. It then made enquiries about the extent and functioning of vocational organisation in a selected number of other countries.[3] In dealing with twelve foreign states it obtained its data from a variety of sources. Official documents and books by 'authoritative' writers were examined. Information was sought from the Department of External Affairs, foreign politicians and diplomatic staff. The commission communicated with a number of experts abroad including a Dutch sociologist, P.J. Spoorenberg, and R.J.P. Mortished of the International Labour Office.

In September 1939 the Second World War erupted in Europe. Browne was quick to realise the implications it had for the work of the commission. The nation faced great uncertainty and he anticipated that some of the members might be unable to maintain their commitment due to pressing business difficulties. The Commission on Agriculture had suspended its activities and Browne felt that the Commission on Vocational Organisation might also be obliged to do so.

By early October 1939 the commission had studied the functioning of vocational organisations in a number of European countries. Labour courts and national economic councils had also been examined and analysed by Browne and his colleagues. They were about to embark on a study of the work and development of vocational organisations in Ireland. However, in view of the radically changed circumstances Browne wanted the government to decide whether or not the commission should suspend its activities until after the war was over. The taoiseach was invited to address the commission and the chairman declared himself quite amenable to any decision reached by Éamon de Valera and his ministers because, in his opinion, they knew better than anyone else the needs of the country and the dangers facing it.[4] De Valera now had an excellent opportunity to suspend the work of the commission without losing credibility. That he chose not to do so indicates that more than political considerations influenced his thinking when he agreed to set up the commission.

In his speech to the commission on 5 October 1939 de Valera urged it to continue with its labours, and if possible, to accelerate the pace of the work.[5] The chairman, evidently encouraged by de Valera's speech, reassured the taoiseach that the commission would do its utmost to present a report at an early date.

Browne may also have received encouragement from another quarter. When the commission had initiated, or was about to initiate, its enquiries, the Irish Catholic hierarchy received a query from the Vatican. The secretary of state, Cardinal Luigi Maglione, requested information about the instruction of priests in the social teaching of the church. At the June meeting of the bishops an episcopal sub-committee was formed for the purpose of facilitating an appropriate response. The episcopal sub-committee was composed of Bishop John Dignan of Clonfert, Bishop James Roche of Cloyne, and Bishop Patrick Lyons of Kilmore. At the October meeting the sub-committee issued its report and emphasised that this important aspect of priestly education was receiving close attention. Apparently, the bishops were anxious to reassure the Vatican that papal social teaching was being taken seriously. For several years social science had been a formal subject in all the diocesan colleges. In June 1937 a professorship of social science was established in St Patrick's College, Maynooth. Social science was made a 'special' subject in this college of 600 students. The measures adopted were 'adequate to meet any possible danger to religion.'[6]

The authors of the report noted that the population of the entire island was 75% Catholic. There was 'very little danger of Socialism or Communism obtaining a footing' in Ireland. The bulk of the population lived in rural areas and Catholics in the countryside were diligent in attending to their religious duties. Generally, rural workers were not unionised – the inference being that there was no danger of socialism. Even in the cities the vast majority of Catholics were regular in attending the sacraments. The close contact that existed between priests and workers was paralleled by the good relationship between Labour leaders and the bishops. Priests throughout the country were actively involved in a multitude of educational and social organisations. A bishop was chairman of the National Health Insurance Society that insured thousands of workers against sickness and disability. Another bishop was chairman of the Commission on Vocational Organisation.[7] Browne, as a member of the hierarchy, was probably familiar with the findings of his clerical colleagues. He had some reason for optimism.

The commission depended very much on public goodwill in the pursuance of its enquiries. Browne was acutely aware of this and, through the medium of the press, in mid-October 1939 he appealed for co-operation from employers' and workers' organisations. The commission had sent dozens of questionnaires to those who had experience of industrial and social problems. Browne feared that there would be a poor response to the initiatives of the commission because of a misunderstanding about its fundamental objectives. Some trade unionists in particular were suspicious that the bishop and his colleagues were busily devising a scheme for the establishment of a dictatorial corporate state. Thus, Browne felt it necessary to emphasise the commission's commitment to democracy.[8]

Opposition to the commission's endeavours did not emanate entirely from some sectors of the trade union movement. The secretary of the Irish Banks Standing Committee (I.B.S.C.), T.F. Hennessy, did not co-operate with the commission when it sought information on financial matters.[9] After a protracted series of discussions and correspondence Browne, determined to gain compliance, wrote to de Valera, informing him that

> the refusal of the Standing Committee of the Banks would seriously impede the work of the Commission and would lead to painful publicity. Further, if there were resignations from the Commission on this question the effect on the public mind would be bad, not merely for the Commission, but also for the Standing Committee of the Banks. It would also raise the whole question of the status and powers of a Government Commission.[10]

De Valera informed Browne that enquiries would be made.[11] On the same day the secretary of the Department of the Taoiseach, Maurice Moynihan, wrote to the secretary of the Department of Finance, J.J. McElligott. McElligott had been making his own enquiries and had communicated with Hennessy. Moynihan found it difficult to understand why the I.B.S.C. objected to giving oral evidence.[12] McElligott was clearly sympathetic towards Hennessy and the I.B.S.C. He claimed that Browne's letter was unwarranted and concluded by stating 'the Banks were for years being grilled by the Banking Commission and are now entitled to a little respite.'[13] On 14 February 1940 Browne met with de Valera, and with Seán T. O'Kelly who was Tánaiste (deputy prime minister) and Minister for Finance. An agreement was reached to organise a meeting between Hennessy and Browne for the purpose of settling their differences.[14] The outcome was successful. Browne's demands were complied with and on 3 May 1940 Hennessy and Lord Glenavy (Director, Bank of Ireland) attended to give evidence before the commission.[15]

Browne did not always succeed in extracting information from unwilling sources. When the commission requested a copy of the *Report of the Inter-departmental Committee on Sugar Beet* its application was refused. It was informed that some of the information had been obtained on the basis of confidentiality. Furthermore, there was a risk that the public disclosure of some parts of the report would 'seriously embarrass' state departments when government intervention in the sugar industry was deemed necessary.[16] De Valera sent Moynihan to meet Browne to explain why the government did not accede to the commission's request. At the meeting Browne alleged, repeatedly, that government departments, and organisations associated with the government, had not co-operated with the commission. He was particularly critical of the Department of Industry and Commerce. He asserted that there was excessive reliance on the need for official secrecy as a reason to withhold information from the commission. This, he contended, was not consistent with the taoiseach's undertaking when the commission was being set up.[17] Browne's hard-line stance did not win friends for the commission in high places.

The commission continued with its enquiries against a background of wartime restrictions. J.J. McElligott demanded an immediate and drastic reduction in government expenditure. He had adopted an extremely pessimistic view of the Irish economy as the gap between revenue and expenditure began to grow rapidly from 1939. But his endeavours to bring about financial rectitude were tainted by ulterior motives. Vocationalists were well known for their harsh criticisms of the civil service which they equated with bureaucracy. Browne, O'Rahilly and Tierney made no secret of their contempt for bureaucracy. Consequently, there was some opposition in the civil service towards the commission and its objectives. This opposition manifested itself when McElligott attempted to terminate the work of the commission. On 31 May 1940, he advocated that the two main commissions operating at the time should be suspended. These related to vocational organisation and to agriculture. He gave two reasons: (1) both commissions were making heavy demands on staff which could be ill-afforded and, (2) were examining conditions which were likely to be completely changed in the near future.[18] In response to McElligott's memorandum, Seán T. O'Kelly, Minister for Finance, wrote to de Valera on the same day reiterating McElligott's recommendations.[19]

De Valera gave serious consideration to O'Kelly's advice and on 5 June he telephoned the secretary of the commission. The taoiseach enquired about what progress was made and O'Toole made it clear to him that there would not be a report in the near future. The secretary stated that after the taoiseach's visit to the commission in October of the previous year the commission had intensified its endeavours in response to the advice given. But despite its best efforts progress was slow. A vast quantity of records had been obtained and the commissioners – 'all busy men and women, were experiencing some difficulty . . . in adequately analysing and digesting these'. De Valera was left with the impression that it might take years to complete the task and contemplated suspending the work of the commission in view of the wartime exigencies. O'Toole advised him to contact the chairman about this matter. De Valera readily agreed and enquired when Browne would next be in Dublin. O'Toole informed him that Browne was due to visit the capital on 13 June but de Valera felt unable to wait until then because he had to make some decisions for Finance before that date.[20] Prompted by O'Toole's advice the taoiseach agreed to write to Browne.[21]

Browne was not prepared to passively accept the suspension of the commission's work – instigated as it would be by less than honourable motives. The threat of suspension had come as no surprise to him[22] and he reacted angrily. On 7 June he wrote to O'Kelly suggesting that his department wished to suppress the Commission on Vocational Organisation because of its recent examination of Joseph Brennan. Brennan, Chairman of the Currency Commission, submitted oral evidence to the Commission on Vocational Organisation on 30 May, the day before McElligott's memorandum was issued. Circumstantial evidence supported Browne's case.[23] Brennan was a close friend of

McElligott and made it clear to the commission that he only came in compliance with the terms of reference of the commission and did not attend willingly.[24]

In the course of being questioned Brennan had shown himself reluctant to give information, sometimes declining on the basis that either it was not pertinent to the commission's terms of reference or that the information sought could be obtained in the *Report of the Commission of Inquiry into Banking, Currency and Credit*.[25] Brennan was not sympathetic towards vocationalism and his manner throughout most of the interrogation was firm and laconic. A clash between Browne and himself was virtually inevitable because: 'Among officials, Mr Brennan was not always the most willing or the most fluent in oral communication. Among bishops, Dr Browne was not the most modest or the most patient in demeanour.'[26] Brennan was most unhappy with the commission's line of questioning and later informed his colleagues that he never had a more unsatisfactory experience with any government commission than with the Commission on Vocational Organisation.[27]

Browne, in his letter to the Minister for Finance alleged that McElligott 'would regard the Commission as a most inconvenient body and that there would be a certain grim satisfaction in getting rid of the Bishop of Galway, on the ground of war economy'.[28] In his reply the minister denied that the proposal to suspend the commission was so motivated and repeated the two reasons advanced by McElligott. He also put forward a third reason, arguing that the pressure of urgent work on government ministers and on their officials was so great that it precluded the possibility of giving attention to any report that the commission might submit in war time.[29] But the bishop's intervention was regarded as so important by O'Kelly that he decided to forward the correspondence to the taoiseach.

The department's demand for the suspension of the commission was rejected by the government on 23 July 1940.[30] Yet the real decision had been already taken well before this date. De Valera had decided to withstand the pressure exerted by Finance. On 13 June he met Browne in Dublin. Evidently Browne did some tough talking on that occasion because 'it was agreed that the Commission would carry on, as at present, with the existing staff'.[31] It would not have enhanced popular support for the government if it became known that the main motive for suspending the commission's work was political expediency. The reasons advanced by O'Kelly and McElligott for suspending the commission were not considered adequate. The commission was serviced by a very small number of civil servants. The civil servants who appeared before the commission lost no more than one or two hours in the course of giving evidence. Some time was required for the compilation of departmental submissions but the overall commitment of resources by the civil service was small.[32] This is not to say that McElligott's arguments were without merit. The socio-economic conditions which had existed in the late 1930s were undergoing sweeping changes in the early 1940s and it was difficult to forecast with any degree of accuracy what postwar conditions would be like.

McElligott, notwithstanding his disdain for the commission's work, appeared before it to give oral evidence; so did several other senior civil servants. They were pressed for their opinions on vocational organisation. J.H. Whyte describes their reactions as varying from

> the comparative open-mindedness of the Secretary of the Department of Education, Mr J. O'Neill, through the non-committal politeness of the Secretary of the Department of Industry and Commerce, Mr R.C. Ferguson, to the freezing lack of sympathy of Mr J.J. McElligott.[33]

In general, the civil servants who were interviewed by the commission seemed reluctant to approve of vocational organisation if it involved the adoption of new practices and procedures.

The commission had found itself 'peculiarly dependent' on the expertise of Industry and Commerce when studying industrial courts.[34] On 5 March 1940 the commission felt it necessary to remind the department that, in common with other government departments, it was duty-bound to co-operate with a commission established by the government in the public interest. Nearly two months elapsed before the department replied but its response was clearly positive when it stated that it was prepared to place its knowledge and its experience, unreservedly, at the disposal of the commission.[35] R.C. Ferguson, the acting secretary of the Department of Industry and Commerce, restated the department's position when he appeared before the commission on 26 September 1940 to give evidence. He told Browne and his colleagues

> my Minister is very anxious that we should give every facility we possibly can to this Commission. Personally, I feel in the same mood because I quite realise that any recommendation which this Commission may make will almost certainly have very far-reaching effects, if adopted by the Department, on the trade and industry of the country and for that reason I think it is necessary to disclose everything we possibly can.[36]

Apparently, his political master, Seán Lemass, envisaged that the report of the commission would fulfil a vital role in postwar planning.[37]

Vocationalists believed that the primary function of vocational organisations was to serve the common good. The belief that interest groups would give priority to the welfare of the community was fundamental to vocationalist thought and was frequently articulated by its most prominent advocates. The social encyclicals stressed that Catholic associations should function on the basis of Christian moral principles. Nevertheless, there was a wide gulf between Christian aspiration and economic reality. The profit motive had little in common with Christian idealism. Michael Browne's outlook epitomized the vocationalist perspective. He was particularly insistent that experienced business men, when vocationally organised, would serve the public interest in the course of representing their own economic interests. The evidence presented to him indicated to the contrary but the chairman remained steadfast in his opinion.[38] R.C. Ferguson attempted to enlighten Browne, and his colleagues, about the cruder realities of Irish economic life. He informed the commission that when a number of associations assemble to consider an issue an opinion is formed which is always in keeping with the interests of the group and it will not give much consideration to the welfare of other allied groups.[39] Browne was reluctant to accept that voluntary associations were primarily motivated to serve their own interests with little regard for the community. Ferguson, in a futile effort to change the chairman's point of view, declared

> I never came across a move that was actuated by patriotic motives. I have known quite a lot of cases where an Association has not arrived at a very intelligent view sometimes because they did not know some of the larger issues outside the industry, the result being they made mistakes from their own point of view.[40]

Not only would the national community have to be protected against associations of businessmen but also these associations would need to be protected against the consequences of their own narrow perceptions which were based on self-interest. Only government departments had the necessary strength to ensure that sectional interests would not exploit the community. This power, therefore, would not be diminished by a devolution of authority to vocational organisations.

The secretary of the Department of Education, Joseph O'Neill, was interviewed by the commission on 11 October 1940. His friendly and supportive demeanour was similar to Ferguson's attitude. Browne posed the question: 'But you think Mr O'Neill that a council of education, consisting of independent, competent and learned persons, but representing what you might call the interests of the community, would be very valuable?' O'Neill's answer was not ambiguous: 'I think that it would be extremely valuable'.[41] This reply would be misleading if taken in isolation – in its context it gave little reason for optimism. O'Neill stated that it was departmental policy to consult all the interested organisations. The department had a preference for dealing with combinations of associations because matters would be easier to deal with. This, however, had not been possible because there was no significant tendency for associations to combine.[12]

Browne and his colleagues had been 'most impressed' with O'Neill's 'evident desire to help the Commission' and with his ability in answering a 'great variety' of questions.[43] O'Neill, in correspondence with the bishop of Galway, expressed the opinion that the country would benefit enormously if 'some weighty body', with Browne as its first chairman, was established to profoundly influence educational policy.[44] However, contrary to what the vocationalists believed, the civil service did not dictate government policy and O'Neill's views in the end counted for nothing more than a brief morale booster to the commission.

As the commission proceeded with its enquiries one of its members, Senator Michael Tierney, called for the establishment of a council of education. His motion in the Senate on 22 January 1941 proposed

> that Seanad Éireann is of opinion that the Government should establish a council of education to advise the Minister for Education in matters submitted to it by the Minister in relation to the working of his Department.[45]

Tierney discovered that the Fianna Fáil government was still implacably opposed to the idea and, anticipating defeat, he withdrew his proposal.[46] The stance of Thomas Derrig, Minister of Education, did not indicate a flexibility of attitude essential for the implementation of vocationalist recommendations – the significance of this may have been perceived by some members of the commission, especially by Tierney, who were at this juncture trying to compile a report from the vast volume of evidence before them. Sharp differences of opinion amongst the commissioners did not make the task easier.

At its meeting of 27 September 1940 the commission had discussed Document no. 172. This document, prepared by Fr Coyne, summarised the work of the commission between 1 February 1940 and 26 September 1940.[47] No firm conclusions were drawn and the document was intended as a basis for further discussions.[48] Luke J. Duffy was absent from the meeting. He was secretary of the Labour Party and had joined the commission after Senator Thomas Foran's resignation on 17 April 1939. When he read over the report of the proceedings, he noted that Browne had invited proposals or suggestions relating to the issues raised by Coyne's memorandum.[49] Accordingly, he submitted his observations which were later classified as Document 172(B). This document, dated 1 January 1941, was submitted to the commission six days later.[50]

On 11 January, Coyne wrote to Browne declaring that Duffy had 'prematurely and unnecessarily, got anxious about the ultimate lines of our findings'. Notwithstanding this, Coyne still felt that Duffy's submission was 'a most useful document, revealing as it does many constructive ideas and giving us a number of good points to discuss'.[51] Duffy expressed the assumption that the commission had not yet decided to advise for or against the establishment of an elaborate system of vocational organisations.[52] He then proceeded to express his views on vocationalism. The main reason for the setting up of vocational organisations was to serve the common good.[53] Unless the entire community gained from vocational organisation then the public interest was not promoted. The poorer section of the community, especially the unemployed, had to be protected against the evils of the prevailing economic system which sustained poverty and social injustice. It was the primary duty of the state to promote social justice by providing secure employment.[54] Existing economic conditions should be adjusted by the regulation of currency and credit to safeguard, in particular, the economic welfare of the poorer classes.[55]

Duffy strenuously argued that the entire socio-economic system had to be reformed before the development of a vocational system could take place. Full employment was an essential prerequisite. Otherwise a vocationalist system would only benefit part of the community, much to the detriment of the common good.[56] If vocational organisations were set up under existing conditions then the resultant formation of cartels and the growth of monopolistic practices would dominate economic activities.[57] Consumers would be forced to pay higher prices for essential goods and services. Rationalisation would enhance productivity but an adverse consequence of this was increased unemployment. More and more families would find themselves economically marginalised and Duffy even envisaged the spectre of a Malthusian catastrophe if this was allowed to happen.[58]

Senior civil servants had stressed the costs, dangers and problems that would occur if powerful vocational organisations were created, promoted, or allowed to develop. Even some of the commissioners, in the course of their discussions, were forced to acknowledge that cartels and monopolies were detrimental to the common good due to their tendency to impose excessive prices and restrictive trading practices while securing exorbitant profits and inflated salaries. Dr Henry

Kennedy argued that powerful organisations could work against the public interest. Statements made by Browne, Coyne and Walsh indicated how persuasive Kennedy was.[59] Luke J. Duffy was quick to remind his colleagues about what had been acknowledged and also drew attention to McElligott's evidence in order to bolster his contention that Irish society was not yet ready for an elaborate scheme of vocational organisation.[60]

If the state was to protect the national community against the ravages and excesses of sectional interests then it would find itself compelled to exercise a degree of supervision and control over various interest groups. It would be extremely difficult, if not impossible, for the state to avoid an increasing regulatory role and ultimately this would lead to the kind of 'bureaucratic fascism' which the commission had been so anxious to avoid.[61] Duffy concluded

> To proceed with the organisation of pseudo-functional (vocational) interests into something that might well become legally entrenched rackets before the social-economic foundation was developed functionally would be a deleterious putting of the cart before the horse and not even the right horse at that.[62]

Document 172(B) was debated by the commission on 13 March 1941.[63] There was a distinct lack of support for Duffy's views and Browne was quick to go on the offensive, aided by the intermittent contributions of Coyne, Hayes, Kennedy, Wilson, Harvey, and O'Mara. Even two of Duffy's labour colleagues, Campbell and Bennett, did not assist him. Confronted by this formidable alliance of his fellow commissioners he resorted to *Quadragesimo Anno* for ideological support.[64] After two years of studying the subject of vocational organisation, the commission had still not defined exactly what vocational organisation was and this failure tended to complicate the debate.[65] Duffy's assertion that unemployment had to be completely eradicated, before a system of vocational organisation could be developed, wilted in the course of the debate.[66] However, some of the other points raised by him were sustainable. He had questioned the practicability and merit of establishing an elaborate network of vocational organisations within the existing socio-economic order. He had highlighted the dangers of cartels and monopolistic practices and he emphasised that the basic criterion for evaluating any proposals for a vocationalist system was whether or not the common good would be promoted. The commission should have given greater consideration to his views.

Duffy's labour colleague, James Larkin, was also opposed to vocationalist schemes. Larkin's wariness and contempt for corporatism was shared by many of his colleagues in the Workers' Union of Ireland. In a memorandum submitted to the commission, the executive committee (and subordinate officials) of the union candidly expressed their disdain for vocationalism. The declared attitude of the W.U.I. was that it was prepared to consider any scheme designed to promote the co-ordination of Irish economic life – but an elaborate scheme designed to promote vocational organisation would be 'not merely futile but foolish'. The view was expressed that

> Schemes of vocational organisation, of planned direction, are merely cloaks to hide the festering sore in the economic and social body and fail to go to the root of the problem . . . a planned system or even planned direction can only come when the basis of the system is not profit and exploitation of human beings but the principle that service begets service, that every man and woman who will give service to the community shall receive service from the community in return and not otherwise.[67]

Although Larkin did not officially participate in the drafting of the memorandum[68] it is most likely that the document reflected his own thinking about vocationalism. But his outlook, and the expressed views of Luke Duffy, exerted little influence in a commission of 25 members.

THE COMPILATION OF THE REPORT 1941–1944

When studying the extent, structure, activities, and functioning of vocational organisation in Ireland the commission sent questionnaires to 333 organisations and received 150 replies. Also, it heard oral evidence from 174 organisations; some of these were state organisations and government departments.[69] By January 1941 the commission had obtained the bulk of this information. From then on it spent most of its time examining the data and only sought information that was needed to clarify particular points that arose in the course of its discussions.[70] In June of that year the work of the commission was well advanced and a large portion of the report was rough drafted. Coyne hoped that by mid-July the members of the commission would have a draft of the entire first three of four sections of the report. This first draft was then to be examined by the members over the summer holidays. Coyne expected that by September of that year there would be a broad consensus on what had been ascertained and this in turn was to constitute the basis for the fourth section of the report – the most important section which was to contain the recommendations.[71]

Although Browne relied heavily on Coyne to prepare the first draft of the report he expected that Tierney and O'Rahilly would also play a central role. The task envisaged for O'Rahilly was that he would assist Coyne in drafting the report, and he was to assist Browne in responding to dissenting voices from some members of the commission – especially those of Larkin and Bennett.[72] However, O'Rahilly's contribution fell far short of the expectations of his colleagues – this was mainly due to his heavy workload at U.C.C.

While O'Rahilly was present at a meeting of the commission on 16 January 1942 his attendance since the previous autumn had been particularly poor. By this time, Browne was anxious to have the first draft of the report approved. At the meeting Mary MacGeehin put forward the proposal that adequate provision be made for 'homemakers' (i.e. those who cared directly for the family and the home) in the vocational scheme which was being devised. Browne disagreed with the proposal but he agreed to incorporate it temporarily in the draft report. This concession was probably motivated by his determination to avoid the delay that a discussion would entail. Much to his annoyance O'Rahilly's firm opposition to the proposal upset his strategy. An acrimonious exchange ensued as Browne and O'Rahilly clashed on the issue. The chairman put the matter to a vote and MacGeehin's proposal was incorporated in the draft report.

In the aftermath of the quarrel O'Rahilly threatened to resign from the commission.[73] He was convinced that Browne, by his heavy-handed action, had undermined his position.[74] He objected to the hasty incorporation of documents into the first draft of the report. New principles and schemes had been adopted 'practically without discussion.'[75] Coyne, who played a pivotal role in the commission's proceedings, acted quickly to heal the rift. He had a very high regard for O'Rahilly's capabilities and exhorted Browne to write a conciliatory letter to the disaffected professor.[76] On 9 February the chairman wrote to O'Rahilly but his letter aggravated rather than settled the dispute.[77] Coyne continued to apply pressure and by 12 February Browne's attitude had changed. He encouraged O'Rahilly to continue serving on the commission and expressed the wish that their relationship could be 'in the former friendly state'.[78] This appeasing gesture did not have the desired effect. O'Rahilly was not satisfied and continued to exert indirect pressure on Browne through his colleagues. Throughout the remainder of the month he threatened to quit. Some members of the commission, including Luke J. Duffy, C.P. McCarthy, and Seán Campbell, had advised him not to do so.[79] Duffy anticipated that O'Rahilly's resignation would create unfavourable publicity for the commission.[80]

On 28 February O'Rahilly wrote to Hayes declaring 'I am old and tired and overwhelmed with work at present. As to Commission (sic) I have delayed my resignation till next week . . . I see no way out of it, in order to avoid further unpleasant or disedifying scenes.'[81] Coyne believed that the commission would be severely handicapped by the loss of O'Rahilly and he pressed Browne to make another attempt to bring about a satisfactory settlement. The chairman reluctantly acceded to Coyne's appeal.[82] O'Rahilly was sufficiently mollified by Browne's response and changed his mind about resignation.

Browne persisted in pressing ahead at maximum speed. On 17 March 1942 he wrote to the Jesuit provincial in Tullamore (Offaly) requesting that Coyne be granted permission to devote more time to the commission's work. The bishop explained that his episcopal duties and 'other circumstances' restricted his own contribution. In Browne's opinion few members were as diligent or as well informed about vocational organisation as Coyne. Browne sensed a serious problem with motivation when he wrote '. . . not all the members of the Commission have the same interest or attitude to the subject: to convince them is a slow process'.[83] Coyne's professorial duties at Milltown Park in Dublin were not 'very exacting' and Browne's wishes were easily facilitated.[84]

As chairman, Browne faced a daunting task. The commission had an enormous quantity of information to examine and a wide range of views had to be dealt with. Browne was determined to maintain satisfactory progress and preserve unity amongst the majority. With this in mind, he persuaded the commission to hastily process the data with minimal discussion. Consequently, the quality of the first draft left much to be desired. Coyne believed that it was necessary to purge the draft report of much irrelevant and excess material that had been inserted 'to keep people quiet'.[85] Duffy was most unhappy with the document and he feared that there was an underlying tendency to favour the establishment of a fascist state.[86] As the work proceeded Stephen O'Mara and Fr Coyne had reason to worry about the contents of the draft report, especially the fourth section which contained the recommendations. Browne's *modus operandi* had not changed. On 16 August 1942 Coyne wrote to O'Rahilly, complaining that when an idea was expressed in print and circulated to the members Browne was 'too ready to accept it as final with only minor modifications'.[87]

In early 1943 the work of the commission was at an advanced stage. On 18 June the commission decided that minority reports, addenda and reservations were to be submitted no later than 30 September.[88] On 1 July, after several reminders from the commission's office, Browne sent a personal letter to each member of the commission, repeating the closing date. All addenda, reservations and minority reports received were to be circulated to all members by 15 October and it was intended that the commission would discuss and consider these about five days later. The draft report, which was signed on 4 November 1943, was issued in sections to members of the commission from March to August 1943.[89]

No document or communication was received from Luke Duffy by 30 September. On 4 October, the secretary informed the members – including Duffy – that the closing date had expired. On the morning of 21 October, just before the beginning of a commission meeting, O'Toole received a telephone call from a female clerk in Duffy's office. The secretary was informed that Duffy wished that a document, which he had submitted about two years previously, should be taken as representing his views. The document in question was not identified, nor was it even stated that Duffy wanted it put forward as a minority report. Furthermore, no signed statement, verifying Duffy's views or intentions, was received.[90] O'Toole immediately reported the telephone communication to the commission. At the morning and afternoon sessions of 21 October the commission discussed what course of action to take. Hayes argued that procedure had to be adhered to. Otherwise members could keep sending in minority reports over an indefinite period. Bennett expressed a more tolerant attitude. So also did Tierney, he felt that Duffy deserved more flexibility because of his prolonged illness.[91] At the beginning of the afternoon session Alfred O'Rahilly adopted a tough stance on the issue. He proposed the rejection of any document submitted weeks after the closing date. Algernon A. Odlum seconded O'Rahilly's motion. O'Rahilly argued his case vigorously and in the end his motion was passed unanimously.[92]

The commission had dealt decisively with Duffy's oblique communication but this did not mean that it was impervious to labour sensitivities. In the recent past trade unions throughout mainland Europe had been suppressed by dictatorial regimes. In Northern Ireland the imperatives of war had led to severe restrictions on trade unions. Strikes and lockouts were, in practice, forbidden and arbitration was the only option. All this intensified the sense of vulnerability among trade unionists and induced a deep suspicion of any reforms that might threaten or infringe upon their liberties.[93] The commission's report indicates that it took cognisance of Labour's concerns.[94]

Duffy was not the only commissioner dissatisfied with the draft report. As the work of the commission was nearing completion, Coyne expressed some doubts about it. On 17 September 1943 he wrote to Browne outlining his reservations. He was in broad agreement with

Mary MacGeehin's proposal that more attention should be given to the family in the scheme of vocational organisation. MacGeehin had consulted Coyne about her 'homemakers' proposal and he eagerly availed of the opportunity to stress the role of the family in the context of a new vocationalist order. After examining her document he modified it considerably but even after this he feared that the majority of his colleagues would reject it.[95] His pessimism was well founded. Coyne himself gives a vivid description of what was probably a distressing compromise

> I had a first-class row with His Lordship over the omission of sufficient reference to the Family in the scheme: but after a dog fight, in which O'Rahilly joined in and maintained that it was a doctrinal question among Catholics, I said that I was always ready to accept my doctrine from Bishops and left it at that. However, we are as good friends as ever . . .[96]

O'Rahilly's stance on the issue was vindicated and MacGeehin's views were expressed in an addendum.[97]

Stressing the importance of the family was not the only issue that weighed on Coyne's mind. He wished to emphasise that

> the introduction of any form of vocational organisation must be an affair of gradual change and relatively slow growth, commencing from the existing institutions and organisations of our present social life. Our Report is meant, chiefly, to bring down the idea of vocational organisation from the realm of vague generalities and abstract principles and to show how that idea might be realised . . . It is not meant to be a fully-elaborated and final set of engineer's or architect's plans for some great mechanical or structural enterprise . . .[98]

Coyne believed that Transport and Finance, and Commerce to a lesser extent, were too elaborately structured. But he did not enter an addendum to this effect because of his opinion that

> the Report rests on the underlying assumption that vocational organisation should come by a slow process of deliberately controlled and guided quasi-organic growth rather than by any sudden and abrupt mechanical manipulation or setting up of councils, boards or other bodies . . .[99]

He thought it necessary to point out the importance of natural growth which would inevitably lead to many changes in the proposed vocationalist structure. This opinion seems to have profoundly influenced Browne's writing of the fourth paragraph of the foreword which appeared in the final draft of the report. More significantly, it may have been indicative of suppressed doubts about the feasibility of creating and maintaining such an artificial and highly complicated network of vocational organisations described in the draft report.

Some other aspects of the commission's findings were also sources of concern to Coyne. When working out the fine details of the report the members of the commission had disagreed on the exact limit of the terms of reference. Compromise had been reached on this but Coyne felt that the commission had interpreted its terms of reference too broadly. However, he felt that too broad rather than too narrow an interpretation was the preferred option if a mistake of this nature was made. Another reason for worry was the commission's inaccuracies in points of fact or understanding when discussing solicitors. Having discovered this by accident he suspected that mistakes might also have been made when studying the other professions.[100] Up to 29 September 1943, the day before the closing date, Coyne agonised about whether or not to submit an addendum reiterating some of the points he had raised twelve days earlier.[101] Apparently, he had satisfied himself about the accuracy of the commission's findings. Despite his unease, the contemplated addendum was not formalised and Coyne reconciled himself to the report as it was then drafted.

The commission had attempted to assuage the apprehension of its labour members. It efforts did not meet with resounding success. Two of the Labour representatives, James Larkin and Luke Duffy, declined to sign the report. According to John Swift, Larkin regarded the commission and its work 'with more or less silent contempt' while Luke Duffy 'ridiculed the recommendations, in spoken and written comment'.[102] The other two Labour representatives were not fully satisfied with the commission's findings. Louie Bennett and Seán Campbell took care to explicitly disavow any potential fascistic attributes that might be read into the commission's proposals. They declared

> Parliament should retain supreme power under a system of vocational organisation, in order to avoid the danger of Corporatism and a dictatorship, whether individual or bureaucratic . . . although the Report offers safeguards against totalitarian developments, we feel it necessary to emphasise our conviction that the only reliable safeguard will be the conservation of freely elected Parliamentary institutions and of the subordination of the Executive Government to Parliament.[103]

There were 23 signatories to the report (including the secretary). Two signed with addenda only, two signed with reservations only, and two signed with both addenda and reservations.[104] This represents a remarkable degree of consensus, especially when cognisance is taken of the size of the commission and the magnitude of its enquiry. That such broad agreement was achieved may be mainly attributable to Browne. He was a man of strong views and tended to state his opinions robustly. The report, with its highly elaborate recommendations, reflected his desire for 'a complete system' of vocational organisation. He was aware of the potential for monopolistic practices within the vocationalist system. In order to provide the 'necessary correctives', as a safeguard against this danger, he believed it was essential 'to get all the necessary checks and safeguards in at once.'[105]

A prodigious amount of work had been invested in assessing the huge volume of evidence which came before the commission.[106] A unique mass of information was accumulated on Irish associations, including professional organisations, employers' organisations, trade unions, farmers' organisations, banks and the civil service. Despite its cumbersome composition and the complexity of its inquiry the commission had managed to complete its draft report. But this document, signed on 4 November 1943, was not yet suitable for presentation to the government. In September 1943 Coyne had informed Browne that the whole report was in need of 'a good deal of verbal chiropody'.[107] Coyne thought it necessary that two or three members of the commission should work together to improve the quality of the text and Browne readily agreed to this proposal.[108] On 21 October 1943 the commission set up an editing committee and this included Coyne, Browne, Harvey, and Tierney. The editing committee was assigned the task of revising the report together with the addenda and reservations, so that it would be suitable for publication.[109]

The editing committee held its first meeting on the day the report was signed. Before it set about its arduous task the committee informed the taoiseach that a considerable amount of editing work had to be completed before the document could be formally presented to him. Éamon de Valera agreed to wait until the editing work was finished but he requested that he should be given some details, informally, about the recommendations in the report as soon as possible. He agreed to let the committee finish its work as far as the printing of the final draft of the report. The committee responded by promising to send him the first 'fair' copy of the corrected text issued by the printer.[110]

The editing committee found much repetition, faulty classification, superfluous wording, and a distinct lack of uniformity in form and style. These defects had to be eradicated while at the same ensuring that the substance of the report was not altered. Brevity of expression had to be introduced, diction required improvement, facts needed to be verified and much work had to be done with the references. By 22 March 1944 the committee had, after 80 meetings, revised the main typescript of the report. The addenda and reservations then came under the scrutiny of the committee and the authors were consulted as it was deemed necessary.[111] The revised report was forwarded to the

Stationery Office in instalments. The committee corrected the first galley proofs on 17 February and those for the final instalment of the main typescript were forwarded on 2 May. De Valera received the first instalment of page proofs on 22 May.[112] By the end of July 1944 the committee had accomplished its mission.[113]

The commission had been very critical of the expansion of state power. The civil service, regarded as synonymous with bureaucracy, was thought to be the main defect in the Irish political system. It was castigated for its inefficiency and for its undemocratic practices. Vocational organisation was then presented as an antidote to bureaucracy and was also proposed as an alternative to the excesses of free enterprise capitalism. The commission proposed an elaborate system of interconnected vocational organisations, some endowed with statutory powers. These organisations, by enabling people in various occupations to regulate their own affairs, would diminish state intervention in a wide range of social and economic activities (see Appendix 2 for a summary of the *Commission on Vocational Organisation Report*). Politicians and civil servants would have to drastically change their outlook and work practices if such a scheme was to be implemented. This essential condition gave little reason for optimism.

The commission was aware of the possibility that its findings might be ignored. On 25 November 1939 the editorial of *The Irish Times* had noted that the reports of several tribunals and commissions were ignored by successive Fianna Fáil governments during the 1930s. Arising from government inaction was the widespread belief that 'the appointment of a commission is merely a convenient means to shelve an inconvenient problem'. The newspaper article received the attention of the commission and was filed for further reference.[114] It was clear that if the commission's report was shelved by the government this would not be without precedent.

CHAPTER SIX

In Defence of the *Status Quo*

The Commission on Vocational Organisation had been extremely critical of politicians and civil servants. On 28 October 1943, only a few days before the signing of the draft report, an early warning of official dissatisfaction was issued which seemed to anticipate the commission's findings. When Seán Lemass, Minister for Industry and Commerce, gave a speech at a meeting of the T.C.D. Philosophical Society he vigorously defended the role of politicians and civil servants. His opinions contrasted sharply with the outlook of the vocationalists. He claimed that there was widespread recognition of the need to extend government control over commercial activities. Many of those whose acceptance had been gained were not reconciled to some of the consequences that were to follow and they suspected that government planning was a device by civil servants to display their own indispensability. Lemass stated that

> A great deal of nonsense was talked about bureaucracy. It was not true that all extensions of Government control were devised in government buildings and forced on an unwilling people. It was the characteristic of democratic governments that they were always reluctant to extend the area of their responsibility and they only did so with the pressure of public opinion when it was obvious that the public interest so required. Many of those who would be associated with greater State control in particular matters would be found denouncing government interference in business in general.[1]

Even the commission, despite its extreme fear of excessive state intervention, had to agree with the opinion expressed by Lemass that the increase of state intervention in recent years had been mostly due to public pressure.[2]

Having defended the role of the 'bureaucrats' Lemass next turned his attention to the politicians. He condemned the cynical attitude, expressed in some newspapers, which attributed ulterior motives to politicians *en masse*. He felt that 'there must be something fundamentally wrong in the society where 'politician' has become a term of disparagement, if not a term of actual abuse'. Like the commission, Lemass had strong views about the avoidance of dictatorship and he expressed the opinion that if widespread cynicism about politicians continued to manifest itself then democracy itself would be endangered. Nor was he to be impressed by the notion of a National Vocational Assembly as a vital organ in the planning process. He believed that

> If the advantages of planned progress were to be secured without the risks of a dictatorship, the planning authority must be responsible to the people and removable by them. That in practice meant that it would be controlled by the class of person called politicians.[3]

Lemass's speech was made against a background of wartime restrictions. In Ireland, like the rest of Europe, the economic difficulties imposed by World War II prompted greater state intervention in the economy.[4] Declining incomes, rising prices, and the irritating intervention of the civil service in economic affairs had severely dented the popularity of Fianna Fáil.[5] Evidently, Lemass had become increasingly intolerant of the barrage of criticism which both the civil service and Fianna Fáil had been subjected to. Therefore, he was in no mood to adopt a diplomatic stance when politicians and civil servants alike were criticised at length in the chapters of the *Commission on Vocational Organisation Report*. His outlook indicated the prevailing attitude in official circles.

NEGATIVE REACTIONS TO VOCATIONALIST PROPOSALS

The report of the Commission on Vocational Organisation was formally presented to the taoiseach on 1 August 1944. Ten days later members of the government discussed the document and decided that

- the Report should be published at an early date, and
- Departments should be asked to undertake forthwith a cursory examination of the Report and
  - to submit their preliminary observations on its chief recommendations as soon as possible, and
  - to indicate any recommendations which it might be desirable and practicable to implement by legislation at an early date (including especially recommendations which have a bearing on post-war planning) without committing the Government at this stage to the acceptance in principle of the main features of the Report as a whole.[6]

The report was published within the month and this may have induced a transient mood of optimism amongst the vocationalists. In early September Bishop Michael Browne received good news. The first issue of 1,500 copies was sold in two weeks and a further 500 had been ordered from the printer. In comparison, three months had elapsed before 1,000 copies of the Banking Commission report were sold. The Stationery Office claimed that the order would be larger only for the shortage of good quality paper due to wartime trading difficulties (poor quality paper was not considered appropriate).[7] However, any optimism, which may have arisen amongst the vocationalists, was not well founded. After the cabinet meeting of 11 August attitudes in government circles hardened against the report. At the cabinet meeting of August 18 it was decided that

> in their examination of the Report of the Commission on Vocational Organisation Departments should be asked to note specially any statements relating to the practice or procedure adopted by the Government or by Ministers or by Departments in regard to any of the matters mentioned in the Report which are in any way inaccurate or not strictly in accordance with facts and should prepare suitable material to enable replies to be made to such statements if it should be necessary to do so.[8]

It should not have surprised the authors of the report that the 'bureaucrats' diligently set about the task assigned to them. The report had, explicitly and at length, criticised the civil service. Officials in government departments were eager to retaliate but the bulky document first required a detailed and careful examination. In the meantime a sector of the trade union movement expressed criticism of the commission's proposals. Many trade unionists and members of the Labour party had been uneasy about corporatism. The recommendations of the commission were not motivated by hostility to Labour but those individuals in Labour who had been deeply suspicious of corporatism chose to interpret the proposals as an attack on independent working-class organisations.[9] A former member of the commission, Luke J. Duffy, was anxious to highlight his opposition, and resorted to unfair tactics in the process.

On 26 August 1944 *The Irish People* published an article entitled 'Vocational Organisation Requires a Correct Foundation'. The newspaper article summarised the main arguments in document 172(B), which had been submitted to the commission on 7 January 1941. It was understood that, shortly before the completion of the commission's report, Duffy had indicated his intention not to sign it. The inference was made that Duffy then requested memorandum 172(B) to be published as a minority report in his name. The decision to exclude the document from the published volume was taken as equivalent to a refusal to publish a minority report and was regarded as a gross violation of Duffy's rights as a commissioner.[10] However, Patrick O'Toole, who had served as secretary to the commission, argued that this claim was not in accordance with the facts.

There were some major obstacles which made it extremely difficult, if not impossible, to facilitate Duffy's indirect communication. Firstly, there had to be some finality in the proceedings of the commission. The final closing date, which had been set by the commission for the submission of minority reports, addenda, and reservations, was 30 September 1943. Duffy had not complied with this requirement. Secondly, he had not clearly stated his wish to submit a minority report. Thirdly, he had not specified the document although it was assumed that the document referred to was 172(B). As if all this had not been enough to preclude the publication of 172(B) other impediments were also discerned. Patrick O'Toole maintained that memorandum 172(B) would not qualify as a minority report because the commission had not even started to consider the first rough draft of its report when the document was submitted. O'Toole argued that, because 172(B) was cross-referenced with other documents, it was unsuitable for publication. These documents would also have to be published with it. Finally, O'Toole claimed that if document 172(B) were published then other members would also have the right to demand publication of documents that they had submitted.[11]

On 6 September 1944, O'Toole wrote to Bishop Michael Browne informing him that Louie Bennett was anxious for the publication of the facts behind the rejection of Duffy's memorandum. Both Bennett and Campbell were 'in difficulties' with their colleagues in Labour due to the widespread opinion that the commission had unreasonably refused to publish a document by the secretary of the Labour Party. Bennett was confused over what action to take and felt that the Bishop of Galway was the only individual who could correct the false impression that had been created. O'Toole had visited Fr Edward Coyne the previous day and the priest's advice was to ignore the matter. Later, if the adverse publicity grew more serious something might be done about it. O'Toole did not inform Bennett of Coyne's opinion but she suspected that Browne would refrain from intervening in the controversy.[12] O'Toole was acutely aware of how difficult it would be to confront Duffy through the medium of the press. Allegations of suppression had not come from Duffy himself but from 'subsidiary or outside persons'.[13] O'Toole suspected that Duffy was trying to provoke a reaction from Browne. If the weight of evidence discredited the complaints made against the commission then Duffy could easily say that he had not even expressed a grievance.

Browne was troubled by the controversy and believed that O'Toole should issue a letter clarifying the exclusion of document 172(B) from the bound volume of the report. However, when O'Toole wrote to the Bishop on 23 September 1944 he had serious misgivings about this. He was extremely apprehensive because he sensed Duffy had him at a disadvantage. Browne was informed that

> If he finds the case for the Commission in the hands of a mere civil servant his confidence will grow, for he will know that I have put my neck out too far. If he were bent on making trouble he could make a lot for me, and more important even than that, for the Commission also, if I were to slip up on any point. I think that in these circumstances, you ought to reconsider the question of issuing the letter through me. I should have to get sanction for it, situated as I am now.[14]

O'Toole was of the opinion that, because the commission no longer existed, his superiors would not approve of him issuing a letter of clarification that was likely to involve him in public debate. If Duffy had a genuine grievance he should have expressed it several months earlier. His methods were 'furtive and wanting in candour' and O'Toole, although angry over Duffy's dishonest tactics, believed that if the Labour politician was openly challenged on the issue this might only serve his ulterior motives rather than clarifying what had happened.[15] Therefore, it was considered best to refrain from making a response.

Duffy, not content with his indirect offensive, bluntly criticised the report in public. In a lecture to the Labour Party at Rathmines (published in *The Irish Press*, 13 October 1944) Senator Duffy emphasised that the commission had not advocated a corporate state. Nevertheless, in evaluating the commission's work, he believed that its 'whole approach to the subject was regrettable'. He claimed that those who signed the report were motivated by 'a sincere desire to afford organised groups of producers and of those engaged in services an opportunity of acting collectively, in their own rather than in the public interest no doubt, as a safeguard against an expanding cynical bureaucracy'.[16] Furthermore, he stated that if producers were organised on a vocational basis the state would be unable to protect consumers against ruthless exploitation where monopolies would dominate the new order.

Duffy's stance had caused much disappointment and unease amongst his former colleagues but there was, for them, a far more important consideration. After the formal presentation of the report several weeks had passed without a public comment from any member of the government. The suspicion prevailed in some quarters that a favourable response would not be forthcoming. Many of those who were favourably disposed towards the commission's recommendations were aware of the obstacles to the establishment of a new vocationalist order. On 4 October 1944 John J.M. Ryan, editor of *The Irish Catholic*, wrote to Rev T. Morris (later Archbishop of Cashel), expressing the fear that

> Yes, the Vocational Commission Report is being quietly ignored . . . The recommendations cut too deeply at the roots of politics here for it to be a popular document, and there are minor difficulties such as the ordinary man's inability to see how he'll be any better off as a result of it and the rather steep price of the Report itself. Perhaps things will get moving when there is talk of implementing, even in a provisional way, some of the recommendations. On the other hand, the Government is probably waiting for some upsurge of popular enthusiasm about it; in that way it bids fair to rival the language revival question.[17]

Ryan's assessment was far from accurate. The government was not waiting for an upsurge of popular approval for vocationalist schemes – it was firmly opposed to such proposals. Its attitude towards vocationalism was strongly indicated by the reaction of Seán MacEntee (Minister for Local Government and Public Health) to another vocationalist scheme.

On 11 October 1944 Bishop John Dignan of Clonfert, chairman of the National Health Insurance Society (N.H.I.S.), addressed a meeting of the society's committee of management. The subject of his presentation was a paper entitled *Outlines of a Scheme of National Health Insurance*. The N.H.I.S. committee, he believed, was 'the nearest approach to Vocational Organisation in this country.'[18] Those in attendance were told

> As Ireland is a Christian and Catholic country, our Social Services ought to be Christian, that is, the spirit and the teaching of Christ must be their life and their soul. That spirit and teaching are found chiefly in the Social Encyclicals and consequently it is to them we are to look for light to guide us in our planning. The Health Services taken over from Great Britain were not noted for their Christian spirit, as they were materialistic and merely palliative . . .[19]

Dignan envisaged a reformed and greatly enlarged N.H.I.S. presided over by a governing body 'with full autonomous powers'. The new organisation was to benefit up to 90% of the population, providing health care and, if thought possible, a number of 'kindred' social services also.[20] The state, employers and employees jointly financed the N.H.I.S. insurance services. This was to continue but the amounts had to be increased if the scheme was to be extended.[21] No financial calculations, however, were given to indicate how much would have to be paid by the contributors.[22] Dignan hoped that many workers and self-employed, who were not members of the N.H.I.S., would join voluntarily. If large numbers declined to do so then membership would have to become compulsory.[23] If this was regimentation then, he believed, there was no escape from it.

The new N.H.I.S. was to be reformed in accordance with the principle of subsidiarity. Decentralisation required the setting up of regional committees. Dignan was of the opinion that the Catholic Church – 'the greatest force in the country for the social uplifting of the people' – should be represented on the regional and central committees of the society.[24] The bishop did not present the insurance scheme as perfect. He was acutely aware that it was open to criticism, especially in regard to its economic aspects. He stated

> This Paper clamours for criticism and I am thoroughly aware of the many objections that may be made against the principles of the Plan I have outlined. I have no objection to helpful and constructive criticism: the only criticism I shall resent is that the plan is not Christian.[25]

In his closing remarks Dignan appealed to Catholic loyalty.

> Except the teaching of Christ guides us in our personal lives and in our social life, it is vain to expect peace and happiness in our hearts or the kind of social services that is the birthright of a Catholic people. Our whole Social Structure must be built on the strong foundations of Christianity and not on the shifting sands of 'economics'.[26]

Dignan's paper was summarised in the press on 18 October 1944. Seán MacEntee was not overwhelmed by the spiritual values underlying Dignan's proposals. It was not that he had been opposed to the implementation of policies based on Catholic social teaching. He had expressed opinions that were critical of the expansion of state power and the concomitant proliferation of bureaucracy. He had declared himself in support of defending personal and familial autonomy against the advances of state control. Although he occasionally invoked Catholic principles he did not consistently act in conformity with his expressed opinions.[27] On 19 October 1944, the day after the Dignan plan was published, MacEntee rejected the insurance scheme.[28] He dismissed the document as impracticable. Although the financial aspect left much to be desired it should not have aroused such an antagonised response from him in view of his professed regard for Catholic teaching.

There was, however, a personal as well as a policy dimension to the controversy. The National Health Insurance Society (N.H.I.S.) had been established under the terms of the National Health Insurance Act of 1933.[29] The Minister for Local Government and Public Health appointed the chairman and the management committee of the N.H.I.S. and he had the power to remove them.[30] When the N.H.I.S. published its scheme, under the chairmanship of Dr Dignan, it did so without MacEntee's prior knowledge or approval. This lack of courtesy and tact was one of the main reasons for MacEntee's negative response.[31] The minister, much renowned for his vanity, was incensed when he learnt of the Dignan plan through the newspapers.[32] Furthermore, the publication of the N.H.I.S. scheme had the effect of putting pressure on the minister to implement it – and MacEntee tended to react negatively when pushed.[33] Even if the Dignan plan had been submitted to MacEntee before publication he would still have rejected it but his response would have been more conciliatory.

On 30 October 1944, only eleven days after MacEntee's harsh criticism of the Dignan plan, James Ryan, Minister for Agriculture, indicated the government's attitude towards the report of the Commission on Vocational Organisation. Speaking at the opening of the Catholic Social Week in the Mansion House, Dublin, he referred to the report only to defend his department's performance while at the same time expressing scepticism about the spontaneity of vocational organisation. Ryan's speech drew attention to the fact that in the previous ten or twelve years, many unsuccessful attempts had been made to organise and maintain parish guilds and parish councils.[34] These bodies represented the first stage in the vocational organisation of the rural community. The minister was pessimistic about the prospects of parish guilds and councils that had been organised on a voluntary basis and in conformity with the recommendations of the commission.

If vocational organisations were to be spontaneous then voluntary co-operation would have to be forthcoming. Yet the experience of Ryan, and that of his predecessor (Patrick Hogan), was that co-operation was in short supply – even when the Department of Agriculture took positive steps to encourage it. To substantiate his claim, Ryan singled out the creameries for criticism. The marketing of dairy produce, like other agricultural produce, needed to be carried out by a large central organisation. This could be done more efficiently by those involved in the business rather than by civil servants. In 1928 a central marketing organisation was established but within three years the scheme ended in failure because of lack of commitment.

In 1935, when Ryan was Minister for Agriculture, the Dáil decided that the minister should have the authority to grant larger subsidies to those creameries which agreed to participate in the central marketing scheme. Central marketing did not meet with the approval of most of the creameries and it had to be operated by civil servants. Creameries participated only because they wanted to get the higher subsidies. When the scheme was well established the minister told the creameries to take over its operation. After prolonged negotiation the minister obtained agreement on the condition that a civil servant would be chairman of the organisation. Ryan drew two conclusions from this experience. Firstly, it demonstrated how difficult it was to motivate people to organise on a vocational basis in their own interests. Secondly, it refuted the allegation, which had been made repeatedly by the commission, that civil servants intervened excessively in economic matters and against the wishes of the people. It was the very opposite. Civil servants, far from interfering in the business affairs of the agricultural sector, only responded to requests to become involved and were anxious to have people regulate their own activities as much as possible.[35]

Ryan assured his audience that there would be no opposition from the government, or from senior civil servants, to the growth of vocational organisation in the agricultural sector. He claimed that if Fr Hayes and other enthusiasts set themselves the task of forming vocational organisations in the agricultural sector of the economy then they would find a 'fair amount' of such organisation in place already.[36] Ryan had been cautious in that he tempered his critical remarks with conciliatory statements. However, his public statements strongly indicated the government's intention not to implement the elaborate vocationalist scheme described in the report.

THE RETALIATIVE RESPONSE OF THE CIVIL SERVICE

By November 1944 civil servants had made considerable progress in analysing the report. Their observations exposed many fundamental errors of judgement in the report. Criticism was focused on numerous points of detail. The remainder of this chapter examines the reaction of the state departments but, for the sake of brevity, attention is confined mainly to the major points of contention.

The Department of Education completed its preliminary observations on 17 November 1944. The commission had criticised the educational system at length. It had been particularly critical of the existing system of vocational education.[37] The official reaction to this criticism was that the commission was not sufficiently informed to make an overall judgement. The department noted that vocational education was under the direct control of local committees. These committees included representatives of the various trades, professions and occupations. It was argued that these committees were aware of the educational requirements of the young people of their districts. Departmental officials also claimed that the committees were very much in touch with the wishes of the local parents concerning the education of their children. The department concluded: 'it is difficult to reconcile the Commission's severe strictures on Vocational Education with some of its later arguments in support of the appointment of a Council of Education'.[38] The commission's recommendation for the establishment of a council of education, in paragraph 540 of its report, did not meet with the department's approval. A major difficulty was that the national vocational assembly would have to be set up first. The council, as described by the commission, would be unable to fulfil its advisory function to a satisfactory standard. Furthermore, the council would be incompatible with ministerial authority and control.[39] The department's attitude towards the report was distinctly negative.

The Department of Finance submitted its preliminary observations on 30 November 1944. The minister, Seán T. O'Kelly, and the secretary of the department, J.J. McElligott, had both opposed the commission's work. A generous assessment of the report was not forthcoming. It was claimed that the commission had strayed far beyond its terms of reference and that it contained many inaccuracies. Concern was expressed that the report contained no critical evaluation of vocational organisations and assumed that such forms of organisation were beneficial to society. The department was critical of the commission's enquiries about vocational organisations in foreign countries because it was felt that the commission all too often assumed the practical functioning of these bodies which, apparently, was far from the truth.[40]

It was claimed that the foreword by the chairman 'detracts considerably from the force of the recommendations contained in the Report'.[41] The department argued that the proposals were too complicated to be implemented successfully. It was contended that the vast network of organisations proposed by the commission would lead to a 'violent conflict with the principles of organic, vital growth' and this in turn was most likely to obstruct the gradual and natural development of vocational organisations.[42] In response to the question of legislation, the department felt that the commission's organisational scheme was so closely integrated that it would be difficult to give legislative effect to a phased programme of implementation.[43]

The preliminary observations of the Department of Finance had criticised the report in general terms. Its 'further' observations were more detailed.[44] The commission had expressed the view that it would cost the Exchequer no more than £100,000 per annum to finance the upper echelons of vocational organisation.[45] By failing to substantiate its estimates the commission left itself vulnerable to eager critics in the civil service, especially in the Department of Finance. The attitude of the department was that the estimate was 'worthless'. In view of the absence of spontaneous growth it was thought that members of vocational organisations would tend to look beyond their members for finance to cover their costs.[46] The commission overlooked the fact that the total cost of administering the plethora of associations, conferences, councils, and assemblies, if not financed by the state, would have to be met by the professions, industries and services concerned.

Ultimately, the cost would be passed on to the consumer in some form – probably through higher prices. Since consumers were, in the majority of cases, taxpayers also, the extra charges would, in effect, give rise to a system of double taxation. The commissioners seemed to think that the consumer would be delighted to pay, to maintain a new non-governmental bureaucracy because the taxes were not paid to the state. As if all this extra cost was not enough the consumer would be exposed to the higher prices imposed by monopolistic practices. The commission's answer to this problem was that consumers should form their own protective associations. Yet it did not attempt to explain how these associations could be formed or how they would function. In fact the commission acknowledged that this weakness existed throughout its proposals generally when it stated in paragraph 657 of its report

> In many of the vocational and functional councils recommended by us we have felt the need to include a representative of consumers, but have found it difficult to designate a particular organisation that could claim to represent this interest and to be able to supply trained and competent delegates.

One of the great virtues of the new order, according to the report, would be its freedom from the burden of bureaucracy. The Department of Finance observed that the commission carried out its task with the preconceived idea that the best and only satisfactory form of society was one entirely organised on a vocational basis. The commission's fear of bureaucracy was accompanied by a rather naive belief that efficiency and co-operation would be the outstanding features of vocational organisations.[47] Understandably, this utopian view was sharply criticised by the department. It argued that an elaborate system of vocational organisation would tend to destroy community cohesion by placing individuals in rigidly defined vocational compartments – this in turn creating a series of new sectional allegiances. Ironically, this effect would be contrary to a fundamental tenet of vocationalist thought which stressed harmony between the various sectors of society. There was a danger that those economic interests which were most capable of effective organisation would exercise undue power, much to the detriment of the community as a whole. The farmers, who were poorly organised, were likely to be particularly disadvantaged. This factor alone would adversely effect the national economy.[48]

Officials of the Department of Finance did not argue that vocational organisation was without merit. They conceded that vocational organisation was beneficial and that its development should be encouraged by the government but it was contended that vocational organisations had the right to advise government only on those issues which related directly to their own welfare. It was imperative that the government should be absolutely free to accept or reject the advice given to it, bearing in mind the welfare of the national community. However, in view of the huge and complicated network of vocational organisations envisaged by the commission, the government might find itself receiving dictation instead of advice. Contrary to paragraph 513 of the report, vocational bodies could not remain above and outside politics. The fear was expressed that it was only a matter of time before the more powerful interest groups would dominate the new political machinery. Vocational organisation might eventually lead to vocational government.[49]

The commission seemed to be oblivious to the possibility of a clash between the political and vocational authorities, believing that the political could be neatly separated from the socio-economic. It failed to devise a satisfactory relationship between the national vocational assembly and the Dáil. Although the commission did not set out to undermine the authority of the Dáil its recommendations, if implemented, would inevitably have caused conflict between the Dáil and the national vocational assembly.[50]

The danger of excessive state power had been exaggerated in the report and the conditions that existed during World War II may have contributed significantly to this. The Department of Finance acknowledged this probability but it still scorned the exaggerated fears of the commission. While agreeing that state intervention could be dangerous the department pointed out that in a democratic state, such as Ireland, it did not pose a threat. State intervention represented the will of the national community and the state did not exceed its jurisdiction if it intervened to ensure that the needs of the community were adequately served.[51]

An increase in state intervention led to a greater involvement of the civil service in the affairs of society. In the commission's report the civil service was condemned because of its alleged deficiencies; i.e. its preoccupation with record keeping, its rigid adherence to regulations and devotion to precedent, its poor understanding of technical and industrial matters, its lack of personal responsibility and its detachment from those who were affected by its decisions. The department repudiated this assessment. The work of the civil service was (and still is) subject to parliamentary control. Departmental decisions are subject to parliamentary criticism and must be in conformity with what parliament decides. The parliamentary system required an elaborate system of accountancy therefore it was deemed essential to maintain comprehensive records of all financial transactions, details of authority for payments, and justification for decisions which had been acted upon.[52]

With regard to slowness of decisions the point was made that problems big and small often concern several departments and consultation with these was required to ensure consistency of policy. Caution had to take priority over swiftness if consistency of policy was to be preserved. Adherence to precedent was defended on the basis that the effects of legislation could not always be predicted. Frequently, the value of precedent had to be relied upon because, in proving itself to have worked in the past, it provided a clue to what might work in the future and was believed to be better than mere guesswork. Further to this it was contended that civil servants had reason to be cautious because they were answerable for their actions to a government minister who would demand an explanation for actions taken in his name if these actions violated policy or were contrary to what common sense indicated.

The submission of the Department of Finance had identified a number of fundamental errors in the report of the Commission on Vocational Organisation. Individual civil servants were also anxious to make their views known because they deeply resented the commission's allegations against them. The secretary of the Land Commission, M. Deegan, was provoked to write

> I don't pretend for a moment that I can read, calmly, insulting and unsubstantiated references to the doubtful loyalty of the higher Civil Service when changes of policy or changes of Government are in question, to bureaucratic interference and ineptitude, to the inefficient and unbusinesslike and red-tape methods of the Civil Service, to their political subservience to Ministers and so on . . .[53]

Deegan argued that the welfare of the ordinary citizen was better served by government ministers than by vocational organisations that would bring workers and employers together to fix prices, tariffs, quotas and licences. He was puzzled by the commission's attribution of altruistic qualities to employers and their workers as they fixed the prices of the commodities they manufactured, as they allocated production quotas, import quotas and export licences. Would not monopolistic practices develop much to the cost of the consumer? The commission thought not despite the fact that opinions were expressed and arguments articulated which strongly indicated that vocational groups could not be relied upon to willingly subordinate their self-interest to the public interest.[54]

Another individual submission, unsigned and entitled 'Report of Commission on Vocational Organisation 1943: Reactions of a Bureaucrat', attacked the ideological core which underpinned the commission's proposals and was very similiar to Deegan's robust argumentative style. No system of government, it was pointed out, could operate without rules and officials. Civil servants were needed to implement government policies.[55] The commission was castigated for its act of faith in vocationalism. Evidently, the anonymous official regarded paragraph 359 of the report as extremely offensive towards civil servants and politicians when he stated

> Vocational Organisation might, the Commission feel, perform functions of great social and economic importance if 'government by Ministerial order' is to continue after the war. It might, *inter alia*, 'limit bureaucratic interference and ineptitude and eliminate political corruption'. The charming simplicity of our Commissioners could hardly be better illustrated. The Civil Servant, the Minister, cannot avoid interference, ineptitude and political corruption – these good qualities are part of their nature. But hand over their functions to their brothers, cousins or friends who happen to be organised vocationally as professional men, businessmen or craftsmen and all is harmony, efficiency and integrity.[56]

An excellent portrayal of declared self-interest had appeared in *The Irish Times* (9 December 1944) – much to the satisfaction of the aggrieved 'bureaucrat'. The Guild of Irish Bakers congratulated the commission for producing a valuable report. In a resolution that was adopted unanimously the Guild pointed out that since its foundation it had 'worked for the objects and methods suggested in the report, so as to aid the common good of the baking industry'. This gem of a news item supported the civil servant's contention that vocational organisations were primarily concerned with serving their own interests. The

Guild of Irish Bakers had no doubts about vocationalism – or the 'common good' which it was most likely to serve.[57] The implication of this observation was clear – a similar attitude was held by other occupational groups.

The commission had refused to accept that the staffs employed in the administration and functioning of an intricate network of vocational organisations would lead to the creation of a new bureaucracy that would in turn impose a huge cost on the consumer. It denied that there would be a duplication of services. With regard to the former point, the civil servant argued, rather convincingly, that a new bureaucracy would indeed emerge. The commission had assumed that, by denying security of tenure to the directors and staffs of vocational bodies, the bureaucratic mentality would not occur. He predicted

> – that within five years the new Directors will have qualified for the title of Bureaucrats with as much justification as I have . . . ;
> – that within five years the staffs of the new bodies will have formed a vocational organisation the main object of which will be the obtaining of security of tenure, full pension rights, and so on and that they will be successful . . .[58]

A conspicuous irony of the vocationalist scheme was that the despised bureaucrats were to be instrumental in setting up the new vocational structures before many of them were made redundant.

The report conveyed a sense of urgency when it stressed the need for constructive reform. This, together with its commitment to the concept of planning, should have appealed to the instincts of Seán Lemass who was hopelessly endeavouring at the time to imbue his colleagues with a similar sense of urgency.[59] He was Minister for Industry and Commerce and was also Minister for Supplies when the report was published. Lemass had co-operated with the commission in 1940 and had expressed a supportive attitude towards it enquiries. It is remarkable how he drastically changed his stance when the commission's report was published. Despite the fact that he would have had to withhold support for party political reasons this was far removed from the scathing criticism which he directed against the report (this will be discussed in the next chapter). Lemass was needlessly alienated because the report had singled out the Department of Industry and Commerce for particularly harsh criticism. Although some of the comments may have been justified, most of them were of little consequence and were unnecessarily provocative; and those criticisms which were of significance were not substantiated. It was a serious tactical blunder to adopt a disparaging approach towards the minister and his officials when he shared some common ground with the vocationalists.[60]

The Department of Industry and Commerce, in compliance with the cabinet decision of 18 August 1944, issued its preliminary observations on the *Commission on Vocational Organisation Report* on 11 January 1945. According to Industry and Commerce there was a lack of clarity, precision and accuracy in the report. It was pointed out that recommendations were made which contradicted others elsewhere in the report and there seemed to be a duplication, and even a triplication (in some cases), of functions assigned to different vocational bodies.[61] The lack of precise allotment of executive and administrative functions had led to this wasteful duplication. The department anticipated that appeals on disputed issues, from associations to joint boards and later to functional councils or to the national industrial office, could lead to a paralysis of the system if too many cases went to the highest body of appeal.[62]

The commission had proposed that industries should be given a large measure of control over their own affairs with minimal interference by a department of state. This did not mean that industries and their organisations would cease to be subject to laws passed by the Oireachtas. However, the Department of Industry and Commerce stressed that attempts to promote vocational organisation in Ireland contrasted sharply with emerging trends in the advanced industrial countries.[63] In these countries, it was argued, there had been a pressing need for stricter control by legislation, and consequently by government departments, of all industrial and commercial organisations in order to protect the public interest. The need for tighter government control had been growing since before 1939 because of the development of strong monopolistic tendencies which frequently impeded trade and were in conflict with the welfare of the community at large.

The department anticipated that the British government intended to enforce stricter legal controls over industrial and commercial organisations in the United Kingdom. Previously, British legislation and administrative practices had allowed industrial associations and cartels much more freedom in comparison with other countries. It was noted that in the United States of America, and in some European countries, legislation was already in place to control cartels and large industrial associations. Circumstances in Ireland were similar to those in Britain regarding the above except that commercial and industrial organisations were not as well developed.[64] It seems reasonable to infer that, as far as the Department of Industry and Commerce was concerned, conditions abroad militated against the promotion of vocational organisation in Ireland.

The official attitude of the department was that there was 'a certain atmosphere of unreality' about the vocationalist scheme because it was believed that employers and trade unions would not willingly participate in it.[65] The department had encouraged the establishment of a number of industrial associations and joint industrial councils. Its policy was based on voluntary association – not on legislative compulsion. Joint industrial boards (representing both employers and workers in each industry) and industrial associations were thought to be beneficial because they could give valuable advice to the government. However, the opinion was expressed that to confer more than advisory and consultative functions would be incompatible with the public interest. Furthermore, the department was adamant that industrialists did not want an association with powers of enforcement, inextricably linked to powers of prosecution, for noncompliance with regulations.[66] Powers of law enforcement had to remain with departments of state.

The fallacy of 'organic growth' was also emphasised by the Department of Industry and Commerce and provided it with one reason amongst many to echo the widespread sentiment in the civil service that the report contained many contradictory statements. Reference was made to paragraph 567 which dealt with employers' associations.[67] The commission was 'not convinced that it would be wise or necessary to make membership compulsory on all individuals or firms'. The growth of vocational organisation should be encouraged rather than forced. But in paragraph 565 it was stated 'All persons or firms engaged in an industry in which an employers' association has been registered, whether members of the association or not, should be bound by the regulations made by the association and should pay the annual registration and membership fees.' This statement clearly advocated compulsory membership (de facto if not de jure) and violated a fundamental principle of vocational organisation. Government ministers and civil servants alike did not have much faith in the notion of spontaneous or organic growth of vocational organisations. Their sceptical attitude was well founded.[68] Therefore they tended to emphasise it as the only way forward when opposing demands or proposals to stimulate the development of vocational organisations by legislative action. The vocationalists would be forced to rely on 'the laws of organic, vital growth', as outlined in the foreword of the report, as the only mechanism of development of vocational organisations.

The Department of Industry and Commerce rejected the commission's scheme for industry. After examining the proposals concerned with commerce the department concluded that these would be 'even more difficult in actual operation than those relating to Industry, as organisation in Commerce is not so complete and in certain ways is more complicated'.[69] In regard to transport the department dismissed the recommendations in the report as 'extraordinarily cumbersome' and detrimental to any possibility of co-ordination.[70]

On 13 January 1945 the Department of Industry and Commerce submitted its final observations on the report. It vigorously defended its record of consulting various organisations, industrialists and business firms. The commission had alleged that, although consultative councils had been established for agriculture, similar councils had not been set up for industry.[71] This criticism was unjustified. The Department of Industry and Commerce, in the course of defending its record of consulting industrial firms, claimed that since its establishment it had been responsible for the creation of over 50 industrial advisory committees.[72] These committees met when summoned by the department or at the request of the committees themselves. The promotion of trade and industrial associations for purposes of consultation was a central feature of departmental policy.[73] The text of paragraphs 335 to 339 (inclusive) of the report was found to be particularly offensive because it created the false impression that the Department of Industry and Commerce was hostile towards organisations representing commercial and industrial interests. These paragraphs gave only 'some slight acknowledgement' of the evidence that had been submitted by the department. The commission's assessment of the policy and work of the department was denounced as 'unfair, frequently inaccurate' and 'distorted'.[74]

Unlike the Department of Industry and Commerce, the Department of External Affairs had not been criticised by, nor was it affected by, the commission's recommendations. However, these considerations did not dissuade it from making critical comments about the commission's findings. On 19 January 1945 the secretary of the Department of External Affairs, Joseph Walshe, wrote to the Department of the Taoiseach expressing concern about the commission's sources of information about Portugal. Colman O'Donovan, the chargé d'affaires at Lisbon, had drawn Walshe's attention to the inadequacy of paragraph 54 of the commission's report which stated

> The Commission is unable to give a complete description of the corporations, the second stage of the Portuguese system; for as these

> were established only on 12th November, 1938, we were not able, owing to the outbreak of war, to procure the text of the Decree and relevant official documents.

O'Donovan stated that the legation had been in existence since February 1942 – about 18 months before the completion of the report. At no time was he asked to assist their enquiries. This was a serious omission because the document sought by the commission could have been obtained at any time through the legation.[75] This in turn cast a shadow of doubt over paragraph 40 of the report which, in general terms, listed the commission's sources of information for the twelve foreign countries studied. Adequate consultation with the Department of External Affairs was obviously in question.

Walshe expressed his regret that the censorship authorities had not discouraged the advocacy of the Portuguese corporatist system in the periodical press when the commission was pursuing its enquiries. He felt that those who advocated vocationalism had influenced public opinion in favour of the Portuguese type of corporatism. This was a cause for concern because the main sources of information about Portugal were apparently derived from the publications of the Propaganda Secretariat. Walshe, although acknowledging that the commission had not recommended the establishment of a corporate state, felt that it was highly probable that members of the commission had been unduly influenced by what they had read about Portugal.[76]

On 21 February 1945, the Department of External Affairs supplied more information about Portugal to the Department of the Taoiseach. This data was received from the Research Department of the British Foreign Office. The Research Department had undertaken a confidential review of the Portuguese press. The newspaper *Voz* had highlighted the shortcomings of Portuguese corporatism. From the study it was evident that all was not well with corporatism in Portugal. The Corporate Technical Council had major problems in dealing with abuses that were rampant amongst the existing 297 corporatist organisations. The legation at Lisbon added that the censorship authorities in Portugal would, ordinarily, never allow press criticism of the corporatist organisations – but public discontent was so strong against the inefficiency and corruption of these bodies that the authorities thought it prudent to allow the expression of some dissatisfaction. The 'Gremios' (associations of employers) were high on the list of offenders.[77]

Bureaucracy had been castigated by the commission as the antithesis of vocationalism. Now the unthinkable had occurred in

Portugal – corporatist organisations had become infected with bureaucracy. This affliction was manifested by 'incompetence or lack of zeal'. Many people had sought employment in corporate organisations 'not to serve them but merely to get a job'.[78] The Gremios had come to resemble the public service where disinterested and poor service was not unknown. The commission had denied, rather naively, that vocational organisation in Ireland, as proposed in the report, would lead to the creation of a new form of bureaucracy. Such a view was patently unsubstantiated.

The commission, when describing the corporatist system, made it clear that the ideal it supported was societal corporatism – not a corporate state. In devising its corporatist scheme for Ireland the commission was anxious to limit the power of the state and it expressed concern about the growing practice of legislation by statutory orders and regulations because this tended to transfer legislative and sometimes even judicial powers to the executive. The commission's extreme fear of excessive state intervention in the social and economic aspects of Irish national life is somewhat mitigated by the fact that, when the report was drafted in November 1943, Hitler and Stalin were still in power and dictatorship was rampant throughout war-torn Europe. Also, the exigencies of wartime planning had induced greater state intervention in the Irish economy. Nevertheless, it is ironic that the commission chose to express a deep mistrust of politicians in a liberal democracy and harshly criticised the institutions of a popularly elected government. In doing so it incurred the wrath of the civil service and the opposition of government ministers.

Some government departments were relatively slow in completing their assessment of the *Commission on Vocational Organisation Report*. In March 1945, observations on the document were submitted by the departments of Justice, Local Government and Public Health, Supplies, and Agriculture. The Department of Justice did not find fault with the report to the same extent as Finance or Industry and Commerce but it declined to approve of the commission's proposals.[79] The Department of Local Government and Public Health, presided over by Seán MacEntee, adopted a negative approach to the commission's recommendations in common with other state departments. Paragraphs 437 to 440 of the report of the Commission on Vocational Organisation addressed the issue of national health insurance. The opinion of the Department of Local Government and Public Health was that the commission's findings were misleading – an outcome which could have been avoided if the commission had consulted more extensively with the department.[80] The view was expressed that

> vocationalism in the sphere of national health insurance, of a kind corresponding exactly to the definition of vocational organisation in the Commission's Report, and having its origin in British legislation, was abandoned here over ten years ago, and is now likely to be discarded in Great Britain.[81]

The department did not trust the National Health Insurance Society to administer the compulsory scheme of national health insurance in a fair manner. The organisation would not be allowed to decide who was or who was not insurable because it had been found that 'its attitude towards a particular case is in fact determined by the probable effect on the funds of the Society'.[82]

The department asserted that only the minister was capable of protecting individual rights which would otherwise be violated by corporate or institutional interests.[83] Only the minister could administer an Act of the Oireachtas because he was responsible to the Oireachtas and its Public Accounts Committee. Through the Oireachtas he had the power to enforce compliance with regulations. The N.H.I.S. scheme was financed mainly by employers and workers but the state also contributed a substantial proportion of the revenue. The suspicion prevailed that the employers and workers might conspire to circumvent the law at the expense of the taxpayer.[84]

The department was sharply critical of paragraph 543 of the commission's report which recommended the establishment of a council of health. Its functions of co-ordination and planning were regarded as untenable – these functions were for the minister. The Department of Local Government and Public Health rejected the proposal to set up a council of health on the basis that it would violate ministerial authority. However, it was feasible for the council to serve as a consultative body 'possessed of specialised knowledge, information and experience, to which the Minister could look for technical advice on public health problems.' But this function was not acknowledged because it was felt that such a heterogeneous council would not be able to give worthwhile technical advice. What the department needed, it was claimed, was advice from outside groups whose members were selected on a 'narrow basis of excellence' rather than on the broadness of their representation.[85]

The Commission on Vocational Organisation had accumulated a vast amount of information on the many facets of Irish social and economic life but it had failed to consult some departments of state on a number of important matters which were pertinent to its investigations and subsequent assessment.[86] The Department of Supplies felt aggrieved because 'the Commission either pronounced judgment or quoted at length erroneous statements submitted to them without hearing the views of the Department.'[87] The department was dismissive of those proposals in the report which it felt qualified to evaluate; these were concerned with industry, commerce and transport.[88] The proposed organisation for industry was thought to be too complicated and top-heavy.[89] There was more than a suspicion that workers and employers in particular industries would connive with each other to further their joint interests at the expense of the community at large. The scheme devised by the commission did not allow adequate protection for consumers.[90]

The vocationalist scheme for organising the rural population, especially those engaged in agriculture, fared no better than those already discussed. The opinion of the Department of Agriculture was that the commission should have taken due cognisance of failed attempts to organise the rural sector of the population over the preceding fifty years. Parish organisations were not only difficult to organise – they were extremely difficult to maintain. These bodies lacked the vitality to endure for any significant length of time, except those that were located near the parish church.[91] A major problem, according to the department, was that the rural population was so dispersed, and rural people were so heavily burdened with their daily work, that there was little inclination and even less capacity to undertake any duties of parochial organisation. The few people in the parish who had sufficient spare time, such as the clergy and local school teachers, did not give cause for optimism. School teachers in particular had not encountered remarkable success in their efforts to promote local schemes; neither had the Department of Agriculture.[92]

The organisation of farmers was crucial to the viability of any rural plan because they were by far the dominant socio-economic sector. There had been many attempts to stimulate a co-operative spirit amongst them but what had been achieved was not impressive.[93] The Farm Improvement Scheme in some areas had been obstructed by a minority of farmers. Land drainage was particularly dependent on full co-operation between farmers and this was, all too frequently, not forthcoming. Occasionally the department attempted to organise cow-testing associations and agricultural credit societies but the response of farmers was not encouraging. When farmers did not react positively to such concrete projects, specifically designed to assist them, how could they be expected to take an active interest in parish organisations where the objectives were not well defined?

The commission had emphasized the need to devise a scheme to organise the entire rural population. Failure to do so would result in 'a very partial and unbalanced plan for the vocational organisation of the country.' The commission did not believe that it was practicable to organise the non-farming sector of the rural community on 'a strict and rigid vocational basis' because of its low population density.[94] Therefore it was not considered necessary 'to establish, for the purposes of general rural organisation, any bodies higher than the Parish Guild . . . i.e., county or national bodies to co-ordinate and supervise the activities of Parish Guilds'. Instead, the commission was content to speculate that parish guilds would decide to group themselves for purposes such as pooling information, consultation, and adopting joint strategies to pursue common objectives.[95] An important distinction was made between the agricultural and non-agricultural sectors of rural Ireland.[96] Agriculture was to have its own hierarchy of vocational organisations, presided over by a national agricultural conference.[97]

The commission had proposed a very disjointed scheme of rural organisation. The official view of the Department of Agriculture was that the parish guilds 'would stand somewhat in a position of isolation and unlinked with the general network of vocational bodies'.[98] In its assessment of the report the department revealed an extreme fear of the commission's proposals. Of course there were dangers to parliamentary democracy inherent in some of the commission's recommendations – but the response of the Department of Agriculture was excessive when dealing with the higher echelons of vocational organisation. The department feared that, like some other government departments, it would be stripped of many of its functions, and might even be abolished. This apprehension was expressed forcefully:

> It is obvious that the idea underlying the whole of these proposals leading up to the establishment of a National Agricultural Conference with its appendages, the Governing Body and the National Agricultural Office, is to replace the whole of the present organisation, including Committees of Agriculture and the Department of Agriculture itself.[99]

In the final paragraph of its observations the department described a catastrophe of Armageddon proportions arising from a conflict between the Dáil and the national vocational assembly. Contrary to paragraph 513 of the report, the political structure of the state would be transformed as vocational organisation led to vocational government. With its multitude of Guilds, Councils and Conferences *et cetera*, the new system would be extremely complex and burdened with cumbersome procedures, making it unworkable. Furthermore, national unity would be destroyed as sectional interests competed with each other. The proposed implementation of the commission's plan conjured up the spectre of 'chaos and national disintegration'.[100] This unprecedented calamity had to be prevented. Radical change would not to be brought about by the implementation of the vocationalist grand plan.

AN ASSESSMENT OF THE CIVIL SERVICE REACTION

Civil servants challenged, sometimes to the extent of ridiculing, the findings of the commission. They castigated the assumptions, misconceptions, and misinformation which seemed to underlie many of its recommendations. It was stated that the report was self-contradictory in parts and that its proposals could neither be understood nor implemented due to ambiguity. Also, civil servants who commented on the report believed that the commission had strayed far beyond its terms of reference. It was noted that 'in the Bible and in Shakespeare one could find a reference to anything whatever – past, present or future. The Report of the Banking Commission set up a rivalry for this distinction. And this Report runs it close . . .'[101]

It should not have surprised those who were members of the commission that government departments were extremely critical of their report. The Departments of Agriculture and of Industry and Commerce were those most in contact with economic interest groups and suffered the brunt of the commission's criticisms. In the case of Finance, James McElligott was still secretary of the department and had already shown himself hostile to the commission's endeavours. These three departments were to the forefront in denouncing the report. Other government departments either stated a policy of absolutely no implementation of the commission's recommendations or approved of only trivial aspects of the commission's proposals. The Department of Lands, for instance, could only bring itself to concede that playing fields were very suitable for administration by parish councils and parish guilds.[102] The departments of External Affairs, Education, Defence, and Local Government and Public Health had no plans to implement any of the vocationalist proposals. The Department of Posts and Telegraphs and the Minister for the Co-ordination of Defensive Measures made no observations.[103]

A fundamental weakness of the report was that it focused criticism mainly on administrative practices and institutional defects. Instead, the core of the problem was due to

> the pervasive mediocrity of the Irish public mind – the sheer dearth of trained and disciplined intellect – that made the recommendations of the Report so generally impractical at that time. Until the quality was improved, systems could make little difference.[104]

The commission had insisted that men of public spirit, integrity, and intelligence were essential for the development of vocational organisation and that organisational structure alone was not enough[105] – but it then forgot about this stipulation and proceeded to construct its recommendations on the assumption that men of high calibre were available in sufficient numbers and all that needed to be done was to create the right structures.

The civil service was not without fault but the commission's inordinate criticism alienated potential supporters of vocationalism and strengthened the position of the reactionaries. Consequently, the Fianna Fáil government found a willing ally in the civil service when it rejected the commission's major recommendations. Therefore

> By the mid-nineteen-forties a rift had emerged in Ireland between two philosophies of government. One could be labelled 'vocationalist', and called for the diffusion of responsibility among vocational groups. The other could be called 'bureaucratic' and defended the centralisation of authority in government departments.[106]

A rigidity and extremity of views arose on both sides which was not conducive to a positive synthesis. The civil service could not have been expected to share the aspirations of the vocationalists who held it in low regard. Consequently, its response to the commission's recommendations was so emotive that rationality was substantially compromised. Ministers and civil servants invoked the doctrine of ministerial responsibility as a reason to obstruct the promotion of vocational organisation in Ireland. In doing so they failed to see the weaknesses of their own system.[107]

The emphasis on the British-derived principle of ministerial responsibility was not entirely justifed. Dozens of public bodies existed in Britain with varying measures of freedom from direct ministerial management. These organisations included the British Broadcasting Corporation and the London Passenger Transport Board. Circumstances were similar in Ireland where a number of semi-independent public bodies had been created and these included the Irish Sugar Company, Aer Lingus and the Electricity Supply Board. The principle had been established that semi-autonomous vocational organisations could exist without necessarily conflicting with the doctrine of ministerial responsibility.[108] Yet civil servants and politicians alike repudiated the proposals of the commission without acknowledging due merit. Their negative response was made easier by the defective reasoning which underpinned so many recommendations in the report.

The proposals in the report were based on the assumption that once practical men, truly representative of their economic constituencies, came together, they would subordinate their self-interest to the public interest. Despite the evidence to the contrary the commission had remained unshaken in its faith in vocationalism. The vulnerability of the public to exploitation by sectional interests was a major flaw in the commission's recommendations and government departments were only too eager to emphasise this weakness. A fundamental weakness of the report was the failure to reconcile vocationalist aspirations with the existing system of parliamentary democracy. The proposals of the commission could not have been implemented exactly as recommended without causing conflict between the new vocational organisations and parliament, but some of the vocationalist schemes could have been put into effect if substantial modifications had been made. Even the most hardened critics of the commission's proposals acknowledged that there was some good in the concept of vocational organisation.[109] Their approval, however, was confined to the realm of theory and the forces of reaction resisted, with ease, the demands of the vocationalists.

CHAPTER SEVEN

The Rejection of Vocationalist Proposals, 1945

AN ACRIMONIOUS DEBATE

The Department of Industry and Commerce had been extremely critical of the *Commission on Vocational Organisation Report* when it submitted its assessment to the Department of the Taoiseach in January 1945. Seán Lemass, still presiding over the department, had no intention of pressing ahead with the implementation of any of the commission's recommendations but the propensity of his political opponents to quote the report during Dáil debates made it difficult for him to ignore it. Fr Edward J. Coyne was aware of this and informed Dr Michael Browne that two Dáil deputies, Eamonn Coogan and Patrick McGilligan, were 'always baiting Lemass with the Commission's views'.[1] The minister was so incensed with the commission's findings that it required very little aggravation to push him beyond the limits of prudence. Senator Gerard Sweetman's lengthy invocation of the report[2] finally exhausted the last vestiges of his restraint.

On 21 February 1945 Lemass bluntly stated his views on the report of the Commission on Vocational Organisation. In the course of a Senate debate on the Minerals Company Bill he launched a scathing attack which articulated his sense of outrage – an outrage that was shared by many civil servants, especially those in the Department of Industry and Commerce. He declared

> I find it not easy to speak about the report of the Vocational Commission . . . I have read the report of that commission on more than one occasion and I have been unable to come to any conclusion as to whether the querulous, nagging, propagandist tone of its observations is to be attributed to unfortunate drafting or to a desire to distort the picture. The commission spent a great deal of energy upon its researches, and a very long time in preparing its report, and I think it is unfortunate that the report, when published, should be such a slovenly document. I think

> that that is a fair description of it, because it contains an extraordinary number of mis-statements of fact which could easily have been rectified by a telephone enquiry to the Department or organisation concerned. In some respects, its recommendations are self-contradictory.[3]

Understandably, these bitter words provoked an angry response from the Bishop of Galway and the ensuing debate received much press coverage in March 1945. Other members of the commission too had reason to feel aggrieved, especially Coyne, who had invested so much time and effort in the commission's work.

Coyne wrote to Browne the day after Lemass's blunt criticism of the report. The bishop was advised to request from Lemass examples of where the commission had made mistakes. Coyne anticipated that Lemass's reply would reveal the most damaging errors discovered by the minister's officials. This, of course, would facilitate an effective retaliatory response. If Lemass refused to specify what errors had been made then he could be discredited on the issue because Browne could inform the media of his request and the minister's refusal. Coyne was not particularly worried about minor mistakes – the important point was that, in his opinion, the commission had not made any major errors. Evidently, he suspected that the report had not been well received in official circles and he felt that Lemass's insulting criticisms presented an opportunity not to be missed. He impressed upon Browne that

> This is the first time that anyone in a position of authority has come out with something definite to catch hold of – and unless it is scotched at once, the ordinary people will just take it as true and as a proof that the Report has no practical value. Moreover, it is a very good opportunity to arouse interest in the Report once again and to carry war into the other camp.[4]

Browne acted on Coyne's advice and wrote to Lemass on 23 February. While Browne awaited Lemass's reply Coyne offered more advice

> Before making any direct answer to Lemass I would make sure that I know the full weight of the metal that he can bring to bear on me: I can judge this even from a few instances, if he gives them. But to go blindly into a defensive document not knowing exactly where and what his attack would be merely to supply him with ammunition and give ourselves a decided handicap.[5]

The Jesuit priest then explained his strategy in detail. Lemass had to be challenged to substantiate his allegations so that an effective response could be made. The bishop of Galway was urged, at length, to keep the public debate at 'a very high level' and care had to be taken so that it did not disintegrate into a 'private brawl'. Above all Browne was not to betray any trace of anger or personal irritation. He was to exhibit a 'cool, objective, liberal, tolerant attitude' while Lemass would be left to struggle vainly from the quagmire of insults and false accusations to which he had descended. Catholic loyalty, it was hoped, would be a decisive factor in winning support for the commission's recommendations. Furthermore, this debate would serve the vocationalist cause by acting as the springboard of a long-term campaign to promote support for the commission's proposals.[6]

Lemass replied to Browne on 2 March. The minister complained, with a great deal of justification, that the report disclosed an attitude towards the Department of Industry and Commerce which was 'unfair' and which gave a 'distorted' account of its policy and work. He failed to comprehend how the majority of members of the commission signed their names to the 'masterpiece of innuendo' which was expressed in paragraph 359 of the report.[7] This paragraph warned that bureaucratic interference, ineptitude and political corruption could become so great as to endanger individual liberty, impartial administration and public honesty. It was thought that vocational organisations might function as an effective antidote to such diseases of the body politic and assist in the wise drafting of regulations. Furthermore, it was anticipated that vocational organisations would assist the state in securing co-operation from the business community so that the enforcement of such regulations could be done more efficiently and justly. It was with these considerations in mind that the commission had examined the role of vocational organisations in commercial activities.

Lemass's harsh criticism of the report, although justified to some extent, revealed a deficiency of objective assessment. In his letter to Browne he declared

> I have tried in these observations to avoid making any comments on the merits of the commission's recommendations, to the extent that I have been able to understand them, and to confine myself to drawing attention to the defects of the Report as such . . .[8]

Coyne was eager to challenge Lemass and others who dared to denigrate the findings of 'the 22 Don Quixotes' who signed the report.[9] On 5 March he wrote again to the bishop of Galway. Browne was informed that Lemass had 'the whole civil service trying to pick holes in the report'.[10] Coyne believed that a number of errors would be discovered but he was confident that none of these would be of major importance.

Coyne's advice was shrewd, calculated and of crucial importance to Browne. The bishop was clearly influenced by what Coyne recommended when he spoke out publicly in defence of the report at University College, Galway.[11] He stressed the need to defend 'high and sacred principles' and expressed concern that Ireland should be safeguarded against totalitarianism. The objectives he had in mind when he spoke about vocational organisation were justice, order, efficiency, brotherhood and freedom; these, he believed, should get a 'fair chance' in Ireland. He was anxious to teach politicians to refrain from uttering gratuitous insults and false accusations. Thus, he was duty-bound to defend the members of the commission against injustice. The public were informed that: 'It is well known that immediately our Commission's report was published, the Civil Service set itself to search out every defect.'[12] Browne challenged Lemass to substantiate his allegations. Attention was drawn to the fact that the commission had to make the first survey of its kind, covering hundreds of vocational and functional bodies in every branch of Irish economic life. It was understandable that the report contained some inaccuracies because of the limited clerical assistance given to the commission. Reference was made to paragraph 720 of the report which informed the reader that, despite all the care in the preparation of the document, there was bound to be some errors in point of detail. However, the assertion was made that the broad outline of the survey was substantially correct and it was argued that the recommendations were not invalidated by errors of detail. Furthermore, Browne claimed that the report could not be conveniently dismissed as out of touch with reality because of the broad membership of the commission.

Browne believed that the use of the word 'slovenly', which perhaps caused the greatest offence, was based mainly on the opinion that the report lacked clarity. He was quick to observe

> It is a strange irony that at the very moment Mr Lemass was making this charge in the Senate the Dáil was engaged in debating the Military Pensions (Amendment) Bill – a measure necessitated by the fact that the courts found that even the Government and Parliament, with all their official draftsmen, could not say exactly what they meant in the original act. How often has this happened in other acts, not to speak of orders.[13]

He repudiated Lemass's objection to paragraph 359 of the report by asking a series of rhetorical questions

> Does the Minister really deny that regulations could be more wisely drafted? . . . Does he deny that there could be better public co-operation?

> Does he claim that bureaucrats are never inept? Does he think that people in this age of licences and controls are never afraid that their rivals in business get some advantage?[14]

He declared his respect for the office of the minister and for the minister's abilities but he protested strongly against the injustice and insults which he felt the former members of the commission had been subjected to. Finally, he recognised that it was the prerogative of the government to accept or reject the report but he made it clear that if the government decided on the latter option then it was in danger of rejecting Catholic social teaching because the report was based on principles enunciated by Pope Pius XI.[15]

Coyne was very satisfied when Browne's speech was published on 8 March and promptly congratulated the bishop on his performance.[16] Coyne's sense of triumph was intensified by his perception that Lemass had committed a serious tactical blunder by being so offensive in his remarks. Whatever the merit of the minister's case there was no justification for his insulting remarks. As a result, public sympathy had, apparently, shifted in support of the commission on the issue.[17]

The minister's intemperate outburst may have caused some concern amongst his cabinet colleagues. Dr Maurice Moynihan (then secretary to the Department of the Taoiseach) informed the author that it induced an 'atmosphere of disapproval' in official circles.[18] However, de Valera did not make any conciliatory statements in reference to Lemass's remarks. On 14 March 1945 he was asked in the Dáil if the government intended to implement the commission's recommendations. He replied

> it is necessary to bear in mind what the Most Reverend Chairman has pointed out clearly in his Foreword, namely, that vocational organisations should develop in accordance with the laws of natural organic growth, that not all the suggestions in the Report are immediately operable and that some must await the development of others as their foundation.[19]

This was, effectively, a subtle repudiation of the commission's findings.[20]

Seán T. O'Kelly, whose Department of Finance had not rendered a kind verdict on the report, adopted a conciliatory approach. He told the Senate on 20 March that Lemass had reacted impulsively in the course of a heated debate and would not have used the same words if he had more time to calmly express his opinions. However, O'Kelly cautiously added that he had not consulted Lemass on this matter. He acknowledged that the commission had given excellent public service and he conceded to opposition criticism that people who volunteer to give public service by serving on government commissions should not be subjected to abuse.[21] On the same occasion, O'Kelly took the opportunity to denigrate the work of another Catholic bishop. In reference to the Dignan plan he sarcastically observed that the suggestions made by the Bishop of Clonfert

> would have been much more helpful if the financial aspects of these had been considered at the same time. The foundation of social security is finance. All the lovely ideas in the world are of no use unless you are able to implement them financially.[22]

The confrontation between the vocationalists and the government was at its most intense in March 1945. Seán MacEntee engaged in a bitter public debate with Bishop John Dignan while Lemass and Browne publicised their grievances.[23] Lemass and MacEntee were not overawed by the invocation of the papal encyclicals to bolster vocationalist contentions and they maintained a hard-line attitude towards the vocationalist lobby. In the editorial of *The Irish Times* (10 March 1945) it was argued that the perception of southern Ireland as a state ruled by the Catholic bishops was now difficult to sustain. The notion, expressed particularly in Northern Ireland, of Éire as a 'priest-ridden community', could be refuted with greater confidence because two government ministers were clearly rejecting proposals advocated by two Catholic bishops.[24]

Lemass's views were published again on 23 March. He claimed that he had compiled a list of 27 errors. These errors did not account for the total number in the report as Browne had claimed.[25] The 27 mistakes were in the chapters of the report which dealt only with the policy and work of the Department of Industry and Commerce. Lemass's main criticism was not with errors of statistical detail which could be attributed to the limited staff resources of the commission. Instead he took issue with the incorrect conclusions which were based on errors that could have been avoided if the commission took the time to check the details. Furthermore, he felt that 'the facts ascertained in the course of the commission's enquiries were interpreted and presented as if to justify preconceived conclusions'.[26] He defended his objection to paragraph 359 of the report but he did not clearly explain his reasons. In reply to Browne he declared

> It is not correct, as His Lordship is reported to have said, that I objected to any reference by the Commission to the dangers of Government intervention in any form and to the effects of bureaucracy in particular. I object most strongly to insinuations in paragraph 359 which the Commission made no attempt to substantiate and the implications of which, I feel sure, cannot have been fully appreciated by many of the signatories of the Report.[27]

Lemass believed that the report, as a public document, was not of much value and only slightly modified his stance on the word 'slovenly' when he declared

> Having re-read my comments, I have no desire to modify them, except in one particular. In the course of them I used the word 'slovenly' which I regret, not because I regard it as fundamentally inaccurate, but because it has connotations other than I had in mind. I used the word as synonymous with 'lacking precision and thoroughness', a characteristic which the Report displays in exceptional degree, and the appropriateness of the description can be amply demonstrated.[28]

This was regarded as an 'ungracious withdrawal' by the Bishop of Galway.[29] Lemass did not satisfactorily demonstrate to the public that the report lacked precision and thoroughness. His letter to Browne listed 27 alleged errors and these had been challenged one by one by the bishop who dismissed them as false. Browne stated that the commission had been thorough in its investigation. The report was only a summary of the evidence taken by the commission. The volume of evidence was in excess of 3,400 folio pages and the documents submitted amounted to no less than 2,000 pages.[30]

According to the historian, J.H. Whyte, the bishop was the clear winner of the debate.[31] This judgement seems to be fair and may be partly attributable to the fact that Lemass, instead of concentrating attention on the fundamental weakness of the report, had allowed himself to become trapped in an argument which focused too much attention on points of detail. His unrestrained criticism of the commission probably alienated support for his grievance and anything less than an overwhelming weight of logic and evidence in his favour to counteract this could only have led to defeat in the bitter controversy which followed. Another major advantage enjoyed by Browne was the good advice he received from Coyne. As well as advising Browne on tactics Coyne had also supplied the bishop with detailed information relating to the mistakes which had been alleged by Lemass.[32]

Coyne was jubilant after Browne's 'wielding of the sledge'. His own workload had increased and left him insufficient time to enter the public arena in defence of the report. But elation gave way to apprehension as he reflected on the aftermath of victory – a victory portentous of renewed hostility from official circles. Coyne had learnt from a 'a very high officer' in the civil service that after Browne's last reply to Lemass there had been a frantic effort to 'retrieve the situation'. It was feared that Lemass would, with the backing of the civil service, persuade the government to issue a White Paper discrediting the report of the commission. It was anticipated that this document would allege and specify: errors of fact; prejudiced conclusions or unfair criticisms of government policy or administrative procedures; impracticable recommendations. Coyne had learned from a 'very good authority' that an inter-departmental committee had reported 'very unfavourably' on the commission's findings.[33] However, Coyne's fears did not materialise. The government would not shower fire and brimstone on the report – it was much safer to quietly banish it to the outer darkness.

A CHALLENGE TO THE GOVERNMENT

The rejection of vocationalist proposals by Seán Lemass signified the government's intention to shelve the *Commission on Vocational Organisation Report*. Bishop Michael Browne was not comforted by Fine Gael's apparent support for the implementation of the commission's proposals. When he was defending the report against the disparaging statements of Lemass he received disturbing news which indicated that both Fianna Fáil and Fine Gael were endeavouring to politicise the commission's findings for party political purposes. On 14 March 1945 he was informed by Fr John Hayes of Muintir na Tíre that, after the publication of his riposte to Lemass on 8 March, a Fianna Fáil senator, William Quirke, had approached Senator P.J. O'Reilly of Clonmel and had urged him to put forward a motion in the Senate 'that the findings of the Vocational Commission should be implemented'. O'Reilly then spoke to Hayes on the matter. Hayes did not have a high opinion of Quirke and told Browne

> I know Quirke, he is just a party hack and a politician. O'Reilly is an independent member, an innocent man. Why has Quirke asked him to do this? Why would not Quirke do it himself as an FF member . . . I suspect Quirke. I suspect FF.[34]

Hayes advised O'Reilly to do nothing until the matter was given further consideration – but there was not much to consider. Evidently, O'Reilly, much enlightened by Hayes, thought it better not to facilitate Fianna Fáil's strategy at his expense.

At this juncture Browne realised that politicians of the two main political parties were not seriously committed to the implementation of the commission's recommendations. On 16 March he wrote to Alfred O'Rahilly, stating that

> there is one thing that could well be stressed and it is that the Report is entirely non-political. At the moment it is being used by the political

> opponents of the Government and I think it was really that which provoked Mr Lemass's outburst. I have reason to believe that some Government supporters are trying to force the other side to identify themselves with the Report officially so as to give more reason for its rejection by the Government. Fr Hayes sent me some evidence of this.[35]

He was determined to avoid becoming embroiled in any political controversy because it had been deemed essential by the commission that politics should be kept out of vocationalism and vocationalism out of politics.

Browne was, apparently, well informed about the activities of politicians on both sides of the political divide. On 23 March 1945 the leader of Fine Gael, Richard Mulcahy, introduced a motion in the Dáil for the establishment of a council of education in conformity with the guidelines laid down in paragraph 540 of the report.[36] This paragraph recommended 'the establishment of a Council of Education as a permanent institution to act as the accredited advisory body to the Minister for Education'. It was to be 'a vocational non-political body without any executive or administrative powers'. Mulcahy also called for the setting up of an Oireachtas committee under the chairmanship of the Minister for Education to examine the best method of setting up the council. He quoted from paragraph 513 of the report which stressed that no changes in the political system were recommended or implied. In his opinion, therefore, the recommendations of the commission did not detract in any way from the authority of the state.[37]

Mulcahy's Dáil motion was the first test case of the government's determination not to implement any of the major recommendations contained in the report of the Commission on Vocational Organisation. It unwittingly served Fianna Fáil's strategy of rejecting the vocationalist proposals with greater effectiveness than Lemass's verbal barrage. On 23 March and 18 April, the Minister for Education, Thomas Derrig, defended the centralisation of authority in government departments and revealed a hypersensitivity towards upholding the sovereignty of parliament. The old arguments against the establishment of a council of education were resurrected. The government was entrusted with the responsibility for administration and with the formulation of policy therefore responsibility could not be delegated to a select committee. Derrig argued that the Dáil had delegated to him, as Minister for Education, responsibility for education. In turn he was responsible to the Dáil and in the course of the annual estimates for the department, or in dealing with motions concerned with his work, there were sufficient opportunities for public debate and public criticism. Therefore the national representatives and the people were kept informed about ongoing developments and the reasons for them.[38]

Derrig feared that conflict might arise between himself and the council because of an overlap of functions. The minister regarded the duties of the council as an encroachment on his right to decide educational policy. Although paragraph 540 of the report specified that the council was to be an advisory body the minister was convinced that it would not confine itself to mere enquiry.[39] Even if the minister and his council were in full agreement there was still the possibility of conflict between the Minister for Education and the government, where issues of large expenditure (such as salary scales for teachers) were concerned.[40] The composition of the council also presented problems. Derrig believed that the commission's proposal would make for a very large and unwieldy body.[41]

When Éamon de Valera contributed to the debate on 18 April he reiterated many of the points made by the minister. He was convinced that even if the government took the initiative to implement Mulcahy's motion there might still be a major obstacle to its formation. He doubted that the representatives of the various organisations involved in education would be willing to come together to discuss different aspects of educational policy with the minister.[42] Consultation with separate associations would be more conducive to forthright criticism and frank advice. Even if the various organisations did co-operate such a broad-based council would be unsuitable for discussing narrow issues. The system of consultation between the department and the various professional bodies was to everyone's satisfaction. What government ministers needed, it seemed, was specialist advice – not counsel of a general nature.

Thomas Derrig not only disagreed with the proposal to establish a vocational council of education, he also argued against the acceptance of an important idea underlying the proposal. The commission harboured the fear that 'the State may be urged to go beyond its legitimate sphere and to usurp the sacred rights of parents . . . State control of education had proved to be the most effective means of introducing totalitarian regimentation'.[43] The most effective precaution against this threat was the establishment of a council of education that would elicit 'the ready co-operation of all concerned in education to make fully effective the national educational policy as determined by the Government and the Oireachtas'.[44] There was some difficulty in reconciling the above two statements where the council of education would simultaneously limit the power of the state and assist it in implementing its policies.

The notion that the Irish state might 'usurp the sacred rights of parents' was preposterous – especially when cognisance is taken of the fact that southern Ireland was a democracy where the Roman Catholic Church exerted a dominant influence. Successive ministers for education had expressed agreement with the extent of church control over education. In fact the Roman Catholic Church had won greater control over education in Ireland than in any other country. A striking feature of educational policy in Ireland since independence was the reluctance of the state to interfere in any way with church control.[45] Derrig was quick to point out in the Dáil that education was regulated on a denominational basis.[46] He claimed that, in view of events in other countries, a national educational council could not by itself prevent the state from obtaining a stranglehold over the educational system. The attitude of his department was that the extensive control exercised by the church would provide a more effective protection against the danger envisaged by the commission. Furthermore, there were safeguards in the constitution. If the Oireachtas passed legislation which was unconstitutional then this could be remedied by legal action. Another restriction on his control over the educational system was the need to obtain the agreement of the Minister for Finance to make new regulations or change existing structures where funding was concerned. He may have felt that his freedom of action was already so limited that any erosion of his authority – even if it was minimal – would be intolerable.

Derrig assured the Dáil that the government had not closed its mind to the possibility of establishing a council of education but the whole question of vocational organisation had to be examined before a council of education could be properly discussed.[47] For example, the establishment of the national vocational assembly would have to precede the formation of a council of education if paragraph 540 of the report was to be strictly adhered to. De Valera also argued that vocationalism had to be studied on a broad basis. He stressed that the government was not against vocational organisation in principle. Vocational organisation presented 'a very broad question' and the government would have to examine it 'from every particular angle'.[48] In effect, this meant that investigations would continue indefinitely and the government could procrastinate with impunity.

During the debate on the proposed council of education on 18 April 1945 de Valera referred to an aspect of the commission's work which was of particular interest to him. It was concerned with the commission's endeavour to create a scheme of rural organisation. He was not satisfied with the commission's scheme for organising the rural community and he told the Dáil

> when the Commission was being set up, I did say that, if it failed in one thing, it would have failed practically completely, that is, if it failed in getting a satisfactory organisation of the rural community. One of the principal difficulties we have in regard to agriculture is that it cannot organise itself to protect its own interests . . . I am very doubtful if the solution that has been suggested is adequate to the task.[49]

De Valera's message was clear – the commission had 'failed practically completely' in its task. Irish society was predominantly rural and was so structured that it was extremely difficult to vocationalise it. The implication was that the government would not attempt to implement the commission's main recommendations. This, however, conflicted with other statements that de Valera made on the same occasion. He indicated that the government was still seriously considering the commission's recommendations. He claimed that no final decision had been reached because the state departments had not submitted all their observations to the government.[50] His ambivalence contrasted sharply with Lemass's outspoken approach.

De Valera rejected Mulcahy's Dáil motion on the basis that it was contrary to the tenets of parliamentary democracy.[51] Mulcahy's motion had called for the setting up of an Oireachtas committee, under the chairmanship of the Minister for Education, to examine the proposal for the establishment of a council of education. Mulcahy specified that the committee, under the chairmanship of the Minister for Education, would be representative of parliament because Fianna Fáil would have its full majority on it.[52] De Valera had argued that the acceptance of this proposal was equivalent to the government abandoning its constitutional duty to govern. He, rather conveniently, had chosen to interpret the issue as a thinly disguised motion of no confidence in the government.[53] On 26 April 1945 the motion was put to a vote in the Dáil and the government easily defeated it with 51 against and only 26 in favour.[54] The Fianna Fáil leadership had reacted negatively towards the report of the Commission on Vocational Organisation, but de Valera seemed anxious to salvage some practical advantage from the commission's arduous labours.

DE VALERA'S CAUTIOUS STRATEGY

On 17 April 1945, in the aftermath of the debate between Lemass and Browne, the government decided that the large volume of information, which had been accumulated by the commission, should be published.[55] De Valera and his colleagues had strongly indicated that the *Commission on Vocational Organisation Report* would not be acted upon but they may have been concerned that the shelving of the report would lead to unfavourable publicity. Apparently, the data obtained by the commission was valuable for purposes of economic planning and its publication would demonstrate to the public that the work of the commission had not been a complete waste of taxpayers' money.

Browne had plenty of time to clarify his thoughts about how he might respond to the government's intentions, having heard by unofficial means what was afoot. His informant (probably Fr E.J. Coyne) stated that an indirect communication from Seán T. O'Kelly indicated that the government intended to publish either an inter-departmental report on the commission's findings or the evidence of the commission. An official in the Department of Agriculture confirmed that it was to be the evidence.[56] Although Browne and Coyne resolved to make matters difficult for de Valera they both felt that it would be better not to convey a very negative attitude. Coyne believed that the evidence was so bulky and so costly to publish that the price would be far too high for the majority of those who would be interested. Consequently, he anticipated, sales might not even reach the paltry figure of half a dozen. The commission might then be blamed for the unmitigated waste of public money, time, and resources involved. However, Coyne did not want to give de Valera the impression that the former members of the commission were opposed to either the publication of the evidence or to some other means of making it accessible to the public.[57]

De Valera decided to consult Browne as a matter of courtesy because the bishop had served as chairman of the commission. On 2 May he wrote to Browne explaining the government's intentions. He referred to the first footnote on page 98 of the report which stated that copies of the evidence obtained by the commission had been deposited in the National Library. He pointed out that no such deposit had taken place. The evidence in its existing form was deemed to be unsuitable for deposit and two reasons were advanced to justify this. Firstly, the evidence contained many manuscript alterations. There would be no means of preventing those who consulted it from making further additions or alterations and these would not be distinguishable from those already made by the commission. Secondly, there was no comprehensive index except an official one which was retained exclusively for official use. Therefore, the evidence could not be conveniently consulted. The government's answer to the problem was to publish the evidence which was to include an index. All the evidence, both oral and documentary, was to be published except documents which were already available to the public such as the articles of association of various companies. The report had to be reprinted and de Valera proposed that a prefatory note, opposite the Table of Contents, should be inserted as follows: 'Copies of the evidence submitted to the Commission are at present (May 1945) being prepared for printing and will be published in due course'. This insertion then required the replacement of footnote 1 on page 98 with a statement directing the reader to the prefatory note.[58]

Once more Coyne was discreetly active. On 8 May he wrote to Browne and urged him to adopt a tough stance. Browne needed little prompting in this direction. De Valera's request for Browne's approval elicited a frosty response from the bishop of Galway who was still upset over Lemass's remarks. His inclination from the onset was to 'lay down the law'.[59] Coyne's advice was to serve as the basis of Browne's justification in refusing to oblige de Valera.[60] On 12 May, Browne replied to de Valera, arguing at length why he was unable to facilitate the government's intentions. However, the genuine reason for his refusal to co-operate became clearly evident when he stated

> You mention in your letter that it may interest me to know that the Report has to be reprinted. It was more of interest to me, and of regret, to read your letter and to note that it contained not the slightest reference to the insulting attack made on the Report and on the motives of the members of the Commission by one of your Ministers. It has been a matter of very great pain to me in more senses than one that a Minister of State should have treated the Commission in such a manner and should have attempted, apparently quite deliberately, to denigrate the Report – an attempt made, as we now know, from insufficient knowledge as to what his own Department had told us.[61]

On 19 May, Browne wrote again to de Valera, reiterating his objections to the government's intentions. He refused to approve of any changes to the report. Browne anticipated that if he did agree to de Valera's proposal then he might be open to criticism and protestations from his former colleagues. If the government wished to secure the approval of the commission on the issue then the only option open to it was to request the former members to convene again to consider the government's proposals. Of course, as Browne pointed out, the government had the power and resources to make whatever changes it liked.[62] But unilateral action was not a realistic option. If the government did not secure the agreement of the commission it would be vulnerable to adverse publicity. Neither would de Valera attempt to convene the commission in response to Browne's suggestion. The public statements of James Ryan had not pleased the vocationalists; Lemass's speech in the Senate and his subsequent press statements had outraged them. Goodwill had been eroded and the government's request would probably have been turned down by an overwhelming majority of those individuals whose work had been described as 'slovenly'. The resurrection of the commission would only have served to stimulate more public controversy, giving the vocationalists valuable publicity in the process.

On 28 May 1945, de Valera wrote to Browne, declaring himself very surprised at the bishop's response. He had not foreseen any difficulties. He had not proposed any changes to the substance or wording of the report itself. He informed Browne that he was enquiring into a number of points raised. In due course he intended to reply in full to the objections which had been put forward.[63] In the meantime Browne was not to remain silent about the way the commission's work had been treated. He was in poor health in early June and wrote to Hayes, declaring '. . . the kingdom of Heaven suffereth violence and I shall yield to your invitation to speak in Waterford on Sunday 5th. August.'[64] Several angry ex-commissioners attended the Muintir na Tíre Rural Week, including Browne, Harvey, Coyne, Bennett, and of course Hayes. Browne took the opportunity to 'clarify his position', while Coyne made a 'spirited defence' of the report. Hayes, however, declined to make any critical statements.[65]

The government was in no mood to appease the vocationalists. When Bishop John Dignan's term as chairman of the National Health Insurance Society came to an end in August 1945 it was not renewed. Seán MacEntee, despite his condemnation of bureaucratic centralism, replaced the bishop with a civil servant.[66] Furthermore, it seems that *The Irish Press* (which had been founded by de Valera) became the instrument of the government's public criticism of the report. On 11 August, Frank Pakenham's scathing analysis was published in the national newspaper. The article, entitled 'An examination of Commission Report' repeated, almost verbatim in some paragraphs, criticisms from civil servants, mainly those in the Department of Finance.[67] Five days later Fr E.J. Coyne responded with an article in *The Irish Catholic*, repudiating some of the criticisms directed against the report.[68] *The*

Irish Press was quick to retaliate with an article by an anonymous author on 18 August. Browne was under no illusions about de Valera's attitude. In correspondence with Hayes he expressed the view that 'It was evident that *The Irish Press* on instructions from above was very hostile. The article by an anonymous writer was proof of how sore they felt.'[69] Browne was anxious to have the last word but he was disappointed when Coyne did not again rise to the challenge.

Meanwhile, the Department of the Taoiseach gave further consideration to the vocationalist scheme. The commission had undertaken an examination of the professions and subsequently issued its findings in parts three and four of the report.[70] The Department of the Taoiseach reserved for itself the task of examining the commission's scheme of vocational organistion for the nineteen professional groups which were identified.[71] The department observed that the proposal to establish a permanent professional commission[72] was in line with the broader recommendations of the commission which, if implemented, would thoroughly vocationalise Irish society and the economy. Taking cognisance of this the department adopted a policy which was extremely cautious. The above recommendation would not be implemented because: 'if adopted, it would have the effect of applying to the professions the principles of a fully developed vocational organisation.' What was wrong with this? The answer was not ambiguous. It was believed that

> To select from the many recommendations in the Report and to accept now such a fundamental recommendation (apart altogether from any consideration of its merits in relation to the community or to the professions) would, undoubtedly, create an important precedent which might tend to give rise later on to very embarrassing difficulties when the other fundamental recommendations of the Commission come up for consideration. There is also a risk that the adoption now of this particular recommendation might create in the minds of the public an impression that the Government were favourably disposed towards the main principles of the Report and that certain sections of the community might avail of the opportunity arising out of the acceptance of one such principle to start a campaign in favour of the adoption of the Report as a whole.[73]

Almost as an afterthought departmental officials outlined the difficulties and disadvantages inherent in adopting the commission's recommendation. It was unclear whether or not the professions as a whole were sufficiently well organised to justify the setting up of a professional commission. Ten of the nineteen professions examined by the commission were not organised on a legal statutory basis and these included engineers, accountants and architects. Apparently, there were obstacles to granting these professions statutory status. Some problems arose due to internal difficulties. Accountants, for example, were represented by a number of different organisations. External problems were caused by conflict of interests between associated professions such as engineers and architects.

The fourth paragraph of the foreword in the report, emphasising the importance of organic development, was also invoked to reject the recommendation for a professional commission. Another reason for declining to establish a professional commission was that, apparently, the professions would not welcome it. Furthermore, the professional commission could not be set up until the national agricultural conference, the national industrial conference and the council of education had been established.[74]

The Department of the Taoiseach gave serious consideration to the extension of statutory registration to professions organised on a voluntary basis and, on 14 August, it sent its observations to the other departments of state.[75] From the memorandum it was clear that the proposal to establish a professional commission had been ruled out. The department referred to paragraph 517 of the report which stated that on several occasions the legislature had accepted the principle that registration of a profession is socially sound and beneficial provided certain conditions are met. Two preconditions were specified. Professions had to be well organised and of sufficiently numerous membership to justify statutory registration. The government would then be prepared to sponsor the necessary legislation if further conditions were met. These were

- The government had to be satisfied that the enactment of such a scheme was in the public interest. The rights of the community had to be adequately protected.
- The overwhelming majority of the membership of the profession had to support the scheme.
- It was essential that such a scheme did not injure the interests of allied or associated professions.

The taoiseach's department considered that the government might publicise its readiness to consider an extension of the principle of statutory registration, subject to the above conditions.[76]

At a government meeting on 14 December 1945 it was decided that no public announcement would be made indicating the government's

ABOVE: Pope Leo XIII (1878–1903). His encyclical, *Rerum Novarum* (1891) became the foundation document of modern Catholic social teaching. Photograph from *Life of Leo XIII* by Bernard O'Reilly (Sampson Low, Marston, Searle & Rivington; London, 1887).

TOP RIGHT: Pope Pius XI (1922–1939). The encyclical *Quadragesimo Anno*, issued by him in 1931, celebrated the fortieth anniversary of *Rerum Novarum* and stimulated much interest in social Catholicism, especially in Ireland. Photograph from *Pope Pius XI and World Peace: An Authentic Biography* by Lord Clonmore (The Catholic Book Club, London, March 1938).

RIGHT: Michael Collins, Chairman of the committee that drafted the constitution of the Irish Free State (1922). Photograph R28,905, courtesy of the National Library of Ireland.

The Minister for Industry and Commerce, Seán Lemass (left), with the Minister for Agriculture, James Ryan (right) at an industrial fair, 14 April 1932. Photograph courtesy of *The Examiner* (formerly *The Cork Examiner*).

ABOVE: The Fianna Fáil Cabinet, 1933. *Left to right, seated*: Joseph Connolly, Seán T. O'Kelly, Éamon de Valera, PJ Ruttledge, Seán Lemass. *Standing*: Conor Maguire, Gerald Boland, Thomas Derrig, Frank Aiken, Seán MacEntee, Dr. James Ryan and M. Moynihan. Maguire (Attorney-General) and Moynihan were not members of the Executive Council.

LEFT: General Eoin O'Duffy, shown here in the Spanish uniform of the Irish brigade, circa 1936. In 1936 he organised the Irish Brigade to fight for the armies of General Franco in the Spanish Civil War. Photograph by kind permission of Monaghan County Museum.

John Charles McQuaid (*left*) with Éamon de Valera (*right*), date unknown. Photograph courtesy of Dublin Diocesan Archives, Drumcondra, Dublin.

The Commission on Vocational Organisation, meeting at the Shelbourne Hotel, Dublin, 18 April 1940. *Front row*: Henry P. Boland, Fr. Edward J. Coyne S.J., Lucy Franks, Bishop Michael Browne of Galway (chairman), Louie Bennett, Rev. Dr. J.A.H. Irwin and Richard Wilson. *Middle Row*: C.P. McCarthy, Patrick Gallagher, Rev. John M. Hayes, M. MacGeehin, Francis A. Lowe, Senator Prof. Michael Tierney, Algernon A. Odlum. *Back Row*: Senator Seán Campbell, Dr. Henry Kennedy, Prof. Alfred O'Rahilly, James J. Walsh, Luke J. Duffy, P.A. O'Toole (Secretary). Photograph courtesy of John Carroll, Lafayette Photography.

Left to right: Alfred O'Rahilly, Edward J. Coyne, and Michael Tierney; circa 1941. Photograph courtesy of The Diocesan Office, The Cathedral, Galway.

Handing over of the Office of Arms (renamed The Genealogical Office), 4 April 1943. *Left to right*: Thomas Ulick Sadlier, Seán T. O'Kelly (Tánaiste), Éamon de Valera (Taoiseach), Edward McLysaght, Richard J. Hayes, and Thomas Derrig (Minister for Education). Photograph R18,482, courtesy of the National Library of Ireland.

The Commission on Vocational Organisation presenting its report to the Taoiseach at his office in Iveagh House, Dublin; 1 August 1944. *At front*: Éamon de Valera (*left*) receiving the report from Bishop Michael Browne (*right*). *At back*: Senator Seán P. Campbell, Dr. Henry Kennedy, Rev. John M. Hayes, Louie Bennett, Rev. Dr. J.A.H. Irwin, G.H.C. Crampton, Prof. Michael Tierney, Francis A. Lowe, Lucy Franks, Richard Wilson, and P.A. O'Toole (Secretary). Photograph by permission of Irish Press Plc.

Dr. John Dignan, Bishop of Clonfert from 1924 to 1953 and chairman of the National Health Insurance Society 1936–1945. The *Outlines of a Scheme of National Health Insurance* which he announced to the press in October 1944 was based on vocationalism and was harshly rejected by Seán MacEntee, Minister for Local Government and Public Health. Photograph courtesy of Ms. Terry Dignan.

Canon John M. Hayes, founder of Muintir na Tíre. Photograph courtesy of Muintir na Tíre.

General Mulcahy in Cork at a Fine Gael meeting, 3 February 1948. Photograph courtesy of *The Examiner*.

The Taoiseach, John A. Costello at an Inter-Party meeting in Fermoy, 30 April 1949. Costello is in the front row, second from the right. Photograph courtesy of *The Examiner*.

The Taoiseach, John A. Costello shortly before his departure for Canada, 22 August 1948. Costello is on the right with the cigarette. Photograph courtesy of *The Examiner*.

The Fianna Fáil Cabinet, 1951. *Front row, left to right*, Maurice Moynihan, Frank Aiken, Éamon de Valera (Taoiseach), President Seán T. O'Kelly, Seán Lemass, Seán MacEntee, James Ryan, Thomas Derrig. *Second row, left to right*, Patrick Smith, Thomas Walsh, Sean Moylan, Gerald Boland, Oscar Traynor, Erskine Childers. *Back row,* Colonel O'Sullivan, Cathal Daly, Eamonn Dunphy. Moynihan, O'Kelly, O'Sullivan, Daly and Dunphy were not members of the Cabinet.

willingness to sponsor legislation designed to give effect to schemes of statutory registration. Instead, only 'sympathetic consideration would be given to any scheme of statutory registration that might be submitted by representatives of a particular profession' subject to the conditions specified on 14 August.[77] In reality 'sympathetic consideration' was no more than a pious platitude. The government did not wish to extend statutory registration to those professions which were organised on a voluntary basis because this was likely to lead to demands for the establishment of a professional commission with all its accompanying risks. Rejecting all major recommendations outlined in the report had been, and was to be, a persistent feature of government policy.

In the meantime de Valera once again turned his attention to the evidence of the commission. On 26 September 1945, the government discussed, informally, whether or not the evidence should be published. No firm decision was reached and de Valera decided to give further consideration to the matter.[78] However, he was by now doubtful about the advantages of printing and publishing the information.[79] He had satisfied himself that the objections raised by Browne were not sustainable[80] but he did not issue a directive to publish the evidence. The data was printed and, in March 1946, it was decided to make it available to the public through the National Library of Ireland.[81]

The evidence of the commission may have been more valuable than its report, containing as it did much valuable information about the socio-economic aspects of Irish life. The problem with the report was that it manifested a prejudiced interpretation and analysis of the facts. Evidently, de Valera and his colleagues in government recognised the value of the evidence – why else would they have wished to publish it? However, in treating the commission so shabbily they provoked a response which made publication extremely unlikely. Thus, the commission's work was a waste of time, effort and taxpayers' money.

De Valera and his government colleagues did not feel inclined to make any placatory gestures towards the vocationalists. All but the most naive of vocationalists would have been aware of Fianna Fáil's attitude towards the report by November 1945. James Ryan, however, seemed determined to deflate the last remnants of vocationalist aspirations. When, as Minister for Agriculture, he presided at the opening of the Catholic Social Week on 30 October 1944 the overall thrust of his speech had been defensive and conciliatory. Thirteen months later, this time addressing the Fianna Fáil faithful in the Mansion House, Dublin, he was far more dismissive of the commission's recommendations. In his speech of 20 November 1945, (this was one of a number of lectures which had been organised by the National Executive of Fianna Fáil) Ryan declared

> I am not objecting to the merits of the Commission's scheme of organisation but I think it is impracticable and could only, if at all, be achieved by gigantic efforts. The position aimed at is not so substantially different from the *status quo* as to warrant the vast amount of organisation and work that will be required.[82]

He assured his audience that the dangers to society, which were present in the 1930s, were now no more. The capitalists could no longer exploit the community at will. Unbridled capitalism was in sharp decline and squalid living conditions were being eliminated. His remarks implied that *Quadragesimo Anno* and vocationalism were obsolete.

Ryan drew attention to the growing trend of nationalisation. Many states had embarked on a policy of state ownership of utility services and essential industries. Ireland was no exception where, for example, there was state ownership of electricity, transport, and of the sugar industry. According to the minister the capitalists had less room for economic activity and the need for vocational organisation was diminishing. State ownership did not preclude vocational organisation. Workers would still have their trade unions and employers their associations. The amount of vocational organisation that did exist could continue to do so and was desirable when it served a purpose. But the era of Pius XI was over and, in the new post-war world, a new order was emerging. Ryan proclaimed: 'The State-appointed Manager or the Managerial System is coming – the popular demand will enforce it. As services and industries come under this system the necessity for, and the urge towards Vocationalism will become less.'[83]

There was now little doubt about the government's rejection of the commission's proposals, especially when cognisance was taken of the public statements of Seán Lemass and James Ryan.[84] The official consensus was that vocationalism was obsolete. The aspirations of the vocationalists had been subjected to severe criticism, scepticism and ridicule by politicians, civil servants and journalists. Corporatist proposals had been rejected but the vocationalists had not abandoned their aspirations. They were determined to win public support for the recommendations put forward in the *Commission on Vocational Organisation Report*.

CHAPTER EIGHT

The Decline of the Vocationalist Movement

A FUTILE CAMPAIGN, 1945–1947

The publication of the report of the Commission on Vocational Organisation in August 1944 gave new life to the vocationalist movement and made it difficult for the government to dispense quietly with its recommendations. Several weeks after the publication of the lengthy document the Catholic Young Men's Society organised a series of lectures which took place in the Mansion House, Dublin, from 30 October to 3 November.[1] The main topic of interest was the *Commission on Vocational Organisation Report*. The Minister for Agriculture, James Ryan, had attended and he expressed grave doubts about the feasibility of the commission's scheme.[2] However, his views did not dispel the enthusiasm of those in the central executive of the Catholic Young Men's Society. After the Catholic social week had ended, they established a sub-committee to ascertain the best means of pressing for the implementation of the report. The sub-committee organised a meeting of representatives of several Catholic organisations at the C.Y.M.S. hall in North Frederick St., Dublin, on 12 February 1945. The Professor of Sociology at Maynooth, Dr Peter McKevitt, adressed the meeting and afterwards the following motion was unanimously adopted:

> That this meeting, representing Catholic social organisations in Dublin, believing in the urgent necessity for a new social order based on the teachings of the Papal Encyclicals, calls on the people of Ireland to take the necessary action to bring into operation the recommendations contained in the Report of the Commission on Vocational Organisation.[3]

A provisional committee was elected and on 16 March 1945 it held its first formal meeting. An organisation was to be formed to publicise the report and to press for its implementation but disagreement arose about how the organisation was to be structured. The editor of *The Standard*, Peadar O'Curry, was in agreement with the aims of the provisional committee but not with the way the new organisation was to be formed. He had been asked to serve on the provisional committee because of his position as editor of the weekly newspaper. The committee decided 'that membership of the proposed Vocational Organisation Conference be open to every member of a Catholic organisation'.[4] O'Curry objected to this policy on the basis that it excluded all non-Catholics and Catholics who were not members of Catholic social action organisations. He was not the only dissatisfied member. The issue was debated and it was put to a vote. Six members of the committee voted in favour of permitting all citizens to join but eight members voted to postpone such a decision to an unspecified future date.

O'Curry believed that the committee's decision was symptomatic of an attitude that placed too much reliance on the clergy for vocationalist initiatives. He feared that if there was widespread anticipation of 'intervention' by the clergy this might have a negative effect. Already, it seemed, there were suspicions in trade union and labour circles that a 'clerical movement' was conspiring to 'impose vocationalism'.[5] O'Curry believed that the laity should take the initiative to promote the vocationalist cause but he was unsure of what course of action to take in order to convince his colleagues to reverse what had been decided. Bishop Michael Browne's advice was most emphatic. It was a basic principle of democracy that the will of the majority should be accepted. Furthermore, it would not be wise to divide the committee, especially when the issue of broader participation had been left open to a later date. Browne believed that while some non-Catholics and unorganised Catholics approved of vocational organisation the main impetus would come from organised Catholics.[6]

On 25 May, after eight meetings, the provisional committee submitted policy documents to a general meeting of Catholic societies, explaining its objectives and the strategy to be pursued. The delegates present approved of the documents submitted and on 1 June 1945 the executive committee of the Catholic Societies' Vocational Organisation Conference (C.S.V.O.C.) held its first meeting.[7] The Aims and Programme of the C.S.V.O.C. included the following clauses

- That the ultimate object of the C.S.V.O.C. is to secure the establishment of a social structure in this country based on the principles of vocational organisation, with particular regard to the recommendations of the Report of the Vocational Organisation Commission.

- That the immediate object of the C.S.V.O.C. is, primarily, to enthuse the members of the Catholic Societies in favour of vocational organisation on the general lines of the Commission's Report and also, to influence in that direction by propaganda as many other members of the community as possible.[8]

Through its constituent organisations (see Appendix 3) the C.S.V.O.C. had the support of thousands of Catholics in the archdiocese of Dublin although most of this was not active support.

On 31 May, the editor of *The Irish Catholic*, John J.M. Ryan, in correspondence with the future archbishop of Cashel, Dr Thomas Morris, had explained what may have been the opinion of the majority of those who served on the C.S.V.O.C. executive committee. It was observed that there had been a very weak public response to the report and the view was expressed that the government would only move to implement the report if public opinion clearly supported this. Therefore, the primary objective of the C.S.V.O.C was to rally sufficient public support for the commission's recommendations. The first task was to motivate the members of the constituent organisations. It was anticipated that once substantial results were forthcoming the organisation would then become more broadly based, extending its activities beyond Dublin.[9]

The strategy of the C.S.V.O.C. was fundamentally in error. The government was not cautious in waiting for public support for vocationalist reforms; it was firmly against the implementation of the commission's proposals. The government's disapproval of the vocationalist scheme had been strongly indicated by the public statements of James Ryan and Seán Lemass. Richard Mulcahy's Dáil proposal of 23 March 1945 had been the first test of Fianna Fáil's determination to reject the commission's proposals. The motion was overwhelmingly defeated. On 21 March 1946, Fianna Fáil's resolve was again tested. During the course of the Dáil debate on the Public Health Bill, 1945, Richard Mulcahy called for the setting up of a council of public health generally in conformity with the findings and proposals contained in paragraphs 541–543 of the report.[10] His motion was pressed to a vote, and like the motion to establish a council of education, it was defeated.[11]

After the defeat of Mulcahy's motion James Larkin (Junior) immediately proposed the establishment of a number of consultative councils to advise and assist the Minister for Local Government and Public Health on particular matters pertaining to public health. This motion was a compromise on Mulcahy's proposal.[12] It specified that the councils in question should be established on a permanent and continuous basis. Larkin did not advocate that the consultative councils should be established 'purely on a vocational basis' but he did argue for the inclusion of non-medical experts in order to facilitate a policy of improving public health on a broader basis. This motion was also defeated.[13]

Fianna Fáil's intentions were clearly unsympathetic to demands for vocationalist schemes. On 2 July 1946, Mulcahy reminded the Dáil that his party had twice challenged the government's attitude to the recommendations of the commission. On both occasions a reactionary response was encountered and the inescapable conclusion was that the government had shown itself to be 'entirely adverse to the proposals contained in the Report of the Vocational Commission and to be somewhat hostile to the principles upon which that report is based'.[14] Mulcahy pressed de Valera for a reply. The taoiseach, in response, pointed out that the commission's work was a failure because it had failed to propose a satisfactory scheme of organisation for the rural community.[15] He referred to the foreword of the report and stressed the need to refrain from imposing vocational organisation upon a community not prepared for it. It was as if any vocationalist initiative taken by the government would invariably conflict with the principle of natural growth.

Another issue which was a source of concern to de Valera was the need to protect the welfare of the community against various sectional groups. *Quadragesimo Anno* had stressed the need to end class conflict. The commission, mindful of this tenet of papal teaching, endeavoured to devise a scheme to bring employers and employees together in vocational organisations. De Valera did not doubt the benefit of uniting employers and workers in the pursuance of their common interests but he was concerned about the possibility 'that the two did not meet just to exploit the rest.'[16] He was suspicious of the influence and motives of corporate interests.

De Valera expressed the view that vocational organisation would be natural and beneficial to the community only if it came from 'below'. Anything 'superimposed from the top' would be artificial and consequently it would not be durable.[17] However, his motivation for refusing to implement any of the commission's major recommendations had more to do with political strategy than with social philosophy. Evidently, he did not believe it prudent to bluntly attack the findings of the commission. Unlike Lemass he indulged in duplicity. He was determined to block the implementation of the commission's major recommendations but he displayed a readiness to support the implementation of some minor recommendations outlined in the report. This enabled him to retain some degree of credibility when he claimed that his government was giving serious consideration to the vocationalist scheme while at the same time ensuring that an irresistible public campaign was not stimulated in support of implementing the major recommendations. On 16 April 1947, he told the Dáil

> Of the recommendations of the commission which are immediately operable, a number have already been implemented by the Government, others are in the course of being implemented, and others are still under examination. As examples of recommendations already implemented, I might cite the Hire Purchase Act, 1946; the Industrial Relations Act, 1946; the Auctioneers and House Agents Act, 1947, which became law a few weeks ago; and the Consultative Medical Council set up by the Minister for Health, which held its inaugural meeting last week. The consolidation of laws, on which the commission also made recommendations, has been under active consideration for several years past, and a number of consolidating measures have been passed both before and since I received the report of the commission. Last May both Houses of the Oireachtas, at the instance of the Government, adopted additional standing Orders to facilitate the passage of consolidation Bills.[18]

The most striking feature of all these initiatives was that most of them were minor and all of them were peripheral to the commission's major proposals.[19] The Industrial Relations Act 1946 was the most significant and it improved the system of industrial conciliation in Ireland by establishing a Labour Court but this Act, helpful as it was, did not set up the vocational structure as recommended by the commission. Neither did the Consultative Medical Council resemble the council of health that the commission had advocated in paragraph 543 of its report.

Despite the government's negative attitude towards the report the C.S.V.O.C. persisted in its campaign to win public support for it. Shortly after the publication of the document it had been recognised by those who preached the gospel of vocationalism that the text (approximately 300,000 words) was beyond the comprehension of most citizens. Brian O'Nolan, alias 'Myles na gCopaleen', had unkindly described it as 'a monument of verbosity'. He was of the opinion that 'the most hardened civil servant would not dream of attempting beaurocratic (sic) prolixity on so grandiose a scale.'[20] In response to the above problem a number of pamphlets were published which summarised and simplified the recommendations in the report.[21] Some newspapers and periodicals also carried articles which summarised sections of the report and elaborated upon the underlying principles. All this was to no avail – the general public remained unmoved. Even some sectors of traditional support declined. Two Irish periodicals, *Studies* and *The Irish Monthly*, ceased to give close attention to vocationalism which they had done throughout the previous decade.[22]

As the C.S.V.O.C. continued with its efforts relatively little was heard from Michael Browne, Edward J. Coyne, John M. Hayes, Michael Tierney, Alfred O'Rahilly and other former members of the commission. At least some of them were aware of the relentless opposition of politicians and civil servants to their ambitious plan. Alfred O'Rahilly resented the government's response to the report and felt that at least it could have formed a council of education as a gesture of appreciation to those who had worked so hard to produce the document.[23]

The formation of a council of education was a long-standing aspiration of the vocationalists. The opposition parties pressed for its establishment[24] but government politicians and civil servants remained as obstinate as ever. The rejection of the commission's recommendations was not the only obstacle to the setting up of the council. The Department of Education was not renowned for taking initiatives; its main concern was to keep the system running smoothly.[25] This inertia was not just a feature of Fianna Fáil administrations. The long established resistance to change, in addition to Fianna Fáil's opposition to the commission's proposals, precluded any possibility of establishing a council of education before the first Inter-Party Government took office in February 1948. After sixteen years as Minister for Education, Thomas Derrig still regarded educational reform, particularly structural reform, as 'interference' with a system which was to his complete satisfaction. The reforms in postwar Europe had done nothing to change his or de Valera's outlook.[26]

Vocationalism *per se* did not command much public support. The vocationalists constituted a weak pressure group but, in seeking to reduce the power of the state, they were to find common cause with the Catholic hierarchy. The principle of subsidiarity underpinned vocationalist ideology but it also had major implications for the status and role of the Roman Catholic Church in society. Long before the publication of *Rerum Novarum* the Catholic Church had become deeply involved in matters of a socio-economic nature. By the late nineteenth century the Catholic Church in Ireland had gained considerable control over education, health and various charitable services. The power of the church derived in large measure from such control.[27] The controversies which arose from the blunt dismissal of the commission's report and the Dignan plan may have predisposed the hierarchy to support demands for the curtailment of state power[28] – especially when the administrative system of government was becoming more centralised. According to J.H. Whyte

> despite the varied nature of 'vocationalist' support, however, the situation had in it the elements of a clash between Church and State. The fact that the most articulate exponents of the 'vocationalist' point of view were two bishops, backed by a number of Catholic organisations, while on the other side the most determined defenders of the 'bureaucratic' viewpoint were ministers and civil servants, served to ensure this.[29]

The growth of state power in Ireland was not entirely a post-war phenomenon. Since independence the higher civil servants had been attempting to maximise the centralisation of administrative authority in Dublin. Although de Valera treasured the notion of a self-reliant rural Christian community he did nothing to reverse the trend of growing state intervention.[30] As far as the political and administrative organisation of society was concerned he continued to cling to the requirements of democratic centralism despite his awareness of the dangers of bureaucracy and over-centralisation. The commission had fulminated against bureaucratic centralisation and attempted to devise a system of governance which would facilitate wider participation in decision-making. De Valera had chosen to reject its recommendations and there emerged a wide and obvious divergence between the idea of the self-reliant community and the reality of the centralising state. In parallel with these developments there was an erosion of the consensus which had previously existed between church and state on moral and social issues. Tension between church and state became more discernible towards the end of the 1940s.

The vocationalists continued to campaign for the implementation of the commission's report but did not meet with success. Their ideology centred around two main principles – one positive, one negative, namely, the establishment of vocational organisations and, the limitation of state intervention in the social and economic aspects of national life. The proliferation and development of vocational organisations proved as elusive as ever. Government assistance was not forthcoming and society lacked the spontaneity which the vocationalists had so often spoken about. Consequently, the main feature of the vocationalist movement was predominantly negative – bordering on an obsessive desire to stop the growth of state power. Vocationalists believed that the threat of totalitarianism had not abated in post-war Europe and developments at home and abroad fuelled their fears. The right-wing dictatorships had been defeated and destroyed but the totalitarian states of the left were made stronger than ever. In the communist states of eastern Europe the state gained complete control over social services and the economy after 1945. From the vocationalist perspective all was not well in the democracies of western Europe either as a trend emerged where state intervention in socio-economic matters became more pervasive. In the post-war period there was an unprecedented expansion of the welfare state, especially in Britain. The improvement of public health and social welfare services in Britain stimulated demands in Ireland for similar improvements.[31]

The first response of the Department of Local Government and Public Health, to the mounting pressure for reform, had manifested itself in the form of the Public Health Bill (1945). This bill was characteristic of the bureaucratic and centralising tendencies of the department and it diverged widely from Catholic social principles.[32] The Health Bill (1947) was similar to the Public Health Bill (1945).[33] When the 1947 bill was enacted it provoked opposition from the Catholic hierarchy. However, Fianna Fáil was able to delay in making a decision on how to respond to the hierarchy's representations. When the first Inter-Party government took office in February 1948 it inherited the thorny problem of improving the health services.

VOCATIONALISM AND THE FIRST INTER-PARTY GOVERNMENT 1948–1951

Fianna Fáil had shown itself hostile to the recommendations of the commission. Therefore when the party was ousted from government in February 1948 it gave the vocationalists some reason for optimism. The first coalition government was composed of all political parties in the Dáil except Fianna Fáil. Fine Gael, National Labour, and Clann na Poblachta to a lesser extent, all had expressed support for vocationalist principles.[34] At the outset the new government seems to have been anxious to stress its allegiance to Catholic social teaching.

Richard Mulcahy, the leader of Fine Gael, was appointed Minister for Education. Mulcahy had issued a statement on 17 February on behalf of Fine Gael, Labour, National Labour, Clann na Talmhan, Clann na Poblachta and the Independents. On that date a ten point programme for government was agreed and this included a commitment to establish a council of education.[35] On 24 February 1948, still in its first week of office, the government conveyed to Pope Pius XII the following message

> On the occasion of our assumption of office and of the first Cabinet meeting, my colleagues and myself desire to repose at the feet of your

> Holiness the assurance of our filial loyalty and of our devotion to your August Person, as well as our firm resolve to be guided in all our work by the teaching of Christ, and to strive for the attainment of a social order in Ireland based on Christian principles.[36]

This declaration was welcomed by the C.S.V.O.C. The association recognised that the growth of vocational organisation had to come from within society if it was to be viable in the long term but it also insisted that the government had a vital role to play. Accordingly, the attention of the taoiseach, John A. Costello, was drawn to paragraph 711 of the report, which called for the enactment of legislation to give effect to recommendations made by the commission. Attention was also drawn to the fact that Dr John D'Alton, Archbishop of Armagh, had expressed his approval of the commission's proposals.[37]

Mulcahy now had the opportunity to give substance to his previous demands but he chose instead to reconsider his declared support for vocationalist recommendations. In March 1948 – within a few weeks of taking office – the minister reassured the annual congress of the Irish National Teachers' Organisation that the government was committed to the establishment of a council of education. He praised the work of the Commission on Vocational Organisation but, instead of quoting paragraph 540, he opted instead to emphasise that he was now inspired by the foreword of the report.[38] The type of council he had in mind would 'induce a vocational organisation devoted to educational thought among the various groups that are working in education at the present time'.[39]

The setting up of a council of education was not without precedent. It had already been pointed out that the Minister for Agriculture had a consultative council to advise him.[40] Other ministers had established similar bodies. The Minister for Health set up a National Health Council; the Minister for Local Government established a Housing Board; and the Ministers for Industry and Commerce and for Social Welfare also set up bodies to advise and assist them.[41] Yet, Mulcahy was reluctant to follow the trend. In his first year as Minister for Education, he had been 'learning quite a lot' and now, much enlightened by his ministerial experience, had come to believe that if the council was to be established on a vocational basis its personnel would be 'as numerous and varied as the contents of Noah's Ark'.[42] Such a council, he said, would not be structured to give the best type of advice. However, despite this impediment, he did eventually establish a council of education, probably because of pressure from the Labour Party.[43] On 4 April 1950 he announced its terms of reference

> To advise the Minister, in so far as pertains to the powers, duties and functions of the State, upon such matters relating to educational theory and practice as they think fit and upon any educational questions and problems referred to them by him.[44]

The general regulations governing the constitution and the procedures of the council specified that it was to have no administrative, executive, or financial powers, duties or functions. The council was prohibited from involving itself with issues that related to salaries, grants and pensions. It was to consist of a chairman and other members and the number of members was to be decided by the minister. All members were to be nominated by the minister.

The proposed council did not bear any resemblance to the one that the Commission on Vocational Organisation had recommended. This was particularly evident where the selection of members was concerned. Paragraph 540 of the report had specified that the council should be representative of parents and of all the organisations directly concerned with the various sectors of education, both religious and secular. Furthermore, representatives of agriculture, industry and commerce were to be granted membership of the council. In contrast to the commission's recommendation, the council of education was formed on a narrow basis. Of the 31 members no less than 26 were, or had been, professors, teachers or inspectors. The editorial of *The Irish Independent* was critical of the fact that the recommendations of the commission had not been complied with.[45] The council was criticised for being too narrow in its representation and for its urban bias. Only four of the members were from rural areas and the president of the Irish National Teachers' Organisation, J. Mansfield, alleged that it was dominated by the urban sector of the population and by higher educational interests.[46]

Various interest groups protested against their exclusion. The National Executive of the Trade Union Congress, the Administrative Council of the Labour Party, and the Vocational Education Officers' Organisation all complained that none of their representatives had been selected to serve on the council.[47] A common criticism of the council was that parent representation had not been specially allowed for. Of course many of the members were parents but none of them had been chosen on that basis. Apparently, *The Irish Times* was in the minority when it expressed the view that the council was broadly representative and that its members were well selected.[48]

From the beginning, Mulcahy had regarded his ministerial role as 'a very, very narrow one' and he persisted in holding this view.[49] It seemed that Mulcahy, unlike Derrig, was not hypersensitive about his ministerial authority being infringed upon. Such an attitude should have enhanced the functioning of the council and should have been conducive to the promotion of vocational organisation. That this was not so can be attributed to the fact that, although Fine Gael had championed the vocationalist cause in the Dáil, its corporatist credentials were far from impeccable. Its flirtation with the discredited ideology was to prove even more lukewarm in the 1940s than in the 1930s. As the major party in government it declined to establish a vocational council of education.[50] Furthermore, it made no positive response when petitioned by the C.S.V.O.C. to implement the recommendations of the Commission on Vocational Organisation.

The C.S.V.O.C. had reminded the taoiseach, John A. Costello, that 'practically all' the government parties, before the general election, had made a commitment to work for social change based on the vocational concept. Therefore it confidently anticipated that the government would endeavour to give practical effect to these statements of intent.[51] On 4 February 1949, Denis Galvin, chairman of the C.S.V.O.C. executive committee, wrote to the taoiseach, requesting an interview in order to ascertain the government's attitude towards vocational organisation. His deputation list gave the names of three employers, three trade-union officials and three members of the C.S.V.O.C.[52] On 28 March 1949, Costello received the deputation. He was asked whether or not the government approved of social reform in Ireland on a vocational basis. Other pertinent questions were asked: Did the government approve of the recommendations of the commission? If it had insuperable objections to the implementation of the plan what precisely was the nature of these objections? What action did the government intend to take to encourage the growth of vocational organisation? Was any government action contemplated under paragraph 711 of the report?[53]

The deputation declared itself satisfied with Costello's response to the representations made but the view was expressed that: 'The success or otherwise of an interview is, however, to be judged solely by its results and the results in this case are yet to come'.[54] This cautious attitude was justified. Further correspondence failed to elicit any firm commitment from the government. The C.S.V.O.C. was informed that the questions raised were 'under consideration' and that a further communication would be sent. It waited in vain as the months passed. On 6 June, 1950 Galvin wrote to the taoiseach, pressing him for a clear response to the questions of 28 March 1949. His concluding paragraph appealed for action; it stated

> The need for the establishment of a Christian social order is every day becoming of greater urgency. While, however, there is distinct evidence of a growing demand for the establishment of such a social order the absence of encouragement by the State is seriously retarding progress towards this end. My Committee therefore feel that the Government should without further delay declare its intentions in the matter.[55]

The government had more pressing matters to attend to, especially in regard to the improvement of the health services. As the state became more involved in health care and social welfare the Roman Catholic Church reacted aggressively – attempting to defend what it regarded as its sphere of influence. Issues of health and social welfare became the main focus of tension between church and state and an open conflict erupted when the Minister for Health in the first Inter-Party Government, Dr Noël Browne, introduced his mother-and-child-scheme. This scheme was constructed within the general framework of the 1947 Health Act and was to provide free maternity care for all mothers and expectant mothers, and free medical care for all children up to the age of 16. In comparison to neighbouring countries the Irish infant mortality rate was high and the scheme was designed to remedy this problem. However, it did require an extension of state control and this elicited a strong protest from the vocationalists.[56]

Bishop Michael Browne of Galway was a vigorous critic of the mother-and-child-scheme. So also was Fr E.J. Coyne; he opposed the tendency of the state to intervene more and more in the social and economic aspects of community life.[57] The Knights of St Columbanus, through their newspaper, *The Standard*, had consistently opposed government health policy since 1945. This organisation, a constituent body of the C.S.V.O.C., had important hierarchical and political contacts.[58] Apparently, the Knights of St Columbanus were of strategic importance. When the crisis developed between church and state in 1951 the Knights may have played an important interconnecting role between the Irish Medical Association, the Catholic bishops's standing committee and the Inter-Party Government. However, there is insufficient evidence to substantiate or clarify this aspect of the mother-and-child scheme controversy.[59]

Opponents of the scheme appealed to the Catholic hierarchy for support on the basis that it violated Catholic social teaching. The bishops decided that the scheme was indeed contrary to Catholic social teaching because it was, they claimed, in direct opposition to the rights of the family and of the individual. Noël Browne's political ineptitude greatly weakened his position. His cabinet colleagues refused to support him, he resigned, and the scheme was abandoned.

He was not the only minister of the Inter-Party government to experience trenchant opposition from those who were hostile to the growth of state intervention. William Norton's proposals to reform and extend the state's system of social insurance provoked criticism from influential clerics such as Fr E.J. Coyne, SJ; Fr Felim O'Briain O.F.M.; Dr Cornelius Lucey (then Professor of Ethics at Maynooth), and Dr Peter McKevitt. The Bill was criticised by *The Standard, An Ríoghacht* and by *Christus Rex*, and the C.S.V.O.C. proposed its own plan. But Norton kept on closer terms with the bishops than Noël Browne had and he experienced no overt opposition from the hierarchy. His knowledge of church social teaching helped him to defend his proposed legislation against those critics who regarded his scheme as an unwarranted extension of state power. Norton also benefited from a better relationship with his cabinet colleagues than Browne had. However, his Social Welfare Bill never became law because the Inter-Party government fell when it had only reached its second reading.[60] In the general election that took place on May 30, Fianna Fáil won 69 Dáil seats and, with the support of a few independent deputies, Éamon de Valera was again appointed taoiseach on 13 June 1951.

THE VOCATIONALIST MOVEMENT 1951–1960

On 16 July 1951, the secretary of the C.S.V.O.C., Thomas C. O'Gorman, wrote to Éamon de Valera, informing him that the C.S.V.O.C. had urged the Inter-Party government to promote the development of vocational organisation in the state but, as it awaited a response to representations made, the government fell from power. The C.S.V.O.C. now looked to Éamon de Valera and his party for support.[61] There was little reason for optimism. Fianna Fáil had not responded favourably to the *Commission on Vocational Organisation Report* after its publication in 1945. At this juncture even the most optimistic and naive of vocationalists suspected that 'the politicians had deliberately shelved the Report in the hope that it would become lost in the limbo of forgotten things'.[62] The new Fianna Fáil administration did not initiate any major changes demanded by the vocationalists. On 18–19 October 1951, the Irish Guild of St Luke, S.S. Cosmas, and Damian (the medical guild of the Knights of St Columbanus[63]) passed a resolution at its annual general meeting which was condemnatory of government policy. The guild deplored

> the failure to implement the recommendations of the Vocational Commission, in particular those which affect the Medical Profession,

> and the consequent general tendency towards the introduction of Socialistic Schemes throughout our whole national life . . .[64]

De Valera's government had trouble with the Catholic hierarchy in 1952–1953 when it attempted to implement a revised version of Noël Browne's scheme. However, a confrontation with the bishops was avoided because Fianna Fáil successively pursued a strategy of appeasement – introducing amendments that were for the most part symbolic.

Vocationalist appeals for radical reforms did not elicit a positive response from the government. By 28 April 1953, nothing substantial had been done to implement the recommendations of the Commission on Vocational Organisation. The departments of Agriculture, Defence, Industry and Commerce, Lands, Posts and Telegraphs, and Social Welfare declared that either no action had been taken to implement the recommendations of the commission or that they were not concerned with such recommendations. The Office of Public Works and the Office of the Revenue Commissioners were also in a similar position.[65]

The Department of Education reported that paragraphs 539 and 540 of the report had been 'put into effect' – this was not true. The Council of Education, which had been set up in April 1950, was fundamentally different from the one proposed by the commission. Likewise, the National Health Council was also very different from the one described in paragraph 543 of the report. This council, also referred to as the Consultative Council of Health, had been established by the Minister for Health, Dr James Ryan, on 10 April 1947. The council did not bear any resemblance to the one proposed by the commission.[66] The selection of its membership was on a much narrower basis – nominations came from four medical organisations and from the Minister for Health. Furthermore, the council lacked autonomy and its functions, duties and responsibilities were not fixed by statute. It could only advise the minister on matters concerned with health administration and the initiative lay entirely with the minister in seeking advice. Significantly, in the period 1953–1954, when vocationalism was a spent force, the council's status was improved substantially and it was given authority to advise the minister on issues of its own choice.[67]

The position of Local Government in regard to the implementation of the commission's recommendations was that some action was being taken to modernise and codify the law affecting the department. The Department of Justice declared that the only part of the report which concerned it was the proposal to establish a council of law. The council had not been set up but a Statute Law Reform and Consolidation

Office was established which performed some of the functions prescribed for such a council. The establishment of the office, however, fell far short of what had been proposed in paragraphs 533 and 534 of the report. The Department of Finance claimed that it had implemented only one recommendation of the commission which was outlined in paragraph 667 of the report. Such a claim, as modest as it was, could only be partially sustained. The paragraph in question specified that a system of negotiation and arbitration should be established for the civil service. The department's claim was not quite true because the commission had recommended that the form and methods of collective bargaining, negotiation, conciliation, and arbitration, were to be determined by the national vocational assembly. The assembly had not been established. Furthermore, the scheme, which had been introduced on 1 June 1950, was only functioning on an experimental basis[68] and its future was very uncertain.

On 16 April 1954, T.C. O'Gorman wrote to the leaders of the political parties, reminding them of the general election which was to take place on 18 May. The political parties were asked whether or not they were in favour of establishing a provisional vocational assembly in accordance with paragraph 711 of the report. Once again the leading politicians were reminded of the fact that Ireland was overwhelmingly Christian and what was being advocated was a type of organisation which was based on Christian principles. As if this argument was not strong enough Article 15 of the new constitution was also invoked – but to no avail. The sense of urgency which had been present in the earlier calls for reform, by the C.S.V.O.C., now descended to dark despair. Thus, O'Gorman wrote

> It is sad to have to relate that in the interval since the Report appeared, practically nothing has been done by any Government towards promoting the implementation of the Commission's recommendations; and this, notwithstanding the expressions of approval by various party leaders of the vocational organisation ideal and ministerial praise of constructive proposals submitted by this Conference. (A number of Consultative bodies have been set up, but on lines radically different from those recommended by the Commission).[69]

This statement succinctly summarised the harsh reality which must now have been obvious to the majority of vocationalists – no Irish government would assist the formation and development of vocational organisations as described in the *Commission on Vocational Organisation Report*. The view was expressed that '. . . we are in the peculiarly illogical position in this predominantly Catholic country that the political authority will not give any assistance towards the establishment of a true vocational order.'[70]

In the absence of government support the realisation of the vocationalist ideal depended on the strength and commitment of the Catholic social movement. In the early post-war period several associations and periodicals had energetically articulated Catholic social teaching. Muintir na Tíre grew in numbers and *The Standard* continued its analysis of events from a Catholic social perspective. New organs of opinion sprang up alongside those which already existed. In 1946 University College Cork initiated a series of courses designed to familiarise trade unionists with Catholic social teaching. In 1948 the Jesuits established the Catholic Workers' College in Dublin for the same reason. The Dublin Institute of Catholic Sociology was set up in 1950 for the purpose of conveying the tenets of Catholic social teaching to the entire population. In 1951 the C.S.V.O.C. commenced publishing *V.O.* and by 1954 the bi-monthly bulletin had reached a circulation figure of 2,300 copies per issue.[71] In 1952 a series of Social Study weeks was organised in Dublin which attracted audiences sometimes numbering in the thousands.[72] However, the number of people who actively promoted the idea of vocational organisation were never more than a small minority and the exponents of vocationalism were few in numbers.[73] The same names occurred again and again, sometimes as speakers at Muintir na Tíre rural weeks or at the Dublin Institute of Catholic Sociology. Their articles were published in periodicals such as *The Standard*.

The Republic of Ireland was over 90% Catholic and there were few exponents of communism, liberalism or democratic socialism. A movement, which was motivated by Catholic social principles, should have met with little resistance – especially when the vocationalist principle was expressed in the 1937 constitution. Yet the resistance was overwhelming. The majority of Irish Catholic bishops and priests either opposed or failed to support the vocationalist cause. Fr John Hayes, founder of Muintir na Tíre, did more than any other vocationalist to translate theory into practice. His efforts to give practical effect to Catholic social teaching met with '. . . stone walls of clerical opposition . . . There was a resistance to Catholic social work in Ireland by the older priests only to be compared with the resistance to Russian communism'.[74] A minority of young priests regarded the guilds of Muintir na Tíre as mere forums for discussion. Others believed 'the movement was fraught with dangers: the laity getting too much control . . . interference in church affairs and, worst of all, the mingling of Catholics and Protestants.'[75] Thus, it worried Fr Hayes that his work might be ' . . . a labour of Sisyphus; it would be so hard to make it prevail against the spirit of the age.'[76] Conservative bishops and priests were quite capable of suppressing vocationalist inspired schemes without any assistance from politicians and civil servants.

Archbishop John Charles McQuaid had successfully frustrated attempts in the 1930s to form a council of education on a vocational basis. His lack of enthusiasm for vocationalism is further indicated by the exclusion of Muintir na Tíre from the archdiocese of Dublin from 1940 (the year he became archbishop).[77] Muintir na Tíre was not prepared to go where it was not welcomed. A disappointed Canon Hayes may have had McQuaid in mind when he quipped 'It is bad enough to be kicked by the Devil, but it is the divil and all to be kicked by angels and archangels.'[78]

Developments abroad also militated against the development and spread of vocational organisations. The Catholic social movement in Ireland was very different from its counterparts in most European countries. The cataclysm of the Second World War had induced a complete change in social Catholicism. Corporatism had been discredited because of its association with fascism and Catholics now gave their support to Christian Democracy. The writings of St Thomas Aquinas, which had played such an important role in the formation of papal corporatist thought, now provided an ideological stimulus for the development of Christian Democracy.[79] The appeal of Christian Democracy was that it promised a new style of politics based on participation, reconciliation and co-operation while still retaining an adherence to traditional moral values.[80] It emerged as a major political force in postwar Europe.

Most countries in western Europe had endured destruction and bloodshed on a massive scale during the Second World War. The ravages of military conflict tended to bring people of different traditions together and stimulated co-operation which lasted beyond the war. In those countries that were able to remain neutral, and free from war, social and political Catholicism remained basically unchanged. In Spain, Portugal and Switzerland the Catholic reforming zeal, which was evident in other parts of western Europe, was subdued or absent. In Ireland many Catholics attached great importance to their traditional identity at a time when the majority of Catholics in mainland Europe sought reconciliation and co-operation with those of other traditions – in particular with democratic socialists. Irish Catholicism had moved closer to the Catholicism of mainland Europe during the 1930s as both embraced corporatist ideology. But in the post-war era corporatism was no longer a politically respectable ideology. From the mid–1940s some exponents of Catholic social teaching continued to advocate vocational organisation when it was no longer in vogue in mainland Europe[81] but they struggled in vain to resist the demise of papal corporatism.

The inordinate distrust of state power which so typified the vocationalist movement up to the mid–1950s was also manifested in the social outlook of the Catholic hierarchy[82] but the majority of Irish Catholic bishops did not support vocationalist demands. The vocationalists were too dogmatic in invoking the principle of subsidiarity.[83] They failed to recognise that state initiatives were sometimes required as a response to social deprivation. An increase in state power and the expansion of 'bureaucracy' were necessary concomitants. This was nowhere more evident than in the health services where the Roman Catholic Church exerted considerable control. A substantial reduction of such control and participation was inevitable due to the rapidly rising costs of modern health care.

From the mid–1950s the Catholic social movement became less ideological and began to adopt a more flexible ethos. Dr Jeremiah Newman's advice to Catholic social activists indicates a substantial change in outlook.

> there are certain things against which we must guard. One is a too great dogmatism in expressing our opinions on social affairs. The principles of the moral law regarding social matters are of a very different kind from those which govern individual conduct . . . they pertain to a much more complex matter than do the principles regarding, for example, murder or lying, and are by no means as easily applicable as are the latter. For these reasons we should be careful, when dealing with State activities, not to oppose every State scheme simply because it is a State scheme.[84]

Towards the end of the 1950s the campaign for vocational organisation slowly came to a halt and the C.S.V.O.C. became extinct around 1960.[85] Suspicion of state power was no longer widely felt.[86]

The Catholic social movement in the 1960s was less dogmatic in its response to complex social issues. A number of concerned Catholics perceived the need to address the intellectual deficiencies of Irish Catholicism. Determined efforts were made in some quarters to promote the development of new ideas and attitudes so that Irish Catholicism would be able to respond positively to a rapidly changing social environment.[87] More effort was spent on obtaining and assessing factual information in order to attend to the actual needs of the Irish people. As Catholic clergymen became more familiar with sociological research studies they perceived that the Irish state was not doing enough for some of its citizens. Ironically, priests and bishops began to advocate more state intervention.

The 1960s therefore witnessed a radical re-orientation of the Irish Catholic social movement which made vocationalist aspirations even less attainable. Furthermore, the political parties had decisively rejected the *Commission on Vocational Organisation Report*. The corporatist scheme envisaged by the commission had failed to win widespread support but, under the aegis of Seán Lemass (he served as taoiseach from June 1959 to November 1966), a new variant of corporatism/neo-corporatism began to emerge in Ireland.

CHAPTER NINE

Revival?

The vocationalist ideal, like the Phoenix, has, apparently, re-emerged from the ashes – 'swiftly and silently Ireland has realised, in practice, the dream of the Vocationalists'.[1] A number of organisational structures, similar to some of those recommended by the Commission on Vocational Organisation, have been formed.

> . . . with the development of economic planning after 1958, there was a multiplication of consultative bodies in Ireland, and by the nineteen-sixties there seemed some sign that the structures recommended by the Vocational Organisation Commission in 1944 were at last coming into existence. The National Industrial Economic Council, established in 1963, which includes representatives of the State and of both employers and workers, bears some resemblance to the National Industrial Conference which the Vocational Organisation Commission had proposed. The Joint Industrial Boards which the commission had proposed for each industry are in some degree paralleled by the Adaption Councils which have been established in twenty-four Irish industries. The National Agricultural Council established in 1967 may . . . come to play a part similar to that proposed by the Vocational Organisation Commission for a National Agricultural Conference. If there is no longer any talk about the need for vocational organisation in Ireland, part of the reason may be that more vocational organisation exists.[2]

The Labour Court and the Labour-Employer Conference together carried out some of the functions that were specified by the commission for joint industrial councils. The Law Reform Commission fulfilled a role which the commission had proposed for the council of law. However, a development of greater significance was that 'a planning civil service found it necessary to secure the co-operation of the organised interest groups, which meant most of the interests nominated by the Commission for representation in the National Vocational Assembly.'[3]

In view of the above, is it now correct to assume that the aspirations of the vocationalists have been fulfilled? The purpose of this chapter is to ascertain to what extent the vocationalist ideal has been realised in Ireland.

Seán Lemass shared with the Commission on Vocational Organisation the belief that consultation between government and various interest groups was of crucial importance in economic planning. But he differed sharply from the commission on social and economic issues. Lemass was more influenced by the writings of John Maynard Keynes and Sir William Beveridge than by the papal encyclicals.[4] His strategy for economic development was based on the planning techniques which were devised, particularly in France and Italy, after the Second World War. Vocationalism, as elaborated by Bishop Michael Browne and his colleagues, had no role to play in government policy formation. In his last year as taoiseach Lemass was still bitterly critical of the *Commission on Vocational Organisation Report*. In early 1966 he stated in an interview

> The basic idea in that Report was not that vocational organisation was something that should be imposed on the community by the Government, but something that should grow naturally. And this didn't quite happen. The forecast that it was going to happen soon proved to be wrong. The present Bishop of Galway was the chairman of that Commission, and he set out with one main ambition – to produce a Report in less time than was ever achieved before. So a lot of the material that went into the Report was not subjected to any very critical examination.[5]

Ironically, it was Lemass, the most outspoken critic of the Commission on Vocational Organisation, who shunted Ireland in the direction of corporatism.[6]

The complexity of modern governance exerted pressure on the state to invite employers, workers and farmers to contribute directly to the solution of contemporary problems. Yet Lemass's readiness to consult the various sectoral interests in Irish society was often frustrated by the fact that they were badly organised and poorly represented. He preferred to negotiate with organisations whose representatives conveyed the interests of an industry as a whole rather than dealing with individual firms. In a democratic state integrated policy-making required consensus which in turn relied on consultation. The interest group representatives who gave evidence before the commission in the early 1940s had complained about the lack of consultation. The commission concluded that

> in the exercise of supervision and control over private enterprise by government departments there is relatively little consultation with vocational organisations. Such consultation as does take place is not continuous or obligatory, but is casual and haphazard. Even where bodies have been statutorily established they have been limited in function, defective in composition, and shortlived in operation.[7]

The commission had found that planning in the industrial sphere was 'sectional, local, piecemeal and unbalanced'.[8] A unified and highly developed socio-economic structure was vital if planning was to be effectively formulated and implemented.

While Lemass and the commission shared the conviction that co-ordinated planning was crucial for maximising the potential for economic development they differed sharply on strategy. The commission abhorred bureaucracy and regarded vocational organisations as alternatives to civil service intervention. Lemass, in contrast, envisaged the civil service and private enterprise as partners in a scheme of national economic development. This constituted a fundamental difference between the corporatism preached by the commission and the neo-corporatist policy of Lemass. His chosen strategy for economic development was based on a corporatist/neo-corporatist national consensus.[9]

In the early 1960s, a vigorous upswing in the global economy was in progress and the prospects for greater free trade emerged. The Irish economy reoriented itself more and more towards production for exports in response to the reduction of protectionist barriers. Simultaneously, it was exposed to greater competition as trade restrictions were dropped. In order to meet the new challenge co-operation between government, employers and trade unions was necessary to maximise efficiency. Consultative bodies were set up to promote co-operation. In 1961 the government established the Committee on Industrial Organisation (C.I.O.). The C.I.O. was made up of representatives of employers, trade unions, and the public service and its objectives were to evaluate the condition of Irish industry and to ascertain the measures that might have to be taken if Irish industry was to adapt to conditions of more intense competition. The C.I.O. believed that co-operation between firms in each industry would greatly alleviate the industrial problems which were so prevalent. The experience of the C.I.O. in this regard indicates clearly why the recommendations of the Commission on Vocational Organisation were so impractical during the 1940s and 1950s. Like the commission, the C.I.O. was unduly optimistic in anticipating the emergence of co-operative effort between Irish industrialists.[10]

The C.I.O. was a precursor of the National Industrial and Economic Council (N.I.E.C.) which was established in 1963. The N.I.E.C. had no representatives from any of the political parties and therefore it was not deeply divided by party political squabbles. Civil service representation was limited to two serving senior civil servants and this precluded the council from being regarded as a mere projection of the public service. The N.I.E.C. was essentially tripartite in nature. It included representatives from the public service, the Irish Congress of Trade Unions (I.C.T.U.), the Federated Union of Employers (F.U.E.) and other employers' organisations. The N.I.E.C. was widely viewed as a council comprised of individuals who genuinely and independently served the public interest. It had the independence to criticise openly and was enabled to submit its reports to government and have them published unaltered. According to Garret Fitzgerald the N.I.E.C. exerted 'the first effective source of outside pressure on the public service that has been created in Ireland . . . '[11] The status and expertise of the council enabled it to challenge the public service, where its performance had been unsatisfactory. Politicians had all too often failed to grapple with policy issues in a sufficiently professional way to induce or enforce constructive change in public service performance. The N.I.E.C. was the main forum through which the state interacted with various interest groups in the economy. Other lesser bodies included the National Agricultural Council which was formed in 1967 and the Committee on Industrial Progress which was set up in 1968.

The N.I.E.C. was disbanded in 1971 but the influences which had stimulated its inception endured and in 1973 the National Economic and Social Council (N.E.S.C.) was established. This was a similar council but had broader terms of reference and a wider membership than its predecessor. The main difference in membership was the rural representation. No representative of the agricultural community had served in the N.I.E.C. because of the fragmentation of rural organisations. N.E.S.C. membership was drawn from agricultural organisations, the Confederation of Irish Industry, the Irish Employers' Confederation, the I.C.T.U., the government, and from various government departments.[12] The council was only an advisory body but it did influence government policy formation.[13]

Why was the government so anxious to consult with, and be advised by, its 'social partners'? Consultation tended to promote consensus which is a vital factor in economic planning. Moreover, consultation was essential because governments needed assistance in order to grapple with a large number of inter-related social and economic problems which beset every modern state. Economic planning also required the regulation of prices and wages. Irish governments prepared legislation or threatened to pass legislation to control prices and wages when voluntary co-operation was not forthcoming.[14] An important feature of Irish economic development was, and still is, the attraction of foreign investment. Multinational corporations are conducive to corporatist arrangements. Corporatist policies involve the creation of a harmonious relationship between employers, trade unions and the state. Stable industrial relations are an essential condition for the attraction of foreign investment.

Income policy tends to form the motive force of corporatism or neo-corporatism. In Ireland wage policies were based on a series of national 'understandings' or national wage agreements. However, wages policy cannot be considered in isolation from budgetary and economic policies in general. Therefore 'understandings' also addressed the issues of employment, taxation, education, health and social welfare.

Why did various interest groups seek representation on consultative councils such as the N.E.S.C.? Membership of advisory councils was eagerly sought after by sectional groups because it effectively enhanced their status and granted them access to organisations which influenced the formation of government policies. Those associations which were broadly representative, such as the I.C.T.U. and the F.U.E., tended to have representation on a wide range of official committees.[15]

Ireland's drift towards corporatism was not unique in the 1960s and 1970s – the western world had moved in that general direction also. The national economic planning throughout western Europe after the Second World War involved the institutionalised integration of employer associations and trade unions with the state in terms of functional representation. These councils or institutes did not declare themselves corporatist – they developed on a pragmatic basis in harmony with the dominant political systems of parliamentary democracy and interest group lobbying. The coercive power of the state was a factor of secondary importance in their emergence.[16] The co-ordination of effort by the state, employers, trade unions and farmers would seem to indicate that Ireland had become corporatist – but was this more apparent than real? If Ireland had succumbed to corporatism was this the same type of corporatism recommended by the Commission on Vocational Organisation?

Whether or not Ireland became corporatist in the 1960s and 1970s is open to debate – a debate which is somewhat confused by the difficulty in devising a broadly accepted definition of what corporatism actually means.[17] In recent years there has been much discussion on the meaning of corporatism but this has tended to confuse rather than clarify the issue. The concept of tripartism[18] may help to provide a more satisfactory explanation of Ireland's economic development. Tripartite negotiations have featured prominently in the decision-making procedures of many Western countries. Ireland's drift towards corporatism may have progressed no further than 'institutionalised tripartism.'[19] This was due to a number of factors which obstructed a 'neo-corporatist concertation of interests'.[20] The 'peak' associations of employers and trade unions were weakly centralised. Trade unions in particular resisted too close a participation in responsibility for public policy. Furthermore, the state had not been firmly committed to corporatism and distanced itself from the 'social partners' on a number of occasions.[21] Thus, Philippe C. Schmitter found that Ireland, like France, Britain and the U.S.A., has 'proven consistently more resistant to the blandishments of corporatism' than Sweden, Denmark, Switzerland, the Netherlands, Finland, Norway and Belgium.[22]

In view of the above it would seem appropriate to describe Ireland, especially in the 1960s and 1970s, as quasi- or neo-corporatist if not tripartite. Tripartite or quasi-corporatist arrangements led to the implementation of some of the commission's recommendations although not exactly as envisaged by the commission. The tension between bureaucratic and vocationalist ideologies, which so strained church-state relations in the 1940s and in the 1950s, had subsided and disappeared by around 1960. Exponents of Catholic social teaching ceased to berate the state for its adherence to bureaucracy.[23] Government ministers and civil servants became more tolerant of, and more inclined to deal with, vocational organisations. All then seemed to be well as far as vocationalist aspirations were concerned – but was the underlying reality radically different?

The commission had expressed the view that a society organised on a vocationalist basis was compatible with any form of political organisation or government. When it proposed a corporatist scheme for Ireland the commission emphasised that its recommendations were in no way to be interpreted as a call for changing the existing political system. It declared that the supreme responsibility for policy formation should remain with the electorate, Oireachtas, and government. Notwithstanding all this the commission's recommendations would inevitably have changed the political structure of the state. Quasi-corporatism, far less radical than the commission's type of corporatism, has exerted a profound influence on the political system. It diminished the authority of the Dáil. In seeking 'social partners' the government had to compromise its position as the only national policy maker. Did the 'social partners' then benefit from a concomitant growth of influence? It would seem not.

Many organisations were frequently consulted by civil servants but some of those who communicated with the civil service believed that such contact was only a means of acquiring information and compliance or was no more than a public relations exercise. There was little confidence in it as a method for genuine consultation or negotiation. Consultation therefore was not seen by sectional interest organisations as a genuinely co-operative activity.[24] If consultative procedures effectively degenerate into one-way channels of communication then vocational organisations become an extension of central government regardless of whether they are trade unions or employer associations.[25] Despite the implementation of some of the commission's recommendations the civil service remained as powerful as ever. If more vocational organisation did exist in Ireland from the 1960s onwards it did not effectively counteract bureaucratic overcentralisation.

A major adverse effect of overcentralised decision-making was that the system tended to become less flexible as the problems became more complicated. Furthermore,

> Another cost of concentrating too much responsibility for too much public business in too few hands is to leave nearly everyone else with little sense of responsibility. Hence widespread irresponsibility. This undermining of responsible democracy comes not from conscious decision but from failure to grasp the undemocratic implications of concentrating responsibility instead of dispersing it.[26]

The commission had vigorously opposed the growth of bureaucratic power. It emphasised that a state which took too much power and responsibility for a wide range of socio-economic concerns would become overburdened and incapable of adequately fulfilling its basic functions. The functions of the state involved the promotion and safeguarding of social justice and the co-ordination of the activities of the various sectors of society. The principle of subsidiarity formed the basis of the commission's recommendations. Structures of governance were proposed which would have permitted a wider participation in decision making. This was intended to have the dual effect of unburdening the state, enabling it to function more effectively, while at the same time giving to subsidiary organisations the duties which they could most effectively discharge.

Bureaucratic centralisation may not be the only development which adversely affected democracy in Ireland. The limited dispersal of power to the 'social partners' did not necessarily enhance the democratic process. It may have created conditions where the essential planning decisions were taken outside of parliament – 'somewhere between the world of political representation and the world of the corporate forces'.[27] The budget, which was formally announced in the Dáil on 30 January 1991, elicited a chorus of complaints from opposition deputies. Protests were made against the marginalisation of the majority of elected representatives in the framing of a new national programme. Opposition deputies protested that the central role of the

Oireachtas had been usurped as the important decisions were taken by the trade unions, employers, farmers, and by the government. Demands were made that the general body of elected representatives should be included in the decision-making process.[28]

Despite the widespread cynicism of the Irish people towards their elected representatives there is still a strong commitment to parliamentary democracy. Any doubts therefore about the democratic credentials of neo-corporatism, especially where the sovereignty of parliament is concerned, tends to promote a strong reaction. The marginalisation of the majority of Dáil deputies was not the only adverse effect of corporatist type arrangements. A parallel development occurred where the rank-and-file members of the various interest groups felt inadequately represented by their own high-ranking officers when central bargaining was under discussion. The social partners made such an extensive use of specialists and technical staff to represent their views that decision-making became more and more concentrated in the hands of experts. Hence the observation that

> the Dáil is rendered less and less capable of not only framing policy but even of fully grasping the implications of policy as it is presented to it. Interesting enough is the parallel between the diminishing authority of the Dáil . . . and . . . the diminishing status of the rank and file members of the various interest groups *vis à vis* their own officers . . . particularly in relation to central bargaining.[29]

It has been argued that, in Ireland, neo-corporatist arrangements did not endanger democracy. When interest organisations are themselves democratic, and when their decisions are in accordance with explicit standards of public policy, then such organisations do not pose a threat to democracy.[30] It has been claimed that interest groups enhance the democratic process. Their contacts with political parties and civil servants are seen as desirable because, it is asserted, they moderate the system and make it more flexible.[31] Yet strong arguments have been advanced to stress that neo-corporatism is incompatible with democracy.[32] The main arguments against neo-corporatism may be summarised as follows

> it offends against the canons of both liberalism and democracy. It takes economic decision-making out of public debate and surrenders it to elites. It forces people to define themselves as members of a bloc and be counted towards that bloc's strength, even if they dissent from its leaders' policies. And it formally grants the representatives of a few thousand business men parity with those of millions of workers – a gross violation of the principle of one person one vote.[33]

The ideology of neo-corporatism aroused considerable scepticism and dissatisfaction in Europe.[34] The economic benefits of corporatist/neo-corporatist arrangements were also called into question. A particular disadvantage of neo-corporatist arrangements was their tendency to fall apart when confronted by economic crises.[35] Generally, neo-corporatist arrangements were progressively weakened since the downturn in the global economy in 1973 and, towards the end of the 1980s; the prognosis for neo-corporatism was not good.[36]

The neo-corporatism which developed in Ireland during the 1960s and 1970s declined in the early 1980s as the alliance between the government and its social partners became more fragile. This decline was reversed in the late 1980s and early 1990s because Fianna Fáil, as the main party in government, was more inclined than other political parties to favour neo-corporatist policies.[37] Government policy favoured 'participative democracy' which involved greater collaboration between state and voluntary organisations.[38] However, neo-corporatism in Ireland has a very uncertain future.[39] Neo-corporatist initiatives may fail, mainly because of the persistent inability of trade union and employer associations to overcome their sectional interests.[40]

Although neo-corporatist structures and 'understandings' indicate a partial fulfilment of the commission's recommendations this is more apparent than real. The spontaneous growth of vocational organisation did not occur to such an extent that the aspirations of the vocationalists were realised. Instead, what emerged in Ireland was 'an especially virulent breed' of neo-corporatism where the government was unable to fulfil its basic functions.[41] Neo-corporatism was induced, primarily, by successive governments, determined to gain compliance from the social partners, in a state where economic development was stultified by bureaucratic and political overcentralisation. Therefore this type of neo-corporatism was ineffectual on the economic front, and it was tainted with illiberal and undemocratic traits which made it repugnant to the dominant political ethos of a liberal democratic state.

The principle of subsidiarity, so central to the commission's recommendations, has not been implemented. The Irish Episcopal Conference, in its document *Work is the Key: Towards an Economy That Needs Everyone*, has acknowledged the importance of subsidiarity.[42] Nearly fifty years after the commission's findings were published the report entitled *Local Government Reorganisation and Reform* (1991) stressed the need to reform the Irish political system on the basis of the principle of subsidiarity.[43] Unlike the commission's scheme, power would be devolved to local government rather than to vocational organisations. However, there would be 'appropriate linkages with the social partners'.[44] Thus, there could still be constructive interaction between 'functional' democracy and 'geographical' democracy – but of course in a much different way to that envisaged by the commission. The anticipated benefits would include a more robust and highly developed democratic system, a more efficient central government, much greater local initiative, and a better use of public resources. It is highly significant that in some of the more prosperous small states such as Denmark, Norway, Sweden, Finland, Switzerland and Austria the regional and local authorities have controlled a much higher proportion of public expenditure than in Ireland.[45] In Europe the general trend is towards increasing decentralisation of decision-making. The notable exceptions are Britain and Ireland.[46]

Today the need to devolve power and responsibility remains as urgent as ever. In the context of Ireland's membership of the European Union there is considerable concern in this country about the power of bureaucracy and the 'democratic deficit' which has emerged. It is feared that as more and more power shifts to Brussels the people will even become more remote from the decision makers and that their concerns will not get due attention. To allay such fears the principle of subsidiarity has once again been resurrected.[47] This, however, is not due to the influence of Catholic social activists.

Unlike the 1930s the Roman Catholic Church no longer preaches with vigour the virtues of subsidiarity – despite the fact that it still acknowledges the fundamental importance of the principle. Ironically, the church itself, from the mid-nineteenth century, has become increasingly bureaucratised and overcentralised.[48] Episcopal conferences in Brazil, Canada, England, Indonesia, North Africa and Scandinavia have felt it necessary to refer explicitly to the principle of subsidiarity. Local churches made demands for greater autonomy and less interference from Rome. Dissatisfaction was also expressed with the level of consultation and communication between the Vatican and the local churches.[49]

Catholic social teaching has changed substantially since the 1930s. The church no longer preaches the gospel of corporatism, it no longer favours a particular socio-economic system.[50] Developments in the intervening years help to explain the profound change in outlook. Corporatist ideology attracted support when class conflict was a major problem in industrial societies. In the early post World War Two period papal corporatism quickly became much less relevant to social issues because vocational organisations proliferated, strikes became less frequent, unemployment abated, and workers became relatively affluent.[51]

After the Second Vatican Council (1962–1965) there was a substantial change in the intellectual climate of Catholicism. In the 1960s Catholic social teaching changed considerably. The church expressed concern for the disadvantaged and the poor in society but it looked mostly to the social welfare state to alleviate their plight. *Mater et Magistra* (1961), *Populorum Progressio* (1967) and *Laborem Exercens* (1981) are less restrictive on state intervention in social welfare than are *Rerum Novarum* and *Quadragesimo Anno*.[52] *Pacem in Terris* (1963) and *Populorum Progressio* indicated the change of emphasis in the church's concerns – international relations and the Third World respectively. It is highly significant that, in 1971, Pope Paul VI abandoned the attempt to formulate a social document which could be universally applied. He declared that: 'In view of the varied situations in the world, it is difficult to give one teaching to cover them all or to offer a solution which has universal value. This is not our intention or even our mission.'[53]

That the papacy might once again champion the cause of societal corporatism is extremely unlikely. Even if it did so it seems inconceivable that the Catholic hierarchy in Ireland would give active and effective support to the cause. Historical and contemporary observations bestow more than credence to this assertion. In a country which was (and still is) overwhelmingly Roman Catholic it would have been reasonable to expect widespread and active support for Catholic social teaching. That such an expectation remains unfulfilled is not seriously in question. This may be attributed to the persistent tendency of Roman Catholics in Ireland to compartmentalise their beliefs (this of course is not a unique trait of Irish Catholicism). Although Irish Catholics profess loyalty to the church they sometimes repudiate or ignore its claim to speak with authority on particular issues.[54]

Frequently, those who advocated the acceptance and implementation of Catholic social teaching expressed robust religious beliefs, sometimes reinforced by patriotic sentiment, to bolster their message. Eugene Goulding believed that the work of the C.S.V.O.C. was inspired by 'the highest motives of true patriotism, for it seeks to transform society and in particular the industrial system so as to win both back to Christ.'[55] Cardinal John D'Alton, in his Lenten Pastoral (1948), declared that the task of instilling Catholic social principles in Irish trade unionism was part of an ongoing struggle between the forces of Christ and the anti-Christ.[56] Alfred O'Rahilly stated that active support for the social encyclicals offered the most effective means of eliminating the 'lamentable dichotomy' between Catholic action and Catholic belief. But there was a major problem in realising the potential of the encyclicals because

> their full import is not always appreciated, at least by lay audiences. There is a temptation to regard them as pious generalisations without any mandatory relevance to the actual problems, social and political, of daily life . . . we have allowed most of our working lives to become secularised and dechristianised. Religion, many of us layfolk are inclined to think, is an affair of individual piety, chiefly exhibited in church.[57]

No substantial change in attitude has occurred since O'Rahilly made the above observation. Kieran Kennedy highlights how ineffective Christian belief has been in motivating constructive social reform when he states: 'Despite the fact that Ireland still remains an overwhelmingly Christian country, religious motivation has never been strong in regard to wider social responsibility'.[58] The reason for this is elucidated by reference to Frank Duff

> Our Christianity . . . is being understood and practised only in a partial sense, that is as an individualistic religion whereby one beautifies and saves one's own soul. It is not being practised as a social religion, . . . Without the practical living of the full Christian duty the theory is fruitless; without it we are thrown back on the caricature of Christianity.[59]

The Roman Catholic Church still plays a pivotal role in Irish society but its influence has been diminished considerably over the last four decades, especially in the 1990s. The church has failed to promote Christian solidarity and has disillusioned, if not alienated, a large sector of its membership.[60] Over the past twenty years church authorities have issued a series of documents on Christian social responsibility. The most outstanding of these is *Work is the Key: Towards an Economy That Needs Everyone*. However, it is most likely that only a small minority of Catholics has studied the document, and there is little if any evidence of Catholics seriously attempting to practise the underlying principles.

The probability of a Christian renaissance stimulating the development of a new vocationalist order can be dismissed with a reasonable degree of certainty. The prospect of political parties initiating, or attempting to initiate, radical reforms on a corporatist basis can also be confidently dismissed. Some of the fundamentals of Catholic social teaching from the 1930s remain fossilised in the *Constitution of Ireland* (1937) – accounting for a substantial portion of its dormant contents. Although Article 45 was inspired by Catholic social teaching it is merely an aspiration and the principles it expresses are not cognisable by the courts. Doubts have been expressed about its value as a source of guidance for the members of the Oireachtas.[61] Contrary to the provisions of Articles 18 and 19 the notion of a vocationalist Senate remains as mythical as ever.[62] Similarly, Article 15.3 remains unfulfilled.[63]

Is it now time to abandon the idea of a Senate supposedly established to function on a vocational basis? It is difficult to avoid answering in the affirmative. The composition and functioning of the Senate has aroused much criticism since its foundation. In 1958, a Seanad Electoral Law Commission, under the chairmanship of Judge Joseph McCarthy, considered whether its shortcomings could be remedied within the provisions of Articles 18 and 19. After nine months of deliberations the twenty member commission came to no firm conclusions.

In March 1966, the taoiseach, Seán Lemass, disclosed an interest in constitutional change. Shortly before his resignation he established an all-party Committee on the Constitution on which he himself served. The committee was of the opinion that if the Senate was to be retained it did not necessarily follow that it should remain unchanged in regard to its composition and methods of election. The constitution was found to be flexible enough to allow for fundamental change of the Senate by the enactment of ordinary legislation.[64] The committee concluded that 'the principle of a second chamber composed on vocational or functional lines should be preserved'.[65] Yet other statements and observations seem to detract considerably from this conclusion. The committee advised that

> The purpose of the Seanad is to deal with the affairs of the community as a whole and not to look after the interests of any special groups or associations. The individual Senators should be capable of taking a broad view of public affairs as a whole, and not restrict themselves to their own sectional interests.[66]

The committee did not recommend that all Senators be elected on a vocational or functional basis.[67] There seemed to be an underlying antipathy towards vocationalism and this was nowhere more strongly indicated when the committee opposed the idea of activating article 19 of the constitution. The stated reason for rejection was mainly on the basis that

> . . . if such an arrangement were introduced the political parties would find it necessary to take a much greater interest in the internal affairs of the Nominating Bodies. The dangers of introducing unnecessary party-political activity in commercial, professional, vocational and cultural bodies has often been adverted to in the past and we are fully satisfied that it should be avoided at all costs.[68]

This statement has implications far beyond the composition and functioning of the Senate and represents a major problem in reconciling vocationalism with parliamentary democracy. Vocational organisations or corporations endowed with statutory powers would be vulnerable to infiltration and manipulation by the political parties. Conversely, sectional interests might exercise undue influence on political parties. Either of these developments would work against the national interest.

If corporatism in some shape or form is to contribute to economic growth and to the consolidation of democracy then its manifestation at national level has to be paralleled by similar developments at local and regional level. The initial steps of constructive change would involve a restructuring of the state and 'raising the standards of citizenship by forging a sense of community'.[69] But creating a sense of community has proved to be an extremely difficult task. The experience of Muintir na Tíre bears testimony to this problem. The organisation declined from its peak strength of nearly 600 registered branches in the 1960s to 135 registered branches in 1994.[70] Unfortunately, as a community development organisation, Muintir na Tíre has been unable to secure widespread public support for its initiatives.[71]

In order to induce greater self-sufficiency at local and regional level power and responsibility have to be devolved from central government. Decentralisation would not inevitably lead to dynamic community development but it is an essential prerequisite for the long-term improvement of national performance. Whether or not corporatism has any positive role to play in this process is open to debate. Societal corporatism or vocationalism is desirable if it promotes social harmony and reduces the adverse effects of conflict between the various interest groups. It is desirable if it promotes self-sufficiency at local and regional level through the mechanism of co-operation. Yet it is fraught with the risks of creating divisions in the community by rigidly compartmentalising people into different functional groups. Contrary to the approach of the Commission on Vocational Organisation, a neatly symmetrical and hierarchical network of vocational organisations cannot be devised from the beginning.

R.J.P. Mortished, who enjoyed a distinguished career in the International Labour Organisation, informed the commission that it was futile to expect the majority of citizens to take an active and continuous interest in national and international affairs. However he believed that most citizens had a natural interest in 'parish pump politics'. He felt that 'political activity and training ought therefore to begin with the parish pump as centre, and develop outwards'.[72] Vocational organisation or societal corporatism too should develop from the 'parish pump' outwards if it is to succeed. Unfortunately the tendency since 1922, in Ireland, has been away from the parish centre.

Canon John Hayes believed that the social virtues, especially charity and patriotism, begin at parish level. He reasoned that

> . . . the person who despises those of his fellow countrymen whom he knows best – namely his fellow parishioners – must have a peculiarly agile mind if he is ardently devoted to the rest of his fellow-countrymen whom he knows but little or not at all.[73]

A core element of his philosophy was the fusion of Christian values and practical patriotism.

Christians, as members of communities, give practical expression to their faith through community action. Ideally, Christians endeavour to promote love, justice and peace, hence the description of the church as a corporate community. The theological basis for this outlook is as follows

> though Christian faith is an eminently personal act that relates the believer to God, it is never the act of an individual apart from the Church as a community of faith. Thus it is evident that the Christian vocation to work for greater justice and peace in society must be a communal undertaking.[74]

However the prospect of Christian renewal ushering in an era of spontaneous societal corporatism seems even more remote than an elevated standard of citizenship. Neo-corporatism has been recast in the late twentieth century and lacks continuity with the corporatism of the 1930s. The new neo-corporatism has been based on economic planning and is not preoccupied with justice. Trade unions and employers are manipulated for the purpose of stability. In Ireland it has consisted of rationalising the pressure group process rather than reforming the socio-economic order.

The Commission on Vocational Organisation proposed the establishment of an elaborate network of vocational organisations which contradicted its expressed wish that vocational bodies should develop spontaneously from existing institutions and organisations, with minimal involvement from the state. The organisational structure was hopelessly impracticable while the 'organic' concept had considerable potential to stimulate a sense of community based on consensus, voluntary effort, and self-sufficiency. This potential is still unfulfilled, and is likely to remain so, until local and regional communities are given more control and responsibility for their own affairs.

Conclusion

Popular support for vocationalism, even in its heyday, was superficial rather than deep-rooted. The conditions that were so conducive to its popularisation were not enough to create a potent force for social reform on the basis of Catholic social principles. When *Quadragesimo Anno* was published in 1931 social Catholicism in Ireland was about to enter a phase of rapid growth. The movement, however, was weak on the intellectual front and it did not have sufficient experience of examining Irish social problems on the basis of Catholic social principles. Consequently, *Quadragesimo Anno* was inappropriately applied, by the vocationalists, to address a number of problems which were not of primary importance in the new state. The lack of vocational organisation, the inadequacies of public administration, and the threat of unchristian ideologies were not amongst Ireland's most serious problems in the 1930s.[1]

Vocationalists were hostile to many modern ideas and developments – this militated greatly against the realisation of their aspirations. Egalitarian and liberal concepts, so prominent in the rhetoric of the French Revolution, were denounced. Free market capitalism and socialism were also condemned. Vocationalists even went so far as to denigrate English parliamentary democracy upon which the Irish political system was based. Consequently, serious doubts were raised about the compatibility of vocationalism with parliamentary democracy, notwithstanding the protestations of the vocationalists to the contrary. The outcome of this was that vocationalism did not command widespread and sustained support. The Catholic majority accepted their church's spiritual authority but on political issues they felt free to make independent decisions. Daniel O'Connell's maxim, 'our religion from Rome, our politics from Ireland', influenced political opinion far more than the papal encyclicals did.[2]

The implementation of vocationalist proposals depended on the commitment of a well-organised pressure group. However, in the late 1930s social Catholicism in Ireland failed to make any significant progress. Those who preached the gospel of corporatism encountered an overwhelming inertia. Alfred O'Rahilly indicated their sense of frustration when he stated in a Radio Eireann broadcast on 20 March 1938

> There is increasing talk of Catholic social principles. Now if there is any one point that emerges clearly and urgently from the Papal Encyclicals, it is the necessity of a functional organisation of society. The passages stare us in the face. Are we ever going to do anything except to read books and to give lectures? An ounce of practical application would be worth a ton of talk.[3]

The vocational movement was incapable of making significant progress and relied on state assistance to achieve its objectives. The *Constitution of Ireland* (1937), drafted under the aegis of Éamon de Valera, reaffirmed the nation's acceptance of Catholic moral and social principles. It expressed support for the vocationalist concept but de Valera, as his subsequent behaviour was to prove, was not committed to promoting the proliferation and development of vocational organisations. The constitutional expression of the vocationalist idea was due mainly to political considerations. De Valera

> could hardly publicly denounce an ideology commended by the papacy. He would instead smother it in his embraces, by incorporating vocational representation into his new constitution. It would have been difficult for him to avoid this in any case. If Article 45 of the 1922 Free State constitution had remained a dead letter in practice, it did genuflect in a vocationalist direction. Eliminating all reference to the subject in the 1937 constitution, when so much else from the Free State constitution was retained, might have provoked awkward questions.[4]

Provision was made in the constitution for the establishment of a Senate on a vocationalist basis but the vocationalist ideal was not adhered to and the Senate functioned instead as a plaything of the political parties – with Fianna Fáil as the dominant player. The priority given to party political interests indicates that de Valera had little regard for vocationalism. There is, perhaps, another dimension to his thinking worthy of consideration – his capacity for self-deception.

> He devised an electoral system for the Senate that invited corruption, and responded to pleas for reform by delicately holding his nostrils. Like his countrymen in general, he combined a rigid concept of private morality with a more selective one of public morality . . . Protected from the contagion of evidence by the metallic carapace of his self-righteousness, he had the invaluable capacity of assuming that what he did not wish to see did not exist. Incapable of hypocrisy, he had a highly refined capacity for self-deception.[5]

De Valera established the Commission on Vocational Organisation in January 1939 but an examination of his motives will indicate that he had not changed his attitude towards vocationalism. His apparent benevolence was probably little more than a cautious strategy – designed to keep the vocationalists busy and safely removed from making trouble for the government at a time of impending war in Europe.[6] The size and composition of the commission made consensus extremely difficult to achieve, composed as it was of 25 members with 'strong-willed personalities' under the chairmanship of Dr Michael Browne who 'might not succeed in always steering the smoothest course'.[7] Furthermore, the magnitude and complexity of the task facing it was unprecedented.[8] Even if the commission managed to produce a report the government was not obliged to implement its recommendations.[9]

The vocationalists were singularly disadvantaged. It is likely that de Valera set up the commission to manoeuvre them into submitting detailed proposals that would expose them to sustainable criticism on a broad range of issues. As if to ensure that the commission would not produce a satisfactory report de Valera appointed only three members with expertise in agricultural matters while at the same time stressing that if the commission failed to devise a satisfactory scheme of rural organisation its findings would be unsatisfactory.

Political expediency accounts for most of the explanation of de Valera's response to vocationalist demands. His *modus operandi* may have been considerably influenced by the political philosophy of Niccolò Machiavelli.[10] However, more than political factors have to be considered if a full explanation of de Valera's reasoning is to be attempted. It seems that vocationalism appealed to his intellectual curiosity and he may also have hoped to extract some practical benefits from vocationalist proposals. Furthermore, he was a devout Roman Catholic and the dictates of his conscience may have compelled him to respond positively to demands for an extensive investigation into the possibilities of promoting vocational organisation in Ireland. The fact that the commission faced an almost impossible task would not have troubled him – he was simply complying with the wishes of the vocationalists by granting them the broad-based enquiry which they had requested. The failure of the commission to devise a satisfactory scheme could only have confirmed de Valera's opinion that vocationalism, although based on Catholic social teaching, was impracticable and incompatible with parliamentary democracy. He could therefore decisively reject, with a clear and informed conscience, an ideology which was not clearly based on Catholic dogma. Perhaps he also considered the political philosophy of Niccolò Machiavelli when the Florentine advised

> . . . there is nothing more difficult to execute, nor more dubious of success, nor more dangerous to administer than to introduce a new order of things; for he who introduces it has all those who profit from the old order as his enemies, and he has only lukewarm allies in all those who might profit from the new . . . many writers have imagined for themselves republics and principalities that have never been seen nor known to exist in reality; for there is such a gap between how one lives and how one ought to live that anyone who abandons what is done for what ought to be done learns his ruin rather than his preservation: for a man who wishes to profess goodness at all times will come to ruin among so many who are not so good . . .[11]

De Valera would have appreciated that, although vocationalism was the pursuit of the ideal, politics was the pursuit of the possible.[12] His version of vocationalism was politically innocuous – it relied almost entirely on voluntary commitment and posed no problems for the democratic process. His outlook contrasted sharply with that of the Commission on Vocational Organisation.

The commission differed from the vocationalists of the 1930s in that it formulated proposals which had been laboriously researched. This was in contrast to the pronouncements of the earlier advocates of corporatism who all too often indulged in vague generalisations and frequently failed to subject their utopian visions to any degree of critical scrutiny. However, despite the broadness of its composition, its assiduous research and the large volume of evidence before it, the commission made serious errors of judgement in constructing its proposals, mainly because of the preconceived opinions of the majority of its members. When describing the conditions necessary for the success of vocational organisation the commission was clearly influenced by *Quadragesimo Anno*. It believed that vocational organisation would foster justice, order, efficiency, freedom, brotherhood and social service. The commission was clearly motivated by Christian philosophy as enunciated by Popes Leo XIII and Pius XI. Vocational organisation was not impracticable in any form but the fundamental weakness with the commission's plan was that it depended on a level of Christian commitment which did not exist in the real world. Those who criticised the report did not believe that powerful vocational organisations would subordinate their vested interests to the common good.

The commission failed to give adequate consideration to some of the shortcomings and problems that were likely to arise from the formation of a new vocational order. Its quixotic outlook is, perhaps, understandable in view of international developments at the time. Economic difficulties, war and social upheaval were unprecedented in devastating effect and magnitude. An awareness of all this tended to intensify aspirations for socio-economic reconstruction. In a world of great uncertainty the concept of harmony and co-operation had a powerful appeal in some circles. *Quadragesimo Anno* was regarded by many people, especially Roman Catholics, as the Christian alternative. It was regarded as a document which outlined the ideological basis of a system that would promote economic prosperity while at the same time safeguarding human rights. Vocationalism emphasised the unity of society, but, ironically, it presented the risk of creating deep divisions because well organised sectional interests, especially those with statutory powers, would have tended to counteract social cohesion. It is particularly noteworthy that civil servants in the Department of Finance criticised the commission's plan for placing individuals in rigid compartments on the basis that it would have led to the creation of limited allegiances. They anticipated that this would be counterproductive to national unity.

The various groups and organisations which gave evidence to the commission had vigorously defended their own interests.[13] Fianna Fáil adopted a similar stance and defended itself against the reforms envisaged by the vocationalists. As the largest political party in the state it had the most to lose because the new order, as visualized by the commission, would have diminished the power of political parties. Central government would be weakened as power was devolved to vocational organisations established on a statutory basis. Civil servants also had their interests to defend. They pointed out to government ministers the many assumptions, prejudices and errors of detail in the commission's report. The report had harshly judged them and if its proposals were implemented many civil servants would have been made redundant. Fianna Fáil therefore found a willing ally in the civil service.

De Valera adopted an uncompromising attitude towards the report but this was moderated by a cautious strategy. He was not as forthright as Seán Lemass in his public statements. Evidently, he still feared that the vocationalists could create serious problems for his government. He was determined to shelve the commission's recommendations while at the same time claiming that his government approved of vocationalism in principle. His response to demands for the establishment of a vocational council of education indicated a rigid adherence to the principles of parliamentary democracy. His strong views, on the powers and duties of government and parliament, left very little room for the devolution of power to a network of vocational organisations endowed with statutory powers.

The commission had failed to explain, satisfactorily, how its scheme could be applied to Irish needs and problems. Like the vocationalists of the previous decade, it did not succeed in clearly demonstrating how vocationalism could be reconciled with parliamentary democracy. The advocacy of societal corporatism by the papacy, and by an influential group of Irish Catholics, undoubtedly had a considerable impact upon Irish political opinion but doubts about the compatibility of vocationalism with parliamentary democracy had not been quelled. The lack of a vigorous commitment from the Catholic hierarchy could only have served to reinforce the widespread ambivalence towards vocationalism. This in turn was conducive to politicians and political parties making a mere plaything of the vocationalist ideal.

In the absence of spontaneous development the vocationalists came to rely almost entirely on the state to set up the complex organisational network which had been described in the *Commission on Vocational Organisation Report*. It was indeed ironic that they had come to rely so heavily on the state which they held in deep distrust. The state did not oblige them. There was no significant degree of genuine support from any of the political parties for the commission's proposals – this made it relatively easy for de Valera to shelve the report. Neither, it seems, was there an economic or social basis for the implementation of the report. According to Philippe C. Schmitter, societal corporatism 'appears to be the concomitant, if not ineluctable, component of the postliberal, advanced capitalist, organised democratic welfare state'.[14] Ireland in the 1940s and 1950s could not be described as 'postliberal' or 'advanced capitalist' and its social welfare system lagged behind those of the more prosperous countries of western Europe.

It would have been reasonable to expect that in a country, which was predominantly Catholic, that Catholic social teaching would have had a powerful impact – but this did not happen. The outlook of the Catholic bishops remained fundamentally unchanged since the foundation of the state. Their main emphasis was on moral codes of conduct and the social teaching of the church was neglected. The response of the Catholic clergy to vocationalist exhortations was matched by a similar reaction from the laity. The potency of church social teaching was diminished by the overriding desire of most Catholics to pursue salvation rather than to practice the social aspects of their religion. This became clearly evident when the Catholic Societies' Vocational Organisation Conference failed to rally public support for vocationalist reforms.

Changes in Catholic social teaching after the pontificate of Pius XI militated against the acceptance of vocationalism. The demise of corporatism in early post-war Europe could not have escaped the attention of the Catholic hierarchy and Catholic social activists. Furthermore, it is most likely that the majority of politicians were conscious of post-war political trends. Vocationalism was obsolete, it no longer warranted serious consideration.

The support of Éamon de Valera had been crucial for the realisation of vocationalist aspirations. He dominated his colleagues more than Cosgrave ever did in his time and he led a united party accustomed to his strong leadership.[15] No policy, requiring active and long-term government support, had any chance of success if he opposed it. He held the reins of power continuously from 1932 to 1948 – these were crucial years for the realisation of vocationalist objectives. His attitude and actions were therefore of central importance in analysing the abysmal failure of the vocationalist movement.

Some ideas and recommendations outlined by the Commission on Vocational Organisation were at least worthy of serious consideration and could have been implemented with some modifications.[16] But the scheme in its entirety was not feasible due to a variety of political, social and economic reasons. The new vocationalist system would have disrupted the workings of the civil service and compromised the sovereignty of parliament. The commission failed to take due cognisance of the reasons for the abolition of the Free State Senate. The national vocational assembly and its ancillary organisations would have, like the old Senate, obstructed the will of the people by coming into conflict with the Dáil.

The state and its organisations had functioned to the reasonable satisfaction of the majority of the Irish people. Vocational organisation on a scale envisaged by the commission had no provable benefit.[17] If a Fianna Fáil or a coalition government had attempted to construct a new vocationalist order, as specified by the commission, it is most likely that there would have been an overwhelming reaction against it. The state was already in place. There were checks and balances on state power. This was manifested in a number of ways. There was for example, a system of electoral representation, judicial review, and the responsibility of government to parliament. Parliamentary democracy was a central feature of Irish political culture and commanded the support of the vast majority of the Irish people.

Notwithstanding the fact that the majority of the members of the Commission on Vocational Organisation embraced a flawed socio-political philosophy it is important to acknowledge that they were, in general, conscientious individuals driven by a sense of urgency, justice and purpose. They were anxious to stimulate constructive reforms at a time of great uncertainty and gave generously of their time in the public interest. The majority of them were public-spirited men and women, motivated by Christian convictions, who undertook a task of enormous magnitude and complexity. The political and economic systems which they criticised were far from perfect. They deserved better treatment from politicians and civil servants than they received.

A number of issues which were addressed by the *Commission on Vocational Organisation Report* have persisted as matters of concern – issues such as the importance of the partnership between capital and labour; the role of the state in regulating social services and the economy; and the principle of subsidiarity which has re-emerged as an important issue in European Union policy. Despite the untenable scheme proposed by the commission some of the issues which it dealt with will continue to be relevant to the social, economic and political aspects of Irish national life.

APPENDIX ONE

Members of the Commission on Vocational Organisation, 1939–1944

Chairman: Dr Michael Browne (Bishop of Galway).

Churches and Universities Group
- Rev Edward J. Coyne S.J., President of the Irish Agricultural Organisation Society.
- The Right Rev Thomas A. Harvey (Church of Ireland), Bishop of Cashel and Emly, Waterford and Lismore.
- Rev J.A.H. Irwin, a republican Presbyterian minister and a friend of de Valera.
- Professor Alfred O'Rahilly, University College, Cork.
- Professor Michael Tierney, University College, Dublin.

Labour
- Louie Bennett, General Secretary of the Irish Women Workers' Union.
- Senator Seán Campbell, Treasurer of the Dublin Typographical Society.
- Senator Thomas Foran, President of the Irish Transport and General Workers' Union. He resigned on 17 April 1939 and was replaced by Luke J. Duffy, a senior member of the Labour Party.
- James Larkin (Senior), General Secretary of the Irish Workers' Union of Ireland.

Employers
- G.H.C. Crampton
- Patrick Gallagher
- Francis A. Lowe

- Sir Alexander Maguire
- C.P. McCarthy
- Algernon A. Odlum, President of the Irish Flour Millers' Association.
- Timothy O'Mahony
- Stephen O'Mara
- James J. Walsh

Agriculture

- Rev John M. Hayes, founder of Muintir na Tíre.
- Dr Henry Kennedy, General Secretary of the Irish Agricultural Organisation Society Ltd.
- Richard Wilson

Miscellaneous

- Henry P. Boland
- Lucy Franks
- Mary MacGeehin[1]

Patrick A. O'Toole was appointed as secretary of the commission at a later date.[2] Premises for the commission were provided at no. 2, Merrion Square, Dublin.

APPENDIX TWO

The Report of the Commission on Vocational Organisation

Throughout the 1930s the vocationalists had proclaimed policies which were often generalised and vague. The *Commission on Vocational Organisation Report* was far more detailed and considered on the subject of vocational organisation than any other document of its kind. Unlike so many advocates of vocationalism, members of the commission carried out detailed research and acknowledged some of the problems inherent in implementing the proposals. An indication of the scope, variety and complexity of the commission's task is provided by the fact that the analytical table of contents, which preceded the 539 page report, extended to over 40 pages.

The report was divided into four main sections. The commission had endeavoured to examine the entire organisation of Irish social and economic life and attempted to present a master plan for a new structure of governance for Irish society.[1] It was required to report on the practicability of developing vocational organisation, taking due cognisance of the social and economic conditions at the time. Therefore, the commission felt compelled to undertake a study of three preparatory topics which corresponded to the first three sections of the report.

Part I examined the theory and history of vocational organisation. The taoiseach, Éamon de Valera, had attended the first meeting of the commission and had told those assembled that vocational organisation did not pertain to the political organisation of the state. He described it as an organisation of society 'in which people who are engaged in similar callings or professions naturally gravitate together to promote the interests of those professions or callings'.[2] The commission did not feel bound to accept the taoiseach's definition and endeavoured to construct one of its own. Vocational organisation was taken to mean 'a form of organisation of human beings based on their occupation or vocation and designed to enable them to fulfil some activity concerned with the occupation.' It was democratic in form; its members would form 'an organic body with power to speak and act for the vocation'.[3] Although the commission recognised the difference between vocational and functional organisations it treated them as being synonymous for practical purposes.[4] As if it recognised the inadequacy of its own definition the commission felt that it would be easier to enlighten the ordinary citizen by summarising the essential features of vocational organisations.[5] The commission recognised that there were different levels in vocational organisation. At the highest level, a vocational organisation would defend and promote the interests of all members of a vocation, trade, or profession as a whole. It would guide the policies and activities of a vocational group so that it did not conflict with the interests of other vocational groups and it would take care to promote the common good of the community.

The commission then proceeded to discuss the legal status and powers of vocational bodies. All vocational organisations started out as voluntary associations.[6] The commission emphasised the importance of giving legal or corporate status to vocational organisations. The corporatist system was not new. The universities, the Incorporated Law Society and the Irish Medical Registration Council were all examples of the incorporation of vocational bodies. The state endowed vocational bodies with legal status which conferred on them certain legal rights. Specific legal responsibilities and duties were also imposed on them in regard to their own members and also certain public duties were specified. The fact that the state had granted legal status and authority to a vocational organisation did not mean that the corporate body ceased to be free from bureaucratic control and political interference. On the contrary, the corporatist system helped to protect vocational bodies, and the community at large, from bureaucracy and tyranny.[7] The commission did not approve of state corporatism because this political system violated the autonomy of vocational bodies by integrating them into its administrative and executive machinery.[8]

In the second chapter of part 1 the commission explained the historical background of vocational organisation, ranging from the guilds of the eighth to the eighteenth centuries and covering the trade unions, employers' associations and other vocational organisations of the nineteenth and twentieth centuries. What emerged was a glorification of medieval society and institutions. Medieval craft guilds were not invested with 'a halo of economic chivalry' but they were regarded as excellent examples of vocational organisation.[9] Trade unions, friendly societies, professional associations, co-operative societies and employers' associations were all seen as the modern successors to the guilds of the Middle Ages.[10]

Part two of the report is entirely concerned with the foreign dimension of the commission's inquiry. The commission was required to ascertain the potential for the development of vocational organisation in Ireland. With this objective in mind it set out to discover the kinds or varieties of vocational organisations which existed abroad and their relationships to different political and social environments. Twelve countries were studied; these were Italy, Portugal, Sweden, New Zealand, Denmark, Finland, Great Britain, Belgium, The Netherlands, France, Germany and Russia. These twelve states were categorised into five different groups. The countries were chosen, not just for their similarities to Ireland but also for their differences. For example, Britain, Belgium, the Netherlands and France were all parliamentary democracies like Ireland but were all far more industrialised. Denmark and Finland were of interest because, like Ireland, their economies were mainly agricultural. Russia and Germany contrasted with Ireland in that they were governed by single-party dictatorial regimes. Part two of the report showed that, despite the differences between these countries, a considerable amount of vocational organisation had developed in all of them. However, in totalitarian states its independence was limited and it was made subservient to the political objectives of the party in power.[11]

Part three of the report was a detailed study of vocational organisations which existed in Ireland at the time. The survey was guided by 'the division of the functional life of a country which has been more or less recognised internationally for statistical purposes'.[12] Separate chapters were devoted to the study of vocational organisation in

- the professions,
- agriculture,
- industry,
- commerce,
- transport,
- finance,
- personal services,
- public administration and social services.

The commission concluded that vocational organisation at the time existed in almost every sector of social and economic life in Ireland and that it served a useful and practical purpose.[13] However, the commission noted many defects and much incompleteness and stressed the need to promote the development of voluntary organisation in all areas of economic and social activity. It also examined the legal status of various institutions and organisations, their rights, duties, privileges and functions. The commission investigated the development of schemes to plan, regulate and direct industrial activities. It concluded that the government planning which had been tried was totally inadequate, and that it was fundamentally flawed because it neglected the necessary unity of the economic structure.[14]

The report was not only important for its analysis of what was wrong with Irish society; it was more significant for the remedies that it proposed. The recommendations of the commission are contained in part four of the report and this section proved to be the most controversial. The commission, mindful of its terms of reference, attempted to devise the best means to promote vocational organisation and to specify the rights, powers, and duties that should be conferred or imposed on vocational bodies, and their relationship to the Oireachtas and government. It was convinced by the outcome of its inquiries that vocational organisation was not only practicable but that 'its possibilities for social good are very great'.[15]

The commission submitted detailed recommendations under the same eight headings that had been used in part three. One uniform system was not proposed for the main branches of social and economic life because each of the main sectors was so different in function, needs and outlook. Therefore, a different organisational structure was necessary. This was in conformity with the organic concept, deemed so essential for the development of vocational organisation. The commission believed that the future development of vocational organisation would depend much more on the individual vocations and the community than on state assistance. Nevertheless, some encouragement from the state was necessary.[16]

In outlining the conditions necessary for the development of vocational organisation, the commission referred to *Quadragesimo Anno* to bolster the theoretical basis of its recommendations. In the preamble to the recommendations five main purposes, common to all forms of vocational organisation, were identified.[17] These involved the promotion of

- justice,
- order,
- efficiency,

- freedom,
- the ideal of brotherhood and social services.

The commission asserted that the alternatives to vocational organisation were either competitive anarchy or state regimentation. It had reported that bureaucracy was the main defect which it detected in Irish government. In part one of the report the undemocratic nature of an expanding bureaucracy had been emphasised. The ability of a democratically elected government to introduce and implement new policies was 'very seriously limited' by the administrative power of civil servants.[18]

In part four of the report the commission described what was wrong with the civil service which it equated with bureaucracy. It pointed out that those who entered the civil service were very young and that consequently they did not have any technical knowledge of industry or business. There was an excessive commitment to recording of decisions and filing. This generated bulky files and made for slowness of decisions. A minister was liable to be questioned in the Dáil and exposed to public criticism for the actions of any of his officials and this made civil servants extremely careful and more inclined to do nothing than to take a risk which might be considered reasonable in the business world.[19] The excess of caution that caused delays and inertia was further aggravated by a lack of individual responsibility. Responsibility was diffused because officials shared the task of formulating specific proposals. A shield of anonymity that protected civil servants facilitated the absence of individual responsibility. Except for the secretaries of the various government departments civil servants could not be discussed personally in the Oireachtas and they were unknown to the vast majority of the general public.

In theory, a minister was responsible for all the actions of the civil servants within his department. In reality the size and complexity of a government department was so great that his control was substantially diminished and the powers of the senior officials were proportionately increased. Therefore, higher civil servants exercised considerable power without corresponding responsibility. Civil servants enjoyed security of tenure provided that they were of good behaviour and they were entitled to a pension on retirement. They were employed under conditions of 'comfort and convenience'.[20] Unlike those in the competitive business world their livelihood was not directly and continually dependent on their own endeavours. Surprisingly, the commission had some nice things to say about civil servants. In the report it was acknowledged that Irish civil servants were highly educated and had a well-deserved reputation for integrity.[21] However, these benign attitudes were transient and were overshadowed by the harsh criticism of bureaucracy that was taken as synonymous with the civil service.

The commission found that civil service procedures were not suitable for the efficient management and planning of the national economy because of the following defects in the system

- a rigidity shown in the tendency to interpret regulations in a narrow legalistic manner, to adhere fixedly to precedent and to refuse to create a new precedent or to experiment;
- a lack of personal responsibility and of inducement to produce results: where remuneration is not dependent on results, either negatively or positively, there is a temptation to adopt the easiest or most convenient course rather than the best;
- a lack of close and effective contact between the official and those affected by his decision . . .[22]

The absence of economic efficiency associated with the growth of bureaucratic power, was not the only major consideration. Of grave importance were the infringements of liberty and the violation of democratic rights as power shifted more and more from the political executive to the bureaucrats. The spectre of totalitarianism was raised and the teaching of *Quadragesimo Anno* was echoed again as the over-burdened state became increasingly interventionist in the social and economic affairs of its citizens. The ultimate scenario depicted was bribery, corruption and favouritism on a grand scale.

The commission did not advocate an unqualified acceptance of *laissez-faire* as a means of counteracting the evils of bureaucracy. It did not question state control. Instead it questioned the nature of state control when it declared 'bureaucracy is not identical with State control. It is but one form or method of State control'. State control was justified only 'where it is necessary for the defence of the good of the people'.[23] The commission then asked itself was there any alternative to bureaucracy and proceeded to devise an elaborate answer. It was acknowledged that the increase of state intervention, in the economic and social affairs of its citizens in recent years, was mostly attributable to public demand which was motivated by a desire to protect and promote the common good.[24] Now that state control was recognised as necessary, how should it be exercised? The commission recommended that the state should act as much as possible through vocational bodies as an alternative to bureaucratic control. Vocational organisations, adequately representative of their respective vocations, were to help the government in two ways: (1) by giving advice, and (2) by assisting with the regulation and control of private enterprise to an extent necessary for the promotion of the common good.[25]

The commission noted that the state already operated through vocational bodies. The professions provided an encouraging precedent for self-regulation by vocational organisation without expense to the taxpayer and without jeopardising the rights of the state. The commission then advised that the same principle should be applied to other socio-economic activities such as agriculture, industry, and commerce.[26] In amplification of this proposal it constructed, in theory, an elaborate hierarchy of interlocking vocational authorities.

Each trade, craft, profession and industry was to have its own vocational organisation and the organisations, consisting of both employers and employees, would represent the views and provide for the needs of their respective vocations. Professions or industries with overlapping interests were to have joint councils. For example, a cereals council would include representatives of farmers, millers, bakers, milling and baking operatives, brewers, distillers, and domestic consumers.[27] Above these councils were to be six assemblies covering a wider range of economic activities.[28] These multi-vocational organisations would serve the need for a higher form of unity and co-ordination. Each main group was provided with a representative body as follows

- The professional commission,
- The national agricultural conference,
- The national industrial conference,
- The national commercial conference,
- The national transport council,
- The national finance council.

The function of these middle-tier organisations, such as the national industrial conference or the national agricultural conference, was to act through their governing bodies as a court of appeal for lower bodies, to settle their disputes and to co-ordinate their plans. It was intended that all these bodies would be national in extent and constructed on a democratic basis.[29] Each body would represent all the vocational elements within its sphere of influence.

In order to prevent any conflict of interests arising between the six principal occupational groups, a national vocational assembly was recommended. Its three main functions were those of co-ordination, consultation, and planning.[30] Its function of co-ordination would involve the promotion of harmony and co-operation between vocational organisations. Each of the six principal occupational groups could not act in complete isolation; price levels and wage rates in one sector might seriously affect the others. The national vocational assembly, at the apex of the vocational hierarchy, would serve as the final court of appeal when disputes arose concerning vocational matters. The six national representative bodies were to elect 100 members to the assembly, and these 100 in turn would elect a further 20 to make a total membership of 120.[31]

The assembly would operate through a governing body of not more than 24 persons and a national vocational office with a full-time director and staff.[32] It was to be invested with authority to assume responsibility for the active and ambitious management of the national economy in conjunction with the Oireachtas and government. With regard to the function of consultation it was recommended that the assembly should be recognised as the consultative body on general economic or vocational issues and that the government should seek advice and information from it concerning the most efficient way of attaining economic objectives. The commission was careful to state that

> In the body politic, the electors, Oireachtas and Government share the supreme responsibility for determining the main principles of policy. The Vocational Assembly should advise on the best means of implementing it and so provide most valuable and powerful collaboration.[33]

In compliance with the last requirement of its terms of reference the commission advocated that enabling legislation should be passed to authorise the establishment of the national councils, conferences, commission, and assembly that it had described in detail.[34] The commission urged that these bodies should have authority conferred on them to exercise their functions in accordance with the recommendations of the report.

Democratic liberties and economic efficiency were seen as inextricably connected. In order to secure maximum efficiency it was deemed necessary to undertake an ambitious planning programme but the civil service was hopelessly ill-adapted to meet the challenge because it was inflexible, lacked initiative and was cocooned from the economic rigours of society at large. In contrast, the national vocational assembly was ideally suited to the planning process. However, it was noted that the word 'planning' was unpopular and conjured up images of compulsion and dictatorship. It was argued that planning could be more effectively implemented by a dictator who compelled co-operation and stifled opposition. Conversely, a democracy was handicapped where co-operation was voluntary and criticism was allowed. At this point the question was asked 'Should it (i.e. planning) then be regarded as impossible?'. If the answer was in the affirmative then this indicated a bleak future for democracies where economic security was desired in conjunction with civil rights.

It was imperative that democracies should plan economic activities in order to make the optimum use of resources while at the same time conforming to the dictates of social justice. Therefore planning had to be based on consensus rather than being imposed on the people by a small minority. The commission could not see how it was possible for the nation to achieve its full potential for economic development other than through the mechanism of a national vocational assembly that would be composed of representatives of every sector of economic life within the state.[35]

The commission pointed out that a network of vocational organisations could co-exist with a political system which was not based on vocationalism. Vocational organisation was not dependent on any form of government and was compatible with democracy, especially since it was a system of social and economic self-government. It was emphasised that the recommendations in the report pertained strictly to the social and economic life of the country and the commission 'endeavoured to keep all irrelevant political influence from impinging on this vocational structure and to keep it, in turn, from becoming involved in political affairs'.[36] In accordance with this objective it was recommended that politicians should be excluded from rural and vocational organisations.[37]

In the concluding paragraphs of the report some potential criticisms of its findings were considered. In paragraph 716 it was denied that vocational organisations would become infected with a bureaucratic mentality. To ensure against this the tenure of officials was to depend on performance. Officials would be promptly removed if satisfactory results were not forthcoming. In paragraph 717 the commission denied that the new vocational organisations would lead to a duplication of staffs and services because of overlap in functions between some sectors of the civil service and the new organisations. This would, if true, lead to an intolerable added financial burden on taxpayers and consumers generally. Such a possibility was denied on the basis that vocational bodies could operate certain public services more efficiently than the civil service, thus facilitating a reduction of the civil service. In paragraph 718, the commission emphasised the need to reduce staff numbers in the civil service in such an eventuality. A third criticism considered by the commission concerned the possible formation of monopolies which would be detrimental to small employers, independent craftsmen and consumers. The commission believed that the various national conferences and the national vocational assembly would provide a safeguard against the growth of monopolies, preventing unfair practices where some trades were better organised than others.[38]

Finally, in paragraph 720 of its report, the commission emphasised that its research was unprecedented because of the scope and complexity of the investigations involved. It had carried out a difficult and arduous task. There were bound to be minor errors but the commission asserted that 'The broad outlines of our survey are substantially correct, and neither they nor the principles on which our recommendations are based can be invalidated by errors of detail'. The commission, however, had made a number of serious mistakes and it was these, rather than errors of detail, which made it vulnerable to the harsh criticism of those who were resolutely opposed to radical reforms based on vocationalist proposals.

APPENDIX THREE

Constituent Associations of the Catholic Societies' Vocational Organisation Conference

- Academy of Christian Art
- An Ríoghacht
- Aurora Society, Blackrock College
- Catholic Association for International Relations
- Catholic Cinema and Theatre Patrons' Association
- Catholic Young Men's Society
- Christian Brothers (James' St Schools) Past Pupils Union
- Crumlin Catholic Action Association
- Guild of Catholic Lawyers
- Guilds of Regnum Christi
- International Catholic Girls' Protection Society
- Irish Guild of Catholic Nurses
- Knights of St Columbanus
- Leo League of Social Reform
- Maria Duce
- Mirror of Justice Praesidium, Legion of Mary
- St Peter's Past Pupils Union.[1]

Notes

TERMS AND ABBREVIATIONS

1 Social Catholicism is defined in: (1) Alfred Diamant, *Austrian Catholics and the Social Question 1918–1933* (University of Florida Press Monographs, Social Sciences, No. 2, Spring 1959), p 4; and (2) A.R. Vidler, *A Century of Social Catholicism 1820–1920* (S.P.C.K., London, 1964), pp ix–xii.
2 Alfred Diamant, *op. cit.*, p 4.
3 There was a slight difference in meaning between 'vocational organisation' and 'functional organisation' but for practical purposes the commission regarded the two terms as synonymous and decided to, with some exceptions, use the former term. See the *Commission on Vocational Organisation Report* (dated 1943, published 1944), paragraph 9.
4 The *Commission on Vocational Organisation Report*, paragraph 9. The commission considered the word 'vocation' to cover all forms of occupation, including professions, industries, trades and crafts.
5 Philippe C. Schmitter, *Corporatism and Public Policy in Authoritarian Portugal* (Sage Publications, London and Beverly Hills, California, 1975) pp 8–9.
6 J.T. Winkler, 'Corporatism', *European Journal of Sociology*, vol 17, part 1 (1976), p 101, in reference to Andrew Shonfield, *Modern Capitalism* (Oxford 1965), pp 160–3, and 230–3.
7 L.P. Carpenter, 'Corporatism in Britain, 1930–45', *Journal of Contemporary History*, 11 (1976), pp 3–4.
8 J.T. Winkler, op. cit., p 101, in reference to C. Delzell, *Mediterranean Fascism 1919–1945* (New York, Macmillan, 1970).
9 Philippe C. Schmitter, 'Still the Century of Corporatism?', in *Trends Towards Corporatist Intermediation*, edited by Philippe C. Schmitter and Gerhard Lehmbruch (Sage Publications, Beverly Hills, California, and London, 1979). See pp 9–10 for an extensive list.
10 Leo Panitch, 'Recent theorizations of corporatism: reflections on a growth industry', *British Journal of Sociology*, vol 31, no. 2 (June 1980), pp 183–184.
11 See J.T. Winkler, *op. cit.*, pp 103–109.
12 Ibid., pp 110–114.
13 Jukka Pekkarinen, Matti Pohjola, and Bob Rowthorn, 'Social Corporatism and Economic Performance: Introduction and Conclusions', in idem (editors), *Social Corporatism: A Superior Economic System?* (Clarendon Press, Oxford, 1992), p 1.

INTRODUCTION

1 Basil Chubb, 'Vocational Representation and the Irish Senate', *Political Studies*, Vol II, No. 2 (1954), pp 97–111.
2 J.H. Whyte, *Church and State in Modern Ireland 1923–1970* (Gill and Macmillan, Dublin, 1971). The second edition was published in 1980.

3 Joseph Lee, 'Aspects of Corporatist Thought in Ireland: The Commission on Vocational Organisation, 1939–43', in Art Cosgrove and Donal McCartney (editors), *Studies in Irish History presented to R. Dudley Edwards* (University College Dublin, 1979), pp 324–346.
4 Ibid., p 346, footnote 126.
5 Most notable amongst the new archival sources is the Bishop Michael Browne papers relating to the Commission on Vocational Organisation (Galway Diocesan Archives, Motunt St Mary's, Galway).

CHAPTER ONE

1 E.N. Williams, *The Penguin Dictionary of English and European History 1485–1789* (Penguin Books, 1980), pp 13, 104. See also Roger King, *The State in Modern Society: New Directions in Political Sociology* (Macmillan, Basingstoke and London, 1986), pp 118–119; and Otto Newman, *The Challenge of Corporatism*, (The Macmillan Press Ltd., London and Basingstoke, 1981) p 3.
2 Hugh Thomas, *An Unfinished History of the World*, Revised Edition (Pan Books, London, 1989), pp 476–480.
3 See Dorinda Outram, *The Enlightenment* (Cambridge University Press, Cambridge, 1995), pp 45, 107; and E.N. Williams, *op. cit.*, p 135.
4 Thomas Bartlett, 'The Catholic Question in the Eighteenth Century', *History Ireland*, vol 1, no. 1 (Spring 1993), p 18.
5 William Doyle, *The Old European Order 1660–1800*, Second Edition (Oxford University Press, 1992), pp 186–192; and E.N. Williams, *op. cit.*, pp 132–133, 281.
6 However, long before the enactment of the legislation, the guilds performed only the functions of friendly societies or satisfied the demand for historical pageantry in civic affairs rather than exerting any control over industry or trade. See the *Commission on Vocational Organisation Report* (dated 1943, published 1944), paragraph 24.
7 Alfred Diamant, *Austrian Catholics and the Social Question, 1918–1933* (University of Florida Monographs, Social Sciences, no. 2, Spring 1959), pp 9–10.
8 Richard L. Camp, *The Papal Ideology of Social Reform* (E.J. Brill, Leiden, The Netherlands, 1969), p 3.
9 See Paul Misner, *Social Catholicism in Europe: From the Onset of Industrialization to the First World War* (Darton, Longman and Todd, London, 1991), pp 3–4.
10 Ibid., p 4.
11 See for example: Franklin L. Baumer, 'Romanticism (ca.1780–ca.1830)' in Philip P. Wiener (Editor in Chief), *Dictionary of the History of Ideas, vol 4: Studies of Selected Pivotal Ideas*, (Charles Scribner's Sons, New York, 1973), pp 198–204 and René Wellek, 'The Unity of the Romantic Movement' in John B. Halsted (Editor), *Romanticism: Problems of Definition, Explanation, and Evaluation* (D.C. Heath & Co., Boston, 1965), pp 45–52.
12 See Anthony Quinton, 'Political Philosophy', in Anthony Kenny (editor), *The Oxford Illustrated History of Western Philosophy* (Oxford University Press, 1994), p 338. The organic concept was elaborated upon as far back as the 12th. century by theorists such as John of Salisbury (1120–1180). Organic analogies used the structures of the human body to describe social organisations. Medieval lawyers resorted to organic metaphors in explaining the legal status of corporate bodies such as guilds and religious orders. See Paul E. Sigmund, 'The Catholic Tradition and Modern Democracy', *Review of Politics*, vol 49, no. 4 (1987), p 533.
13 See Jacques Droz, 'Romanticism in Political Thought', in Philip P. Wiener, *op. cit.*, pp 206–207; David Thomson, *Europe Since Napoleon*, Revised Edition (Pelican Books, 1975), pp 141–142; and William Carr, *A History of Germany 1815–1985*, Third Edition (Edward Arnold, 1987), pp 1, 125.

14 Roger Aubert, 'Internal Catholic Controversies in Connection with Liberalism' (chapter 20), in Hubert Jedin and John Dolan (Editors), *History of the Church: vol 8: The Church in the Age of Liberalism*, (Burns and Oates, London, 1981), p 283.
15 In 1864 Bishop Wilhelm von Ketteler of Mainz, the most prominent Catholic social crusader of his time, had written a book entitled *The Labour Question and Christianity*. In it he condemned the extremes of wealth and poverty which existed under the liberal capitalist system. He believed that the solution to the plight of the workers was not one of charity but of institutional reform. Deeply influenced by the romantic school of thought he hoped for the restoration of a corporative society modelled on that of the Holy Roman Empire. Ibid., pp 302–303.
16 Henri Daniel-Rops, *A Fight For God* (J.M. Dent and Sons, London, 1966), p 129.
17 John H. Whyte, *Catholics in Western Democracies: A Study in Political Behaviour*, First Edition (Gill and Macmillan, Dublin, 1981), pp 47–75.
18 See Paul Misner, *op. cit.*, p 169.
19 Vogelsang was influenced by the romantic social ideas of Adam Müller. See Oskar Köhler, 'Catholicism in Society as a Whole' (chapter 12), in Hubert Jedin and John Dolan (editors), *History of the Church: vol 9: The Church in the Industrial Age* (Burns and Oates, London, 1981), pp 202–203.
20 Gary McEoin, 'The Impact of Catholic Social Teaching', *Doctrine and Life*, vol 41, no. 10 (December 1991), p 532.
21 See Richard L. Camp, *op. cit.*, pp 5–9.
22 David Thomson, *op. cit.*, pp 327–328.
23 Oskar Köhler, 'The Encyclical *Aeterni Patris*' (chapter 20), in Hubert Jedin and John Dolan (vol 9), *op. cit.*, p 307.
24 Frederick Copleston, *A History of Philosophy: Schopenhauer to Nietzsche*, vol 7: Part 2 (Image Books, New York, 1965) pp 161–162.
25 The basis of the reconciliation between Aristotelian philosophy and Christian theology was the principle that truth does not contradict truth. Thomists regarded the philosophy of Aristotle as an excellent exposition of the natural world, unaided by Christian revelation. Since God was regarded as the creator of both the natural and supernatural orders there could be no contradiction between what existed in one and what existed in the other.
26 Gerald A. McCool, 'Neo-Thomism and the Tradition of St Thomas', *Thought*, vol 62, no. 245 (June 1987), p 141. See also Oskar Köhler, 'The Encyclical *Aeterni Patris' op. cit.*, in Hubert Jedin and John Dolan (vol 9), *op. cit.*, pp 310–311.
27 In *Rerum Novarum* Pope Leo XIII referred far more frequently to the Bible than to any other source. However, there is no definitive interpretation of scripture. Therefore, Leo's outlook was mainly determined by a Thomistic explanation of the Bible. But the works of St Thomas Aquinas were also open to different interpretations and Leo's analysis was in error. See Gerald A. McCool, *op. cit.*, pp 137–138, 141–142.
28 Eamon Duffy, *Saints and Sinners: A History of the Popes* (Yale University Press and S4C, 1997), p 241. Leo did not take due cognisance of modern ideas and he regarded Thomism as an 'ultimate philosophical doctrine, rather than merely a profound and admirable work of the human reason at a given epoch.' See James Hennesey, 'Leo XIII: Intellectualizing the Combat with Modernity', *U.S. Catholic Historian*, vol 7, no. 4 (1988), p 397, in reference to Wilfrid Ward, 'Leo XIII', *The Fortnightly Review*, 80 (1903), pp 264–265. Peter de Rosa observed that St Thomas was unable to provide all the answers to the problems of modern Europe. It is most likely that he would have changed his outlook if he had access to the published works of eminent intellectuals such as Galileo Galilei, Isaac Newton, and Charles Darwin. See Peter de Rosa, *Vicars of Christ: The Dark Side of the Papacy* (Corgi Books, 1990), p 372.
29 Leo XIII was also more pragmatic than his predecessors. This he demonstrated in *Au Milieu des Sollicitudes* when he advised French Catholics to reconcile themselves with their republican government even though he believed it had not been established on a legitimate basis. Gary McEoin, *op. cit.*, pp 532, 535.

30 Liam Ryan, 'The Modern Popes as Social Reformers', *The Furrow*, vol 42, no. 2 (February 1991) p 88. See also Donal Dorr, *Option for the Poor: A Hundred Years of Vatican Social Teaching*, Revised Edition (Gill and Macmillan, Dublin, 1992), p 13.
31 Liam Ryan, *op. cit.*, p 88.
32 Frederick W. Powell, *The Politics of Irish Social Policy 1600–1990* (The Edwin Mellin Press, New York, U.S.A., 1992) pp 130–131.
33 Alfred Diamant, *op. cit.*, pp 6–7.
34 Henry Somerville, 'The Rerum Novarum After Forty Years', *Studies*, vol 20 (March 1931), pp 4–5. See also Oskar Köhler, 'Catholicism in Society as a Whole', *op. cit.* in Hubert Jedin and John Dolan (vol 9), *op. cit.*, pp 206–208.
35 J. Derek Holmes, *The Triumph of the Holy See: A Short History of the Papacy in the Nineteenth Century* (Burns and Oates, London, 1978), pp 200–201
36 Ibid., p 201; and Bill McSweeney, *Roman Catholicism: The Search for Relevance* (Basil Blackwell, Oxford, 1980), pp 74–75; and P. McKevitt (The Editor), 'The Background of Rerum Novarum', *Christus Rex*, vol 5, no. 4 (October 1951), pp 341–342.
37 Paul Misner, *op. cit.*, pp 128, 214.
38 See Bill McSweeney, *op. cit.*, introduction xiv; and pp 78–79.
39 John H. Whyte, *op. cit.*, p 58.
40 Leo XIII, 'Rerum Novarum', in *The Pope and the People: Select Letters and Addresses on Social Questions* by Pope Leo XIII, Revised Edition (Catholic Truth Society, London, 1920), p 179.
41 Ibid., pp 180–184.
42 Ibid., pp 207–208.
43 Ibid., pp 208–209.
44 Ibid., pp 187–189.
45 See P. McKevitt, *op. cit.*, pp 342–343.
46 Leo XIII, *op. cit.*, , pp 209–211.
47 Ibid., p 214.
48 Ibid., pp 187, 214–215, 218.
49 J.H. Whyte, *Church and State in Modern Ireland 1923–1979*, Second Edition (Gill and Macmillan, Dublin, 1984), p 63.
50 Richard L. Camp, *op. cit.*, p 28.
51 Leo XIII, *op. cit.*, pp 191, 193, 196.
52 Donal Dorr, *op. cit.*, pp 26–27.
53 J.H. Whyte (1984), *op. cit.*, p 62.
54 The high point of corporatist theory formation probably occurred in the nineteenth and early twentieth century. However, corporatism as proposed by Leo XIII, dates back to the guilds of the Middle Ages. See Andrew Cox, 'The Old and New Testaments of Corporatism: Is it a Political Form or a Method of Policy-Making?', *Political Studies*, vol 36, no. 2 (June 1988), p 295.
55 See Philippe C. Schmitter, 'Corporatism is Dead! Long Live Corporatism!', *Government and Opposition* vol 24, no. 1 (Winter 1989), pp 67–68.
56 Bill McSweeney, *op. cit.*, p 80.
57 Ibid., p 83.
58 A.R. Vidler, *A Century of Social Catholicism: 1820–1920* (S.P.C.K., London, 1964), pp 139–140, 159–160.
59 Richard L. Camp, *op. cit.*, p 14.
60 Donal Dorr, *op. cit.*, pp 63–66.
61 See Friedrich Baerwald, 'The Labour Encyclicals Today', *The Catholic Mind*, vol 49, no. 1066 (October 1951), p 626.
62 Stephen J. Lee, *The European Dictatorships 1918–1945* (Methuen, London and New York, 1987), Introduction, first page.
63 Oswald von Nell-Breuning, 'The Drafting of Quadragesimo Anno', in Charles E.Curran and Richard A.McCormick (editors), *Readings in Moral Theology no. 5: Official Catholic Social Teaching* (Paulist Press, New York, 1986), pp 60–68.

64 (1) Ibid., pp 60–61, 64, 66; (2) George Weigel, 'Catholicism and Democracy: The Other Twentieth – Century Revolution', *The Washington Quarterly*, vol 12, no. 4 (Autumn 1989), p 12. According to Weigel the *Koenigswinterer Kreis* developed the concept of subsidiarity.
65 Oswald von Nell-Breuning, *op. cit.*, pp 61–62.
66 Ibid., p 62.
67 See Oswald von Nell-Breuning, *op. cit.*, p 67.
68 The pope's note is located in paragraphs 91–96; see Oswald von Nell-Breuning, *op. cit.*, p 62. Paragraphs 91–96 can be found in Pius XI, 'Quadragesimo Anno', pp 42–43, immediately after footnote 50, in *Selected Papal Encyclicals and Letters 1928–1932*, Revised Edition (Catholic Truth Society, London, 1933)., Fascism is not explicitly mentioned. Pius expressed his disapproval of state corporatism when he declared (in Pius *op. cit.*, p 43): 'We feel bound to add that to Our knowledge there are some who fear that the State is substituting itself in the place of private initiative, instead of limiting itself to necessary and sufficient help and assistance. It is feared that the new syndical and corporative institution possesses an excessively bureaucratic and political character, and that . . . it risks serving particular political aims rather than contributing to the initiation of a better social order.'
69 See Oswald von Nell-Breuning, *op. cit.*, p 63.
70 Ibid., p 61.
71 The view was expressed that *Quadragesimo Anno* was one of the most appalling cases 'of religious exhortation without knowledge or understanding – of well-meaning people attempting to meddle with the workings of extremely complicated and sensitive machinery which they do not understand.' Frank Knight, 'Ethics and Ecomomic Reform: III, Christianity', *Economica*, November 1939, p 418; quoted in Dale L. Cramer and Charles G. Leathers, 'Schumpeter's corporatist views: links among his social theory, *Quadragesimo Anno*, and moral reform', *History of Political Economy*, vol 13, no. 4 (Winter 1981), p 746. The majority of economists declined to respond positively to the papal encyclical which proposed reforms on the basis of moral principles – hence the complaint by Louis J.Twomey (Director of the Institute of Industrial Relations, Loyola University, New Orleans, U.S.A.) that many Catholic business graduates, even from Catholic business schools, had succumbed to the pervasive Protestant economic liberal ethos. In his opinion there was 'a vast difference between the Catholic business man and the business man who happens to be a Catholic.' See his article 'Papal Social Teaching in Business Education', *The Catholic Mind*, vol 48 (November 1950), pp 669–670.
72 See Francis Xavier Murphy, *The Papacy Today* (Weidenfeld and Nicolson, London, 1981), p 55.
73 Even as early as 1932 Oswald von Nell-Breuning predicted that political extremists would quote *Quadragesimo Anno* to justify the elimination of political parties and parliamentary democracy. See Alfred Diamant, *op. cit.*, pp 28–29; in reference to Oswald von Nell-Breuning, *Die soziale Enzyklika. Erläuterungen zum Weltrundschreiben Papst Pius XI. über die gesellschaftliche Ordnung* (Katholische Tat-Verlag, Cologne, 1932), p 39.
74 Pius denounced the ruthless aggression of the fascist state against the Catholic Church with his encyclical *Non Abbiamo Bisogno* (1931). On 14 March 1937 his encyclical *Mit Brennender Sorge* condemned the Nazi atrocities against the church. Both encyclicals were favourably received abroad. See Anthony Rhodes, *The Vatican in the Age of the Dictators 1922–1945* (Hodder and Stoughton, London, 1973), pp 195–210; and John F. Pollard, *The Vatican and Italian Fascism 1929–32: A Study in Conflict* (Cambridge University Press, Cambridge, 1985), pp 157–161. Pius's encyclical, *Divini Redemptoris* (1937), declared that atheistic communism was intrinsically evil.
75 John F. Pollard describes Pius XI as a realist and an opportunist in the context of his dealings with Mussolini. John F. Pollard, *op. cit.*, pp 193–194.

76 When Pius XI dissolved Luigi Sturzo's *Partito Popolare* (Popular Party) in 1926 he contributed very substantially to the consolidation of fascism in Italy. Pius preferred a network of Catholic social organisations, detached from politics. These organisations, collectively referred to as Catholic Action, were to confine themselves to propagating the faith amongst Italians. See Stuart E. Knee, 'The Strange Alliance: Mussolini, Pope Pius XI, and the Lateran Treaty', *Mediterranean Historical Review*, vol 5, (December 1990), p 186. After the signing of the Lateran Treaty in February 1929 the pope felt compelled to criticise Mussolini's fascist regime when its aggressive actions threatened both the independence and the influence of the church in Italy. Albert C. O'Brien, 'Italian Youth in Conflict: Catholic Action and Fascist Italy, 1929–1931', *The Catholic Historical Review*, vol 68, no. 4 (October 1982), pp 625–635.

77 See Martin Broszat, *The Hitler State* (Longman, London and New York, 1981), pp 82–83, 88–91. Shortly afterwards Pius became implacably opposed to Hitler's government when the Nazis subjected the church in Germany to brutal attacks, violating the terms of the Concordat in the process. Peter C. Kent, 'A Tale of Two Popes: Pius XI, Pius XII and the Rome – Berlin Axis', *Journal of Contemporary History*, vol 23, no. 4 (October 1988), pp 589–608.

78 John F. Pollard, *op. cit.*, p 169; and Anthony Rhodes, *op. cit.*, pp 212–213.

79 The papacy was severely criticised abroad for signing the Lateran Treaty with a fascist dictator. This treaty was regarded in many circles as compromising the moral status of the Catholic Church. Furthermore, in conjunction with this, Pius XI's failure to condemn Mussolini's aggressive foreign policies was widely misinterpreted as silent assent. See Stuart E. Knee, *op. cit.*, pp 192, 200, 202.

80 Stephen J. Lee, *op. cit.*, p 108.

81 However, it should not be inferred from this that Pius was influenced by fascist ideology to support Franco or any other fascist dictator. By the end of 1935 the Vatican had established a satisfactory working relationship with the Republican government in Spain and was very reluctant to grant recognition to Franco's regime. But the republican regime was unable to protect the Catholic Church in Spain against the anti-religious fanaticism of left-wing extremists. As the atrocities against the church grew in frequency and magnitude the Vatican gradually turned against the republicans. It supported Franco because he defended the church – albeit for his own political interest. See Anthony Rhodes, *op. cit.*, pp 123–127.

82 According to John Swift, the Lateran Treaty and *Quadragesimo Anno* were interpreted by some people in Ireland as Papal approval of Italian, and later, of Portuguese fascism. See his article 'Report of Commission on Vocational Organisation (and it's Times, 1930–'40's)', *Saothar*, vol 1, 1975, p 56.

83 See John H. Whyte (1981), *op. cit.*, p 84

84 Richard L. Camp, *op. cit.*, pp 66–67.

85 J.H. Whyte (1984), *op. cit.*, p 67.

86 In *Quadragesimo Anno* the organic metaphor was very much inspired by Ephesians 4:15–16, Romans 12:4–5, and 1 Corinthians 12:12–27. See Pius XI, *op. cit.*, pp 41–42, and 64–65. The Commission on Vocational Organisation was deeply influenced by *Quadragesimo Anno* and invoked the organic concept in support of socio-economic reform on a corporatist basis. See the *Commission on Vocational Organisation Report* (1943), paragraphs 19–20.

87 Pius XI, *op. cit.*, p 37.

88 Ibid.

89 Ibid., pp 62–65.

90 Ibid., p 38.

91 Ibid., pp 4, 47, 49–50, 54–55.

92 Richard L. Camp, *op. cit.*, pp 146–147.

93 Ibid., p 127; in reference to Terence P. McLaughlin (Editor), *The Church and the Reconstruction of the Modern World: The Social Encyclicals of Pius XI*, p 250. See Pius XI, *op. cit.*, pp 42–43.

CHAPTER TWO

1 Liam Kennedy 'The early response of the Irish Catholic clergy to the co-operative movement', *Irish Historical Studies*, vol 21, no. 81 (March 1978), p 56.
2 See John H. Whyte, *Catholics in Western Democracies: A Study in Political Behaviour*, First Edition (Gill and Macmillan, Dublin, 1981), pp 7–9, 69–75.
3 John H. Whyte, *op. cit.*, pp 66–67.
4 See: Terence Brown, *Ireland: A Social and Cultural History 1922–1985* (Fontana Press, London, 1985), pp 30–32; Tom Garvin, 'Priests and patriots: Irish separatism and fear of the modern, 1890–1914', *Irish Historical Studies*, vol 25, no. 97 (May 1986), pp 71–72.
5 L. Paul-Dubois, *Contemporary Ireland* (Maunsel and Co., Dublin, 1911) p 496.
6 Ibid.
7 Ibid., p 497.
8 Finín O'Driscoll, *The Search for the Christian State – An Analysis of Irish Social Catholicism, 1913–1939* (M.A. thesis, University College, Cork, 1994), pp 48–49.
9 J.H. Whyte, *Church and State in Modern Ireland 1923–1979*, Second Edition (Gill and Macmillan, Dublin, 1984), p 66.
10 Finín O'Driscoll, *op. cit.*, pp 37–39.
11 Ibid., p 51.
12 Thomas Morrissey, 'The Paradox of James Connolly, Irish Marxist Socialist (1868–1916) and the Papal Social Encyclicals (1891–1991)', *Milltown Studies* no. 28 (Autumn 1991), p 24.
13 Ibid., p 25.
14 Ibid.
15 Dermot Keogh, *The Rise of the Irish Working Class: The Dublin Trade Union Movement and Labour Leadership 1890–1914* (Appletree Press, Belfast, 1982), pp 49, 51.
16 'Pastoral Address of the Archbishops and Bishops of Ireland, Assembled in Special Meeting, to Their Flocks, February, 1914', *Hibernia*, vol 12, no. 6 (June 1948), p 10.
17 Thomas Morrissey, *op. cit.*, p 25.
18 Finín O'Driscoll, *op. cit.*, p 65.
19 Ibid., pp 67–72.
20 See Henry Boylan, *A Dictionary of Irish Biography*, Second Edition (Gill and Macmillan, Dublin, 1988), p 309; and J. Anthony Gaughan, *Alfred O'Rahilly I: Academic* (Kingdom Books, Dublin, 1986), pp 51–54.
21 Finín O'Driscoll, *op. cit.*, p 78.
22 J. Anthony Gaughan, *Alfred O'Rahilly III: Controversialist: Part 2: Catholic Apologist* (Kingdom Books, Dublin, 1993), p 85.
23 Schoolmen were medieval philosophers, versed in scholasticism. Scholasticism was the system of philosophy, theology, and teaching that dominated medieval western Europe. It was based on the writings of the Church Fathers and (from the twelfth century) on Aristotelian philosophy.
24 J. Anthony Gaughan, *Alfred O'Rahilly II: Public Figure* (Kingdom Books, Dublin, 1989), p 282.
25 Finín O'Driscoll, *op. cit.*, pp 78–79, 81–83; and J.Anthony Gaughan, *Alfred O'Rahilly III: Controversialist Part 1: Social Reformer* (Kingdom Books, Dublin, 1992), pp 28–30.
26 J. Anthony Gaughan (1992), *op. cit.*, pp 30–35.
27 Sinn Féin ('Ourselves') was a movement which developed in the period 1905–1908 under the guidance of Arthur Griffith and Bulmer Hobson. After the civil war, those who had fought against acceptance of the Anglo – Irish Treaty (1921) retained the name and this party became the political wing of a well known subversive organisation, the Irish Republican Army (IRA), from the 1920s.
28 Myles V. Ronan, 'Catholic Action in France, Germany, Switzerland, Italy (and Ireland?)', *The Irish Ecclesiastical Record*, Fifth Series, vol 13 (January–June 1919), p 289.

29 Ibid., p 290.
30 Patrick Boylan, *Catholicism and Citizenship in Self-Governed Ireland* (Pamphlet no. 14 in the 'Irish Messenger' Social Action Series, Dublin, n.d.), p 10. This 19 page pamphlet was based on a lecture delivered to St Andrew's Temperance Association, Dublin.
31 Ibid., p 2.
32 Document entitled 'Extract from Sean MacBride's Submission to the New Ireland Forum in 1984', p 2; in Box no. 6 ('A O'R Draft Constitution'), Alfred O'Rahilly papers, University College Cork; D.H. Akenson and J.F. Fallin, 'The Irish Civil War and the Drafting of the Free State Constitution: The Drafting Committee and the Boundaries of Action', *Éire-Ireland*, vol 5, no. 1 (Spring 1970), p 13.
33 D.H. Akenson and J.F. Fallin, *op. cit.*, p 23.
34 D.H. Akenson, and J.F. Fallin, 'The Irish Civil War and the Drafting of the Free State Constitution: The Drafting Process', *Éire-Ireland*, vol 5, no. 2 (Summer 1970), p 43.
35 J. Anthony Gaughan (1989), *op. cit.*, p 160.
36 D.H. Akenson, and J.F. Fallin, ' . . . The Drafting Process', *op. cit.*, pp 47–48, 51. Collins and O'Sheil did not sign any of the drafts. Collins maintained a neutral stance as the final arbiter among the competing groups. O'Shiel was too busy as a legal advisor to the Provisional Government to attend meetings on a regular basis. D.H. Akenson and J.F. Fallin, ' . . . The Drafting Committee and the Boundaries of Action', *op. cit.*, pp 14–15; and Idem, ' . . . The Drafting Process', *op. cit.*, p 48.
37 See D.H. Akenson and J.F. Fallin, ' . . . The Drafting Process', *op. cit.*, pp 53, 57. Article 37 of Draft C is almost identical to Article 37 of the 'A O'R Draft Constitution' in folder C, marked 'A O'R Corrected', Box 6, Alfred O'Rahilly papers, University College Cork.
38 J. Anthony Gaughan (vol 3, Part 1, 1992), *op. cit.*, pp 192–193.
39 'Footnotes to the Draft Constitution of 1922', p 3, Box 6, Alfred O'Rahilly papers, University College Cork.
40 See D.H. Akenson and J.F. Fallin, ' . . . The Drafting Process', *op. cit.*, pp 55, 57.
41 Ibid., see pp 43, 48, 52–54.
42 Alfred O'Rahilly, 'The Constitution and the Senate', *Studies*, vol 25, (March 1936), p 12.
43 J. Anthony Gaughan (1989), *op. cit.*, p 156.
44 'Extract from Seán MacBride's Submission to the New Ireland Forum in 1984', *op. cit.*, p 4, Box 6, Alfred O'Rahilly papers, University College Cork. According to J. Anthony Gaughan (1989) *op. cit.*, O'Rahilly's document was not entirely ignored; it 'influenced considerably the final shape of the 1922 constitution.' Drafts A and C were used to make amendments to Draft B. See pp 159–160.
45 J. Anthony Gaughan contends that O'Rahilly, despite his poor attendance record, 'made important contributions to the proceedings of the committee', and persuaded Douglas, Kennedy and France to include God in the preamble of Draft B. J. Anthony Gaughan (1989) *op. cit.*, p 155.
46 'Memorandum on Executive', n.d., signed by 'HK', P4/308, Hugh Kennedy papers, University College Dublin.
47 Letter by James Douglas to *The Irish Independent*, 26 June 1922, P4/315 (6), Hugh Kennedy papers, University College Dublin.
48 Reproduction of Draft B, in D.H. Akenson, and J.F. Fallin, ' . . . The Drafting Process', *op. cit.*, p 87.
49 Ibid., Article 52.
50 Letter by James Douglas to *The Irish Independent*, 26 June 1922, *op. cit.*, P4/315 (5), Hugh Kennedy papers, University College, Dublin.
51 Copies of both documents, translated into English, were consulted in P4/309 and P4/320 of the Hugh Kennedy papers, University College, Dublin.
52 Article 45 of Draft A stated: 'The Oireachtas may provide for the establishment of Councils representing functions of the national life, such as Education, Agriculture,

Transport and Fisheries. A law establishing any such Council shall define its rights and duties and its relation to the government of Saorstát Éireann.' Article 44 of Draft B was similar; it declared: 'The Oireachtas may provide for the establishment of Functional or Vocational Councils representing branches of social and economic life, such as, Education, Agriculture, Transport, Labour and Industry, Fisheries, Co-operative development. A law establishing any such Council shall determine its powers, rights and duties and its relation to the government of Saorstát Éireann and may provide for the introduction into the Oireachtas of Bills approved by such Council.' See D.H. Akenson and J.F. Fallin, '... The Drafting Process', *op. cit.*, pp 68, 85.

53 J. Anthony Gaughan (1989), *op. cit.*, p 160–161.

54 D.H. Akenson, and J.F. Fallin, 'The Irish Civil War and the Drafting of the Free State Constitution: Capitulation to the British', *Éire-Ireland*, vol 5, no. 4 (Winter 1970), p 54.

55 'Extract from Sean MacBride's Submission to the New Ireland Forum', *op. cit.*, p 3, Box no. 6, Alfred O'Rahilly papers, University College, Cork. See also J.J. Lee, *Ireland 1912–1985: Politics and Society* (Cambridge University Press, 1989), p 59; and Tim Pat Coogan, *De Valera: Long Fellow, Long Shadow* (Hutchinson, London, 1993), pp 319–321.

56 O'Rahilly to M. MacDonnchada, 2 September 1922, P4/315 (37), Hugh Kennedy papers, University College Dublin.

57 James Douglas to Hugh Kennedy, 26 June 1922, P4/315 (2), Hugh Kennedy papers, University College Dublin.

58 P.J. Connolly to the Secretary of the Provisional Government, 10 August 1922, P4/315 (14), Hugh Kennedy papers, University College Dublin.

59 'Footnotes to the Draft Constitution of 1922', p 1, *op. cit.*, Box 6, Alfred O'Rahilly papers, University College Cork; Figgis to Kennedy, 24 August 1922, P4/314 (10), Hugh Kennedy papers, University College Dublin.

60 O'Rahilly to M. MacDonnchada, 2 September 1922, *op. cit.*, P4/315 (37), Hugh Kennedy papers, University College, Dublin.

61 See D.H. Akenson, and J.F. Fallin, 'The Irish Civil War and the Drafting of the Free State Constitution: Draft Constitution', *Éire-Ireland*, vol 5, no. 4 (Winter 1970), p 47, reproducing Article 42 of Collins' unaltered draft; and the corresponding Article 44 in the *Draft Constitution of the Irish Free State to be submitted to the Provisional Parliament* (Dublin, 1922), p 12.

62 See Joseph Lee, 'Aspects of Corporatist Thought in Ireland: The Commission on Vocational Organisation, 1939–43', in Art Cosgrove and Donal McCartney (editors), *Studies in Irish History presented to R.Dudley Edwards* (University College Dublin, 1979), p 324, in reference to Commission on Vocational Organisation: Minutes of Evidence, N.L.I. MS 932, Document no. 9, p 18; and Alan J. Ward, *The Irish Constitutional Tradition: Responsible Government and Modern Ireland, 1782–1992* (Irish Academic Press, Dublin, 1994), pp 186, 367, in reference to Figgis to Kennedy, 16 March 1922, P4/309 (1), Hugh Kennedy papers, University College Dublin. On 16 March 1922 Figgis brought Collins' attention to Article 68 of the Polish Constitution which made provision for the formation of vocational councils.

63 See F.S.L. Lyons, *Ireland Since the Famine*, Second Edition (Fontana Press, London, 1985) pp 471–476.

64 Ibid., pp 472–473; and Thomas Garvin, *The Irish Senate* (Institute of Public Administration, Dublin, 1969), pp 4, 9.

65 Finín O'Driscoll, *op. cit.*, p 117.

66 Ibid., see p 125.

67 Alfred O'Rahilly, 'Educational Reform', in *Irish Educational Problems: Addresses at I.N.T.O. Congress 1923* (Irish National Teachers' Organisation, Dublin), p 15. O'Rahilly's lecture to the I.N.T.O. was not delivered with the help of a well prepared script. The subsequent article (pp 14–28) was written from memory and the aid of 'a few jottings.'

68 Séamas Ó Buachalla, *Education Policy in Twentieth Century Ireland* (Wolfhound Press, Dublin, 1988), pp 53, 67.
69 Alfred O'Rahilly (1923), *op. cit.*, p 16.
70 Ibid., p 17.
71 Ibid., pp 25–28.
72 Pádraig Ua Murcada, 'The Labour Question', *The Catholic Bulletin*, vol 14, no. 2 (February 1924), pp 117–118.
73 *The Catholic Bulletin*, vol 13, no. 11 (November 1923), pp 738–739. See also Right Hon. Lord Ffrench, 'The Economic Future of Ireland', *Studies*, vol 15 (September 1926), pp 353–367. His article epitomizes the vagueness of Catholic social thought in Ireland during the 1920s. He observed that 'the spirit informing the Government cannot be otherwise than Catholic in the long run' (p. 359). However, he was not sure what developments would occur because Irish Catholics had not been in control of their own affairs for centuries (pp 359–360). Ffrench predicted that peasant proprietors would be the mainstay of the economy of the Irish Free State and went on to declare – 'the donkey and cart and not the motor car will be the symbol of the general standard of living' (p. 364). The fundamental consideration for him, when pondering the economic future of Ireland, was whether or not the people would be influenced by the principles outlined in the encyclicals of Pope Leo XIII.
74 Henry Somerville, 'An Alternative to Capitalism', with comments by John A. Ryan, Hilaire Belloc, John Kelleher, George O'Brien, and Joseph E. Canavan; *Studies*, vol 14 (December 1925), pp 521–530.
75 Ibid., pp 530–532. John Ryan was Professor of Moral Theology at the Catholic University of America. He was also the director of the Department of Social Action, N.C.W.C., Washington.
76 Ibid., pp 532–534.
77 Ibid., pp 534–539. Rev John Kelleher was Professor of Theology at St John's College, Waterford.
78 Ibid., p 541.
79 See J.H. Whyte (1984), *op. cit.*, pp 24–34; Dermot Keogh, *The Vatican, the Bishops and Irish Politics 1919–1939* (Cambridge University Press, 1986), pp 127–129, 161, 163–166, 174, 205–207; and Idem, 'The Catholic Church and the Irish Free State 1923–1932', *History Ireland*, vol 2, no. 1 (Spring 1994), p 48.
80 See John Kelleher, 'Catholic Rural Action: A Pointer for Ireland', *Studies*, vol 17 (September 1928), pp 429–430. After the Civil War the Catholic hierarchy resolved that the clergy would not involve themselves in party politics; see Dermot Keogh (1986) *op. cit.*, pp 127, 265.
81 John Kelleher, *op. cit.*, pp 430–433, 435–436.
82 *The Synod of Maynooth 1927: Decrees Which Affect the Catholic Laity*, translated with some notes by Rev M.J. Browne (The Catholic Truth Society of Ireland, Dublin, 1930), Decree no. 238, pp 11–12.
83 E. Cahill, S.J., 'The Catholic Social Movement', *The Irish Ecclesiastical Record*, Fifth Series, vol 36 (July-December 1930), p 585.
84 E. Cahill, *op. cit.*, pp 585–586.
85 John Busteed, 'The World Economic Crisis and Rerum Novarum', *Studies*, vol 20 (March 1931), pp 21–22.
86 J.H. Whyte (1984), *op. cit.*, pp 66–67.

CHAPTER THREE

1 The *Commission on Vocational Organisation Report* (dated 1943, published 1944), paragraph 5.

2 Dermot Keogh, *Twentieth Century Ireland: Nation and State* (Gill and Macmillan, Dublin, 1994), pp 68–69.
3 Finín O'Driscoll, *The Search for the Christian State – An Analysis of Irish Social Catholicism, 1913–1939*, (M.A. thesis, University College Cork, November 1994), p 158.
4 See J.H. Whyte, *Church and State in Modern Ireland 1923–1979*, Second Edition, (Gill and Macmillan, Dublin, 1984), p 71.
5 Cornelius Lucey, 'The Vocational Group Movement', *The Irish Monthly* (April 1938), pp 236–237.
6 C. Lucey, 'On a Recent Social Study in Social Science', *The Irish Ecclesiastical Record*, Fifth Series (Volume 41, January – June, 1933), pp 372–373.
7 'Résumé for the Press', Document no. 23, p 2, Edward J. Coyne papers, Jesuit Archives, Dublin.
8 For an account of the power and influence of the Jesuits, the suppression of their order, and their support for papal power and religious conservatism see H.M. Scott (editor), *Enlightened Absolutism: Reform and Reformers in Later Eighteenth-Century Europe* (Macmillan, London, 1990), especially pp 53, 60, 161, 175–176; and William Doyle, *The Old European Order 1660–1800*, Second Edition (Oxford University Press, 1992), pp 205–207.
9 'The Historical Background to Rerum Novarum;', (typescript of a lecture delivered by E.J. Coyne S.J., at St Ruskin's College, Oxford, 30 July 1934), Document no. 19, p 3, Edward J. Coyne papers, Jesuit Archives, Dublin.
10 Ibid.
11 'The Historical Background to Rerum Novarum', *op. cit.*, Document no. 19, p 8; Edward J. Coyne papers, Jesuit Archives, Dublin.
12 Ibid., pp 10–12.
13 Ibid., p 12.
14 Ibid., p 13.
15 'The Catholic Doctrine of Labour', Document no. 14, p 1, Edward J. Coyne papers, Jesuit Archives, Dublin.
16 Ibid.
17 Damian F. Hannan and Patrick Commins, 'The Significance of Small-scale Landholders in Ireland's Socio-economic Transformation', pp 101–102, in J.H. Goldthorpe and C.T. Whelan (editors), *The Development of Industrial Society in Ireland* (Oxford University Press, 1992).
18 Michael Peillon, *Contemporary Irish Society: An Introduction* (Gill and Macmillan, Dublin, 1982), p 91.
19 Evelyn Bolster, *The Knights of St Columbanus* (Gill and Macmillan, Dublin, 1979), p 64.
20 Ibid.
21 Coyne to Hayes, 25 November 1937, John Hayes papers, Muintir na Tíre Archives, Tipperary.
22 J.H. Whyte, *op. cit.*, p 69.
23 M.J. Browne, 'The World Economic Crisis and Catholic Teaching', *The Irish Ecclesiastical Record* (5th Series, vol 41), January – June 1933, pp 345–346. Randall Collins, in his article 'The Rise and Fall of Modernism in Politics and Religion', argues that Protestantism was not an essential element for the development of modern capitalism. Although his contention must remain within the realm of speculation it is reasonable to make the point that similiar modern social and economic structures would have evolved if the Protestant schism had not occurred. See *Acta Sociologica*, vol 35 (1992), p 177.
24 M.J. Browne, *op. cit.*, p 343.
25 Dr Cornelius Lucey, an influential advocate of corporatism, warned that social services, such as the dole and old-age pensions, should not be part of the state's permanent duties – but there could be no solution without state intervention. The

state was obliged to initiate reforms so that the propertied classes provided adequately for workers. Therefore, state social services, according to Lucey, should only represent emergency measures until the necessary changes had been made. See Cornelius Lucey, 'The Message of the Social Encyclicals', *The Irish Ecclesiastical Record* (5th. Series, vol 52), August 1938, pp 120–121. In countries with strong Protestant state churches the principle of state responsibility for public welfare developed earlier than in countries which were either religiously mixed or predominantly Catholic. In the latter two groups of countries private charity and the principle of subsidiarity, relying heavily on smaller collectivities, remained vigorous. See Peter Flora and Jens Alber, 'Modernization, Democratization, and the Development of Welfare States in Western Europe', in Peter Flora and Arnold J. Heidenheimer (editors), *The Development of Welfare States in Europe and America* (Transaction Books, New Brunswick, U.S.A.; and London, U.K., 1981), p 43.

26 See Richard Breen, Damian F. Hannon, David B. Rottman, and Christopher T. Whelan, *Understanding Contemporary Ireland: State, Class and Development in the Republic of Ireland* (The Macmillan Press, London, and Gill and Macmillan, Dublin, 1990), pp 26–27.

27 F.S.L. Lyons, *Ireland Since the Famine*, 2nd. Edition (Fontana Press, London, 1985) p 476.

28 Richard Breen, Damian F. Hannon, David B. Rottman, and Christopher T. Whelan, *op. cit.*, p 27.

29 Pamphlet entitled 'Muintir na Tíre: A Brief Sketch of its History' p 3, Muintir na Tíre Archives, Tipperary.

30 Joseph Lee, 'Aspects of Corporatist Thought in Ireland: The Commission on Vocational Organisation, 1939–43', in Art Cosgrove and Donal McCartney (Editors), *Studies in Irish History presented to R.Dudley Edwards*, (University College Dublin, 1979) p 325.

31 *The Irish Times*, 14 August, 1954, Department of the Taoiseach, S10816A, National Archives, Dublin; and Italian minister (signitature not decipherable) to Hayes, 24 July 1943, John Hayes papers, Muintir na Tíre Archives, Tipperary.

32 J.H. Whyte, *op. cit.*, p 83.

33 Document entitled 'Statement on the Constitution of the Irish Labour Party', dated 11 October 1937; in box file 'Archbishop Byrne (1921–1940): Meetings of the Hierarchy: Agenda and Notes', Edward Byrne papers, Dublin (R.C.) Diocesan Archives. The other two 'experts' who signed the document were Bishop Jeremiah Kinane of Waterford and Dr Patrick O'Neill.

34 The socialism of James Connolly was not compatible with Catholic teaching. By April 1940 the Labour constitution had been redrafted in accordance with the suggestions of the Committee of Experts. See J.H. Whyte, *op. cit.*, pp 82–84.

35 Dermot Keogh, *The Vatican, The Bishops and Irish Politics 1919–1939* (Cambridge University Press, Cambridge, 1986), p 204.

36 Maurice Manning, *The Blueshirts* (Gill and Macmillan, Dublin, 1987), p 228.

37 See John Swift, 'Report of Commission on Vocational Organisation (and it's Times, 1930–'40's)', *Saothar*, vol 1, no. 1 (May 1975), p 57.

38 Daniel A. Binchy, 'Proposals for a New Senate', *Studies*, vol 25, no. 97 (March 1936), p 23; and The *Commission on Vocational Organisation Report* (1943), paragraph 16.

39 There seems to be agreement amongst historians on this. See for example: Dermot Keogh, 'The Irish Constitutional Revolution: An Analysis of the Making of the Constitution', in Frank Litton (Editor), *The Constitution of Ireland 1937–1987* (Institute of Public Administration, Dublin, 1988), p 5; John A.Murphy, *Ireland in the Twentieth Century* (Gill and Macmillan, Dublin, 1975), p 82; J.J. Lee, I*reland: 1912–1985 Politics and Society* (Cambridge University Press, Cambridge, 1989), pp 181–182.

40 Eugene Broderick, *Irish Corporatism 1931–1939*, (M.A. University College, Cork, 1991), pp 185–186.

41 See Eugene Broderick, *op. cit.*, pp 103–104, 108, 187–188.
42 See, for example, William Norton's views; *Dáil Debates*, vol 50, cols 2380–2382, 1 March , 1934.
43 Charles McCarthy, *Trade Unions in Ireland 1894–1960* (Institute of Public Administration, Dublin, 1977), pp 115–116.
44 *Seanad Debates*, vol 18, col 846, 21 March, 1934.
45 Ibid; see also *Seanad Debates*, vol 17, col 1173, 22 August 1933.
46 Eugene Broderick, *op. cit.*, p 183.
47 *Dáil Debates*, vol 50, cols 2227–2228, 28 February, 1934.
48 Ibid., vol 53, col 915, 21 June 1934.
49 Dermot Keogh, *Ireland and Europe 1919–1989: A Diplomatic and Political History* (Hibernian University Press, Cork and Dublin, 1990), p 47.
50 J.J. Lee (1989), *op. cit.*, p 271. Fr Edward J. Coyne had rather perceptively observed that government ministers and civil servants would not be sympathetic towards vocational organisations because they were 'not enthusiastic for having any brother near their throne'. Edward J. Coyne, 'National Economic Councils', *Studies*, vol 22 (June 1933), p 292.
51 *The Irish Times*, 4 November 1936.
52 J. Anthony Gaughan, *Alfred O'Rahilly III: Controversialist Part 1: Social Reformer*, (Kingdom Books, Dublin, 1992), pp 192–203.
53 Invitations to send representatives were issued to: The Association of Secondary Teachers' of Ireland; Irish Technical Education Association; Vocational Officers' Association; Managers' Associations; Headmasters', Schoolmasters' and School Mistresses' Associations; Universities (Trinity College, University Colleges, Cork, Dublin and Galway), Christian Brothers Training Colleges, Association of Assistant Mistresses in Secondary Schools, and the Conference of Convent Secondary Schools. The above list was obtained from *The Irish Press*, 9 November 1933, in folder 'C.H.A. 1933', AB8/A/VI (62–65), John Charles McQuaid papers, Dublin (R.C.) Diocesan Archives. All references to the McQuaid papers in this chapter are from the above file.
54 Letter signed by T.J. O'Connell, 3 October 1933, in folder 'C.H.A. 1933' John Charles McQuaid papers.
55 'Memorandum on Proposed (Advisory) Council of Education: First and Second Meetings', n.d., signed by McQuaid and sent to Archbishop (Byrne) of Dublin, folder 'C.H.A. 1933' (also in folder 'C.H.A. 1934'), John Charles McQuaid papers. The above document is virtually identical to 'Memorandum on Proposed (Advisory) Council of Education', in box file 'Education – Secondary', Edward Byrne papers, Dublin (R.C.) Diocesan Archives. All subsequent references to the Byrne papers in this chapter are from the above box file.
The I.N.T.O. was represented by six delegates. The Technical Schools and Protestant Associations were 'strongly represented'. The National University of Ireland declined the I.N.T.O. invitation. Trinity College decided not to send delegates to the convention because the proposal to form a council of education was seen as 'hostile' to the government.
56 Memorandum by John C. McQuaid, 11 November 1933, folder 'C.H.A. 1933', John Charles McQuaid papers; and in box file 'Education – Secondary', Edward Byrne papers. Handwritten at the top of the first page of the memorandum (of document in McQuaid papers only) is 'Read at first meeting'; i.e. the meeting of 11 November 1933 organised by the I.N.T.O. The objections raised by McQuaid are summarised in 'Memorandum on Proposed (Advisory) Council of Education. First and Second Meetings', n.d., *op. cit.*
57 Ibid.
58 Ibid. McQuaid's claim is corroborated by the letter issued by the I.N.T.O. on 3 October 1933 *(op. cit.)* inviting several educational institutions and organisations to discuss the formation of a council of education. The I.N.T.O. stated that, shortly

after the foundation of the state, it had called for the establishment of an advisory council. It noted that the Minister for Education, Thomas Derrig, and his predecessor, John M. O'Sullivan, had 'definitely refused' to comply with its demands.

59 'Memorandum on Proposed (Advisory) Council of Education: First and Second Meetings', n.d., *op. cit.*

60 Ibid.

61 Letter signed by T.J. O'Connell, 3 October 1933, *op. cit.*

62 'Memorandum on Proposed (Advisory) Council of Education: First and Second Meetings', n.d., *op. cit.*

63 Ibid.

64 Ibid.

65 McQuaid to Byrne (letter 'by hand'), 23 May 1934, folder 'C.H.A.1934', John Charles McQuaid papers; and in box file 'Education – Secondary', Edward Byrne papers.

66 'Second Memorandum: Education Council: Third Meeting', presumably issued by McQuaid, folder 'C.H.A. 1934 Council on Education', John Charles McQuaid papers.

67 Ibid.

68 Memorandum by McQuaid for submission to the hierarchy, 15 June 1934, folder 'C.H.A. 1934 Council on Education', John Charles McQuaid papers.

69 Letters dated 5 October 1934 in 'C.H.A.1934 Council on Education', John Charles McQuaid papers. The alternative strategy, which McQuaid was anxious to avoid, was to declare, at the November convention, the intention of the C.H.A. to separate from the lay associations. The other professedly Catholic associations would have followed the example of the C.H.A.

70 McQuaid to Archbishop (Byrne), 1 October 1934, 'C.H.A. 1934 Council on Education', John Charles McQuaid papers; and in box file 'Education – Secondary', Edward Byrne papers. A copy of this letter is also to be found in file 1440/4, Éamon de Valera papers, Franciscan Archives, Dublin.

71 Ibid.

72 Letters issued by McQuaid, dated 5 October 1934, *op. cit.*

73 'Memorandum on Proposed (Advisory) Council of Education: First and Second Meetings', n.d., *op. cit.*

74 This is clear from the correspondence in 'C.H.A. 1933' and 'C.H.A. 1934 Council on Education', John Charles McQuaid papers. McQuaid corresponded with Cardinal Joseph MacRory, Archbishop Edward Byrne of Dublin, Archbishop John Harty of Cashel, Archbishop Joseph Walsh of Tuam, and Bishop Thomas O'Doherty of Galway. At their June meeting the bishops condemned the attempt to set up a federation of educational associations.

75 McQuaid to Archbishop (Byrne), 1 October 1934, *op. cit.*

76 'Memo. on an Annual Education Day in C.T.S. Week', folder 'C.H.A. 1933', John Charles McQuaid papers. See also McQuaid to Archbishop Byrne, 1 October 1934, *op. cit.* The above memorandum was issued by McQuaid. This is indicated by McQuaid to 'Lord Bishop' (presumably Thomas O'Doherty of Galway), 14 June 1934, folder 'C.H.A. 1934 Council on Education', John Charles McQuaid papers.

77 'Second Memorandum: Education Council: Third Meeting', *op. cit.*; and 'Memorandum on Proposed (Advisory) Council of Education: First and Second Meetings', *op. cit.*

78 Alfred O'Rahilly, praised the interdenominational nature of the I.N.T.O. in a speech at its congress, held at U.C.C. in March 1937. On the same occasion he stressed once again the need for a council of education. See J. Anthony Gaughan, *op. cit.*, pp 195–199. In June 1938 Rev Cornelius Lucey called for 'a devolution of some of the powers at present vested in the Department of Education to a vocational council for education, representative of all parties charged with the formal education of the child, and responsible immediately to these parties for the fulfilment of its trust'. See Cornelius Lucey, 'A Guild for Education', *The Irish Ecclesiastical Record*, 5th. Series, vol 51, no. 6 (June 1938), p 585.

79 See Dermot Keogh, 'Church, State and Society', in Brian Farrell (editor), *De Valera's Constitution and Ours* (Gill and Macmillan, Dublin, 1988), p 107; and Finín O'Driscoll, *op. cit.*, pp 202, 206–208.
80 Finín O'Driscoll, *op. cit.*, p 279.
81 Ibid., p 214.
82 Ibid., pp 234–235.
83 Ibid., p 238.
84 *Commission of Enquiry into Banking, Currency and Credit 1938: Reports*, Majority Report: Appendix 15, paragraph 2.
85 Ibid., paragraph 9.
86 Ibid., paragraph 19.
87 Ibid., paragraph 6.
88 J. Anthony Gaughan, *Alfred O'Rahilly II: Public Figure* (Kingdom Books, Dublin, 1989), p 313.
89 *Commission of Enquiry into Banking, Currency and Credit 1938: Reports*, Minority Report no. I, Appendix B, p 607.
90 Ibid.
91 Ibid., p 597.
92 J. Anthony Gaughan (1989), *op. cit.*, p 312.
93 Ibid., pp 312–313; and Finín O'Driscoll, *op. cit.*, pp 245–246.
94 *Commission of Enquiry into Banking, Currency and Credit 1938: Reports*, Minority Report no. III, p 628.
95 See J.J. Lee (1989), *op. cit.*, pp 199–200.
96 Finín O'Driscoll, *op. cit.*, pp 273–275, and J.J. Lee (1989), *op. cit.*, pp 563–565.
97 Dermot Keogh (1988) in Frank Litton *op. cit.*, p 67.
98 *Dáil Debates*, vol 51, cols 1829–1830, 18 April 1934; and vol 69, cols 1608– 1609, 2 December 1937.
99 Thomas Garvin, *The Irish Senate* (The Institute of Public Administration, Dublin, 1969), pp 11–12.
100 Two reservations to the minority report were issued and jointly signed by John Keane and Frank MacDermot.
101 *Report of the Second House of the Oireachtas Commission* (Government Publications, Dublin, 1936), paragraph 12, p 30. The proposal of a Senate constituted on a vocational basis was not a new one. Thomas Johnson, leader of the Labour Party, had first put forward the proposal in the Dáil on 4 October 1922. *Dáil Debates*, vol 1, cols 1139–1142, 4 October 1922. The idea was not acted upon but it lingered on persistently. It was revitalised again in 1928 when a Joint Committee on the Constitution of Seanad Éireann re-examined the matter. Once again no one succeeded in formulating a satisfactory proposal and the idea of a vocational Senate was dropped. De Valera opposed the proposal in 1928 as he had done in 1922 – not because he was opposed to vocationalism but because he was hostile to the Senate, as it was then constituted. Thomas Garvin, *op. cit.*, p 7.
102 *Report of the Second House of the Oireachtas Commission* (1936), paragraph 13, p 30.
103 Ibid., paragraph 14, pp 30–31.
104 Ibid., paragraph 19, p 33.
105 Dermot Keogh (1988), in Brian Farrell, *op. cit.*, p 108.
106 Seán Faughnan, 'The Jesuits and the drafting of the Irish constitution of 1937', *Irish Historical Studies*, vol 26, no. 101 (May 1988), p 85, in reference to The Earl of Longford and Thomas P. O'Neill, *Éamon de Valera* (Dublin, 1970), p 295; Browne to de Valera, 23 September 1936; de Valera to Browne 26 September 1936; and 'Good Government' by Dr Cornelius Lucey; 1093/3, Éamon de Valera papers, Franciscan Archives, Dublin.
107 Dermot Keogh, 'The Jesuits and the 1937 Constitution', *Studies*, vol 78, no. 309 (Spring 1989), p 94; see also pp 91–92.

108 McQuaid to de Valera, 16 March 1937, file 1091 (p. 42), Éamon de Valera papers, Franciscan Archives, Dublin. McQuaid had extensively studied *Rerum Novarum and Quadragesimo Anno*. This is evident from the above file. See McQuaid to de Valera, 16 February 1937, 17 February 1937, and n.d. (file pages 35, 36 and 58 respectively).
109 Cahill to de Valera, 4 September 1936, pp 2–3 of document, 1095/2A, Éamon de Valera papers, Franciscan Archives, Dublin.
110 De Valera to Cahill, 19 September 1936, 1095/2A, Éamon de Valera papers, Franciscan Archives, Dublin.
111 Cornelius Lucey, 'Good Government', *op. cit.*, p 18. See also p 6. Document in file 1093/3, Éamon de Valera papers, Franciscan Archives, Dublin.
112 Michael Browne disagreed with some of the views expressed in Cornelius Lucey's paper on 'Good Government', *op. cit.*, file 1093/3, Éamon de Valera papers. John Charles McQuaid also took issue with Alfred O'Rahilly over 'donation and designation theories of power'. See McQuaid to de Valera, 25 May 1937, file 1091, Éamon de Valera papers, Franciscan Archives, Dublin.
113 D.J. Hickey and J.E. Doherty, *A Dictionary of Irish History 1800–1980* (Gill and Macmillan, Dublin, 1987), p 91. De Valera's party also won the general election held on the same day as the referendum.
114 *The Irish Independent*, 14 May 1937, in the Alfred O'Rahilly papers, Blackrock College, Dublin. Within two weeks of forming his first government in 1932 de Valera had requested, from Alfred O'Rahilly, a copy of his draft constitution of 1922. O'Rahilly duly obliged and subsequently observed that the 1937 document closely resembled his own. J.Anthony Gaughan (1989), *op. cit.*, pp 278, 285. This similarity, however, did not prevent him from being harshly critical of the 1937 draft when it was published on 1 May.
115 The Irish Independent, 14 May 1937, *op. cit.*
116 Ibid.
117 Dermot Keogh (1988) in Frank Litton *op. cit.*, p 66.
118 The first paragraph of the article stated: 'The principles of social policy set forth in this Article are intended for the general guidance of the Oireachtas. The application of those principles in the making of laws shall be the care of the Oireachtas exclusively, and shall not be cognisable by any Court under any of the provisions of this Constitution.'
119 Unsigned document entitled 'Directive Principles', n.d., file 1056/3, Éamon de Valera papers, Franciscan Archives, Dublin.
120 Words in quotation marks from the previous document.
121 Thomas Garvin, *op. cit.*, p 12.
122 *Dáil Debates*, vol 69, col 1607, 2 December, 1937.
123 For de Valera's exposition of this see *Dáil Debates*, vol 51, col 1830, 18 April 1934.
124 *Dáil Debates*, vol 69, col 1611, 2 December 1937.
125 Ibid., col 1418, 1 December 1937.
126 Ibid., cols 289–290, 7 October 1937.
127 Ibid., col 1613, 2 December 1937.
128 Ibid., col 1626, 2 December 1937.
129 Ibid., col 1619, 2 December 1937.
130 Ibid., col 1627, 2 December 1937.
131 Alan J. Ward, *The Irish Constitutional Tradition: Responsible Government and Modern Ireland, 1782–1992* (Irish Academic Press, Dublin, 1994), p 246.
132 Basil Chubb, 'Vocational Representation and the Irish Senate', *Political Studies* vol II, no. 2 (1954), pp 102, 106.
133 Ibid., p 104.
134 *Dáil Debates*, vol 69, col 1431, 1 December 1937.
135 See Basil Chubb, *op. cit.*, p 107.
136 F.S.L. Lyons, *op. cit.*, p 543.

137 The Senate Returning Officer, Wilfred Brown, had not understood this term when he gave evidence before the Commission on Vocational Organisation on 23 November 1939. By this time he had presided at two elections and had been responsible for determining the eligibility of candidates representing 'vocational' interests as specified in Article 18.7. Brown admitted '"I am at a great loss to know what anyone means by the word "vocation"'. The chairman of the commission, Bishop Michael Browne was also 'grasping' for a definition. Brown, failing to enlighten himself or the commission on this occasion, could only declare 'Article 19 is the place where the word vocation is used . . . the term "vocational" frankly left me in the air'. Quotations from Commission on Vocational Organisation : Minutes of Evidence, National Library of Ireland, MS 922, 23 November 1939, q.1515 and q.1524.
138 *Dáil Debates*, vol 73, cols 1–2, 26 October 1938. The Minister for Justice, Patrick J. Ruttledge, also denied the existence of corrupt electoral practises. See *Dáil Debates*, vol 73, cols 378–379, 9 November 1938.
139 Joseph Lee (1979) in Art Cosgrove and Donal McCartney, *op. cit.*, p 325.
140 See, for example, *Dáil Debates*, vol 69, col 304 et. seq., 7 October, 1937; cols 1701–1702, 3 December 1937; and col 2041 et. seq., 9 December 1937.
141 De Valera told the Dáil on 11 May 1937 ' . . . we are not organised in a way that would make such a Seanad immediately practicable, nevertheless there was a germ of a suggestion which we tried to work up and to make practicable.' Maurice Moynihan (Editor), *Speeches and Statements by Éamon de Valera 1917–1973*, (Gill and Macmillan, Dublin, 1980), p 317.
142 The *Commission on Vocational Organisation Report* (1943), paragraph 696.
143 Thomas Garvin, *op. cit.*, p 24; in reference to *The Irish Times*, 30 March 1938 and *The Irish Independent*, 12 May 1938.
144 Dermot Keogh (1990), *op. cit.*, p 112.
145 Basil Chubb, *The Government and Politics of Ireland* (Stanford University Press, Stanford, California, and Oxford University Press, 1970), p 205.

CHAPTER FOUR

1 See Dermot Keogh, *Ireland and Europe 1919–1989: A Diplomatic and Political History* (Hibernian University Press, Cork and Dublin, 1990), p 113.
2 Maurice Moynihan, *Speeches and Statements by Éamon de Valera 1917–1973*, Edited by Maurice Moynihan (Gill and Macmillan, Dublin, 1980), pp 128, 131, 153, 189, 383–384. See also J.J. Lee, *Ireland* 1912–1985: *Politics and Society* (Cambridge University Press, 1989), pp 187, 215, 232.
3 Dermot Keogh, *op. cit.*, p 112.
4 See J. Anthony Gaughan, *Alfred O'Rahilly II: Public Figure* (Kingdom Books, Dublin, 1989) p 328.
5 M. Moynihan to T.J. Kiernan, 10 February 1938, Department of the Taoiseach, S10812, National Archives, Dublin.
6 The *Commission on Vocational Organisation Report* (1943), paragraph 100.
7 Cornelius Lucey, anxious to rid vocationalism of the suspicion of fascism, stressed that Catholic social reformers had advocated vocational organisation long before Mussolini embraced fascist ideology. Cornelius Lucey, 'The Vocational Group Movement', *The Irish Monthly*, April 1938, p 235. The growing public perception of the connection prompted Alfred O'Rahilly to suggest that the word 'corporatism' should be substituted by the word 'conciliarism' to describe the vocational organisation of society because corporatism had 'acquired a bad flavour through bad associations and misunderstandings.' *The Irish Press*, 19 July 1938, in Department of the Taoiseach file S10813, National Archives, Dublin. O'Rahilly's suggestion was not original. Over

two years previously Joseph Bracken had observed: 'Corporativism has a bad name – so bad that its best friends do not call it Corporativism at all; they call it Vocationalism or Functionalism.' Bracken was anxious to emphasize the difference between the fascist and Catholic variants of corporatism and he expressed a preference for the term 'Functionalism' with this in mind. Joseph Bracken, 'The Corporate State and the Fascist Tyranny – a Challenging Distinction', *Hibernia*, vol 1 (January 1937), pp 15, 19.

8 The *Commission on Vocational Organisation Report* (1943), paragraph 31, and paragraphs 99–100.

9 The series was as follows and the transcripts were later published in the Jesuit periodical, *The Irish Monthly*: (1) Alfred O'Rahilly, 'Vocational Organisation in the Past', 20 March 1938 (I.M., May 1938, pp 295–304); (2) The Ven. Archdeacon John Kelleher, 'The Encyclicals and Vocational Organisation', 27 March 1938 (I.M., May 1938, pp 305–315); (3) Michael Tierney, 'Vocationalism and Parliamentary Democracy. Are They Reconcilable?', 3 April 1938 (I.M., June 1938, pp 369–377); (4) Hugh O'Neill 'How Vocational Organisation Would Promote Social Justice', 10 April 1938 (I.M., June 1938, pp 378–385); (5) M.P. Linehan, 'Vocational Organisation and the Wage Earner', 17 April 1938. (I.M., June 1938, pp 386–393); (6) C.P. McCarthy, 'Vocational Organisation for Industrialists', 24 April 1938 (I.M., July 1938, pp 444–453); (7) Rev J.M. Hayes, 'Vocational Organisation for Farmers and Farm Labourers', 1 May 1938 (I.M. September 1938, pp 596–604); (8) John J. Horgan, 'A Vocational Second Chamber', 8 May 1938 (I.M., August 1938, pp 526–534); (9) T.J. McElligett, 'How the Farmers Can Organise', 15 May 1938 (I.M., January 1939, pp 51–58). The transcripts of the radio broadcasts are located in Department of the Taoiseach file S10812B, National Archives, Dublin.

10 J.M. Hayes, 'Vocational Organisation for Farmers and Farm Labourers', The Irish Monthly, September 1938, *op. cit.*, p 596.

11 Ibid., p 598.

12 Ibid.

13 Maurice Moynihan (1980) *op. cit.*, 'The Ireland That We Dreamed Of', radio broadcast of 17 March 1943, p 466.

14 Michael Tierney, 'Vocationalism and Parliamentary Democracy. Are They Reconcilable?' The Irish Monthly, June 1938, *op. cit.*, pp 371, 373 and 376.

15 Ibid., p 371.

16 Rev J.M. Hayes, *op. cit.*, pp 596–597.

17 Michael Tierney, *op. cit.*, p 374.

18 *The Irish Times*, 28 May 1938.

19 See John, J. Horgan, 'A Vocational Second Chamber', The Irish Monthly, August 1938, *op. cit.*, pp 532–533.

20 Ibid.

21 *Seanad Debates*, vol 21, col 300, 13 July 1938.

22 Ibid.

23 Popes Leo XIII and Pius XI had asserted the church's right to deal authoritatively with social and economic issues because these were not separate or exempt from Christian moral principles. Pius XI, 'Quadragesimo Anno', *Selected Papal Encyclicals and Letters 1928–1932*, Revised Edition (Catholic Truth Society, London, 1933), pp 18–19.

24 Cornelius Lucey, 'The Message of the Social Encyclicals', *The Irish Ecclesiastical Record*, 5th. Series, vol 52, no. 2 (August 1938), p 113.

25 Louis McRedmond, *To the Greater Glory: A History of the Irish Jesuits* (Gill and Macmillan, Dublin, 1991), pp 278–280.

26 *Seanad Debates*, vol 21, col 301, 13 July 1938.

27 Hence the complaint by Pat Murphy: 'That large and languid number of Catholics who are content to accept things as they are, so long as they themselves suffer no inconvenience, are a bit amazed that the Pope should expect them to put the

doctrines they believe into practise in everyday life.' See Pat Murphy, 'Reform: His Holiness Desires Real and Radical', *Hibernia*, vol 3, no. 1 (January 1939), p 6.
28 *Seanad Debates*, vol 21, col 301, 13 July 1938.
29 Ibid., col 302.
30 Ibid., cols 306–311.
31 Ibid., cols 312–313.
32 Untitled document, obviously in reference to the Commission on Vocational Organisation, n.d., Box AB8/A/ VII–IX (73–87), in folder marked 'Undated' (pre 1940), John Charles McQuaid papers, Dublin (R.C.) Diocesan Archives.
33 Ibid.
34 *Seanad Debates*, vol 21, col 438, 21 July 1938.
35 Ibid.
36 Ibid., cols 439 and 462.
37 Seanad Debates, vol 21, cols 325–326, 439, 13 and 21 July 1938, *op. cit.*
38 See Dermot Keogh, *op. cit.*, p 113.
39 See J.J. Lee (1989), *op. cit.*, p 274.
40 Dermot Keogh, *op. cit.*, p 113.
41 John Swift in 'Report of Commission on Vocational Organisation (and it's Times, 1930–'40's).', *Saothar*, vol 1, no. 1 (May 1975), p 54.
42 Maurice Moynihan (1980), *op. cit.*, p 273.
43 Interview with Dr Maurice Moynihan, 3 August 1993.
44 Ibid.
45 The draft terms of reference was enclosed with the letters of Moynihan to MacDermot and Moynihan to Tierney, 26 July 1938, Department of the Taoiseach, S10677A, National Archives, Dublin. The wording of the draft terms of reference is almost identical to that of the final terms of reference as outlined in the *Commission on Vocational Organisation Report* (1943), paragraph 1.
46 Tierney to Moynihan, 28 July 1938, Department of the Taoiseach, S10677A, National Archives, Dublin.
47 The *Commission on Vocational Organisation Report* (1943), paragraph1.
48 Moynihan to O'Ryan, 5 December 1938, Department of the Taoiseach, S10677B, National Archives, Dublin.
49 From Moynihan to the private secretary of each minister, 11 November 1938, Department of the Taoiseach, S10677A, National Archives, Dublin.
50 De Valera to Gregg and de Valera to Currie, 17 November 1938, Department of the Taoiseach, S10677A, National Archives, Dublin.
51 *The Irish Times*, 22 April 1938. The Minister for Industry and Commerce did not have confidence in the ability of parliament to deal adequately with economic matters. J.J. Lee, 'Seán Lemass', in J.J. Lee (editor), *Ireland 1945–1970*, (Gill and Macmillan, Dublin, 1979), p 22.
52 Letter from the Department of Finance, dated 16 November 1938, Department of the Taoiseach, S10677A, National Archives, Dublin. Minority Report no. 1 was signed, not just by Alfred O'Rahilly, but also by Seán P.Campbell and by William O'Brien. It is not clear from paragraph 623 (p. 369) of the *Reports of Commission of Inquiry into Banking, Currency and Credit* (1938) that O'Rahilly refused to allow discussion on Minority Report no. 1 at the commission's last session. In reference to the three minority reports submitted, paragraph 623 of the Majority Report states: 'We regret that the representations therein made were not brought before us by these members during the course of the discussions on which we have for so long been engaged, and that they have been submitted only at our final session.'
53 Appendix no. 1 of the majority report (p. 415) reveals that O'Rahilly's attendance record was the poorest of the 21 member commission. He was present for only 37 of the 150 meetings. The appendix did not cover meetings of sub–committees.
54 Correspondence from the Department of Finance, dated 16 November 1938, *op. cit.*

55 O'Rahilly did criticise his former colleagues through articles in *The Standard* and *The Irish Press* but MacEntee did not explain the circumstances which provoked O'Rahilly's criticism. George O'Brien, professor of political economy at U.C.D., had played a dominant role in the proceedings of the Commission of Inquiry into Banking, Currency and Credit. O'Brien and other influential members of the commission anticipated that O'Rahilly would attempt to influence the findings of the commission with the introduction of papal social teaching. To guard against this prospect it was decided to compile an appendix entitled 'A Note on Some Aspects of Papal Encyclicals in Relation to the Terms of Reference of the Commission' (Appendix no. 15, signed by O'Brien and the 'unsuspecting' Bishop William MacNeely of Raphoe). Their scheme to deflect him misfired and elicited an aggressive response instead. In appendix 15 of the majority report the signatories indicated that they had taken due cognisance of the papal encyclicals concerning matters of social justice. O'Rahilly, Seán P.Campbell and Peadar S. O'Loghlen disagreed with this and, in the first and third minority reports, they expressed their dissenting views. See J. Anthony Gaughan, *Alfred O'Rahilly 1: Academic* (Kingdom Books, Dublin 1986), p 186; and idem (1989), *op. cit.*, pp 314–318.

56 Letter from the Department of Education to the Department of the Taoiseach, dated 14 November 1938 including an attached memorandum entitled 'Vocational Councils', Department of the Taoiseach, S10677A, National Archives, Dublin. The churches and university list included Michael Tierney, Alfred O'Rahilly, E.J.Coyne, Cornelius Lucey, J.A.H. Irwin and a Church of Ireland representative (not named). The names were obtained from an incomplete list (n.d., untitled) of proposed personnel in the above file. Coyne had recommended that Mary McGeehin (Inspector of Schools and President of the Catholic Women's Federation of Secondary Schools Union) should be invited to serve on the commission. Document entitled 'Proposed Commission on Vocational Organisation', 27 August 1938, S10677A.

57 Documents entitled 'Vocational Organisation 1938: Names suggested for Commission', Department of the Taoiseach, S10677A, National Archives, Dublin.

58 Ibid. The members were Bishop Michael Browne of Galway, Edward J. Coyne S.J., Henry Kennedy (I.A.O.S.), Michael Tierney (recommended by Senator MacDermot), Alexander Maguire, Alfred O'Rahilly, Seán Campbell, and James J. Walshe.

59 Document entitled 'Vocational Organisation Commission. Discussions and conversation with Most Reverend Dr M. Browne,' n.d. Department of the Taoiseach, S10677B, National Archives, Dublin.

60 Robinson to Browne, 3 September 1938, B/8–1, Michael Browne papers, Galway Diocesan Archives, Mount St Mary's, Galway.

61 Michael Browne papers, B/8–1, Galway Diocesan Archives, Mount St Mary's, Galway. The letters in question are not reliably decipherable due to very poor handwriting but it seems that both Cardinal Joseph MacRory and the Archbishop of Tuam approved of Browne's acceptance of the chairmanship of the commission. See also document entitled 'Commission on Vocational Organisation: Summary of the Facts' n.d., Department of the Taoiseach, S10677B, National Archives, Dublin.

62 Untitled memorandum dated 22 May 1940, Department of the Taoiseach, S13550A, National Archives, Dublin.

63 'Vocational Organisation Commission. Discussions and conversation with Most Reverend Dr M. Browne', n.d., *op. cit.*

64 See R.M. Fox, *Jim Larkin* (International Publishers, New York, 1957), pp 168–169.

65 Charles McCarthy, *Trade Unions in Ireland 1894–1960* (Institute of Public Administration, Dublin, 1977), p 139.

66 J. Anthony Gaughan (1989), *op. cit.*, pp 330–331.

67 O'Rahilly's proposed draft of a reply to de Valera's invitation to serve on the commission, enclosed with his letter to Browne, 1 December 1938, B/8–1, Michael Browne papers, Galway Diocesan Archives, Mount St Mary's, Galway.

68 Ibid.

69 Ibid.
70 O'Rahilly to Browne, 1 December 1938, *op. cit.*, B/8–1, Michael Browne papers, Galway Diocesan Archives, Mount St Mary's, Galway.
71 'Vocational Organisation Commission. Discussions and conversation with Most Reverend Dr M. Browne', n.d., *op. cit.*
72 O'Rahilly to Browne, 14 December 1938, B/8–1, Michael Browne papers, Galway Diocesan Archives, Mount St Mary's, Galway.
73 See J. Anthony Gaughan (1989), *op. cit.*, p 331.
74 Memorandum dated 17 January 1942, enclosed with a letter from O'Rahilly to Coyne, 19 January 1942, Alfred O'Rahilly papers, Blackrock College, Dublin.
75 *The Irish Times*, 3 March 1939, Department of the Taoiseach, S10677B, National Archives, Dublin.
76 Ibid.
77 See J.J. Lee (1989) *op. cit.*, p 274.
78 *Cabinet Minutes*, Cab. 2/2, G.C. 2/38, 10 January 1939, National Archives, Dublin.
79 De Valera to Browne, 18 January 1939, Department of the Taoiseach, S10677B, National Archives, Dublin.
80 Browne to de Valera, 20 January 1939, Éamon de Valera papers, file 1093/6, Franciscan Archives, Dublin.
81 Ibid.
82 See 'Memorandum for the Government: Proposed Commission on Vocational Organisation' 3 January 1939, Department of the Taoiseach, S10677A, National Archives, Dublin); and the *Commission on Vocational Organisation Report* (1943), paragraph 1.
83 De Valera to Browne, 21 January 1939, Éamon de Valera papers, 1093/6, Franciscan Archives, Dublin.
84 Moynihan to Browne, 23 January 1939, B/8–1, Michael Browne papers, Galway Diocesan Archives, Mount St Mary's, Galway.
85 Moynihan to Browne, 24 January 1939, B/8–1, Michael Browne papers, Galway Diocesan Archives, Mount St Mary's, Galway.
86 O'Curry to Browne, 13 February 1939, B/8–1, Michael Browne papers, Galway Diocesan Archives, Mount St Mary's, Galway.
87 *Seanad Debates*, Volume 21, Col. 300, 13 July 1938.
88 This is indicated by the presence of a copy of McQuaid's letter to Archbishop Byrne, dated 1 October 1934, in file 1440/4, Éamon de Valera Papers, Franciscan Archives, Dublin. Another copy of this letter is to be found in 'C.H.A. 1934 Council on Education', AB8/A/VI (62–65), John Charles McQuaid papers, Dublin (R.C.) Diocesan Archives. Furthermore, de Valera was probably kept informed of the Catholic hierarchy's response to the initiative of the I.N.T.O. by his Minister for Education, Thomas Derrig, who discussed the issue of a council of education with McQuaid.
89 Quirke to McQuaid, 28 May 1938, folder 'C.H.A. 1938', AB8/A/VI (66–68), John Charles McQuaid papers, Dublin (R.C.) Diocesan Archives.
90 McQuaid to Quirke, 1 June 1938, folder 'C.H.A. 1938', AB8/A/VI (66–68), John Charles McQuaid papers, Dublin (R.C.) Diocesan Archives.
91 Untitled document giving details of the half-yearly meeting of the C.H.A., held on 13 October 1938, folder 'C.H.A. 1938', AB8/A/VI (66–68), John Charles McQuaid papers, Dublin (R.C.) Diocesan Archives.
92 Joseph O'Neill, 'Vocational Councils', document attached to letter from the Department of Education to the Department of the Taoiseach, dated 14 November 1938, *op. cit.*, Department of the Taoiseach, S10677A, National Archives, Dublin. McQuaid informed the minister that he refused to support the advocacy of such a council because he feared that the establishment of the council might be the first step in the secularisation of education. Furthermore, he believed that a major difficulty with a council covering all sections of education was that the experts in any one sector would be in a minority and their views might be over-ruled by other

representatives who had little knowledge of their problems. This latter view was also held by the Department of Education.

93 See R.F. Foster, *Modern Ireland 1600–1972* (Penguin Books, London, 1988), pp 545–546. The Irish National Teachers' Organisation carried out an enquiry amongst its members for the purpose of ascertaining the effect of teaching through the medium of Irish. In 1941 it published the outcome of its investigations which revealed much dissatisfaction but the report received a hostile response in official circles. John Coolahan, *Irish Education: Its History and Structure* (Institute of Public Administration, Dublin, 1981), p 44. Significantly, the I.N.T.O. was probably also in favour of the establishment of a council of education at that time. See *Dáil Debates*, vol 114, col 259, 17 February 1949.

94 Letter from the Department of Education to the Department of the Taoiseach, 14 November 1938, *op. cit.*, and attached 'Vocational Councils' memorandum, *op. cit.*

CHAPTER FIVE

1 *The Irish Times*, 3 March 1939, Department of the Taoiseach file S10677B, National Archives, Dublin.

2 Joseph Lee, 'Aspects of Corporatist Thought in Ireland: The Commission on Vocational Organisation 1939–1943', in Art Cosgrove and Donal McCartney (Editors), *Studies in Irish History presented to R. Dudley Edwards* (University College Dublin, 1979), p 344. See also Patrick Clancy, Sheelagh Drudy, Kathleen Lynch, and Liam O'Dowd (editors), *Ireland: A Sociological Profile* (Institute of Public Administration, Dublin, 1986), pp 6–8.

3 The *Commission on Vocational Organisation Report* (1943), paragraphs 3, 39 and 40.

4 Address by An Taoiseach on 5 October 1939, Document 19, p 1, Box no. 1, Papers of the Commission on Vocational Organisation, National Archives, Dublin.

5 Ibid., p 2.

6 Document entitled 'Report on Education of Clergy in Social Science', 'Clonfert' folder, in box file 'Archbishop Byrne (1921–1940) Bishops of the Province of Tuam', Edward Byrne papers, Dublin (R.C.) Diocesan Archives.

7 Ibid.

8 *The Irish Press*, 14 October 1939; and *The Standard*, 20 October 1939, in Box no. 21, Papers of the Commission on Vocational Organisation, National Archives, Dublin.

9 O'Toole to Browne, 5 February 1940; 'Irish Banks Standing Committee', 30 January 1940, Document no. 62, pp 2–3; Browne to Hennessy, 1 February 1940. All documents in file E4/50, Box no. 2, Papers of the Commission on Vocational Organisation, National Archives, Dublin.

10 Browne to de Valera, 1 February 1940, file E4/50, Box no. 2, Papers of the Commission on Vocational Organisation, National Archives, Dublin.

11 De Valera to Browne, 3 February 1940, Department of the Taoiseach, S13550A, National Archives, Dublin.

12 O'Muimhneacháin to McElligott, 3 February 1940, Department of the Taoiseach, S13550A, National Archives, Dublin.

13 McElligott to Moynihan, 6 February 1940, Department of the Taoiseach, S13550A, National Archives, Dublin. Browne assured de Valera that it was not the intention of the Commission on Vocational Organisation to review the report of the Banking Commission. Browne to the Department of the Taoiseach, 12 February 1940, file S13550A, National Archives, Dublin.

14 Memorandum dated 16 February 1940, Department of the Taoiseach, S13550A, National Archives, Dublin.

15 Commission on Vocational Organisation: Minutes of Evidence, National Library of Ireland, MS926, 3 May 1940, Qs. 8964–9109.

16 Letter to the secretary of the commission, 26 April 1940, Department of the Taoiseach, S13550A, National Archives, Dublin.
17 Memorandum entitled 'Commission on Vocational Organisation', and untitled memorandum dated 22 May 1940, Department of the Taoiseach, S13550A, National Archives, Dublin.
18 Ronan Fanning, *The Irish Department of Finance 1922–1958* (The Institute of Public Administration, Dublin, 1978), pp 322–323.
19 O'Kelly to de Valera, 31 May 1940, Department of the Taoiseach, S11926, National Archives, Dublin.
20 O'Toole to Browne, 6 June 1940, B/8–1, Michael Browne papers, Galway Diocesan Archives, Mount St Mary's, Galway.
21 No letter from de Valera to Browne on this matter was located in the Michael Browne papers.
22 Browne to O'Toole, 7 June 1940, B/8–1, Michael Browne papers, Galway Diocesan Archives, Mount St Mary's, Galway.
23 Joseph Lee, *op. cit.*, p 330.
24 Commission on Vocational Organisation: Minutes of Evidence, National Library of Ireland, MS 926, 30 May 1940, Q. 10509.
25 See, for example, Commission on Vocational Organisation: Minutes of Evidence, National Library of Ireland, MS 926, 30 May 1940, Qs. 10516 and 10522.
26 Maurice Moynihan, *Currency and Central Banking in Ireland 1922–1960* (Gill and Macmillan, Dublin, 1975), p 250.
27 Ibid., pp 253–254.
28 Browne to O'Kelly, 7 June 1940, B/8–1, Michael Browne papers, Galway Diocesan Archives, Mount St Mary's, Galway.
29 O'Kelly to Browne, 13 June 1940, B/8–1, Michael Browne papers, Galway Diocesan Archives, Mount St Mary's, Galway.
30 McElligott and O'Kelly also failed to persuade the government to terminate the work of other commissions, committees and tribunals. The Interdepartmental Committee of Inquiry regarding Shooting Rights, the Town Tenants (Occupation of Tenancies) Tribunal, the Committee on Summer-Time, and the Irish Manuscripts Commission were allowed to continue functioning. The government decided to suspend the Commission on Agriculture when its Interim Report on Silage was completed. For the purpose of pacifying Finance it was decided that 'the responsible Ministers should, where appropriate, make every effort to expedite the furnishing of reports in all cases'. Department of Finance memorandum for the government dated 19 July 1940; and copy of an extract from the *Cabinet Minutes*, G.C.2/190, item 4, 23 July 1940, both documents in Department of the Taoiseach file S11926, National Archives, Dublin.
31 Handwritten postscript dated 26 June 1940 in memorandum dated 10 June 1940, Department of the Taoiseach, S11926, National Archives, Dublin.
32 Joseph Lee, *op. cit.*, p 330.
33 J.H. Whyte, *Church and State in Modern Ireland 1923–1979*, Second Edition (Gill and Macmillan, Dublin, 1984), pp 113–114.
34 P. O'Tuathail to the secretary, Department of Industry and Commerce, 5 March 1940, Department of Labour, file W43, National Archives, Dublin. The commission expressed a strong interest in the role of Industrial Courts and Courts of Inquiry (established by leglislation in 1919). The subject of Industrial Courts was regarded by the commission as 'of great importance' for the purpose of studying vocational organisation.
35 R.C. Ferguson to the secretary of the Commission on Vocational Organisation, 3 May 1940, Department of Labour file W43, National Archives, Dublin.
36 Commission on Vocational Organisation: Minutes of Evidence, National Library of Ireland, MS 929, 26 September 1940, Q14826.
37 This is indicated by statements made by Seán Lemass in the Dáil. See (1) *Dáil Debates*, vol 88, col 94, 7 July 1942; (2) *The Sunday Independent*, 12 July 1942, in Box no. 21, Papers of the Commission on Vocational Organisation, National Archives, Dublin.

38 Joseph Lee (1979), *op. cit.*, pp 337–339.
39 Commission on Vocational Organisation: Minutes of Evidence, National Library of Ireland, MS 929, 26 September 1940, Q14828.
40 Ibid., Q.14829.
41 Ibid., 11 October 1940, Q15425.
42 Ibid., Qs. 15414–15416.
43 Browne to O'Neill, 21 October 1940, B/8–1, Michael Browne papers, Galway Diocesan Archives, Mount St Mary's, Galway.
44 O'Neill to Browne, 22 October 1940, B/8–1, Michael Browne papers, Galway Diocesan Archives, Mount St Mary's, Galway.
45 *Seanad Debates*, vol 25, cols 13–14, 22 January 1941.
46 Ibid., col 155, 29 January 1941.
47 Document no. 172, p 1; and Document 172(C) p 1; Box no. 10, Papers of the Commission on Vocational Organisation, National Archives, Dublin.
48 Document no. 172(C), *op. cit.*, p 2.
49 Document no. 172(B) paragraph 1, Box no. 10, Papers of the Commission on Vocational Organisation, National Archives, Dublin.
50 Letter from P.A. O'Toole, n.d., B/8–43, Michael Browne papers, Galway Diocesan Archives, Mount St Mary's, Galway.
51 Coyne to Browne, 11 January 1941, B/8–7, Michael Browne papers, Galway Diocesan Archives, Mount St Mary's, Galway.
52 Document no. 172(B), *op. cit.*, paragraphs 1–2.
53 Ibid., paragraph 3.
54 Ibid., paragraph 4.
55 Ibid., paragraphs 21–24.
56 Ibid., paragraphs 11–12.
57 Ibid., paragraphs 15–16.
58 Ibid., paragraph 17.
59 Document no. 172(A) pp 22–26, Box no. 10, Papers of the Commission on Vocational Organisation, National Archives, Dublin.
60 Document no. 172(B) *op. cit.*, paragraph 15.
61 Ibid., paragraph 20.
62 Ibid., paragraph 25.
63 Letter from P.A. O'Toole, n.d., *op. cit.*
64 Document no. 172(C), *op. cit.*, p 6. For the context of Duffy's quote see 'Quadragesimo Anno', pp 34–35, in Pius XI, *Selected Papal Encyclicals and Letters 1928–1932*, Revised Edition (Catholic Truth Society, London, 1933).
65 Document no. 172(C) *op. cit.*, pp 12–14, 19.
66 Ibid., pp 15–19.
67 Commission on Vocational Organisation: Minutes of Evidence, National Library of Ireland, MS 939, Document 136, p 7.
68 Ibid., introductory note.
69 The *Commission on Vocational Organisation Report* (1943), paragraph 3, and the footnote in p 2.
70 *The Sunday Independent*, 12 July 1942, in Box no. 21, Papers of the Commission on Vocational Organisation, National Archives, Dublin.
71 Coyne to Browne, 19 June 1941, B/8–1, Michael Browne papers, Galway Diocesan Archives, Mount St Mary's, Galway.
72 J. Anthony Gaughan, *Alfred O'Rahilly II: Public Figure* (Kingdom Books, Dublin, 1989), p 335.
73 O'Rahilly to Browne, 16 January 1942, Alfred O'Rahilly papers, Blackrock College, Dublin.
74 Memorandum dated 17 January 1942, enclosed with a letter from O'Rahilly to Coyne, 19 January 1942; O'Rahilly to Coyne, 11 February 1942; and 'Note on the Bishop's Reply', 11 February 1942; Alfred O'Rahilly papers, Blackrock College, Dublin.

75 Memorandum dated 17 January 1942, *op. cit.*
76 Coyne to O'Rahilly, 5 February 1942, Alfred O'Rahilly papers, Blackrock College, Dublin.
77 Browne to O'Rahilly, 9 February 1942; O'Rahilly to Coyne, 11 February 1942, *op. cit.*; and 'Note on the Bishop's Reply', 11 February 1942, *op. cit.*; Letter by O'Rahilly, 12 February 1942; Alfred O'Rahilly papers, Blackrock College, Dublin.
78 Browne to O'Rahilly, 12 February 1942, Alfred O'Rahilly papers, Blackrock College, Dublin.
79 Duffy to O'Rahilly, 3rd., 5th. and 10th. February 1942; McCarthy to O'Rahilly, 13 February 1942, Alfred O'Rahilly papers, Blackrock College, Dublin.
80 Duffy to O'Rahilly, 18 February 1942, Alfred O'Rahilly papers, Blackrock College, Dublin.
81 O'Rahilly to Hayes, 28 February 1942, John Hayes papers, Muintir na Tíre Archives, Tipperary.
82 This is indicated by Coyne to O'Rahilly, 5 March 1942, Alfred O'Rahilly papers, Blackrock College, Dublin.
83 Browne to Jesuit Provincial, 17 March 1942, Edward J. Coyne papers, Jesuit Archives, Dublin.
84 Jesuit Provincial to Browne, 20 March 1942, Edward J. Coyne papers, Jesuit Archives, Dublin.
85 Coyne to O'Rahilly, 1 February 1942, Alfred O'Rahilly papers, Blackrock College, Dublin.
86 Duffy to O'Rahilly, 3 and 10 February 1942, op. cit.
87 Coyne to O'Rahilly, 16 August 1942, Alfred O'Rahilly papers, Blackrock College, Dublin.
88 O'Toole to Browne, 11 September 1944, B/8–43, Michael Browne papers, Galway Diocesan Archives, Mount St Mary's, Galway.
89 Letter from P.A. O'Toole, n.d., op. cit.
90 Ibid.
91 Verbatim report of Duffy's memorandum, morning session, 21 October 1943, pp 1–2, B/8–43, Michael Browne papers, Galway Diocesan Archives, Mount St Mary's, Galway.
92 Ibid., afternoon session, pp 1–3.
93 See Charles McCarthy, *Trade Unions in Ireland 1894–1960* (Institute of Public Administration, Dublin, 1977), pp 114–115, 196.
94 The commission was careful to reassure the trade union movement that it had nothing to fear in the event of its recommendations being implemented. The commission stated that trade unions should retain their existing rights. It advised against abrupt state intervention because it believed that trade unions had the ability and the desire to adapt to a changing environment. Although anxious that trade unions should not lose any of their existing privileges the commission hoped that they would relinquish their individual and independent status to form registered associations which were to act as negotiating bodies for each industry. *The Commission on Vocational Organisation Report* (Dublin, 1943), paragraphs 568–569. Browne and the majority of his colleagues recommended that trade unions and employers alike should submit their demands and grievances to Conciliation Courts which would be convened to effect settlement of disputes. This did not place trade unions at a particular disadvantage relative to employers. The decision of Conciliation Courts was to be binding on employers and workers but the commission was vague (probably deliberately) on the details of enforcement so as not to alienate trade unionists. Unlike *Quadragesimo Anno*, the commission did not advocate a complete prohibition on strikes and lock-outs. (Ibid., paragraph 588; and Pius XI, *op. cit.*, p 43).
95 Coyne to Browne, 17 September 1943, B/8–38, Michael Browne papers, Galway Diocesan Archives, Mount St Mary's, Galway.

96 Coyne to Jesuit Provincial, 15 November, 1943, Edward J. Coyne papers, Jesuit Archives, Dublin.
97 The *Commission on Vocational Organisation Report* (1943), Addendum no. 3, pp 471–474.
98 Document D.R. (S) 4, Box no. 29, Papers of the Commission on Vocational Organisation, National Archives, Dublin.
99 Ibid.
100 Coyne to Browne, 17 September 1943, *op. cit.*
101 Coyne to O'Toole, 29 September 1943 and attached copy of Document D.R. S(4) *op. cit.*; Box no. 29, Papers of the Commission on Vocational Organisation, National Archives, Dublin.
102 John Swift, 'Report of Commission on Vocational Organisation (and it's Times, 1930–'40's)', *Saothar* (vol 1, no. 1, May 1975), p 55.
103 The *Commission on Vocational Organisation Report* (1943), Reservation no. 1, p 477.
104 Ibid., p 453. The third member of the commission who did not sign was Sir Alexander Maguire; he had attended only two of the eighty four meetings of the commission. (Ibid., Appendix 1, p 489).
105 Document no. 172 (C), p 11, op. cit.
106 This is evident from *The Commission on Vocational Organisation Report* (1943); see paragraphs 3 and 721, and Appendix 1 (p. 489).
107 Coyne to Browne, 17 September 1943, *op. cit.*
108 Browne to Coyne, 19 September 1943, B/8–38, Michael Browne papers, Galway Diocesan Archives, Mount St Mary's, Galway.
109 Report of the Editing Committee, 5 May 1944, B/8–11, Michael Browne papers, Galway Diocesan Archives, Mount St Mary's, Galway.
110 Ibid.
111 Ibid.
112 De Valera to Browne, 23 May 1944, B/8–1, Michael Browne papers, Galway Diocesan Archives, Mount St Mary's, Galway.
113 Browne to McEvoy, 18 September 1944, B/8–1, Michael Browne papers, Galway Diocesan Archives, Mount St Mary's, Galway.
114 *The Irish Times*, 25 November 1939, in Box no. 21, Papers of the Commission on Vocational Organisation, National Archives, Dublin. The reports of the Canals and Inland Waterways Commission, the Port and Harbours Tribunal, and the Greater Dublin Tribunal were not acted upon. The report of the Banking Commission (1934–1938), despite all the publicity focused on it, had little effect on government policy.

CHAPTER SIX

1 'Seán Lemass on Bureaucracy and Politicians' (reported in *The Irish Press*, 29 October 1943), Department of the Taoiseach, SI0813, National Archives, Dublin.
2 The *Commission on Vocational Organisation Report* (1943), paragraph 668.
3 'Seán Lemass on Bureaucracy and Politicians', *op. cit.*
4 *Raymond James Raymond*, 'De Valera, Lemass and Irish Economic Development: 1933–1948' in John P. O'Carroll and John A.Murphy (editors), *De Valera and His Times* (Cork University Press, Cork, 1983), pp 115, 130.
5 J.J. Lee, *Ireland 1912–1985: Politics and Society*, (Cambridge University Press 1989), pp 239–240.
6 Extract from the Cabinet Minutes, G.C.4/9, item 2, 11 August 1944, in Department of the Taoiseach file S13552; National Archives, Dublin.
7 O'Toole to Browne, 6 September 1944, B/8–43, Michael Browne papers, Galway Diocesan Archives, Mount St Mary's, Galway.

8 Extract from the *Cabinet Minutes*, G.C. 4/10, item 3, 18 August 1944, in Department of the Taoiseach file S13552, National Archives, Dublin.
9 See Joseph Lee, 'Aspects of Corporatist Thought in Ireland: The Commission on Vocational Organisation, 1939–43', in Art Cosgrove and Donal McCartney (Editors), *Studies in Irish History presented to R. Dudley Edwards* (University College Dublin, 1979), p 332.
10 Letter from P.A. O'Toole, n.d., B/8–43, Michael Browne papers, Galway Diocesan Archives, Mount St Mary's, Galway. According to O'Toole the same allegation was also made in *The New Statesman*.
11 Ibid.
12 O'Toole to Browne, 6 September 1944, *op. cit*.
13 O'Toole to Browne, 11 September 1944, B/8–43, Michael Browne papers, Galway Diocesan Archives, Mount St Mary's, Galway.
14 O'Toole to Browne, 23 September 1944, B/8–43, Michael Browne papers, Galway Diocesan Archives, Mount St Mary's, Galway.
15 Ibid.
16 *The Irish Press*, 13 October 1944, Department of the Taoiseach, S13540, National Archives, Dublin.
17 Ryan to Morris, 4 October 1944, Thomas Morris papers, Muintir na Tíre Archives, Tipperary.
18 John Dignan, *Outlines of a Scheme of National Health Insurance* (paper read at the meeting of the committee of management of the National Health Insurance Society, 11 October 1944), p 15. The committee of management of the N.H.I.S. consisted of: a chairman appointed by the Minister for Local Government and Public Health; three trustees appointed by the minister; three members, nominated to the minister by the Trade Union Congress and appointed by him; three members, representing the employers, appointed by the minister; five members elected by a 'college' of 'Insured Persons'. The 'college', elected by county and city borough councils, consisted of about 115 members. It met annually to elect representatives by private ballot.
19 Ibid., p 2.
20 Ibid., pp 3–4. The total membership of the N.H.I.S. in October 1944 was approximately 610,000 (i.e. about 20% of the total population). An estimated 759,000 employed persons were not members, therefore the potential membership was nearly 1,370,000. It was calculated that the enlarged Society would have benefited approximately 2,600,000 persons (Ibid., p 13).
21 Ibid., p 17.
22 Ibid., p 16.
23 Ibid., p 13.
24 Ibid., p 16.
25 Ibid., p 19.
26 Ibid.
27 J.J. Lee, *op. cit*., pp 283–287.
28 J.H. Whyte, *Church and State in Modern Ireland 1923–1979*, Second Edition (Gill and Macmillan, Dublin, 1984), pp 109–110. Whyte critically analyses the Dignan plan in pp 101–106.
29 The *Commission on Vocational Organisation Report* (1943), paragraph 438.
30 J.H. Whyte, op. cit., p 111. Dignan was appointed chairman of the N.H.I.S. in 1936 when Seán T. O'Kelly was Minister for Local Government and Public Health. Ibid., p 74; and D.J. Hickey and J.E. Doherty, *A Dictionary of Irish History 1800–1980* (Gill and Macmillan, Dublin, 1987), p 199.
31 Interview with Mr Tom Barrington, 18 August 1993. Mr Barrington was private secretary to Seán MacEntee at the time.
32 Ibid.
33 Ibid.

34 *The Irish Press*, 31 October 1944, in Department of the Taoiseach file S13540, National Archives, Dublin.
35 Ibid.
36 Ibid.
37 The *Commission on Vocational Organisation Report* (1943), paragraphs 351–357.
38 Preliminary observations of the Department of Education on the report of the Commission on Vocational Organisation, section (A), paragraph 3, Department of the Taoiseach, S13552, National Archives, Dublin. Section (C) of this document, dated 17 November 1944, is also in file S12753A.
39 Ibid., Section (C), paragraph 6.
40 'Preliminary observations of the Department of Finance on Report of Commission on Vocational Organisation', 30 November 1944, paragraphs 1–2, Department of the Taoiseach, S13552, National Archives, Dublin.
41 Ibid., paragraph 7.
42 Ibid, paragraph 8.
43 Ibid., paragraph 9.
44 The preliminary observations were contained in 3 pages of text. The 'further' observations were 13 pages in length, with an additional 6 page appendix which focused criticism on specific points of detail.
45 The *Commission on Vocational Organisation Report* (1943), paragraph 715.
46 'Further observations of the Department of Finance on the Report of the Commission on Vocational Organisation', n.d., unsigned, paragraph 5. Department of the Taoiseach, S13552, National Archives, Dublin.
47 Ibid., paragraph 1.
48 Ibid., paragraph 2.
49 Ibid., paragraphs 3–4.
50 Ibid.
51 Ibid., paragraph 8.
52 Ibid., paragraph 9.
53 M. Deegan, 'Commission on Vocational Organisation 1943', 8 January 1945, first page, Department of the Taoiseach, S13552, National Archives, Dublin.
54 Ibid., second and third pages.
55 'Report of Commission on Vocational Organisation 1943: Reactions of a Bureaucrat', n.d., unsigned, p 1, Department of the Taoiseach, S13552, National Archives, Dublin.
56 Ibid., p 2. The commission had not been entirely unrealistic in its expectations. It was admitted that vocational bodies might not co-operate and serve the public interest and might even regard their kindred organisations as rivals (The *Commission on Vocational Organisation Report*, 1943, paragraph 510). Where parish guilds were concerned fears were expressed that there might be a lack of public spirited individuals who were prepared to devote considerable time to voluntary effort in the interests of the community. Private interests and family considerations might also interfere with the functioning of the guilds (Ibid., paragraph 547). But these penetrating perceptions were transient and did not dissuade the commission from formulating its radical plan.
57 'Report of Commission on Vocational Organisation 1943: Reactions of a Bureaucrat', n.d., *op. cit.*, p 15.
58 Ibid.
59 J.J. Lee (1989), *op. cit.*, p 276.
60 Joseph Lee (1979), *op. cit.*, p 331.
61 R.C. Ferguson, observations of the Department of Industry and Commerce on the report of the Commission on Vocational Organisation, 11 January 1945, paragraphs 1–2, Department of the Taoiseach, S13552, National Archives, Dublin.
62 Ibid., paragraph 3.
63 Ibid., paragraph 4.

64 Ibid.
65 Ibid., paragraph 5.
66 Ibid., paragraph 6.
67 Ibid., paragraph 9.
68 Vocationalists realized that government assistance was crucial for the emergence of a highly developed network of vocational organisations. Their plight can be appreciated from the following quotation: '. . . one must be prepared to wait for years before organic growth becomes a reality; if early results are required, something of the ideal must be sacrificed and Government initiative not only accepted but expected. Indeed, it is difficult to conceive of vocational organisation developing here without a good deal of benevolent direction on the part of the Government. Will this be forthcoming, and when?' Quotation from John J.M. Ryan, 'Vocational Organisation in Industrial Britain', *The Irish Monthly*, vol 73 (December 1945), p 509.
69 R.C. Ferguson, observations of the Department of Industry and Commerce on the report of the Commission on Vocational Organisation, 11 January 1945, *op. cit.*, paragraph 28.
70 Ibid., paragraphs 29–30.
71 The *Commission on Vocational Organisation Report* (1943), paragraph 339
72 R.C.Ferguson, 13 January 1945, observations of the Department of Industry and Commerce on the report of the Commission on Vocational Organisation, paragraph 2, Department of the Taoiseach, S13552, National Archives, Dublin.
73 Ibid., paragraph 3. The department's policy of encouraging the formation of business associations and industrial groups, and its readiness to consult with these organisations, is evident from Mary E. Daly, *Industrial Development and Irish National Identity 1922–1939* (Syracuse University Press, New York, 1992), p 118.
74 R.C. Ferguson, 13 January 1945, Observations of the Department of Industry and Commerce on the report of the Commission on Vocational Organisation, *op. cit.*, paragraph 1.
75 J.P. Walshe to the Secretary of the Department of the Taoiseach, 19 January 1945, Department of the Taoiseach, S13552 Annex, National Archives, Dublin,
76 Ibid.
77 Letter from the Department of External Affairs (author's name not reliably decipherable) to the secretary of the Department of the Taoiseach, 21 February 1945, Department of the Taoiseach, S13552 Annex, National Archives, Dublin.
78 Typescript of 'Article over the initials C.M. (Correai Marques) in the *Voz* of 18 October 1944', Department of the Taoiseach, S13552 Annex, National Archives, Dublin.
79 'Commission on Vocational Organisation: Final observations by Department of Justice on the recommendations in the Commission's Report for the setting up of a Council of Law (Paragraphs 530 to 534 of Report)', March 1945, Department of the Taoiseach, S13552, National Archives, Dublin.
80 T.J. Barrington, 'Department of Local Government and Public Health: Report of Commission on Vocational Organisation', 7 March 1945, paragraph 2, Department of the Taoiseach, S13552, National Archives, Dublin. The commission did not seek evidence from the Department of Local Government and Public Health in regard to the important proposals concerned with: (1) the establishment of a council of health and (2) the setting up of a national construction council (Ibid., paragraphs 49, 64).
81 Ibid., paragraph 6.
82 Ibid., paragraph 20.
83 Ibid., paragraph 23.
84 Ibid., paragraph 21.
85 Ibid., paragraph 49.
86 The commission did not inform the Department of Justice about its enquiries, pertaining to issues of legal clarification and reform, nor was it anticipated by the

department that the commission would be studying these matters. Consequently, the commission deprived itself of valuable advice. This resulted in a gross underestimation of the difficulties associated with legal reform. 'Commission on Vocational Organisation: Final observations by the Department of Justice on the recommendations in the Commission's Report for the setting up of a Council of Law (Paragraphs 530 to 534 of Report.),' March 1945, *op. cit.*, paragraphs 2–3.

87 'Report of the Commission on Vocational Organisation: Observations by the Department of Supplies', March 1945, paragraph 2, Department of the Taoiseach, S13552, National Archives, Dublin.

88 The Department of Supplies was destined for termination at the end of World War II and therefore was not directly concerned with the question of implementing any of the commission's major recommendations which might have been adopted by the government. Yet, it was considered desirable to submit observations because of the experience and knowledge that the department had acquired during the war years. (Ibid., paragraph 1).

89 Ibid., paragraph 26.

90 Ibid., paragraph 27.

91 'Observations of the Department of Agriculture on the Report of the Commission on Vocational Organisation,' paragraph 11, Department of the Taoiseach, S13552, National Archives, Dublin.

92 Ibid., paragraphs 11–12.

93 Ibid., paragraphs 11, 13–14.

94 The *Commission on Vocational Organisation Report* (1943), paragraph 544

95 Ibid., paragraph 547. It had already been suggested (paragraph 545 and footnote 1, p 340) that Muintir na Tíre might assist in formulating guidelines and rules for the formation of parish guilds.

96 Ibid., paragraph 544.

97 Ibid., paragraphs 544, 550–560. The organisation of agriculture was proposed on both a territorial and a commodity basis. The scheme, based on territorial units, grouped all farmers, irrespective of what they produced, into parish and county organisations. The second scheme was based on the production and marketing of certain commodities. Some points of contact were to exist between the two types of organisation; complete integration would be achieved at the highest level of organisation which was the national agricultural conference.

98 'Observations of the department of Agriculture on the Report of the Commission on Vocational Organisation', *op. cit.*, paragraph 15.

99 Ibid., paragraph 28.

100 Ibid., paragraph 36.

101 'Report of Commission on Vocational Organisation 1943: Reactions of a Bureaucrat', *op. cit.*, p 1.

102 M.Deegan, Observations of the Department of Lands, 18 January 1945, paragraph 3, Department of the Taoiseach, S13552, National Archives, Dublin.

103 Copy of a document from file S13636 entitled 'Commission on Vocational Organisation', n.d., unsigned, Department of the Taoiseach, S13552, National Archives, Dublin.

104 Joseph Lee (1979), *op. cit.*, p 343.

105 The *Commission on Vocational Organisation Report* (1943), paragraph 505.

106 J.H. Whyte, *op. cit.*, p 117.

107 Ibid.

108 The *Commission on Vocational Organisation Report* (1943), paragraph 14.

109 'Further observations of the Department of Finance on the Report of the Commission on Vocational Organisation', *op. cit.*, paragraph 22; R.C. Ferguson, Preliminary observations of the Department of Industry and Commerce on the Report of the Commission on Vocational Organisation, 11 January 1945, *op. cit.*, paragraph 20; 'Report of the Commission on Vocational Organisation: Observations by the Department of Supplies,' March 1945, *op. cit.*, paragraphs 11–12.

CHAPTER SEVEN

1 Incomplete letter, signed E.J.C., B/8–44, Michael Browne papers, Galway Diocesan Archives, Mount St Mary's, Galway. See *Dáil Debates*, vol 95, col 1717, 25 January 1945; and cols 2180–2181, 2 February 1945; vol 96, cols 45–48, 14 February 1945. A third Dáil deputy, James Hughes, also quoted the report when debating the Minerals Company Bill with Lemass. *Dáil Debates* vol 95, col 1709, 25 January 1945.
2 *Seanad Debates*, vol 29, cols 1306–1311, 21 February 1945.
3 Ibid., cols 1323–1324.
4 Coyne to Browne, 22 February 1945, B/8–44, Michael Browne papers, Galway Diocesan Archives, Mount St Mary's, Galway.
5 Coyne to Browne, 28 February 1945, B/8–44, Michael Browne papers, Galway Diocesan Archives, Mount St Mary's, Galway.
6 Ibid.
7 Lemass to Browne, 2 March 1945, B/8–44, Michael Browne papers, Galway Diocesan Archives, Mount St Mary's, Galway.
8 Ibid.
9 Coyne to (Seán) Moynihan, 3 March 1945, Department of the Taoiseach, S13550A, National Archives, Dublin.
10 Coyne to Browne, 5 March 1945, B/8–44, Michael Browne papers, Galway Diocesan Archives, Mount St Mary's, Galway.
11 Coyne to Browne, 28 February 1945, *op. cit.*; and *The Irish Press*, 8 March 1945, in Department of the Taoiseach file S13540, National Archives, Dublin.
12 *The Irish Press*, 8 March 1945, *op. cit.*
13 Ibid.
14 Ibid.
15 Ibid.
16 Coyne to Browne, 8 March 1945, B/8–44, Michael Browne papers, Galway Diocesan Archives, Mount St Mary's, Galway.
17 Coyne to Browne, 12 March 1945, B/8–44, Michael Browne papers, Galway Diocesan Archives, Mount St Mary's, Galway.
18 Interview with Dr Maurice Moynihan, 3 August 1993.
19 *Dáil Debates*, vol 96, col 1377, 14 March 1945.
20 The elaborate hierarchy of vocational organisations, councils and governing bodies proposed by the commission did not seem consistent with the foreword in the report. This had been emphasised by the Department of Finance when it submitted its preliminary observations to the Department of the Taoiseach. See the previous chapter.
21 *Seanad Debates*, vol 29, cols 1905–1907, 20 March 1945. O'Kelly found himself in a difficult position because he was friendly with both Lemass and Browne; this is indicated by col 1907 of the above reference.
22 Ibid., col 1910.
23 See J.H. Whyte, *Church and State in Modern Ireland 1923–1979*, Second Edition (Gill and Macmillan, Dublin, 1984), pp 111–112.
24 *The Irish Times*, 10 March 1945, in Department of the Taoiseach file S13540, National Archives, Dublin.
25 *The Irish Press*, 8 March 1945, *op. cit.*, and 23 March 1945 in Department of the Taoiseach file S13540, National Archives, Dublin.
26 *The Irish Press*, 23 March 1945, *op. cit.*
27 Ibid.
28 Ibid.
29 *The Irish Press*, 28 March 1945, in Department of the Taoiseach file S13540, The National Archives, Dublin; and in file 1410/1, Éamon de Valera papers, Franciscan Archives, Dublin.
30 Ibid.

31 J.H. Whyte, *op. cit.*, p 108.
32 Coyne to Browne, 24 March 1945, B/8–44, Michael Browne papers, Galway Diocesan Archives, Mount St Mary's, Galway. Coyne obtained some of the data from two civil servants who had assisted the commission – Patrick O'Toole and C. O'Connor.
33 Coyne to Browne, 11 April 1945, B/8–44, Michael Browne papers, Galway Diocesan Archives, Mount St Mary's, Galway.
34 Hayes to Browne, 14 March 1945, B/8–44, Michael Browne papers, Galway Diocesan Archives, Mount St Mary's, Galway.
35 Browne to O'Rahilly, 16 March 1945, B/8–44, Michael Browne papers, Galway Diocesan Archives, Mount St Mary's, Galway.
36 *Dáil Debates*, vol 96, cols 1744–1746, 23 March 1945.
37 Ibid., cols 1746–1747.
38 Ibid., col 1761, 23 March 1945; and col 2147, 18 April 1945.
39 Ibid., cols 2153–2154, 18 April 1945.
40 Ibid., cols 1763–1764.
41 Ibid., col ,2156.
42 Ibid., cols 2173–2174.
43 The *Commission on Vocational Organisation Report* (1943), paragraph 539.
44 Ibid., paragraph 540
45 See J.H. Whyte, *op. cit.*, pp 16–21, 37–38.
46 *Dáil Debates*, vol 96, cols 1762–1763, 23 March 1945; and cols 2151–2152, 18 April 1945.
47 Ibid., col 1762, 23 March 1945; and cols 2157–2159, 18 April 1945.
48 Ibid., col 2174.
49 Ibid., col 2176.
50 Ibid., col 2177.
51 Ibid., cols 2167–2169.
52 Ibid., col 2600, 26 April 1945.
53 Ibid., cols 2169 and 2178.
54 Ibid., cols 2601–2602.
55 Memorandum dated 10 November 1945, Department of the Taoiseach, S13758, National Archives, Dublin.
56 Letter addressed to Browne, probably from Coyne, 24 April 1945, B/8–43, Michael Browne papers, Galway Diocesan Archives, Mount St Mary's, Galway. The official in question was named as 'Bradley'. He was probably E.S. Ó Brolcháin, one of the civil servants who had been assigned to assist the commission. See the *Commission on Vocational Organisation Report* (1943), paragraph 721.
57 Coyne to Browne, 26 April 1945, B/8–43 Michael Browne papers, Galway Diocesan Archives, Mount St Mary's, Galway.
58 De Valera to Browne, 2 May 1945, B/8–43, Michael Browne papers, Galway Diocesan Archives, Mount St Mary's, Galway.
59 Coyne to Browne, 8 May 1945, B/8–43, Michael Browne papers, Galway Diocesan Archives, Mount St Mary's, Galway.
60 This is evident from a comparison of Coyne to Browne, 8 May 1945, B/8–43 *op. cit.* to: Browne to de Valera, 12 May 1945, B/8–12 and Browne to de Valera, 19 May 1945, B/8–11. The above documents are in the Michael Browne papers, Galway Diocesan Archives, Mount St Mary's, Galway.
61 Browne to de Valera, 12 May 1945, *op. cit.*
62 Browne to de Valera, 19 May 1945, *op. cit.*
63 De Valera to Browne, 28 May 1945, B/8–11, Michael Browne papers, Galway Diocesan Archives, Mount St Mary's, Galway. Details of de Valera's enquiries are contained in a memorandum dated 24 May 1945; a copy of 'Commission on Vocational Organisation: Minute of Meeting held on 4th. November, 1943' enclosed with a letter from O'Toole to Moynihan, 24 May 1945; Moynihan to O'Toole, 25 May 1945 and O'Toole to Moynihan, 25 May 1945. All of the above documents are in Department of the Taoiseach file S13550A, National Archives, Dublin.

64 Browne to Hayes, 2 June 1945, John Hayes papers, Muintir na Tíre Archives, Tipperary.
65 Stephen Rynne, *Father John Hayes: Founder of Muintir na Tíre* (Clonmore and Reynolds, Dublin, 1960), pp 190–191.
66 J.H. Whyte, *op. cit.*, p 112; and J.J. Lee, *Ireland 1912–1985: Politics and Society*, (Cambridge University Press, Cambridge, 1989), p 286.
67 *The Irish Press*, 11 August 1945 in Department of the Taoiseach file S13540; National Archives, Dublin; and the observations (both 'preliminary' and 'further') of the Department of Finance, Department of the Taoiseach, S13552, National Archives, Dublin. The wording between the above documents and the newspaper article is strikingly similar in places.
68 *The Irish Catholic*, 16 August 1945, in Department of the Taoiseach file S13540, National Archives, Dublin.
69 Browne to Hayes, 22 August 1945, John Hayes papers, Muintir na Tíre Archives, Tipperary.
70 The *Commission on Vocational Organisation Report* (1943), paragraphs 157–196, and 514–543.
71 The nineteen professions identified were medical doctors, barristers, solicitors, dentists, veterinary surgeons, midwives, pharmacists, nurses, teachers, architects, engineers, accountants, surveyors, analytical chemists, musicians, librarians, auctioneers and estate agents, insurance officials and journalists. Nine professions were organised on a legal statutory basis. These registered professions included medical doctors, barristers, solicitors, dentists, veterinary surgeons, midwives, pharmaceutical chemists, nurses and teachers. (Ibid., paragraphs 157–158).
72 The professional commission was to represent the various professions. It would have the duty and the power to examine schemes of registration and organisation submitted by the professions. The professional commission would have the authority to function as the supreme domestic tribunal of the professions, dealing with appeals from the decisions of professional boards relating to the removal of members from the register or complaints received from the public. See the *Commission on Vocational Organisation Report* (1943), paragraphs 523–528.
73 'Memorandum for the Government: Commission on Vocational Organisation', paragraph 4, issued by the Department of the Taoiseach, S13552, National Archives, Dublin. In handwriting over the title of the document is: 'Draft memorandum and appendix to Rúnaí, gach Roinn and A.G. for observations on 14/8/45 . . . ' The three page appendix summarised the commission's recommendations in paragraphs 514–528 which dealt with the professions.
74 Ibid.
75 P. Ó Cinnéide to the Secretary of the Department of External Affairs, 14 August 1945, Department of Foreign Affairs, D/FA 238/70, National Archives, Dublin.
76 'Memorandum for the Government: Commission on Vocational Organisation', *op. cit.*, paragraphs 5–6.
77 (1) P. Ó Cinnéide to the secretary, Department of Foreign Affairs, 17 December 1945, D/FA 238/70; National Archives, Dublin; and (2) 'Commission on Vocational Organisation: Recommendations regarding the professions', 24 June 1946, paragraph 4, the Department of the Taoiseach S13636B, National Archives, Dublin.
78 Memorandum dated 10 November 1945, *op. cit.*
79 Memorandum dated 26 September 1945, Department of the Taoiseach, S13550A, National Archives, Dublin.
80 This is evident from a draft letter from de Valera to Browne, n.d., Department of the Taoiseach, S13550A, National Archives, Dublin.
81 Ó Cinnéide to the Director of the National Library of Ireland, 5th. and 23rd. of March 1946, Department of the Taoiseach, S13550A, National Archives, Dublin.
82 *The Irish Press*, 21 November 1945, in Department of the Taoiseach file S13540, National Archives, Dublin.
83 Ibid.

84 This observation was made in *The Sunday Independent*, 25 November 1945. A copy of the relevant article is located in B/8–11, Michael Browne papers, Galway Diocesan Archives, Mount St Mary's, Galway.

CHAPTER EIGHT

1 *The Irish Press*, 28 October 1944, in Department of the Taoiseach file S13540, National Archives, Dublin.
2 See chapter 6.
3 Eugene Goulding, 'Report on the C.S.V.O.C.', *Christus Rex*, vol 8, no. 2 (April 1954), p 112.
4 O'Curry to Browne, 7 May 1945, B/8–11, Michael Browne papers, Galway Diocesan Archives, Mount St Mary's, Galway.
5 Ibid.
6 Browne to O'Curry, 10 May 1945, B/8–11, Michael Browne papers, Galway Diocesan Archives, Mount St Mary's, Galway.
7 Eugene Goulding, *op. cit.*, p 112. Each Catholic organisation was entitled to nominate not more than two representatives to the Executive Committee. The committee had power to co-opt additional members but the number of co-opted members was limited to one third of the total membership.
8 Ibid., pp 112–113. Clauses (3) and (4) were incorporated into the constitution and rules of the C.S.V.O.C which were passed unanimously at its annual general meeting on 17 November 1948. Provision was made in the C.S.V.O.C. constitution for the expansion of the organisation outside the Archdiocese of Dublin.
9 Ryan to Morris, 31 May 1945, Thomas Morris papers, Muintir na Tíre Archives, Tipperary. From the text of the letter it seems that John J.M. Ryan was a member of the C.S.V.O.C. executive committee.
10 *Dáil Debates*, vol 100, cols 292–296, 21 March 1946.
11 Ibid., cols 309–312.
12 Ibid., cols 311–312.
13 Ibid., cols 318–322.
14 *Dáil Debates*, vol 102, col 30, 2 July 1946.
15 Ibid., col 141.
16 Ibid., cols 141–142.
17 Ibid., col 142.
18 *Dáil Debates*, vol 105, cols 569–570, 16 April 1947.
19 J.H. Whyte, *Church and State in Modern Ireland 1923–1979*, Second Edition (Gill and Macmillan, Dublin, 1984), p 109
20 *The Irish Times*, 5 September 1944, in Department of the Taoiseach file S13540, National Archives, Dublin.
21 C.S.V.O.C. publications included (1) *A Synopsis of the Recommendations of the Commission on Vocational Organisation; and* (2) *A Diagrammatic Representation of the Recommendations in the Report of the Commission on Vocational Organisation* (Dublin, 1947). The first edition of the first pamphlet (5,000 copies) was sold out and a second edition was issued. See Eugene Goulding, *op. cit.*, p 114; and Joseph Lee, 'Aspects of Corporatist Thought in Ireland: The Commission on Vocational Organisation, 1939–43', in Art Cosgrove and Donal McCartney (editors), *Studies in Irish History presented to R. Dudley Edwards* (University College Dublin, 1979), p 334. Bishop Michael Browne's pamphlet, *Bulwark of Freedom: Vocational Organisation – Democracy in Action*, was published by the Catholic Truth Society (Dublin, 1945).
22 Joseph Lee, *op. cit.*, pp 328–329.
23 J. Anthony Gaughan, *Alfred O'Rahilly III: Controversialist Part I: Social Reformer* (Kingdom Books, Dublin, 1992), p 200.

24 See *Dáil Debates*, vol 102, cols,142–148, 2 July 1946; vol 106, cols 475, 550, 554–561, 21 May 1947. The Labour Party in government also pressed for the establishment of a council of education. See *The Irish Times*, 10 December 1949, in Department of the Taoiseach, file S12753A, National Archives, Dublin.
25 See John Coolahan, 'Educational Policy for National Schools 1960–1985' in D.G. Mulcahy and Denis O'Sullivan (editors), *Irish Educational Policy: Process and Substance* (Institute of Public Administration, Dublin, 1989), pp 27–28.
26 See Séamas Ó Buachalla, *Education Policy in Twentieth Century Ireland* (Wolfhound Press, Dublin, 1988), p 268. Éamon de Valera had discharged the role of Minister for Education from September 1939 to June 1940. His outlook was conservative and he was quite content to maintain the *status quo*. (Ibid., pp 65–66, 268.)
27 Tom Inglis, *Moral Monopoly: The Catholic Church in Modern Irish Society* (Gill and Macmillan, Dublin, 1987), Chapter 3.
28 See J.H. Whyte, *op. cit.*, p 153.
29 Ibid., p 118.
30 See Joseph Lee, 'Centralisation and Community', in Joseph Lee (editor), *Ireland: Towards a Sense of Place* (Cork University Press, Cork, 1985), p 84.
31 See J.H. Whyte, *op. cit.*, pp 126–127.
32 Ibid., p 134. According to J.H. Whyte, the Department of Local Government and Public Health 'perhaps exhibited more purely than any other department the 'bureaucratic' attitude . . . It showed a readiness to concentrate authority, a lack of interest in the maintenance of autonomous groups, a reluctance even to consult outside groups, that made a sharp contrast with the 'vocational' principles which were being propagated by exponents of Catholic social teaching. It is perhaps no accident that the sharpest conflict between the 'bureaucratic' and 'vocational' attitudes should have arisen in a field controlled by this department' (Ibid., p 130). The new Department of Health was staffed 'almost entirely' by officials from the old Department of Local Government and Public Health (Ibid., p 140).
33 Ibid., p 141.
34 Ibid., p 157.
35 Memorandum entitled: 'The following will be the main features of the policy of the Irish Government', February 1948, Department of the Taoiseach, S12753A, National Archives, Dublin. See also *The Irish Independent*, 18 February 1948. Fianna Fáil was the only political party to consistently oppose the setting up of a council of education and occasionally this opposition seemed to be motivated by the notion that such a council would be used as 'an instrument to make war' on the Irish language policy in the schools. See *Dáil Debates*, vol 110, col 1090, 4 May 1948.
36 *Irish Catholic Directory* (1949), p 705.
37 'Memorandum for presentation to the Taoiseach', issued by the C.S.V.O.C., n.d., Department of the Taoiseach, S13636B, National Archives, Dublin. See also 'Vocational Organisation', *Hibernia*, vol 12, no. 3 (March 1948), p 6.
38 *The Irish Independent*, 31 March 1948, in Department of the Taoiseach file S12753A, National Archives, Dublin.
39 *Dáil Debates*, vol 110, col 1092, 4 May 1948.
40 *Dáil Debates*, vol 106, col 475, 21 May 1947.
41 *Dáil Debates*, vol 114, col 259, 17 February 1949.
42 Ibid., cols 271–272.
43 *The Irish Times*, 10 December 1949, in Department of the Taoiseach file S12753A, National Archives, Dublin.
44 Document entitled: 'Council of Education', n.d., Department of the Taoiseach, S12753B, National Archives, Dublin.
45 *The Irish Independent*, 5 April 1950, in Department of the Taoiseach file S12753A, National Archives, Dublin.
46 *The Irish Independent*, 12 April 1950, in Department of the Taoiseach file S12753A, National Archives, Dublin.

47 *The Irish Independent*, 6 April, 8 May and 10 July 1950, in Department of the Taoiseach file S12753A, National Archives, Dublin.
48 *The Irish Times*, 6 April 1950, in Department of the Taoiseach file S12753A, National Archives, Dublin.
49 *Dáil Debates*, vol 110, col 1089, 4 May 1948. On 19 July 1956 Mulcahy told the Dáil: 'I regard the position as Minister in the Department of Education as that of a kind of dungaree man, the plumber who will make the satisfactory communications and streamline the forces and potentialities of the educational workers and educational management in this country. He will take the knock out of the pipes and will link up everything'. Ibid., vol 159, col 1494, 19 July 1956.
50 The Council of Education which was set up did not press for fundamental changes in the educational system. Its reports have been described as sterile and irrelevant and its conservatism may have reflected the opinions of the majority of politicians and those who administered the educational system during the 1950s. See Séamas Ó Buachalla, *op. cit.*, p 68; and John Coolahan, *Irish Education: History and Structure* (Institute of Public Administration, Dublin, 1981), pp 45, 80–81.
51 'Catholic Societies' Vocational Organisation Conference'; a statement by the C.S.V.O.C. giving a review of its work as presented to the general meeting held on 17 November 1948, p 3, Department of the Taoiseach, S13636B, National Archives, Dublin.
52 Galvin to An Taoiseach (John A.Costello), 4 February 1949, Department of the Taoiseach, S13636B, National Archives, Dublin. The proposed deputation included: Senator E.A. Maguire, Sydney E. Gibson and Joseph H. Bowden, representing employers; Wm. J. Whelan (C.I.U.), Phillip Cairns (T.U.C.) and Wm. McMullan (C.I.U.) were chosen to represent the trade unions; Cornelius Collins, Wm. Phillips and Denis Galvin were selected to represent the C.S.V.O.C.
53 'Memorandum for the Government: Deputation received by the Taoiseach from Catholic Societies Vocational Organisation Conference', 12 September 1949, Department of the Taoiseach, S13636B, National Archives, Dublin.
54 'Vocational Organisation'; a copy of Denis Galvin's address to the C.S.V.O.C., at its annual general meeting (9 December 1949), accompanying the letter from T.C. O'Gorman to the taoiseach, 15 December 1949; Department of the Taoiseach, S13636B, National Archives, Dublin.
55 Galvin to An Taoiseach, 6 June 1950, Department of the Taoiseach, S13636B, National Archives, Dublin.
56 John Whyte, 'Church, State and Society, 1950–70', in J.J. Lee (editor), *Ireland 1945–1970*. (Gill and Macmillan, Dublin, 1979), p 75.
57 Frederick W. Powell, *The Politics of Irish Social Policy 1600–1990* (The Edwin Mellin Press, New York, U.S.A., 1992), pp 257–258.
58 Evelyn Bolster, *The Knights of St Columbanus* (Gill and Macmillan, Dublin, 1979), see pp 95–99. According to Evelyn Bolster the organisation's membership included 16 bishops in 1951, and clerical membership was growing. Even some members of the Inter-Party cabinet ranked amongst the Knights. These were Richard Mulcahy (Education), Seán MacEoin (Justice), William Norton (Social Welfare) and Joseph Blowick (Lands). The Knights did not, however, have a corresponding influence on national policy.
59 Eamonn McKee, 'Church – state relations and the development of Irish health policy: the mother – and – child scheme, 1944–53', *Irish Historical Studies*, vol 25, no. 98 (November 1986), pp 176–177.
60 See J.H. Whyte (1984), *op. cit.*, pp 179–183.
61 O'Gorman to An Taoiseach (Éamon de Valera), 16 July 1951, Department of the Taoiseach, S13636B, National Archives, Dublin.
62 Quotation from 'The Antidote to Stateism', *Hibernia*, vol 15, no. 9 (September 1951), p 12.
63 Evelyn Bolster, *op. cit.*, p 46.
64 J.P. Brennan to the Secretary of the Irish government, 10 November 1952, Department of the Taoiseach, S13636B, National Archives, Dublin.

65 T. Woods to the Irish ambassador in Washington, 28 April 1953, in Department of the Taoiseach file S13636B and in Department of Foreign Affairs file D/FA 238/70, National Archives, Dublin. The correspondence between the Department of External Affairs and other state departments, regarding the implementation of the report, is in file D/FA 238/70. The above letter signed by T.Woods summarises the statements issued by the state departments, and by state offices, such as the Office of the Attorney General.
66 This is evident from a comparison of *Dáil Debates*, vol 106, cols 1043–1044 (30 May 1947), which gives details of the Consultative Council of Health, with the *Commission on Vocational Organisation Report* (1943) paragraph 543.
67 See Brendan Hensey, *The Health Services of Ireland*, Completely Revised Fourth Edition (The Institute of Public Administration, Dublin, 1988), pp 40, 138–139.
68 T. Woods to the Irish ambassador in Washington, 28 April 1953, *op. cit.*
69 O'Gorman to de Valera, 16 April 1954, Department of the Taoiseach, S13636B, National Archives, Dublin.
70 Feirmeoir, 'Agriculture in a Vocational Order of Society', *Christus Rex*, vol 10, no. 1 (January 1956), p 46.
71 Eugene Goulding, *op. cit.*, p 120.
72 See J.H. Whyte (1984), *op. cit.*, pp 160–161, and the editorial in *Hibernia*, vol 15, no. 3 (March 1951), p 13.
73 See J.H. Whyte (1984), *op. cit.*, pp 162–163.
74 Stephen Rynne, *Father John Hayes: Founder of Muintir na Tíre* (Clonmore and Reynolds, Dublin, 1960), pp 169–170.
75 Ibid., p 170.
76 John Ryan, 'The Founder of Muintir na Tíre: John M. Canon Hayes (1887–1957)', *Studies*, vol 46 (Autumn 1957), p 320.
77 Stephen Rynne, *op. cit.*, p 170.
78 Quotation from Stephen Rynne, *op. cit.*, p 171. Bishop Fogarty of Killaloe also adopted a negative attitude towards Muintir na Tíre.
79 See Paul E. Sigmund, 'The Catholic Tradition and Modern Democracy', *The Review of Politics*, vol 49, no. 4 (1987), pp 539–541.
80 The popularity of the Christian Democrat parties was attributable to a number of factors. These organisations included many men who played important roles in various resistance movements during World War Two. The fact that the political parties were formed on a non-denominational basis also enhanced their appeal. Furthermore, they were willing to co-operate with socialists and their members came from different backgrounds right across the social and economic spectrum. See Anthony Trawick Bouscaren, 'The European Christian Democrats', *The Catholic Mind*, vol 47, no. 1041 (September 1949), pp 522–523, 536.
81 J.H. Whyte (1984), *op. cit.*, pp 159–160.
82 Ibid., see pp 307–312.
83 It was easy to criticise the *Commission on Vocational Organisation Report* and the Dignan plan because, in both documents, there was a rather simplistic application of Catholic moral principles to Irish social problems. A characteristic of Irish Catholic moralists in the 1940s and 1950s was their assumption that the moral law was plainly visible for those who cared to see it and that there was only one way to apply it. See Ruth Barrington, *Health, Medicine and Politics in Ireland 1900–1970*, The Institute of Public Administration, Dublin, 1987, pp 151–152.
84 Jeremiah Newman, 'The Catholic Social Movement', *The Irish Ecclesiastical Record*, vol 83, no. 2 (February 1955), pp 106–107.
85 J.H. Whyte (1984), *op. cit.*, pp 331–332.
86 The social liberalism which emanated from the proceedings of the Second Vatican Council diminished the church's opposition towards the welfare state when the state did not encroach on the church's domain in matters of social welfare. See F.W. Powell, 'The Crisis in the Irish Welfare State', in William Reville and Máirtín Ó Fathaigh (editors) *Town and Gown* 1 (The Centre for Adult and Continuing Education, University College Cork, 1994), p 33.

87 See Terence Brown, *Ireland: A Social and Cultural History 1922–1985* (Fontana Press, London, 1985), pp 294–299.

CHAPTER NINE

1 Quote from D.R. O'Connor Lysaght, *The Republic of Ireland* (The Mercier Press, Cork, 1970), p 189.
2 J.H. Whyte, *Church and State in Modern Ireland 1923–1979*, Second Edition (Gill and Macmillan, Dublin, 1984), pp 336–337.
3 Joseph Lee, 'Aspects of Corporatist Thought in Ireland: The Commission on Vocational Organisation, 1939–43', in Art Cosgrove and Donal McCartney (editors), *Studies in Irish History presented to R. Dudley Edwards* (University College Dublin, 1979), p 345.
4 See Raymond James Raymond, 'De Valera, Lemass and Irish Economic Development: 1933–1948':, in John P. O'Carroll and John A. Murphy (editors), *De Valera and His Times* (Cork University Press, 1983), p 131; J.J. Lee, *Ireland 1912–1985: Politics and Society* (Cambridge University Press, Cambridge, 1989), pp 230–231. Lemass's economic strategy, from the mid–forties onwards, has been described as pragmatic rather than ideological; in Brian Farrell, *Seán Lemass* (Gill and Macmillan, Dublin, 1983), p 71. See also J.J. Lee (1989), *op. cit.*, pp 187–188.
5 Quotation from *The Irish Times*, 18 February 1966, in reference to an interview reported in the 'current' issue of *The Word*.
6 See J.J. Lee, 'Seán Lemass', in J.J. Lee (editor), *Ireland 1945–70* (Gill and Macmillan, Dublin, 1979), pp 20–21.
7 The *Commission on Vocational Organisation Report* (1943), paragraph 474.
8 Ibid., paragraph 701.
9 When Éamon de Valera was taoiseach neo-corporatist policies were not pursued. Unlike Lemass, he had not been amenable to institutionalising power outside the political system. J.J. Lee (1989), *op. cit.*, pp 402–403.
10 See Garret Fitzgerald, *Planning in Ireland: A PEP Study* (Institute of Public Administration, Dublin; Political and Economic Planning, London; 1968), pp 61, 65–66.
11 Ibid., p 159.
12 Stephen Lalor, 'Corporatism in Ireland', *Administration*, vol 30 no. 4 (1982), p 82.
13 See Basil Chubb, *The Government and Politics of Ireland*, Third Edition (Longman, London and New York, 1992) p 126.
14 Stephen Lalor, *op. cit.*, p 87.
15 See Basil Chubb, *op. cit.*, p 122.
16 Leo Panitch, 'Recent theorizations of corporatism: reflections on a growth industry', *British Journal of Sociology*, vol 31, no. 2 (June 1980), pp 160–161.
17 See 'Terms and Abbreviations' in this book for a discussion of the meaning of corporatism.
18 Tripartism has been described as 'a hybrid in which parliamentarism and corporatism are combined into a contradictory unity owing to the formal participation in corporatist decision-making of representatives of the parliamentary executive ('government') and/or the delegation of corporatist policy implementation to the parliamentary bureaucracy and/or the formal participation of corporations in the decision-making of the parliamentary executive and/or the delegation of parliamentary policy administration to the corporations.' Bob Jessop, 'Corporatism, Parliamentarism and Social Democracy' in Philippe C. Schmitter and Gerhard Lehmbruck (editors), *Trends Towards Corporatist Intermediation* (Sage Publications, Beverly Hills, California, and London, 1979), pp 195–196.
19 Niamh Hardiman and Stephen Lalor, 'Corporatism in Ireland: An Exchange of Views', *Administration*, vol 32, no. 1. (1984), pp 78–79.

20 Ibid., pp 84–85
21 Stephen Lalor, *op. cit.*, p 84.
22 Philippe C. Schmitter, 'Still the Century of corporatism?' in Philippe C. Schmitter and Gerhard Lehmbruck *op. cit.*, p 24.
23 J.H. Whyte, *op. cit.*, p 337.
24 Basil Chubb, *op. cit.*, p 125.
25 The commission warned of the dangers inherent in circumstances where vocational organisations become subsumed in the administrative apparatus of the state. The *Commission on Vocational Organisation Report* (1943), paragraph 15.
26 T.J. Barrington, 'The Situation of Irish Government', *The Irish Review*, no. 3 (1988), p 23.
27 Ghita Ionescu, *Centripetal Politics: Government and the New Centres of Power* (London, 1975), p 4, quoted in Basil Chubb op. cit., p 126.
28 *The Cork Examiner*, editorial, 31 January 1991.
29 Stephen Lalor, *op. cit.*, p 90. John L. Pratschke pointed out: 'There is now, it would seem, a real danger that the processes of decision-making on economic and social affairs have become too far removed from those most affected by them . . . ' John L. Pratschke, 'Business and Labour in Irish Society, 1945–70' in J.J. Lee (1979), *op. cit.*, p 44.
30 Stephen Lalor, *op. cit.*, p 90.
31 S.E. Finer, *Anonymous Empire*, Second Edition (London, 1966) p 113, quoted in Basil Chubb, *op. cit.*, p 128.
32 Taken to its extreme the debate focuses on the alleged vulnerability of corporatism to fascism. The nature of the historical linkage between fascism and corporatism is open to question. Corporatism 'appears to be intrinsically vulnerable to fascism – even though it has often appealed to men of good will'. L.P. Carpenter, 'Corporatism in Britain, 1930–45', *Journal of Contemporary History* , vol 11 (1976) p 24. For a supporting view see Noel Malcolm, 'Europe's Unholy Godfathers', *The Spectator*, 23 September 1989, pp 8–9. It has also been contended that the link between fascism and corporatism was circumstantial or 'partly accidental'. See Philippe C. Schmitter, *Corporatism and Public Policy in Authoritarian Portugal* (Sage Publications, London and Beverly Hills, California, 1975), p 8; and Joseph Lee (1979), *op. cit.*, p 332.
33 Brian Barry, 'Growth at a price', *Times Literary Supplement*, 26 February–3 March 1988, p 208.
34 Ibid., See also Stuart Hall, 'The state in question', in Gregor McLennan, David Held, and Stuart Hall (editors), *The Idea of the Modern State* (Open University Press, Milton Keynes, 1984), p 13.
35 See Peter Gerlich, Edgar Grande and Wolfgang C. Müller, 'Corporatism in Crisis: Stability and Change of Social Partnership in Austria', *Political Studies*, vol 36 (June 1988), pp 209–213.
36 Brian Barry, *op. cit.*, p 208. For a detailed consideration of the future of corporatism see Jukka Pekkarinen, Matti Pohjola, and Bob Rowthorn (editors), 'Social Corporatism and Economic Performance: Introduction and Conclusions', in *Social Corporatism: A Superior Economic System?* (Clarendon Press, Oxford, 1992), pp 15–20.
37 See Basil Chubb, *op. cit.*, pp 127–128.
38 *Report of the Constitution Review Group* (Government Publications, Dublin, May 1996), p 42.
39 Niamh Hardiman, 'The State and Economic Interests: Ireland in Comparative Perspective', in J.H. Goldthorpe and C.T. Whelan (editors), *The Development of Industrial Society in Ireland* (Oxford University Press, Oxford, 1992), p 357.
40 Richard Breen, Damian F. Hannan, David B. Rottman, and Christopher T. Whelan, *Understanding Contemporary Ireland: State, Class and Development in the Republic of Ireland*, (Gill and Macmillan, Dublin, 1990), pp 180, 221.
41 Thomas J. Barrington, 'Whatever Happened to Irish Government?', in Frank Litton (editor), *Unequal Achievement: The Irish Experience 1957–1982*, (Institute of Public Administration, Dublin, 1982), p 106.

42 The Irish Episcopal Conference, *Work is the Key: Towards an Economy That Needs Everyone*, (Veritas, Dublin, 1992), paragraphs 19–20, pp 81–82.
43 *Local Government Reorganisation and Reform* (Government Publications, Dublin, 1991), p 1.
44 Ibid., pp 2, 29.
45 Joseph Lee, 'Centralisation and Community', in Joseph Lee (editor), *Ireland: Towards a Sense of Place*, (Cork University Press, 1985), pp 93–94.
46 *Report of the Constitution Review Group* (Government Publications, Dublin, May 1996), p 429.
47 The principle of subsidiarity is now explicitly recognised in European Union law. At the insistence of the Germans and the British it was included as a clause in the Maastricht Treaty on European Union. See Anthony L. Teasdale, 'Subsidiarity in Post-Maastricht Europe', *The Political Quarterly*, vol 64, no. 2 (April-June 1993), pp 187, 188–189. In the context of domestic politics and administration, subsidiarity is concerned with addressing demands for stronger local government and complaints about bureaucratic overcentralisation.
48 George Weigel, 'Catholicism and Democracy: The Other Twentieth-Century Revolution', *The Washington Quarterly*, vol 12, (Autumn 1989), p 7.
49 Patrick Granfield, *The Limits of the Papacy: Authority and Autonomy in the Church*, (Darton, Longman and Todd, New York, 1987), pp 125–128.
50 Michael Peillon, *Contemporary Irish Society: An Introduction*, (Gill and Macmillan, Dublin 1982), p 99; and Jean Calvez, 'The Social Teaching of the Church: Growth and Development', *Studies*, vol 79, no. 314 (Autumn 1991), p 239.
51 John H. Whyte, *Catholics in Western Democracies: A Study in Political Behaviour* (Gill and Macmillan, Dublin, 1981), p 107.
52 Anthony Coughlan, 'The Constitution and Social Policy', in Frank Litton (editor), *The Constitution of Ireland 1937–1987*, Special issue of *Administration*, vol 35, no. 4 (The Institute of Public Administration, Dublin, 1987), p 148.
53 John H. Whyte (1981), *op. cit.*, p 108, in reference to *Octogesima Adveniens* which commemorated the eightieth anniversary of *Rerum Novarum*.
54 J.H. Whyte (1984), *op. cit.*, pp 8–12. See also Michael P. Hornsby-Smith, 'Social and Religious Transformation in Ireland: A Case of Secularisation?', in J.H. Goldthorpe and C.T. Whelan (editors), *op. cit.*, p 289.
55 Eugene Goulding, 'Report on the C.S.V.O.C.', *Christus Rex*, vol 8, no. 2 (April 1954), p 120.
56 Most Rev Dr D'Alton, 'The Social Teaching of the Church', *Christus Rex*, vol 2, no. 2 (April 1948), pp 7–8.
57 Alfred O'Rahilly, 'The Function of the State', *Christus Rex*, vol 5, no. 4 (October 1951), p 360.
58 Kieran A. Kennedy, *Facing the Unemployment Crisis in Ireland* (Cork University Press, Cork, 1993), p 40.
59 Ibid., in reference to Frank Duff, *True Devotion to the Nation* (Dundalgan Press, Dundalk, 1966)
60 See Joe McVeigh, *Renewing the Irish Church: Towards an Irish Liberation Theology* (Mercier Press, Cork, 1993), especially pp 91, 121–137; and Gerry O'Hanlon, 'The Christian Vision of Solidarity – Pie in the Sky or Our Daily Bread?', *Studies*, vol 82, no. 328 (Winter 1993), pp 432–435.
61 Arguments for and against the deletion of Article 45 are given in *Report of the Constitution Review Group* (Government Publications, Dublin, May 1996), pp 392–393.
62 The Constitution Review Group was critical of the functioning of the Senate and of its system of representation. It regarded the reform of the Senate as too broad and complex an issue to make specific recommendations within the time set for the completion of its report. The expert body advocated a separate comprehensive review. Ibid., pp 70–71.

63 In the context of greater collaborative efforts between the government and its social partners the Constitution Review Group recommended the amendment of Article 15.3.1. The article would read as follows: 'The Oireachtas may provide for the establishment or recognition of advisory or consultative bodies representing branches of the social, community, voluntary and economic life of the people, with a view to improving participation in, and the efficiency of, the democratic process.' The Review Group stated this amendment would require a consequential change in subsection 15.3.2. Ibid., p 43.
64 *Report of the Committee on the Constitution* (Government Publications, Dublin, December 1967), paragraph 70.
65 Ibid., paragraph 73.
66 Ibid., paragraph 72.
67 Ibid., paragraph 73.
68 Ibid., paragraph 81.
69 Joseph Lee (1985), *op. cit.*, p 95.
70 Interview with Mr Tom FitzGerald (Administrative Officer, Muintir na Tíre), 25 June 1994. Some branches of Muintir na Tíre do not cover an entire parish.
71 Tom FitzGerald (Administrative Officer, Muintir na Tíre) to the author, 7 September 1994. The decrease in the number of branches started to occur from the late 1970s when field officers had to be withdrawn because of lack of finance. Consequently, personal contact with members at local community level declined. This was by far the greatest cause of the organisation's decline. It became so preoccupied with endeavouring to raise funding that there was little time available to pursue its primary objectives. The growth of specialist organisations has also contributed to the decline of Muintir na Tíre. These organisations serve sectional interests rather than the community at large.
72 Document no. 13, p 1, Box no. 1, Papers of the Commission on Vocational Organisation, National Archives, Dublin.
73 Pamphlet entitled 'Muintir na Tíre: A Brief Sketch of its History', p 9, Muintir na Tíre Archives, Tipperary.
74 Patrick Hannon, *Church, State, Morality and Law* (Gill and Macmillan, Dublin, 1992), p 127, in reference to David Hollenbach, *Justice, Peace and Human Rights* (New York, 1988), p 181.

CONCLUSION

1 See J.H. Whyte, *Church and State in Modern Ireland 1923–1979*, Second Edition (Gill and Macmillan, Dublin, 1984), pp 105–106.
2 Quotation from Joseph Lee, *The Modernisation of Irish Society 1848–1918* (Gill and Macmillan, Dublin, 1992), p 49. An anonymous vocationalist expressed the view '... though we are a nation of Catholics, we are a Protestant nation. Our whole political, economic, and social life is based on Protestant philosophy and on Protestant forms. We still assert boldly that we take our religion from Rome and our politics from Ireland.' Debus, 'A Catholic Nation or a Nation of Catholics', *Hibernia*, vol 9, no. 6 (June 1945), p 15. The above opinion was typical of the vocationalist outlook.
3 Alfred O'Rahilly, 'Vocational Organisation in the Past', *The Irish Monthly*, May 1938, p 303. The corresponding transcript of the radio broadcast is in Department of the Taoiseach file S10812B, National Archives, Dublin.
4 J.J. Lee, *Ireland 1912–1985: Politics and Society* (Cambridge University Press, Cambridge, 1989), p 272.
5 Ibid., p 332.
6 See Dermot Keogh, *Ireland and Europe 1919–1989: A Diplomatic and Political History* (Hibernian University Press, Cork and Dublin, 1990), p 113.

7 Words in quotation marks from J.J.Lee (1989), *op. cit.*, p 274; and Joseph Lee, 'Aspects of Corporatist Thought in Ireland: The Commission on Vocational Organisation,1939–43', in Art Cosgrove and Donal McCartney (Editors), *Studies in Irish History presented to R.Dudley Edwards* (University College Dublin, 1979), p 326.

8 The *Commission on Vocational Organisation Report* (1943), paragraph 2.

9 *Seanad Debates*, vol 21, col 438, 21 July 1938. See also *Dáil Debates*, vol 96, col 2174, 18 April 1945.

10 The influence of Machiavelli is claimed by Tim Pat Coogan in his book *De Valera: Long Fellow, Long Shadow* (Hutchinson, London, 1993), pp 118–120.

11 Niccolò Machiavelli, *The Prince* (edited by Peter Bondanella, Oxford University Press, Oxford and New York, 1984), pp 21, 52.

12 De Valera was very much aware of the difficulties and limitations associated with the implementation of Catholic social principles. This is nowhere more clearly evident than in Article 45 of the *Constitution of Ireland* (1937). The principles set forth in the Article are only for the guidance of the Oireachtas and are not legally enforceable under any of the provisions of the constitution.

13 Joseph Lee (1979), *op. cit.*, p 339.

14 Philippe C. Schmitter, 'Still the Century of Corporatism?' in Philippe C. Schmitter and Gerhard Lehmbruch (Editors), *Trends Towards Corporatist Intermediation* (Sage Publications, Beverly Hills, California, and London, 1979), p 22.

15 See Basil Chubb, *The Government and Politics of Ireland*, Third Edition (Longman, London and New York, 1992), p 187.

16 See J.H. Whyte, *op. cit.*, pp 116–117.

17 When Louie Bennett addressed the Labour Party's annual conference on 27 May 1945 she stated that she did not know of any country that could be taken as a model or example to clarify the meaning of vocationalism because no country had yet functioned on a vocationalist basis. *The Irish Press*, 28 May 1945, in Department of the Taoiseach file S13540, National Archives, Dublin.

APPENDIX ONE

1 The *Commission on Vocational Organisation Report* (1943), paragraph 1. The categorisation of personnel is given in 'Memorandum for the Government: Proposed Commission on Vocational Organisation', 3 January 1939, Department of the Taoiseach, S10677A, National Archives, Dublin. The clergy were heavily represented on the commission, accounting for five members. This number could be revised to six if the lay theologian, Alfred O'Rahilly of University College, Cork, is included – he was ordained to the priesthood in 1955. According to Evelyn Bolster, the Knights of St Columbanus were also strongly represented (not officially of course) on the commission. E.J. Coyne, John Hayes, Michael Tierney, and Alfred O'Rahilly were all members. Evelyn Bolster, *The Knights of St Columbanus* (Gill and Macmillan, Dublin, 1979), pp 80–81.

2 De Valera to Browne, 18 January 1939, Department of the Taoiseach, S10677B, National Archives, Dublin.

APPENDIX TWO

1 The commission's field of inquiry covered the vocational activities of 1,339,085 persons engaged in 262 different occupations. Religious, political and recreational activities were not examined. The above figures were obtained from the 1936 census. The *Commission on Vocational Organisation Report* (1943), paragraph 7.

2 The *Commission on Vocational Organisation Report* (1943), paragraph 4.
3 Ibid., paragraph 9.
4 Ibid.
5 Ibid., paragraph 10.
6 Ibid., paragraph 13.
7 Ibid., paragraph 14.
8 Ibid., paragraphs 15–16.
9 Ibid., see paragraphs 19–24; words in quotation marks from paragraph 21.
10 Ibid., paragraphs 25–35.
11 Ibid., paragraph 142.
12 Ibid., paragraph 156.
13 Ibid., paragraph 504.
14 Ibid., paragraph 701.
15 Ibid., paragraph 504.
16 Ibid., paragraph 505.
17 Ibid., paragraphs 506–509.
18 Ibid., paragraph 38.
19 Ibid., paragraph 671.
20 Ibid., paragraph 672.
21 Ibid., paragraph 670.
22 Ibid., paragraph 673.
23 Ibid., paragraph 675.
24 Ibid., paragraph 668.
25 Ibid., paragraph 678.
26 Ibid., see paragraph 677.
27 Ibid., paragraph 596.
28 Ibid., paragraphs 523–528, 554–556, 576–579, 620–621, 634–637 and 651–652.
29 Ibid., paragraph 702.
30 Ibid., paragraphs 706–708.
31 Ibid., paragraph 704.
32 Ibid., paragraphs 709–710.
33 Ibid., paragraph 708.
34 Ibid., paragraph 711.
35 Ibid., paragraph 707.
36 Ibid., paragraph 513.
37 Ibid., paragraph 547.
38 Ibid., paragraph 719.

APPENDIX THREE

1 List of organisations compiled from Eugene Goulding, 'Report on the C.S.V.O.C.', Christus Rex, vol 8, no. 2 (April 1954), p 113; and C.S.V.O.C. correspondence to the Taoiseach between February 1949 and June 1950, Department of the Taoiseach, S13636B, National Archives, Dublin.

Bibliography

PRIMARY SOURCES

The National Archives (Dublin):
Department of the Taoiseach, S files
Cabinet Minutes
Files of the following government departments:
  Finance
  Foreign Affairs (formerly External Affairs)
  Labour
The Report of the Commission on Youth Unemployment (1951)
Papers of the Commission on Vocational Organisation
Frank MacDermot papers

The National Library of Ireland (Dublin):
  Minutes of Evidence of the Commission on Vocational Organisation
Archives of Blackrock College (Dublin)
  Alfred O'Rahilly papers
Archives of the Holy Ghost Congregation (Irish Province, Dublin):
  Denis Fahey papers
  Maria Duce papers
Archives of Muintir na Tíre
  John Hayes papers
  Thomas Morris papers
Archives of University College Cork:
  Alfred O'Rahilly papers
Archives Department, University College Dublin:
  Hugh Kennedy papers
  Seán McEntee papers
Dublin Diocesan Archives (R.C.):
  Edward Byrne papers
  John Charles McQuaid papers
The Franciscan Archives (Dublin):
  Éamon de Valera papers
Galway Diocesan Archives (R.C.):
  Michael Browne papers
The Jesuit Archives (Dublin):
  Edward J. Coyne papers

Edward Cahill papers
Minutes of Jesuit committee on the framing of the Constitution of Ireland (1937)

OFFICIAL PUBLICATIONS

Dáil Éireann Debates
Seanad Éireann Debates
Draft Constitution of the Irish Free State to be Submitted to the Provisional Parliament (1922)
Saorstat Eireann: Status and Constitution: Documents Submitted to the Fourth Assembly of the League of Nations (1923)
Report of the Second House of the Oireachtas Commission (1936)
Bunreacht na hÉireann (Constitution of Ireland, 1937)
Reports of the Commission of Inquiry Into Banking, Currency and Credit (1938)
Commission on Vocational Organisation Report (dated 1943, published in 1944)
Report of the Committee on the Constitution (December 1967)
Local Government Reorganisation and Reform (1991)
Report of the Constitution Review Group (May 1996)

Papal Encyclicals

Rerum Novarum (Leo XIII, 1891)
Quadragesimo Anno (Pius XI, 1931)
Mater et Magistra (John XXIII, 1961)
Pacem in Terris (John XXIII, 1963)

Interviews and correspondence

Mr Thomas J. Barrington, served as private secretary to Seán MacEntee, who was Minister for Local Government and Public Health (1941–1948).
Mr Tom FitzGerald, Administrative Officer, Muintir na Tíre.
Dr Maurice Moynihan, Secretary to Government (1937–1960).

SECONDARY SOURCES

Newspapers

Connacht Tribune
Cork Examiner
Evening Herald
Irish Catholic
Irish Independent
Irish Press
Irish Times
Limerick Leader
Spectator
Standard
Times Literary Supplement

Periodicals

Acta Sociologica
Administration
B.G.A. Record
British Journal of Sociology
Catholic Bulletin
Catholic Historical Review
Catholic Mind
Christus Rex
Cross Currents
Doctrine and Life
Éire-Ireland
English Historical Review
European Journal of Sociology
Fiat
Furrow
Government and Opposition
Hibernia
History Ireland
History of Political Economy
Irish Ecclesiastical Record (5th. series)
Irish Historical Studies
Irish Jurist
Irish Monthly
Irish Review
Irish University Review
Irish Theological Quarterly
Journal of Contemporary History
Mediterranean Historical Review
Milltown Studies
New Blackfriars
Political Quarterly
Political Studies
Position Papers
Review of Politics
Saothar
Studies
Thought
U.S. Catholic Historian
Washington Quarterly

Works of Reference

Boylan, Henry, *A Dictionary of Irish Bibliography*, Second Edition (Gill and Macmillan, Dublin, 1988).

Doherty, J.E. and D.J. Hickey, *A Chronology of Irish History Since 1500* (Gill and Macmillan, Dublin, 1989).

Flew, Antony (editorial consultant), *A Dictionary of Philosophy* (Pan Books, London, 1984).

Helferty, Seamus and Raymond Refaussé (editors), *Directory of Irish Archives*, Second Edition (Irish Academic Press, Dublin, 1993).

Hickey, D.J and J.E. Doherty, *A Dictionary of Irish History 1800–1980* (Gill and Macmillan, Dublin, 1987).

Irish Catholic Directory.

Popkin, Richard H. and Avrum Stroll, *Philosophy*, Third Edition (Made Simple Books, Oxford, 1993).

Williams, E.N., *The Penguin Dictionary of English and European History 1485–1789* (Penguin Books, Harmondsworth, England, 1980).

Theses

Broderick, Eugene, *Irish Corporatism 1931–1939* (M.A. thesis, University College Cork, 1991).

O'Connor, J.D. Raymond, *The Origins, Ethos and Geographical Expansion of Muintir na Tíre: 1931–1970* (M.A. thesis, University College Cork, 1988).

O'Driscoll, Finín, *The Search for the Christian State – An Analysis of Irish Social Catholicism, 1913–1939* (M.A. thesis, University College Cork, 1994).

Books and articles

Ahern, M.J., 'What is The Corporative State?', *The Irish Monthly*, vol 69 (December 1941), pp 572–576.

Akenson, D.H. and J.F. Fallin, 'The Irish Civil War and the Drafting of the Free State Constitution: The Drafting Committee and the Boundaries of Action', *Éire-Ireland*, vol 5, no. 1 (Spring 1970), pp 10–26.

Akenson, D.H. and J.F. Fallin, 'The Irish Civil War and the Drafting of the Free State Constitution: The Drafting Process', *Éire-Ireland*, vol 5, no. 2 (Summer 1970), pp 42–93.

Akenson, D.H. and J.F. Fallin, 'The Irish Civil War and the Drafting of the Free State Constitution: Collins, de Valera and the Pact: A New Interpretation', *Éire-Ireland*, vol 5, no. 4 (Winter 1970), pp 28–40.

Akenson, D.H. and J.F. Fallin, 'The Irish Civil War and the Drafting of the Free State Constitution: Draft Constitution', *Éire-Ireland*, vol 5, no. 4 (Winter 1970), pp 41–53.

Akenson, D.H. and J.F. Fallin, 'The Irish Civil War and the Drafting of the Free State Constitution: Capitulation to the British', *Éire-Ireland*, vol 5, no. 4 (Winter 1970), pp 53–70.

Allum, P.A., *Italy – Republic Without Government?* (W.W.Norton, New York and London, 1973).

Baerwald, Friedrich, 'The Labour Encyclicals Today', *The Catholic Mind*, vol 49, no. 1066 (October, 1951), pp 622–634.

Barrington, Ruth, *Health, Medicine and Politics in Ireland 1900–1970*, (Institute of Public Administration, Dublin, 1987).

Barrington, T.J., 'The Situation of Irish Government', *The Irish Review*, no. 3 (1988), pp 18–25.

Barry, Brian, 'Growth at a price', *Times Literary Supplement*, February 26–March 3, 1988, pp 207–208.

Bartlett, Thomas, 'The Catholic Question in the Eighteenth Century', *History Ireland*, vol 1, no. 1 (Spring 1993), pp 17–21.

Baumer, Franklin L., 'Romanticism (ca.1780–ca.1830)', in Philip P. Wiener (editor-in-chief), *Dictionary of the History of Ideas: vol 4, Studies of Selected Pivotal Ideas*, (Charles Scribner's Sons, New York, 1973), pp 198–204.

Beck, George Andrew, 'Retrospect on Liberalism', *The Catholic Mind*, vol 47, no. 1042 (October, 1949), pp 577–588.

Binchy, Daniel A., 'Proposals For a New Senate', *Studies*, vol 25, no. 97 (March 1936), pp 20–32.

Binchy, Daniel A., 'The Papacy in a Changing World', *Studies*, vol 26 (December 1937), pp 641–647.

Blinkhorn, Martin, *Mussolini and Fascist Italy* (Routledge, London and New York, 1984).

Bolster, Evelyn, *The Knights of St Columbanus* (Gill and Macmillan, Dublin, 1979).

Bouscaren, Anthony Trawick, 'The European Christian Democrats', *The Catholic Mind*, vol 47, no. 1041 (September 1949), pp 522–536.

Bracken, Joseph, 'The Corporate State and the Fascist Tyranny – a Challenging Distinction', *Hibernia*, vol 1 (January 1937), pp 15, 19.

Breen, Richard, Damian F. Hannan, David B. Rottman and Chistopher T. Whelan (editors), *Understanding Contemporary Ireland: State, Class and Development in the Republic of Ireland* (Gill and Macmillan, Dublin, 1990).

Broderick, Eugene, 'The corporate labour policy of Fine Gael, 1934', *Irish Historical Studies*, vol 29, no. 113 (May 1994), pp 88–99.

Broderick, Joe, 'De Valera and Archbishop Daniel Mannix', *History Ireland*, vol 2, no. 3 (Autumn 1994), pp 37–42.

Brophy, Liam, 'Primaute Du Spirituel', *Hibernia*, vol 8, no. 9 (September 1944), pp 5–6.

Broszat, Martin, *The Hitler State: The Foundation and Development of the Internal Structure of the Third Reich* (Longman, London and New York, 1981).

Brown, Terence, *Ireland: A Social and Cultural History 1922–1985* (Fontana Press, London, 1985).

Brown, Tony, '100 Years of Catholic Social Teaching', *Studies*, Autumn 1991, pp 241–252.

Browne, M.J., 'The World Economic Crisis and Catholic Teaching', *The Irish Ecclesiastical Record* (5th series), vol 41 (January – June 1933), pp 337–355.

Browne, Nöel, *Against The Tide* (Gill and Macmillan, Dublin, 1986).

Busteed, John, 'The World Economic Crisis and "Rerum Novarum" ', *Studies*, vol 20 (March 1931), pp 13–23.

Cahill, E., 'The Catholic Social Movement', *The Irish Ecclesiastical Record* (5th series), vol 36 (July – December 1930), pp 572–587.

Cahill, E., *The Framework of a Christian State* (Dublin, 1932).

Cahill, E., 'Capitalism and its Alternatives', *The Irish Ecclesiastical Record* (5th series), vol 45 (February, 1935), pp 113–147.

Calvez, Jean, 'The Social Teaching of the Church: Growth and Development', *Studies*, Autumn 1991, pp 235–240.

Camp, Richard L., *The Papal Ideology of Social Reform: A Study in Historical Development 1878–1967* (E.J. Brill, Leiden, The Netherlands, 1969).

Campbell, J.J., 'To Catholic Action Through Co-operation', *The Irish Monthly*, vol 66 (September 1938), pp 605–611.

Canavan, Joseph E., 'The Virtue of Patriotism', *Studies*, vol 25, no. 97 (March 1936), pp 33–46.

Carlen, M.Claudia, *A Guide To The Encyclicals Of The Roman Pontiffs From Leo XIII To The Present Day* (1878–1937) (H.W. Wilson, New York, 1939).

Carpenter, L.P., 'Corporatism in Britain, 1930–45', *Journal of Contemporary History*, 11 (1976), pp 3–25.

Carr, William, *A History of Germany 1815–1985*, Third Edition (Edward Arnold, London, 1987).

Cawson, Alan (editor), *Organised Interests and the State* (Sage Publications, London, 1985).

Cawson, Alan, 'In Defence of the New Testament: A Reply to Andrew Cox, "The Old and New Testaments of Corporatism" ', *Political Studies*, vol 36 no. 2 (June 1988), pp 309–315.

Chesterton, G.K., 'The Mission of Ireland', *Studies*, vol 21 (September, 1932), pp 374–384.

Chubb, Basil, 'Vocational Representation And The Irish Senate', *Political Studies*, vol II, no. 2 (1954), pp 97–111.

Chubb, Basil (editor), *A Source Book of Irish Government* (Institute of Public Administration, Dublin, 1964).

Chubb, Basil, *The Government and Politics of Ireland*, Third Edition (Longman, London and New York, 1992).

Clancy, Patrick, Sheelagh Drudy, Kathleen Lynch and Liam O'Dowd (editors), *Ireland: A Sociological Profile* (Institute of Public Administration, Dublin, 1986).

Clarke, Desmond M., *Church and State: Essays in Political Philosophy* (Cork University Press, Cork, 1985).

Coffey, P., 'An Injustice of the Capitalist System: Its Monopoly of Financial Credit', *The Irish Theological Quarterly*, vol 16 (1921), pp 34–46.

Coffey, P., 'The Economic World-Crisis: Some Suggestions Towards Diagnosis and Remedy', *The Irish Ecclesiastical Record* (5th series), vol 48 (July-December 1936), pp 131–141.

Coleman, John A. (editor), *One Hundred Years of Catholic Social Thought: Celebration and Challenge* (Orbis Books, Maryknoll, New York, 1991).

Collins, C. and Brendan O'Cearbhaill, 'Joint Industrial Councils', *Christus Rex*, vol 11, no. 2 (April 1957), pp 557–566.

Collins, Edward, 'Distributism', *The Irish Monthly*, vol 72 (January 1944), pp 5–16.

Collins, Randall, 'The Rise and Fall of Modernism in Politics and Religion', *Acta Sociologica*, vol 35, no. 3 (1992), pp 171–186.

Conway, Patrick J., 'The State in Economic Life', *Christus Rex*, vol 2, no. 3 (July 1948), pp 3–16.

Conway, William, 'Industrial Relations: The Principles', *Christus Rex*, vol 4, no. 1 (January 1950), pp 3–15.

Conway, William, 'The Church and State Control', *Christus Rex*, vol 6, no. 2 (April 1952), pp 111–131.

Coogan, Tim Pat, *De Valera: Long Fellow, Long Shadow* (Hutchinson, London, 1993).

Coolahan, John, *Irish Education: Its History and Structure* (Institute of Public Administration, Dublin, 1981).

Cooney, John, *The Crozier and the Dáil: Church and State 1922–1986* (The Mercier Press, Cork and Dublin, 1986).

Copleston, Frederick, *A History of Philosophy*, vol 7, (Image Books, Garden City, New York, 1965).

Copleston, Frederick, *A History of Philosophy*, vol 8 (Image Books, Garden City, New York, 1967).

Corish, Patrick J., *The Irish Catholic Experience: A Historical Survey* (Gill and Macmillan, Dublin, 1985).

Cox, Andrew, 'Corporatism as Reductionism: the Analytic Limits of the Corporatist Thesis', *Government and Opposition*, vol 16, no. 1 (Winter 1981), pp 78–95.

Cox, Andrew, 'The Old and New Testaments of Corporatism: Is it a Political Form or a Method of Policy-making?', *Political Studies*, vol 36 (1988), pp 294–308.

Coyne, Edward J., 'National Economic Councils', *Studies*, vol 22 (June 1933), pp 288–306.

Coyne, E.J., 'The Vocational Structure of Ireland', *The Irish Monthly*, vol 66 (June 1938), pp 394–402.

Coyne, E.J., 'An Economic Council for Ireland', *The Irish Monthly*, vol 68 (June 1940), pp 299–307.

Coyne, Edward J., 'Mother and Child Service', *Studies*, vol 40 (June 1951), pp 129–149.

Coyne, Edward J., 'The Small Farm in Irish Agriculture', *Studies*, vol 47 (Spring 1958), pp 1–20.

Cramer, Dale L. and Charles G. Leathers, 'Schumpeter's corporatist views: links among his social theory, Quadragesimo Anno, and moral reform', *History of Political Economy*, vol 13, no. 4 (Winter 1981), pp 745–771.

Crane, Paul, 'Democratic Capitalism', *Studies*, vol 40 (March 1951), pp 33–46.

Cronin, Mike, 'Blueshirts, Sports and Socials', *History Ireland*, vol 2, no. 3 (Autumn 1994), pp 43–47.

Curran, Charles E. and Richard A. McCormick (editors), *Readings in Moral Theology no. 5: Official Catholic Social Teaching* (Paulist Press, New York, 1986).

D'Alton, John, 'The Social Teaching of the Church' (Lenten Pastoral of the Archbishop of Armagh and Primate of All Ireland), *Christus Rex*, vol 2, no. 2 (April 1948), pp 3–16.

Daly, Mary E., *Industrial Development and Irish National Identity 1922–1939*, First Edition (Syracuse University Press, Syracuse, New York, 1992).

Daniel-Rops, Henri, *A Fight For God: 1870–1939* (London 1966).

Darby, J.H., 'Religion and the Decline of Capitalism', *The Catholic Mind*, vol 49, no. 1066 (October 1951), pp 647–653.

De Fonseka, J.P., 'Some Aspects Of G.K.Chesterton As A Catholic Thinker', *The Irish Monthly*, vol 58 (May 1930), pp 245–257.

De Rosa, Peter, *Vicars of Christ: The Dark Side of the Papacy* (Corgi Books, London, 1990).

Diamant, Alfred, *Austrian Catholics and the Social Question 1918–1933*, (University of Florida Press, Gainesville, Florida, Spring 1959).

Dignan, J., 'The Government Proposals for Social Security', *Christus Rex*, vol 4, no. 2 (April 1950), pp 103–112.

Donnelly, Peter, 'Church and State – Irish Style: Tradition and Innovation', *Studies*, vol 84, no. 335 (Autumn 1995), pp 293–301.

Doolan, Aegidus, 'The Service State in the Light of Catholic Social Principles', *Christus Rex*, vol 1, no. 4 (October 1947), pp 3–13.

Dorr, Donal, *Option for the Poor: A Hundred Years of Vatican Social Teaching*, Revised Edition (Gill and Macmillan, Dublin, 1992).

Dorrien, Gary, 'Beyond State and Market: Christianity and the Future of Economic Democracy', *Cross Currents*, Summer 1995, pp 184–204.

Doyle, William, *The Old European Order 1660–1800*, Second Edition (Oxford University Press, 1992).

Droz, Jacques, 'Romanticism in Political Thought', in Philip P. Wiener (editor-in-chief), *Dictionary of the History of Ideas: vol 4, Studies of Selected Pivotal Ideas*, (Charles Scribner's Sons, New York, 1973), pp 205–208.

Drummond, William, 'Papal Encyclicals and Vocational Order', *The Irish Monthly*, vol 72 (March 1944), pp 101–104.

Dudley-Edwards, Owen, *Éamon de Valera* (GPC Books, University of Wales Press, Cardiff, 1987).

Duffy, Colum Gavan, 'The Irish Constitution and Current Problems', *Christus Rex*, vol 12, no. 2 (April 1958), pp 99–121.

Duffy, Eamon, *Saints and Sinners: A History of the Popes* (Yale University Press and S4C, 1997).

Fahey, Denis, 'Characteristics of St Thomas's Teaching', *The Catholic Bulletin*, vol 15, no. 6 (June 1925), pp 596–608.

Fahey, Denis, 'Off Sterling: The Report of Our Private Banking Commission', *Hibernia*, vol 2, no. 5 (May 1938), pp 9–12.

Fallon, W.G., 'The Bankruptcy of Protestantism?', *Hibernia*, vol 3, no. 6 (June 1939), p 4.

Fanning, Ronan, *The Irish Department of Finance 1922–58* (The Institute of Public Administration, Dublin, 1978).

Fanning, Ronan, *Independent Ireland* (Helicon, Dublin, 1983).

Farrell, Brian, *Seán Lemass* (Gill and Macmillan, Dublin, 1983).

Farrell, Brian (editor), *De Valera's Constitution and Ours* (Gill and Macmillan, Dublin, 1988).

Faughnan, Seán, 'The Jesuits and the drafting of the Irish constitution of 1937', *Irish Historical Studies*, vol 26, no. 101 (May 1988), pp 79–102.

Feirmeoir, 'Agriculture in a Vocational Order of Society', *Christus Rex*, vol 10, no. 1 (January 1956), pp 46–62.

Ffrench, Right Hon. Lord, 'The Economic Future of Ireland', *Studies*, vol 15 (September 1926), pp 353–367.

FitzGerald, Desmond, *Preface to Statecraft* (Sheed and Ward, London, 1939).

FitzGerald, Garret, *Planning in Ireland: A PEP Study* (The Institute of Public Administration, Dublin; Political and Economic Planning, London, 1968).

Flora, Peter and Arnold J. Heidenheimer, *The Development of Welfare States in Europe and America* (Transaction Books, New Brunswick, U.S.A.; and London, U.K, 1981).

Foster, R.F., *Modern Ireland 1600–1972* (Allen Lane, London, 1988).

Fox, R.M. *Jim Larkin: Irish Labour Leader* (International Publishers, New York, 1957).

Freemantle, Anne (editor), *The Papal Encyclicals in Their Historical Context* (Mentor, New York, 1956).

Gaffney, Maurice P., 'The Scope of the Industrial Relations Act', *Christus Rex*, vol 11, no. 2 (April 1957), pp 540–556.

Gallagher, Patrick, *My Story* (Templecrone Co-operative Society, Dungloe, n.d.).

Garvin, Thomas, *The Irish Senate* (Institute of Public Administration, Dublin, 1969).

Garvin, Tom, 'Priests and patriots: Irish separatism and fear of the modern, 1890–1914', *Irish Historical Studies*, vol 25, no. 97 (May 1986), pp 67–81.

Gaughan, J. Anthony, *Alfred O'Rahilly I: Academic* (Kingdom Books, Dublin, 1986).

Gaughan, J. Anthony, *Alfred O'Rahilly II: Public Figure* (Kingdom Books, Dublin, 1989).

Gaughan, J. Anthony, *Alfred O'Rahilly III: Controversialist Part 1: Social Reformer* (Kingdom Books, Dublin, 1992).

Gaughan, J. Anthony, *Alfred O'Rahilly III: Controversialist Part 2: Catholic Apologist* (Kingdom Books, Dublin, 1993).

Gerlich, Peter, Edgar Grande and Wolfgang C. Müller, 'Corporatism in Crisis: Stability and Change of Social Partnership in Austria', *Political Studies*, vol 36, no. 2 (June 1988), pp 209–223.

Girvin, Brian, *Between Two Worlds: Politics and Economy in Independent Ireland* (Gill and Macmillan, Dublin, 1989).

Goldthorpe, J.H. and C.T. Whelan (editors), *The Development of Industrial Society in Ireland* (Oxford University Press, Oxford and New York, 1992).

Goulding, Eugene, 'Report on the C.S.V.O.C.', *Christus Rex*, vol 8, no. 2 (April 1954), pp 109–120.

Granfield, Patrick, *The Limits of the Papacy: Authority and Autonomy in the Church* (Darton, Longman and Todd, New York, 1987).

Grant, Wyn (editor), *The Political Economy of Corporatism* (Macmillan, London, 1985).

Gutmann, James, 'Romanticism in Post-Kantian Philosophy', in Philip P. Weiner (editor-in-chief), *Dictionary of the History of Ideas: vol 4, Studies of Selected Pivotal Ideas* (Charles Scribner's Sons, New York, 1973), pp 208–211.

Hackett, J.P., 'Vocational Groups and Vocational Education', *The Irish Monthly*, vol 66 (November 1938), pp 743–755.

Halsted, John B. (editor), *Romanticism: Problems of Definition, Explanation, and Evaluation* (D.C. Heath, Boston, 1965).

Hannon, Patrick, *Church, State, Morality and Law* (Gill and Macmillan, Dublin, 1992).

Hardiman, Niamh and Stephen Lalor, 'Corporatism in Ireland: An Exchange of Views', *Administration*, vol 32, no. 1 (1984), pp 76–88.

Hayes, J.M., 'Vocational Organisation for Farmers and Farm Labourers', *The Irish Monthly*, vol 66 (September 1938), pp 596–604.

Hebblethwaite, Peter, 'The Popes and Politics: Shifting Patterns in 'Catholic Social Doctrine'', *Daedalus: Journal of the American Academy of Arts and Sciences*, Winter 1982, pp 85–99.

Hennesey, James, 'Leo XIII: Intellectualizing the Combat with Modernity', *U.S. Catholic Historian*, vol 7, no. 4 (1988), pp 393–400.

Hensey, Brendan, *The Health Services of Ireland*, Completely Revised Fourth Edition (Institute of Public Administration, Dublin, 1988).

Higgins, George G., 'Catholic Tests of a Social Order', *The Catholic Mind*, vol 46, no. 1029 (September 1948), pp 565–566.

Higgins, George C., 'After Sixty Years', *The Catholic Mind*, vol 49, no. 1066 (October 1951), pp 606–617.

Hogan, Edward J., 'Democracy in Corporations', *The Catholic Mind*, vol 47, no. 1041 (September 1949), pp 519–521.

Hogan, James, *Modern Democracy* (Cork University Press, Dublin and Cork, 1938).

Holmes, J. Derek, *The Triumph of the Holy See: A Short History of the Papacy in the Nineteenth Century* (Burns and Oates, London, 1978).

Hoppen, K. Theodore, *Ireland Since 1800: Conflict and Conformity* (Longman, London and New York, 1989).

Horgan, John J., 'A Vocational Second Chamber', *The Irish Monthly*, vol 66 (August 1938), pp 526–534.

Hoyt, Robert S. and Stanley Chodorow, *Europe in the Middle Ages*, Third Edition (Harcourt Brace Jovanovich, San Diego, California, 1976).

Hughes, Michael, *Nationalism and Society: Germany 1800–1945* (Edward Arnold, London, 1988).

Hutton, Seán and Paul Stewart (editors), *Ireland's Histories: Aspects of state, society and ideology* (Routledge, London and New York, 1991).

Inglis, Tom, *Moral Monopoly: The Catholic Church in Modern Irish Society* (Gill and Macmillan, Dublin, 1987).

Irving, R.E.M., *The Christian Democratic Parties of Western Europe* (Allen and Unwin, London, 1979).

Jedin, Hubert and John Dolan (editors), *History of the Church: vol 8: The Church in the Age of Liberalism* (Burns and Oates, London, 1981).

Jedin, Hubert and John Dolan (editors), *History of the Church: vol 9: The Church in the Industrial Age* (Burns and Oates, London, 1981).

Jedin, Hubert, Konrad Repgen and John Dolan (editors), *History of the Church: vol 10: The Church in the Modern Age* (Burns and Oates, London, 1981).

John Paul II (Pope), *Crossing the Threshold of Hope* (Jonathan Cape, London, 1994).

Keen, Maurice, *The Pelican History of Medieval Europe* (Penguin Books, Middlesex, England, 1969).

Kelleher, J., 'Priests and Social Action in Ireland', *Studies*, vol 4 (June 1915), pp 169–183.

Kelleher, J., 'Distributive Justice', *The Irish Theological Quarterly*, vol 12, no. 48 (October 1917), pp 342–355.

Kelleher, J., 'Distributive Justice II', *The Irish Theological Quarterly*, vol 13, no. 49 (January 1918), pp 1–18.

Kelleher, John, 'Catholic Rural Action: A Pointer for Ireland', *Studies*, vol 17 (September 1928), pp 421–436.

Kelleher, J., 'Quadragesimo Anno', *The Irish Ecclesiastical Record* (5th series), vol 38 (July-December 1931), pp 337–347.

Kelleher, John, 'The Encyclicals and Vocational Organisation', *The Irish Monthly*, vol 66 (May 1938), pp 305–315.

Kelly, Hugh, 'Hilaire Belloc: Catholic Champion', *Studies*, vol 30 (March 1941), pp 1–16.

Kelly, J.M. (The Editor), 'Revision of the Constitution of Ireland', *The Irish Jurist*, vol 1, Part 1, New Series, (Summer 1966), pp 1–15.

Kennedy, Kieran A., *Facing the Unemployment Crisis in Ireland* (Cork University Press, Cork, 1993).

Kennedy, Liam, 'The early response of the Irish catholic clergy to the co-operative movement', *Irish Historical Studies*, vol 21, no. 81 (March, 1978), pp 55–74.

Kent, Peter C., 'A Tale of Two Popes: Pius XI, Pius XII and the Rome-Berlin Axis', *Journal of Contemporary History*, vol 23, no. 4 (October 1988), pp 589–608.

Keogh, Dermot, *The Rise of the Irish Working Class: The Dublin Trade Union Movement and Labour Leadership 1890–1914* (Appletree Press, Belfast, 1982).

Keogh, Dermot, *The Vatican, the Bishops and Irish Politics 1919–1939* (Cambridge University Press, Cambridge, 1986).

Keogh, Dermot, 'The Jesuits and the 1937 Constitution', *Studies*, vol 78, no. 309 (Spring 1989), pp 82–95.

Keogh, Dermot, *Ireland and Europe 1919–1989: A Diplomatic and Political History* (Hibernian University Press, Cork and Dublin, 1990).

Keogh, Dermot, *Twentieth-Century Ireland: Nation and State* (Gill and Macmillan, Dublin, 1994).

Keogh, Dermot, 'The Catholic Church and the Irish Free State 1923–1932', *History Ireland*, vol 2, no. 1 (Spring 1994), pp 47–51.

Keogh, Dermot, *Ireland and the Vatican: The Politics and Diplomacy of Church-State Relations, 1922–1960* (Cork University Press, Cork, 1995).

King, Roger (with chapter 8 by Graham Gibbs), *The State in Modern Society: New Directions in Political Sociology* (Macmillan, London, 1986).

Knee, Stuart E., 'The Strange Alliance: Mussolini, Pope Pius XI, and the Lateran Treaty', *Mediterranean Historical Review*, Volume 5, no. 2 (1990), pp 183–206.

Lalor, Stephen, 'Corporatism in Ireland', *Administration*, vol 30, no. 4 (1982), pp 74–97.

Lamont, Stewart, *Church and State: Uneasy Alliances* (The Bodley Head, London, 1989).

Larkin, Emmet, *James Larkin: Irish Labour Leader 1876–1947*, (Pluto Press, London, 1989).

Lee, Joseph, 'Aspects of Corporatist Thought in Ireland: The Commission on Vocational Organisation, 1939–43', in Art Cosgrove and Donal McCartney (editors), *Studies in Irish History presented to R. Dudley Edwards* (University College Dublin, Dublin, 1979), pp 324–346.

Lee, J.J. (editor), *Ireland 1945–70* (Gill and Macmillan, Dublin, 1979).

Lee, Joseph, *Reflections on Ireland in the E.E.C.*, Second Edition (Irish Council of the European Movement, Dublin, 1984).

Lee, Joseph, 'Centralisation and Community', in Joseph Lee (editor), *Ireland: Towards a Sense of Place* (Cork University Press, Cork, 1985), pp 84–101.

Lee, J.J., *Ireland 1912–1985: Politics and Society* (Cambridge University Press, Cambridge, 1989).

Lee, Joseph, *The Modernisation of Irish Society 1848–1918* (Gill and Macmillan, Dublin, 1992).

Lee, Stephen J., *The European Dictatorships 1918–1945* (Methuen, London and New York, 1987).

Linehan, M.P., 'Vocational Organisation and the Wage Earner', *The Irish Monthly*, vol 66 (June 1938), pp 386–393.

Litton, Frank (editor), *Unequal Achievement: The Irish Experience 1957–1982* (Institute of Public Administration, Dublin, 1982).

Litton, Frank (editor), 'The Constitution of Ireland 1937–1987', *Administration* (Special issue, published by the Institute of Public Administration, Dublin), vol 35, no. 4 (1987).

Lucey, C., 'On a Recent Study in Social Science', *The Irish Ecclesiastical Record* (5th series), vol 41 (January–June 1933), pp 370–384.

Lucey, Cornelius, 'Christian Corporativism', *The Irish Ecclesiastical Record* (5th series), vol 49 (March 1937), pp 225–241.

Lucey, Cornelius, 'The Vocational Group Movement', *The Irish Monthly*, vol 66 (April 1938), pp 221–237.

Lucey, Cornelius, 'A Guild For Education', *The Irish Ecclesiastical Record* (5th series), vol 51 (June 1938), pp 582–592.

Lucey, Cornelius, 'The Message of the Social Encyclicals', *The Irish Ecclesiastical Record* (5th series), vol 52 (August 1938), pp 113–130.

Lyons, F.S.L., *Ireland Since the Famine* (Fontana Press, London, 1985).

MacArdle, Dorothy, *The Irish Republic*, Fourth Edition (Irish Press, Dublin, 1951).

Machiavelli, Niccolò, *The Prince* (edited by Peter Bondanella, Oxford University Press, Oxford and New York, 1984).

MacLoughlin, James, 'Is Our Culture Threatened?', *The Irish Ecclesiastical Record* (5th series), vol 39 (February 1932), pp 113–123.

Malcolm, Noel, 'Europe's Unholy Godfathers', *The Spectator* (23 September 1989), pp 8–9.

Maloney, Oliver, 'A response to Michael McDowell's views on the value of Catholic socio-economic theory', *Studies*, vol 81, no. 322 (Summer 1992), pp 163–170.

Manning, Maurice, *The Blueshirts* (Gill and Macmillan, Dublin, 1987).

Mansergh, Nicholas, *The Irish Free State: Its Government and Politics* (Allen and Unwin, London, 1934).

Mansergh, Nicholas, *The Unresolved Question: The Anglo-Irish Settlement and its Undoing 1912–72* (Yale University Press, New Haven and London, 1991).

Marshner, W.H, 'Christian Social Order', *Position Papers* 260/261 (August–September 1995), pp 247–250.

Masse, Benjamin L., 'The Popes and the Industrial Revolution', *The Catholic Mind*, vol 49, no. 1066 (October 1951), pp 635–641.

McCarthy, C.P., 'Vocational Organisation For Industrialists', *The Irish Monthly*, vol 66 (July 1938), pp 444–453.

McCarthy, Charles, *Trade Unions in Irseland 1894–1960* (Institute of Public Administration, Dublin, 1977).
McCarthy, John F. (editor), *Planning Ireland's Future: The Legacy of T.K. Whittaker* (Glendale Press, Dublin, 1990).
McCartney, Donal, 'Seán O'Faoláin: A Nationalist Right Enough', *Irish University Review*, vol 6, no. 1 (Spring 1976), pp 73–86.
McCartney, Donal, 'The Quest for Irish Political Identity: the Image and the Illusion', *Irish University Review*, vol 9, no. 1 (Spring 1979), pp 13–22.
McCaughey, Terence P., *Memory and Redemption: Church, Politics and Prophetic Theology in Ireland* (Gill and Macmillan, Dublin, 1993).
McCool, Gerald A., 'Neo-Thomism and the Tradition of St Thomas', *Thought*, vol 62, no. 245 (June 1987), pp 131–146.
McCreesh, Gerard, 'Corporatism as a Solution of Partition', *Hibernia*, vol 3, no. 6 (June 1939), pp 5–7.
McDonagh, Enda, 'Church and State in the Constitution of Ireland', *The Irish Theological Quarterly*, vol 28, no. 2 (April 1961), pp 131–144.
McDowell, Michael H., 'The Questionable Value of Catholic Socio Economic Theory', *Studies*, Autumn 1991, pp 253–258.
McElligott, T.J., 'How The Farmers Can Organise', *The Irish Monthly*, vol 67 (January 1939), pp 51–58.
McEoin, Gary, 'The Impact of Catholic Social Teaching', *Doctrine and Life*, vol 41, no. 10 (December 1991), pp 531–536.
McGuckin, Terence, 'Saint Thomas Aquinas and Theological Exegesis of Sacred Scripture', *New Blackfriars*, vol 74, no. 870 (April 1993), pp 197–213.
McKee, Eamonn, 'Church-state relations and the development of Irish health policy: the mother-and-child scheme, 1944–53', *Irish Historical Studies*, vol 25, no. 98 (November 1986), pp 159–194.
McKevitt, P., 'The Background of Rerum Novarum', *Christus Rex*, vol 5, no. 4 (October 1951), pp 336–349.
McLennan, Gregor, David Held, and Stuart Hall (editors), *The Idea of the Modern State* (Open University Press, Milton Keynes, 1984).
McLeod, Hugh, *Religion and the People of Western Europe 1789–1970* (Oxford University Press, Oxford, 1981).
McPolin, James, 'Public Health Bill', *Christus Rex*, vol 1, no. 3 (July 1947), pp 3–16.
McRedmond, Louis, *To the Greater Glory: A History of the Irish Jesuits* (Gill and Macmillan, Dublin, 1991).
McSweeney, Bill, *Roman Catholicism: The Search for Relevance* (Basil Blackwell, Oxford, 1980).
McVeigh, Joe, *Renewing the Irish Church: Towards an Irish Liberation Theology* (Mercier Press, Cork and Dublin, 1993).
Meenan, James, *The Italian Corporative System* (Cork University Press, Cork, 1944).
Meenan, James, *The Irish Economy Since 1922* (Liverpool University Press, Liverpool, 1970).

Miller, R.J., 'The Revolutionary Encyclical', *The Catholic Mind*, vol 49, no. 1066 (October 1951), pp 654–659.

Misner, Paul, *Social Catholicism in Europe: From the Onset of Industrialization to the First World War* (Darton, Longman and Todd, London, 1991).

Mitchell, Arthur, *Labour in Irish Politics 1890–1930: The Irish labour movement in an age of revolution* (Dublin, 1974).

Mooney, Edward Cardinal, 'Where We Stand Today', *The Catholic Mind*, vol 49, no. 1066 (October 1951), pp 593–597.

Moran, W., 'Some Causes of the Present Unrest', *The Irish Theological Quarterly*, vol 14 (1919), pp 97–109.

Moran, W., 'Social Reconstruction in an Irish State' (parts 1–3), *The Irish Theological Quarterly*, vol 15 (1920), pp 1–10, 101–112, 251–260.

Morrissey, Thomas, 'The Paradox of James Connolly, Irish Marxist Socialist (1868–1916) and the Papal Social Encyclicals (1891–1991)', *Milltown Studies*, vol 28 (Autumn 1991), pp 24–40.

Moynihan, Maurice, *Currency and Central Banking in Ireland 1922–1960* (Gill and Macmillan, Dublin, 1975).

Moynihan, Maurice (editor), *Speeches and Statements by Eamon de Valera 1917–1973* (Gill and Macmillan, Dublin, 1980).

Mulcahy, D.G. and Denis O'Sullivan (editors), *Irish Educational Policy: Process and Substance* (The Institute of Public Administration, Dublin, 1989).

Murphy, Francis Xavier, *The Papacy Today* (Weidenfeld and Nicolson, London, 1981).

Murphy, John A., *Ireland in the Twentieth Century* (Gill and Macmillan, Dublin, 1975).

Murphy, Pat, 'Reform: His Holiness Desires Real and Radical', *Hibernia*, vol 3, no. 1 (January 1939), pp 6–7.

Newman, J., 'Social Justice and the State', *Christus Rex*, vol 6, no. 2 (April 1952), pp 132–143.

Newman, Jeremiah, 'The Catholic Social Movement', *The Irish Ecclesiastical Record*, vol 83, no. 2 (February 1955), pp 96–107.

Newman, Jeremiah, 'Vocational Organisation and the Co-Operative Movement', *Christus Rex*, vol 12, no. 3 (July 1958), pp 171–184.

Newman, Otto, *The Challenge of Corporatism* (The Macmillan Press, London and Basingstoke, 1981).

O'Brien, Albert C., 'Italian Youth in Conflict: Catholic Action and Fascist Italy, 1929–1931', *The Catholic Historical Review*, vol 68, no. 4 (October 1982), pp 625–635.

Ó Buachalla, Séamas, *Education Policy in Twentieth Century Ireland* (Wolfhound Press, Dublin, 1988).

O'Carroll, John P. and John A. Murphy (editors), *De Valera and His Times* (Cork University Press, Cork, 1983).

O'Connor Lysaght, D.R., *The Republic of Ireland* (The Mercier Press, Cork, 1970).

O'Duffy, Eoin, 'General O'Duffy Objects . . . ', *Hibernia*, vol 2, no. 4 (April 1938), p 29.

O'Hanlon, Gerry, 'The Christian Vision of Solidarity – Pie in the Sky or Our Daily Bread?', *Studies*, vol 82, no. 328 (Winter 1993), pp 426–437.

O'Keeffe, Denis, 'The Corporative Organisation of Society', *Studies*, vol 26 (June 1937), pp 177–189.

O'Neill, Hugh, 'How Vocational Organisation Would Promote Social Justice', *The Irish Monthly*, vol 66 (June 1938), pp 378–385.

O'Rahilly, Alfred, 'The Constitution and the Senate', *Studies*, vol 25, (March 1936), pp 1–19.

O'Rahilly, Alfred, 'Vocational Organisation in the Past', *The Irish Monthly*, vol 66 (May 1938), pp 295–304.

O'Rahilly, Alfred, 'The Function of the State', *Christus Rex*, vol 5, no. 4 (October 1951), pp 360–363.

O'Rourke, Kevin, 'Conscience and the Economist', *Doctrine and Life*, vol 45 (May-June 1995), pp 347–352.

O'Rourke, Kevin, 'An Economist Looks at Catholic Social Teaching', *Doctrine and Life*, vol 45 (July-August 1995), pp 405–413.

O'Shea, Eamon, 'The Social Teaching of the Catholic Church: To What Purpose? To What Effect?', *Studies*, vol 79, no. 314 (Summer 1990), pp 116–130.

Panitch, Leo, 'Recent theorizations of corporatism: reflections on a growth industry', *British Journal of Sociology*, vol 31, no. 2 (June 1980), pp 159–187.

Parsons, Stephen, 'On the Logic of Corporatism', *Political Studies*, vol 36, no. 5 (September 1988), pp 515–523.

'Pastoral Address of the Archbishops and Bishops of Ireland, Assembled in Special Meeting, to Their Flocks, February 1914.', *Hibernia*, vol 12, no. 6 (June 1948), pp 10–11.

Paul-Dubois, L., *Contemporary Ireland* (Maunsel, Dublin, 1911).

Peillon, Michael, *Contemporary Irish Society: An Introduction* (Gill and Macmillan, Dublin, 1982).

Pekkarinen, Jukka, Matti Pohjola and Bob Rowthorn, *Social Corporatism: A Superior Economic System?* (Clarendon Press, Oxford, 1992).

Philbin, William J., 'New Directions for the Maynooth Union', *The Irish Theological Quarterly*, vol 22, no. 4 (October 1955), pp 281–292.

Pollard, John F., *The Vatican and Italian Fascism 1929–32: A study in conflict* (Cambridge University Press, Cambridge, 1985).

Powell, Frederick W., *The Politics of Irish Social Policy 1600–1990* (The Edwin Mellin Press, New York, 1992).

Powell, F.W., 'The Crisis in the Irish Welfare State' in William Reville and Máirtín Ó Fathaigh (editors), *Town and Gown 1* (Published by the Centre For Adult and Continuing Education, University College, Cork, 1994), pp 32–42.

Rahilly, Alfred, 'Suarez and Democracy', *Studies*, vol 7 (March 1918), pp 1–21.

Rahilly, Alfred, 'Democracy, Parliament and Cromwell', *Studies*, vol 7 (December 1918), pp 564–583.

Rahilly, Alfred, 'The Catholic Origin of Democracy', *Studies*, vol 8 (March 1919), pp 1–18.

Rahilly, Alfred, 'The Sources of English and American Democracy', *Studies*, vol 8 (June 1919), pp 189–209.

Rhodes, Anthony, *The Vatican in the Age of the Dictators 1922–1945* (Hodder and Stoughton, London, 1973).

Riordan, Patrick, 'Is Altruism the Key to the Common Good?', *Studies*, vol 82, no. 328 (Winter 1993), pp 438–449.

Ritschel, Daniel, 'A Corporatist Economy in Britain? Capitalist planning for industrial self-government in the 1930s', *English Historical Review*, vol 106, no. 418 (January 1991), pp 41–65.

Ronan, Myles V., 'Catholic Action in France, Germany, Switzerland, Italy (and Ireland?)', *The Irish Ecclesiastical Record*, Fifth Series, vol 13 (April 1919), pp 276–290.

Ryan, John A., 'Social Justice: A Rejoinder', *The Irish Theological Quarterly*, vol 13, no. 51 (July 1918), pp 215–219.

Ryan, John J.M., 'Portuguese Corporativism Now', *The Irish Monthly*, vol 72 (March 1944), pp 105–111.

Ryan, John J.M., 'Vocational Organisation In Industrial Britain', *The Irish Monthly*, vol 73 (December 1945), pp 505–509.

Ryan, John, 'The Founder of Muintir na Tíre: John M. Canon Hayes 1887–1957', *Studies*, vol 46 (Autumn 1957), pp 312–321.

Ryan, Liam, 'The Modern Popes as Social Reformers', *The Furrow*, vol 42, no. 2 (February 1991), pp 87–100.

Rynne, Stephen, *Father John Hayes: Founder of Muintir na Tíre* (Clonmore and Reynolds, Dublin, 1960).

Savage, Roland Burke, 'A Problem in Catholic Action: The Formation of Lay Leaders', *The Irish Ecclesiastical Record*, Fifth Series, vol 53 (January 1939), pp 30–46.

Schmitter, Philippe C., *Corporatism and Public Policy in Authoritarian Portugal* (Sage Publications, London and Beverly Hills, California, 1975).

Schmitter, Philippe C. and Gerhard Lehmbruch (editors), *Trends Towards Corporatist Intermediation* (Sage Publications, Beverly Hills, California, and London, 1979).

Schmitter, Philippe C., 'Corporatism is Dead! Long Live Corporatism!', *Government and Opposition*, vol 24, (Winter 1989), pp 54–73.

Schnepp, Gerald J., 'A Catholic Industrial Program', *The Catholic Mind*, vol 47, no. 1040 (August 1949), pp 489–499.

Scott, H.M. (editor), *Enlightened Absolutism: Reform and Reformers in Later Eighteenth-Century Europe* (Macmillan, Basingstoke and London, 1990).

Serrarens, P.J.S., 'Christian Trade Unions', *Christus Rex*, vol 1, no. 3 (July 1947), pp 17–25.

Sigmund, Paul E., 'The Catholic Tradition and Modern Democracy', *The Review of Politics*, vol 49, no. 4 (1987), pp 530–548.

Smith, Gordon, *Politics in Western Europe: A Comparative Analysis*, Third Edition (Heinemann, London, 1980).

Somerville, Henry, 'An Alternative to Capitalism', *Studies*, vol 14, no. 56 (December 1925), pp 521–530; comments on this article by John A. Ryan,

Hilaire Belloc, John Kelleher, George O'Brien and Joseph E. Canavan, pp 530–544.

Somerville, Henry, 'The Rerum Novarum After Forty Years', *Studies*, vol 20 (March 1931), pp 1–12.

Somerville, Henry, 'The Achievement of Rerum Novarum', *The Catholic Mind*, vol 49, no. 1066 (October 1951), pp 598–605.

Sutton, Ralph G., 'A Real Seanad', *Studies*, vol 47 (Summer 1958), pp 169–176.

Swift, John, 'Report of Commission on Vocational Organisation (and it's Times, 1930–'40's).', *Saothar*, vol 1, no. 1 (May 1975), pp 54–63.

Teasdale, Anthony L., 'Subsidiarity In Post–Maastricht Europe', *The Political Quarterly*, vol 64, no. 2, (April-June 1993), pp 187–197.

The Irish Episcopal Conference, Work is the Key: Towards an Economy That Needs Everyone (Veritas, Dublin, 1992).

Thomas, Hugh, *An Unfinished History of the World*, Revised Edition (Pan Books, London, 1989).

Thomason, George F., 'Muintir na Tire's Role in Irish Community Development', *Studies*, vol 51 (Autumn 1962), pp 408–418.

Thomson, David, *Europe Since Napoleon*, Revised Edition (Pelican Books, 1975).

Tierney, Michael, 'Vocationalism and Parliamentary Democracy. Are They Reconcilable?', *The Irish Monthly*, vol 66 (June,1938), pp 369–377.

Toner, Jerome, *Rural Ireland: Some of its Problems* (Clonmore and Reynolds, Dublin, 1955).

Twomey, Louis J., 'Papal Social Teaching in Business Education', *The Catholic Mind*, vol 48, no. 1055 (November 1950), pp 669–672.

Ua Murcada, Pádraig, 'The Labour Question: A Forgotten Document', *The Catholic Bulletin*, vol 14, no. 2 (February 1924), pp 117–120.

Vidler, A.R., *A Century of Social Catholicism 1820–1920* (S.P.C.K., London, 1964).

Von Prondzynski, Ferdinand, 'The Nature of Private Property in Modern Society', *Studies*, vol 72 (Autumn 1983), pp 209–212.

Ward, Alan J., *The Irish Constitutional Tradition: Responsible Government and Modern Ireland, 1782–1992* (Irish Academic Press, Dublin, 1994).

Waters, Dr, 'Diseases of the Social System: The Medical Viewpoint', *Hibernia*, vol 3, no. 9 (September 1939), pp 4–5.

Weigel, George, 'Catholicism and Democracy: The Other Twentieth-Century Revolution', *The Washington Quarterly*, vol 12, no. 4 (Autumn 1989), pp 5–25.

Whyte, John H., *Catholics in Western Democracies: A Study in Political Behaviour*, (Gill and Macmillan, Dublin, 1981).

Whyte, J.H., *Church and State in Modern Ireland 1923–1979*, Second Edition (Gill and Macmillan, Dublin, 1984).

Winkler, J.T., 'Corporatism', *European Journal of Sociology*, vol 17, no. 1 (1976), pp 100–136.

Wood, Anthony, *War in Europe 1939–1945* (Longman, London and New York, 1987).

Pamphlets

Boylan, Patrick, *Catholicism and Citizenship in Self-Governed Ireland* (Office of the Irish Messenger, Dublin, n.d.).

Catholic Education Through the Papal Encyclicals (Extract from the 1949 Lenten Pastoral Letter 'On Living the Faith', by Archbishop D'Alton of Armagh, and issued by the publishers of Fiat – the Key Publishing Society, Dublin, n.d.).

Cosgrave, President, *Policy of the Cumann na nGaedheal Party* (Cumann na nGaedheal, Dublin, June 1927).

Dignan, J., *Outlines of a Scheme of National Health Insurance* (Paper read at a meeting of the committee of management of the National Health Insurance Society held on 11 October 1944).

Faire Bán, *So This Is Ireland* (Kevin J. Kenny, Dublin, n.d.).

Irish Educational Problems: Addresses at I.N.T.O. Congress (Irish National Teachers' Organisation, 1923).

Manual of the Guilds of Regnum Christi (The Central Secretariat of the Guilds of Regnum Christi, Dublin, 1934).

Pastoral Letter of His Eminence Cardinal Logue, the Archbishops and Bishops of Ireland, to the priests and people of Ireland: To be read in all Churches and public oratories at the principal Masses, on Sunday, October 22, 1922 (Browne and Nolan, Dublin, n.d.).

The Synod of Maynooth 1927: Decrees Which Affect the Catholic Laity, translated with some notes by Rev M.J. Browne (The Catholic Truth Society of Ireland, Dublin, 1930).

Index